TANGLED MOBILITIES

Edited by Noel B. Salazar, University of Leuven, in collaboration with AnthroMob, the EASA Anthropology and Mobility Network.

This transdisciplinary book series features empirically grounded studies from around the world that disentangle how people, objects and ideas move across the planet. With a special focus on advancing theory as well as methodology, the series considers movement as both an object and a method of study.

Recent volumes:

Volume 12
TANGLED MOBILITIES
Places, Affects, and Personhood across Social Spheres in Asian Migration
Edited by Asuncion Fresnoza-Flot and Gracia Liu-Farrer

Volume 11
MIGRATION IN THE MAKING OF THE GULF SPACE
Social, Political, and Cultural Dimensions
Edited by Antia Mato Bouzas and Lorenzo Casini

Volume 10
WE ARE ALL AFRICANS HERE
Race, Mobilities and West Africans in Europe
Kristín Loftsdóttir

Volume 9
LIMINAL MOVES
Traveling along Places, Meanings, and Times
Flavia Cangià

Volume 8
PACING MOBILITIES
Timing, Intensity, Tempo and Duration of Human Movements
Edited by Vered Amit and Noel B. Salazar

Volume 7
FINDING WAYS THROUGH EUROSPACE
West African Movers Re-viewing Europe from the Inside
Joris Schapendonk

Volume 6
BOURDIEU AND SOCIAL SPACE
Mobilities, Trajectories, Emplacements
Deborah Reed-Danahay

Volume 5
HEALTHCARE IN MOTION
Immobilities in Health Service Delivery and Access
Edited by Cecilia Vindrola-Padros, Ginger A. Johnson, and Anne E. Pfister

For a full volume listing, please see the series page on our website: https://www.berghahnbooks.com/series/worlds-in-motion

Tangled Mobilities
Places, Affects, and Personhood across Social Spheres in Asian Migration

Edited by
Asuncion Fresnoza-Flot and Gracia Liu-Farrer

berghahn
NEW YORK · OXFORD
www.berghahnbooks.com

First published in 2022 by
Berghahn Books
www.berghahnbooks.com

© 2022, 2024 Asuncion Fresnoza-Flot and Gracia Liu-Farrer
First paperback edition published in 2024

All rights reserved. Except for the quotation of short passages
for the purposes of criticism and review, no part of this book
may be reproduced in any form or by any means, electronic or
mechanical, including photocopying, recording, or any information
storage and retrieval system now known or to be invented,
without written permission of the publisher.

Library of Congress Cataloging-in-Publication Data
Names: Fresnoza-Flot, Asuncion, editor. | Liu-Farrer, Gracia, editor.
Title: Tangled mobilities : places, affects, and personhood across social
  spheres in Asian migration / edited by Asuncion Fresnoza-Flot and Gracia
  Liu-Farrer.
Description: New York : Berghahn Books, 2022. | Series: Worlds in motion ;
  volume 12 | Includes bibliographical references and index.
Identifiers: LCCN 2022004878 (print) | LCCN 2022004879 (ebook) | ISBN
  9781800735675 (hardback) | ISBN 9781800736689 (pdf)
Subjects: LCSH: Asians--Migrations. | Asians--Foreign countries--Social
  conditions. | Immigrants--Asia--Social conditions. | Asia--Emigration
  and immigration--Social aspects.
Classification: LCC JV8490 .T36 2022 (print) | LCC JV8490 (ebook) | DDC
  304.8095--dc23/eng/20220416
LC record available at https://lccn.loc.gov/2022004878
LC ebook record available at https://lccn.loc.gov/2022004879

British Library Cataloguing in Publication Data
A catalogue record for this book is available from the British Library

ISBN 978-1-80073-567-5 hardback
ISBN 978-1-80539-339-9 paperback
ISBN 978-1-80073-568-2 epub
ISBN 978-1-80073-668-9 web pdf

https://doi.org/10.3167/9781800735675

An electronic version of this book is freely available thanks to the support of libraries working with Knowledge Unlatched. KU is a collaborative initiative designed to make high-quality books Open Access for the public good. More information about the initiative and links to the Open Access version can be found at knowledgeunlatched.org.

This work is published subject to a Creative Commons Attribution Noncommercial No Derivatives 4.0 License. The terms of the license can be found at https://creativecommons.org/licenses/by-nc-nd/4.0/. For uses beyond those covered in the license contact Berghahn Books.

Contents

List of Tables		vii
Acknowledgments		viii

Introduction   Tangled Mobilities in the Age of Transnational Migration   1
Asuncion Fresnoza-Flot and Gracia Liu-Farrer

Chapter 1   Sexual Mobility, Migration, and Sexual Fields   26
James Farrer

Chapter 2   Cycles of Irregularity: The Intergenerational Impacts of Trafficking Policies on Migrant Families   48
Pardis Mahdavi

Chapter 3   Mobile Homes, Mobile Objects: Materiality and Mobility of Vietnamese-Belgian Couples   69
Angelie Marilla

Chapter 4   Tangled Intergenerational Mobilities: Maternal Migration and Japanese-Filipino Children in Japan   91
Fiona-Katharina Seiger

Chapter 5   Emotions, Places, and Mobilities: The Affective Drives of the Migration and Settlement Aspirations among Highly Educated Migrants   113
Gracia Liu-Farrer

Chapter 6   Affects, Aspirations, and the Transformation of Personhood: A Case of Japanese-Pakistani Marriages through a Generational Lens   134
Masako Kudo

Chapter 7	Intergenerational Intimacies and Mobilities in Transnational Families: The Experiences of Japanese-Filipino Children *Jocelyn O. Celero*	157
Chapter 8	Truly Liberal and Immensely Oppressive? The Experiences of Returned Queer Vietnamese Migrants from Japan *An Huy Tran*	182
Chapter 9	Social Mobility and Labor Migration under Recession: Exploring Generational Differences among Japanese Migrants in China *Kumiko Kawashima*	205
Chapter 10	Pursuing Respectability in Mobility: Marriage, Migration, and Divorce of Filipino Women in Belgium and the Netherlands *Asuncion Fresnoza-Flot*	227
Conclusion	Empirical Insights, Policy Implications, and COVID-19 Influences *Gracia Liu-Farrer and Asuncion Fresnoza-Flot*	248
Index		257

Tables

Table 2.1	International Migrant Population in Kuwait and the UAE, 2019	55
Table 2.2	Top Five Sending Countries to Host Country—Female Migrant Stock, 2019	56
Table 2.3	Contractual Sterilization Laws in Other Gulf Cooperation Council Countries	59

Acknowledgments

Being ourselves international migrants, tangled mobilities are part and parcel of our lived experiences. These mobilities created opportunities that made our paths cross for the first time in 2018. Specifically, the joint research initiatives between the Université libre de Bruxelles (ULB) and Waseda University have provided us with an encouraging environment in which to engage in a long-term research collaboration. The present edited volume is one outcome of this intellectual enterprise that would not have been possible without the support of different people, centers, and institutions.

We are grateful to Nobue Suzuki (professor of anthropology at Chiba University) who put us in contact with each other in 2017, and to Jean-Louis Moortgat (head of the Waseda University Brussels Office—WBO in the ULB) who has been providing us with ideas, opportunities, and assistance to attain the objectives of our collaboration. Our sincere thanks go to Vanessa Frangville and Frederik Ponjaert of the East Asian Studies (EASt) research center in ULB for their suggestions, encouragement, and support. We appreciate the help of Laura Merla, professor of sociology and our colleague at the Catholic University of Louvain (UCLouvain), who co-organized with us the international workshop "Intimacy, sexuality and family in the process of migration: European/Asian experiences compared" on 18-19 December 2018 at ULB. This workshop led to our efforts to compose this volume. The support of Geneviève Corbisier, secretary of the Laboratory of Anthropology of Contemporary Worlds (LAMC), and the assistance of four master students from ULB (Miriam Diallo, Catherine Gonzalez Alvarez, Nicolas Jacqmin, and Clara Zeltner-Reig) were key to the organizational success of this event.

Aside from a grant from F.R.S.-FNRS (the Belgian national fund for scientific research), the workshop received assistance from the WBO and from the *Maison des Sciences humaines* (MSH) of ULB with the joint support of EASt and of the Interdisciplinary Research Structure on Gender (STRIGES, headed by David Paternotte). The workshop was also sponsored by the Institute of Asian Migrations (IAM) of Waseda University, the Interdisciplinary Research Center on Families and Sexualities (CIRFASE) at the UCLouvain, and the LAMC of ULB. Our collaboration would not have led to interesting exchanges without the following grants: "Waseda-In International Chair" in April 2018, "Subsidy for the Organization of a Scientific Event" from the F.R.S.-FNRS (co-applied for with Laura Merla) in September 2018, and "Impulsion OUT Privilege Partnership Subsidy" from ULB in September 2019.

We offer our heartfelt gratitude to all the authors who have contributed to this volume, and thank them for their patience and active interest in this project, despite the challenges we encountered due to the COVID-19 pandemic. We thank Tony Mason, Tom Bonnington, Amanda Horn, Sulaiman Ahmad, and Caroline Kuhtz from Berghahn Books for their support and faith in this publication project.

Finally, we thank our respective families for their understanding and for continuously inspiring us. Jean-François Flot, a biologist, shared with us the fascinating phenomena of biological and ecological entanglements; and James Farrer, a fellow sociologist, contributed an innovative conceptual framework in our volume building on his long ethnographic experience in China. Our intellectual adventures would also have been lonely without the laughs and distractions of our children, whose lives are so intimately tangled with ours.

Asuncion Fresnoza-Flot and Gracia Liu-Farrer

INTRODUCTION

Tangled Mobilities in the Age of Transnational Migration

Asuncion Fresnoza-Flot and Gracia Liu-Farrer

And now I write you how I am getting along. I am getting along well, very well. I have worked in a factory and I am now working in a hotel. I receive 10 (in our money 32) dollars a month, and that is very good. If you would like it, we could bring Wladzio over some day. We eat here every day what we get only for Easter in our country. We are bringing over Helena and brother now. I had $120 and I sent back $90.
—A passage from the letter of Walercia to Olejnickzka in 1912
(Thomas and Znaniecki 1918: 312)

The excerpt above demonstrates the transformations in a Polish woman's life in the United States of America (USA) in the early twentieth century. This woman's improved economic condition and subsequent reunification with her family members appear tied to her migration. Such spatial movement can be considered "transnational" (Basch, Glick Schiller, and Szanton Blanc 1995). It crosses nation-states' borders and entails various social practices linking the migrants' countries of origin and destination. This transnational migration constitutes a site of transformations for migrants like the Polish woman who wrote the letter above. Over time, transnational migration has become increasingly complex due to the globalization of labor markets, the advent of new technologies of communication and transportation, and the tightening of migration policies in many countries. This complexity involves the intersections and overlaps of different processes in the lives of migrants and their families.

To understand these intertwined processes, the present volume investigates the experiences of migrants into, within, and out of Asia—the largest continent in the world, comprising five geographical regions (East, Southeast, South, Central, and West) and more than forty countries (UNSD 2021). While being traditionally a migrant sending continent, Asia has taken on the status of a major destination of migration since the late twentieth century. In 2019, while it was the birthplace of over "40 percent of all international migrants worldwide" (IOM 2020: 26), Asia also received the highest number (84 million) of migrants in the world (ibid.: 24). It witnessed a 69 percent increase of immigration between 2000 and 2019 (ibid.). The characteristics of this populous and geographically expansive continent—the enormous economic developmental gaps between countries, a broad spectrum of political regimes, and divergent social and cultural contexts—have made Asia a unique context to observe complex transnational migration patterns. The geographic movements of people and their cross-national border practices connect Asia to different regions of the world. The social spaces, both local and transnational, resulting from this situation are therefore an exciting site to consider in examining the intertwined processes that individuals and social groups experience in different stages of their life course. The present volume captures these processes through case studies of migration phenomena involving selected countries in the following Asian regions: East (China, Japan), Southeast (Philippines, Vietnam), South (India, Pakistan), and West (United Arab Emirates). We use the term "Asian migration" to refer to the migration phenomena into, within, and out of these regions.

In this introductory chapter, we present the analytical framework of "tangled mobilities"—a concept inspired by the empirical phenomena observed in the case studies in the volume. We build from the growing literature on human mobility, and incorporate transnational and intersectional approaches to develop this framework. We also revisit and establish dialogue with the recent literature on Asian migration, highlighting the volume's scholarly contributions. After this state of the art, we unveil the different forms of entanglements depicted in our collection of empirical cases. We conclude by emphasizing the added value of "tangled mobilities" as a way of looking at phenomena in contemporary transnational migration.

Tangled Mobilities: Making Sense of Transnational Migration

The "new mobilities paradigm" (Sheller and Urry 2006) in the social sciences provides an innovative approach to studying and conceptualizing transnational migration. In this paradigm, "mobility" has become understood as a social process involving movements, mobility, or the capacity to move, networks, imaginaries, representations, and experiences (Canzler, Kaufmann, and Kesselring 2008; Cresswell 2006; Salazar 2019). This "complex assemblage" (Salazar 2019: 14) also involves affects, ideas, and discourses, which allows for expanded empirical scope and theoretical innovation in transnational migration studies.

From an empirical point of view, the "new mobilities paradigm" brings scholars' attention to the institutional frameworks, material infrastructures, and social systems that facilitate or hamper human mobility. It encourages migration research not only to inquire why some people move from one place to another while others do not, but also to investigate how migrants manage to move. Its focus on the process of mobility, in particular, makes it possible to notice the materiality of movement, the different power dynamics that affect individuals' unequal experiences of mobility, and the relationship between mobility and immobility. It brings into the spotlight the various forms of movements that are not only spatial but also temporal (Kakihara and Sørensen 2001), and not only those traversing national borders, but also those crossing social classes (Noret 2020), cultural realms (Salazar 2010), ethnic boundaries (e.g., Borch 2017), fields of intimacy (Groes and Fernandez 2018), and "regimes of mobility" (Glick Schiller and Salazar 2013). These movements operate according to different logics, and are either interdependent or entail others' movements toward different and sometimes even contradictory directions.

Recently, studies have also brought to attention the entangled nature of these movements. For example, Groes and Fernandez (2018), in their pioneering work on "intimate mobilities," demonstrate the open-ended relations between mobility and intimacy. They elucidate these relations by examining their "three highly entangled and interchangeable fields": "migration regimes and their intimate discontents," "circuits of sex, race and gendered bodies," and "moralities of money, mobility and intimacy" (9-10). This specific work highlights the importance of paying a critical attention to "(en)tanglement" in the study of mobilities, which the present volume takes into account to make sense of contemporary transnational migration.

The focus on "(en)tanglement" in the field of scientific research can be traced back to Darwin's groundbreaking work, *The Origin of Species*, that introduces the theory of natural selection, specifically in his famous description below of a "tangled bank":

> It is interesting to contemplate a tangled bank, clothed with many plants of many kinds, with birds singing on the bushes, with various insects flitting about, and with worms crawling through the damp earth, and to reflect that these elaborately constructed forms, so different from each other, and dependent upon each other in so complex a manner, have all been produced by laws acting around us. (Darwin 1872: 429)

The above description unveils the complexity and interdependency of different forms of life inhabiting such a space at any given moment. The (en)tanglement of these life forms echoes Hernes' (2008) "tangled world," that is, "a world where there are discernable elements, but ones which are twisted together, entwined in ways that add up to an untidy mass" (XIV). Within the "untidy mass," it is possible to "identify and give names to separate strands" that represent "processes" (ibid.). The changes occurring in this mass are individually and collectively experienced as "an unfolding process, a flow of possibilities, and a conjunction of events and open-ended interaction occurring in time" (ibid.; Tsoukas and Chia 2002: 572). Mobility as an assemblage appears akin to this "untidy mass" with different strands in constant change. These strands stand for the different elements (animate and inanimate), components (ideas, representations, practices, imaginaries, and affects), and forms of mobility (spatial, social, temporal, intimate, and temporal). In this case, mobility can be conceptualized as a "tangled" social process, and to understand its dynamics, the tanglement of its different strands should be put to the fore in the analysis rather than treating them separately from one another. Hence, we can speak of "tangled mobilities"—that is, a dynamic, unfolding process in which elements, components, and forms of mobility exist alongside, intersect with, and overlap one another in complex ways, resulting in stasis and movements across different life dimensions (social, legal, intimate, sexual, digital, and temporal).

Given their respective characteristics, each strand of mobility can also be conceived as tanglement in itself. In this regard, strands resemble the "constituent strands" of what Ingold (2008) calls a "meshwork." According to Ingold, "every organism" and "every thing—is itself an entanglement" (ibid.: 1806). Using the metaphor of lines, he explains how individuals become interconnected: "Where inhabitants meet, trails are entwined, as the life of each becomes bound up with each other. Every entwining is a knot, and the more lifelines are entwined, the greater the density of the knot" (Ingold 2011: 149). A "meshwork" appears here as "a tissue of knots" that "become tied up with other strands, in other bundles" (Ingold 2008: 1806). Hence, based on this conception, each "tangled" strand of "tangled mobilities" is critically important in the study of transnational movements of people in order to bring out the nuances and subtleties of this phenomenon. Treating mobilities as both inadvertently and inevitably tangled allows a full understanding of individuals' agency and shifting subjectivity, while also demonstrating mobility and immobility as inseparable and mutually constitutive.

To elucidate the tangled nature of mobilities in the context of migration, a transnational perspective (Basch et al. 1995) seems useful to unveil how migrants and non-migrants, and spaces and places, become interconnected through different human practices and activities traversing the borders of nation-states. Another heuristic approach to highlight the tangled nature of mobility is intersectionality (Crenshaw 1989), which brings scholarly focus to the simultaneous crisscrossing of different categories of difference, notably gender, social class, and "race," producing and reinforcing unequal power relations and marginality of minority groups—not only migrant women but also LGBTQ (lesbian, gay, bisexual, transgender and queer) people. Thus, the present volume considers as much as possible the transnational dimension and intersecting categories in the lives of migrants and non-migrants, thereby illuminating the links between places, affects, and personhood.

In this volume, places refer to geopolitical locations that migrants and their families inhabit, which could be a nation at the macro level, or a city, village, or home at the micro level. Migration and the activities, consciousnesses, memories, and emotions of individuals link various places to one another, creating translocal and/or transnational social spaces and fields. This process informs and is shaped by the affective universe of the migrants. To capture the dynamics of this universe, this volume pays attention to "emotions," which Thrift (2008) defines as the "everyday understandings of affects …, constructed by cultures over many centuries and with their own distinctive vocabulary and means of relating to others" (221). Affect, on the other hand, is understood as "intensity" or the "strength or duration" (Massumi 1995: 84–85) of the effect of objects, images, figures, people, or discourses on individuals, such as "physiological reactions (muscular contraction, secretions) and visible symptoms (voice changes, facial expressions)" (Frykman and Povrzanović Frykman 2016: 14). Understanding emotions can therefore reveal the subtleties of affects in the context of migration, and can also highlight the "personhood" or sense of self of migrants, notably how personhood evolves across time and spaces.

Through the empirical cases of intra-Asia and Asia-Europe/USA mobilities, this volume expands the concept of "mobility" to capture changes in terms of the spatial, social, intimate, and legal positioning that migrants experience during the migration process. It highlights not only the entangled nature of such positional changes but also the entanglement of different forms of mobilities (spatial, social, sexual, intimate, legal). While the empirical focus of the volume is the "spatial mobility" of people across national borders and the phenomena associated with their geographic movement, within the purview of traditional migration research, the concept of "tangled mobilities" allows us to bring in different types of changes in terms of positioning accompanying people's physical movements in the migration process. "Spatial mobility" is defined here as human mobility across socio-geographic spaces that most often unfolds temporally over one's life course and that changes direction due to certain turning points and to the influence of different institutional and cultural norms. The collection of studies in this volume builds on recent developments. It aims to bring the mobility scholarship one step further by focusing on the entanglements of different elements, components, and forms of mobilities.

Mobility Research in the Context of Migrations into, within, and out of Asia

Researchers of Asian migration show that migratory patterns have gradually changed in complex ways, notably from the 1980s onwards with the feminization of Asian migration that strongly contributed to the development of gender and migration research in the Asian continent. This development departs from the gender-neutral approach observed in Asian migration studies from its advent in the latter 1920s to the 1970s (Fresnoza-Flot 2022 forthcoming). Aside from this change, there are also increased intra-Asia movements, new pathways, and intertwined migration channels, which have reinforced the scholarly interest in Asian migration. As Asis, Piper, and Raghuram (2019) observe, "Asia has become an empirical, theoretical and policy exemplar contributing to driving global migration research" (13).

An example of such contributions are the conceptual and theoretical innovations that Asian migration studies brought to the broader field of mobility studies. For example, Asia is the origin and the main destination of women's intimate and labor migrations, which leads to the rise of analytical concepts of "global hypergamy" (Constable 2010), "global householding" (Douglass 2010), and "care chain" (Parreñas 2012; see also Hochschild 2000). The flows of millions of international students and skilled migrants into, within, and out of Asia result in several studies on "brain circulation" (Saxenian 2005) and "educational mobilities" (Waters 2018). The temporary labor migration in and out of Asia that is often mediated by private recruitment agencies causes concerns about "protracted precarity" (Piper, Rosewarne, and Withers 2017). Scholars also remark that Asian labor and intimate migration channels can intersect in the lives of individual migrant women (Lan 2008; Piper and Roces 2003) and that migration can be serial and multiple as migrants seek better pay and work conditions (Paul 2017; Parreñas et al. 2019).

These conceptual and theoretical innovations suggest an increasing complexity of Asian migration. They echo the gradual and complex evolution of the broader field of migration studies that has been witnessing since the 1990s important theoretical developments, such as the rise of the transnationalism perspective and the growing emphasis on sociocultural and intimate factors/dimensions of migration. What is evident is that Asian migration has become characterized by the entanglements of diverse migration paths, places, personhood, and affects, as unveiled in the literature review below, and later in the empirical cases of our volume.

Migration, Personhood, and Affects

The recent literature (1990s–2010s) on Asian migration reveals the link between mobility and personhood. It also highlights the importance of an existential understanding of migration and the heuristic value of an affective lens of analysis.

Although attaining self-actualization through mobility is not a uniquely Asian phenomenon, mobility has an elevated value in Asia. Historically, the modern nation-building process in most Asian countries, by adopting political ideals from the so-called "West" (that is, Europe and North America), economic theories, and political institutions, has been inseparable from international migration to Western countries (Liu-Farrer and Yeoh 2018). Recently, the positive value of international migration is institutionalized through migrant-sending countries' programs that either encourage their nationals to seek overseas work and remit (Palmer 2016; Rodriguez 2010), or implement preferential policies to induce the return of emigrants with foreign educational credentials, professional experiences, and financial resources (Ho 2018). More practically, the material resources and stories of success remitted back home by emigrants have instilled in those in the sending regions a desire to migrate, shaping a culture of migration (Kandel and Massey 2002; Asis 2006). For many Asian people, the capacity to migrate to the West or a developed country in the Asian continent constitutes modern subjectivity (Coates 2018). This applies to the migrants or those waiting to migrate in Chinese villages in Fujian (Chu 2010), to medical tourists in Southeast Asia (Whittaker 2018), as well as to those Chinese millionaires who spend hundreds of thousands of dollars to purchase overseas residency permits and citizenships in order to fashion themselves as members of the global elite (Liu-Farrer 2016). Spatial mobility, therefore, becomes a family strategy for upward class mobility among socially less privileged Asians (Fresnoza-Flot and Shinozaki 2017; Thai 2014), and a way to accumulate cultural capital and facilitate the social reproduction among the middle- and upper-middle-class Asian families (Waters 2008; Liu-Farrer 2016).

The intricate connection between mobility and personhood can also be observed in the case of journeying, an existential need related to one's sense of self. Labeling this form of mobility as existential, Madison (2006) points out that people who volunteer to migrate, ostensibly for practical reasons, sometimes do so out of the desire to escape from a constraining home environment in search of a space to express their independence and freedom. This existential dimension is salient in many strands of migration, and applies to people at different life stages. Many young Japanese working holidaymakers left Japan for Australia in the 1990s and 2000s. They did so to escape the oppressive salarymen lifestyle and a stagnating economy, as well as to fashion a cosmopolitan self through acquiring English skills and living in a Western cultural environment (Kawashima 2010). This lifestyle-driven cross-border mobility applies also to retirees in Asia and the Pacific—for example, Japanese retirees move to Southeast Asia because of their desire for a more leisurely lifestyle after decades of taxing corporate life, their attraction to the warm climate, their quest for the meaning of life, and their assertion of independence in old age (Ono 2010). At the same time, their migration decision is shaped by the fact that only in Southeast Asia can their Japanese pension afford them a comfortable lifestyle (ibid.). This factor also influences the "lifestyle migration" (Benson and O'Reilly 2009) of many middle-class Europeans to Southeast Asian countries such as Thailand (Scuzzarello 2020).

Moreover, the geographic movement of young women toward the domestic service sector or the institution of marriage is another form of existential migration. In many cases, they migrate and enter binational unions to escape their home country's oppressive gender norms, especially the pressure to marry and biologically reproduce (Mahdavi 2016). For example, many Southeast and East Asian women who are highly educated, in their late twenties, or with children from previous relationships, engage in marriage migration to form a family due to the difficulties they encounter in finding a potential partner in their own country's local marriage market (e.g., Lapanun 2012). Their intimate journey to other countries allows them to attain a certain level of social respectability (Suksomboon 2007).

In addition, studies on Asian migration have illuminated the emotional dimension of migration motivation. Studies show that marriage migration of Asian women—initially dubbed as "mail-order" migration (Glodava and

Onizuka 1994)—is not devoid of romantic interests or the possibility to fall in love (Constable 2003; Fresnoza-Flot and Ricordeau 2017). Emotional drivers of migration also exist in most forms of return migration in Asia. Although the ethnic return is often "a project driven by enterprise rather than by nostalgia" (Xiang 2013: 2) and a response to state policies and economic incentives, such migration is also driven by a longing for the ethnic homeland (Tsuda 2018).

The affective lens helps scholars register the entangled forces driving migration and the fact that mobilities yield emotional outcomes. Research employing this lens reviews that career strategies, cultural interests, desires for adventure, and lifestyle choices are tangled together, driving Westerners to move to countries in East and Southeast Asia (Farrer 2019; Debnár 2016; Liu-Farrer 2020; Green 2015; Statham et al. 2020), and pushing Japanese youth and retiring salarymen to find or resume life and careers in China (Kawashima 2018, and this volume). Likewise, the desires for sexual expressions and intimate relationships are both compelling reasons for international migration and inevitable migration consequences, affecting migrants' decisions either to continue moving or to settle (Guzman 1997; Liu-Farrer 2020; Farrer, Liu-Farrer, and Tran, this volume).

The Mediated and Tangled Mobilities

With the political history of colonization, Asian countries' nation-building processes are often hostile to population mobility. They see migrants, especially the ethnic "others," as having no place in the nation-state (Liu-Farrer and Yeoh 2018: 2). Although many Asian countries started to import foreign labor in the late twentieth century, the institutional frameworks for international migration did not develop in some, and are non-existent in others (ibid.). Therefore, empirical studies in the Asian context highlight the role of both the sending and the receiving states (Ortiga 2017) and the migration industry (Asis et al. 2019; Fresnoza-Flot 2012; Liu-Farrer and Tran 2019) in facilitating and hindering cross-border mobilities as well as shaping varied mobility outcomes. "Migration infrastructure" (Xiang and Lindquist 2014) is a concept that emerged out of empirical observations to account for such a heavily mediated process of migration.

Moreover, studying Asian migration allows researchers to gain insights into the tangling of different forms of mobilities. Most Asian countries have had a history of being colonized or occupied by the West. Many sent migrants overseas as farmers and laborers. Asian migrants' international migration to the West and to more advanced economies on the Asian continent has often been accompanied by downward social mobility, career stasis, and legal constraints. Such mobility outcomes result from the unequal positions the sending and the receiving countries occupy in the global political and economic orders, and the difficulty in converting professional credentials or skills across borders (Liu-Farrer, Yeoh, and Baas 2021). Racism, nationalism, and gender hierarchies affect immigrants' skill recognition and consequently their labor market outcomes, even when they enter as professionals or investors, as seen in the labor market experiences of highly skilled Asian and other migrants in Canada and Europe (Bauder 2003; Ley 2011; Nohl et al. 2014). Even the very wealthy Asians with elite North American education feel the constraint of the racialized glass ceiling, having difficulty converting their economic and cultural capital into the kind of symbolic capital recognized by the upper-class white community in North America (Ong 1992).

The same uneven mobilities have appeared in the recent flows of migration into Asia and between Asian countries. First, the concept of "race" and racial hierarchy originated in the West, through military and technological power, and colonization; these have had a lasting influence on Asian people's perceptions of themselves and others (Kowner and Demel 2012). Second, many countries within this continent have experienced rapid but recent economic development, and have not yet solidified their positions in the global economic and political order. Such uncertainties and divergent positions in the global economic, political, and racial hierarchies result in uneven and sometimes contradictory directions of economic, legal, and sexual mobilities of migrants from different continents. Such complex mobility trajectories are reflected in the migration experiences of people from the earlier developed countries in Asia to those that are more recently developed on other continents, and from these continents to Asia. The white Europeans and North Americans in China (Farrer 2019; Farrer, this volume), Japan (Hof 2020; Debnár 2016), and Singapore (Hof 2020) might, on the one hand, enjoy some privileges in the corporate environment because whiteness is traditionally associated with expatriates and highly skilled workers in Asia (ibid.). Some also perceive an elevated social status (Liu-Farrer 2020) or see their sexual capital increasing in value, such as the white men in Shanghai (Farrer 2010; Farrer, this volume) and British women in Dubai (Walsh 2007). On the other hand, in some restrictive immigration regimes in Asia, even rich and successful business people only have access to fixed-term visa categories. Their residence might be terminated when they lose institutional ties to the host countries (Farrer 2019). Professionally, some white migrants, whether they are native English speakers or not, are pigeon-holed into niche occupations such as teaching English, essentially entrapped in a dead-end career with a precarious employment situation (Debnár 2016).

A Way Forward through a "Tangled Mobility" Lens

The literature review in the preceding sections, albeit not exhaustive, points to the contributions of Asian migration scholarship to the larger field of migration and mobility studies. Asian migration research has advanced the field by bringing in plural perspectives on migratory motivations, notably the rising aspirations and desires for mobility among a broad spectrum of people, despite restrictive immigration regimes and competing logics of mobilities operating in individuals' spatial movements. It has changed the scholarly understanding about the driving forces of Asian migration which, rooted in North American experiences, had been dominated by economic analysis (Asis et al. 2010). It points out that affects, emotions, and the desire for social class mobility all play a role in the way individuals experience migration. Interestingly, it unveils the entanglements of different elements, components, and forms of mobilities in the lives of migrants, which have not yet been fully conceptualized in Asian migration in particular, nor in mobility studies in general. The volume's proposed lens of "tangled mobilities" offers researchers a possibility of capturing such complexities of migration through its critical attention to the tangled nature and underlying processes of mobilities. The empirical cases in our edited volume further the discussion on how mobilities are tangled in the different norms, institutional conditions, and power structures. They collectively illustrate how spatial mobilities unfold with such contingencies.

Tangled Social Spheres, Mobilities, and Stasis: An Overview of the Volume

The present volume offers ten empirical case studies featuring intra-Asia migratory phenomenon, Asian migration to Europe, and migration to Asia from Western countries. These case studies carried out by anthropologists and sociologists of migration highlight the voices of diverse actors: both heterosexual and LGBTQ people; mixed couples in which the partners have "different nationalities and/or ethnicities" (De Hart, van Rossum, and Sportel 2013: 995); children of migrants; and highly skilled migrants. It unveils the tangled mobilities in the lives of mainly Asian migrants within the Asian region and beyond. These tangled mobilities involve three strands linking and shaping places, affects, and personhood: the interweaving of social spheres, different forms of mobilities, and mobilities and stasis. These entanglements provide a perspective toward understanding the complexities of transnational migration, and the stakes they entail, in the lives of migrants and their families.

Interweaving Social Spheres

Five chapters in this volume demonstrate the entanglement of the reproductive (family, home) and productive (economic, employment) realms, as well as the so-called "private" (intimate life, family) and "public" (state-regulated social life) spheres. They show the porosity of these socially constructed divisions by revealing how state policies and widely held gender and religious norms regulating and shaping social interactions affect the "private" lives of migrants and their family members.

Two of the chapters (Pardis Mahdavi; Fiona-Katharina Seiger) show how the receiving countries' policies intricately shape the lives of migrants and their children. Through its migration, labor, and citizenship laws, the state governs the family life of migrants and affects their sense of self. The chapter by Mahdavi demonstrates how the "contractual sterilization laws" and the *kefala* (sponsorship) system in Kuwait and the United Arab Emirates determine migrants' access to employment and legal status. In these countries, some migrant women employed as domestic workers, such as Indians and Filipinos, who refused to return to their natal countries after giving birth outside of marriage, found themselves undocumented. Their lack of legal status subsequently puts their children in a more marginal, precarious position than them. Compared to the mothers, who are still citizens of their countries of origin, their children are both undocumented and stateless. These mothers and children are ensnared in what Mahdavi calls "a cycle of irregularity" due to discriminatory state policies.

The porous division between the private and the public is also evident in the case of Filipino mothers who migrated to Japan with their Japanese-Filipino children to work as caregivers. The chapter by Seiger shows that the migration of both mothers and children is inscribed in "a system of brokerage" based on Japan's family reunification policy, and geared toward the Japanese labor market. As "primary carers" to their (soon-to-be) insider citizen children, Filipino mothers qualify as "migrant workforce" catering to the needs of brokers and employers. Without such status of "primary carer," these mothers would not have been able to migrate with their children and work in Japan. This in-tandem migration leads to undesirable separations between mothers and their non-Japanese-Filipino children and situations in which Filipino mothers in Japan have to work and leave their Japanese-Filipino children alone at home. Work and family become intertwined spheres as the brokering system continuously anchors itself to state laws on migration, labor, and citizenship.

The economic sphere of migrants' lives appears twisted with their personal desire to maintain or reinforce their sense of self, which is often alienated due to aging and/or financial difficulties in their natal countries. Two chapters (Kumiko Kawashima; Jocelyn O. Celero) provide examples on this issue. The first example is the case of highly skilled but aging Japanese migrant men in Dalian, China. In her chapter, Kawashima unveils how the downward social mobility of these men due to demotion in their workplaces and the mandatory retirement age in Japan motivated them to migrate to Dalian where they could continue working in a comfortable, rewarding work environment. The impact of the economic recession in Japan on these men's social status affected their sense of self, driving them to migrate to a country where they could enjoy prestige as highly skilled workers. In Celero's chapter, migration to Japan becomes possible for Japanese-Filipinos thanks to Japan's migration policies, which stress a migrant's biological link to a Japanese citizen (in this case, the fathers). Japanese-Filipinos' economically challenging life in the Philippines and their growing up under their kin's care but without their Japanese fathers' support inspired them to engage in Japan's labor market and transnational caregiving. Emphasizing the notion of *utang na loob* (debt of gratitude), these migrants sustain multiple social ties in both Japan and the Philippines.

Finally, one chapter in this volume (Masako Kudo) uncovers how gender-linked and religion-shaped social norms alongside the Japanese state's control of binational marriages influenced the geographic mobilities and the trajectories of family-making of Japanese-Pakistani couples and their children. Kudo describes in her chapter the marriages of Japanese women and their Pakistani husbands as "tangled with law, economy, and religion," which affects these unions' social incorporation in Japan. Aside from the difficulty of accessing the spousal visa, they had difficulty being accepted by their partner's family. Kudo explains how Japanese-Pakistani couples created "affective circuits" characterized by transnational caregiving. Raising children, notably daughters, in an environment where they could easily interiorize Islamic teachings and values, represents another challenge for Japanese-Pakistani couples. As a result, these couples resort to different care arrangements and mobilities, such as relocating to Pakistan, making Pakistani family members visit Japan, or becoming transnationally split families. These complex family lives reflect how the public realm where social and legal norms are located directly affects mixed families' private spheres and intimate lives.

Tanglement of Different Forms of Mobilities

Not only does the migratory journey unfold simultaneously in different spheres, by lifting them out of one social context and inserting them into another; cross-border spatial mobility also entails the individual's changing positions in different social fields. In this volume, empirical studies collectively illustrate how various forms of mobilities—social, economic, sexual, intimate, educational, and legal—occur in different directions. Their trajectories tangle in the migration process because of the changing logic of the fields. Consequently, such divergent mobilities result in affective responses that might trigger the desire for continued geographic movements, if such options are available. Moreover, studies show that different forms of mobilities are not only entangled with each other, but also with material objects, as well as with a person's life course and that of their children.

Several chapters in this volume deal with the entanglement of different mobilities involved in geographic movement. Kawashima's comparison of the experiences of the older and the younger Japanese who migrated to the northeastern Chinese city of Dalian reveals not only that these migrants' geographic, social, and economic mobilities point in different directions, but that such uneven mobilities also affect people differently at various stages of their life course and career progression. The older migrants who had established a corporate career before the economic recession but were marginalized thereafter were able to secure higher status positions and enjoy more professional and social recognition by moving to China. By comparison, the younger migrants whose career development in Japan was stalled by the economic recession underwent downward social class mobility as they were less able to advance their careers by moving to China, and so were more likely to be trapped in a dead end and in precarious conditions.

The chapters by James Farrer and An Huy Tran highlight the entanglement of sexual mobility with spatial, social, educational, and sexual mobilities. Sexual mobility "concerns the relationship between geographic mobility and a larger social field in which sexual desires and sexualities are experienced and defined" (Farrer, this volume). It is tied to a sexual field, which is "constituted by relations among differentially desirable and differently empowered actors in a sexual scene, determining what forms of desire and action are legitimate, who has the power of sexual initiative and refusal, and what is conventionally at stake in sexual interactions" (ibid.). By moving to another society, migrants find their own sexual desirability rising or declining according to the different logic in the new sexual field. Farrer shows that among the elite migrants in Shanghai, white and ethnic Asian male migrants experience elevated sexual status after migrating to China, while white women find themselves less attractive and often have to adopt new sexual strategies to enhance their desirability. Moreover, the local sexual field evolves with the mobilities of people, money, and culture over time. Those who previously occupied higher positions in the sexual hierarchy, such as white male migrants, might find their sexual status drop when the sexual field includes increasing numbers of wealthy return ethnic Chinese migrants.

Tran's chapter investigates the entanglement of sexualities with social and economic statuses in queer Vietnamese' migration journeys, and how such experiences result in conflicting desires, forcing them to re-evaluate their migration decisions and trajectories. While the existing literature on queer migration tends to celebrate such mobility as a form of sexual emancipation, informants in Tran's study experienced the adverse effect of "race," nationality, and social class on their sexual desirability and opportunities upon migration. Regardless of whether achieving freer sexual expressions was part of the motivation to migrate, sexual encounters, or the lack thereof, become part of their migration experience, influencing both their migratory trajectories and sexual orientations. Some migrants, therefore, decided to return to Vietnam, where their status as migrants to Japan and their material resources gained through migration elevated their sexual status in their home country.

Angelie Marilla's study adds a new form of mobility that rarely shows up in migration research—the mobility of the material objects. Her chapter demonstrates that material objects are tangled in people's geographic and social mobilities. Observing the objects displayed in Vietnamese migrant families' homes and businesses in Belgium and those present in the households of Vietnamese-Belgian families, Marilla emphasizes the agency of the mobile objects. The furniture, photos, cups, religious paraphernalia, and print of a famous painting document their owners' journeys, and symbolize the migrant households' spatial and social mobilities. They also accompany, hinder, and sometimes replace human mobilities.

Because different forms of mobilities take place simultaneously during the course of one's geographic movement, and especially because geographic mobility affects one's intimate social and personal life, migration has emotional consequences—and emotions, in turn, matter in one's migration decision-making. Gracia Liu-Farrer's chapter presents highly educated professionals' narratives of their often multinational migratory journeys in Japan and Germany, demonstrating that the outcomes of tangled mobility can be examined through the affective lens. People articulate their motivations through emotional words. What motivates their decision to stay or leave a place often has to do with people's emotional responses to the places they currently dwell, and/or the one they might aspire to move to. The study also highlights the different effects of positive and negative emotions in influencing individual migration decisions. Negative migration, caused by a lack of intimate social or personal relationships and the loss of social recognition, tends to exert a more decisive influence on mobility decisions and to drive people away from where they are.

Finally, it is not only the migrants themselves who get caught in tangled mobilities. For example, in Kudo's study, the migratory directions of the children of Pakistani fathers and Japanese mothers are influenced by their family's social and economic mobility as well as the changing power balance between their parents. In one case, a child hoped to return to Japan to study so as to bring his mother, stuck in his father's family in Pakistan, back to Japan.

Entwined Mobility and Stasis

The entanglement of mobility and stasis is explicit in six chapters of the volume. These chapters expose the relational aspect of personhood, and pinpoint how a migrant's sense of self is challenged, redefined, or reinforced as they inhabit, cross, or connect social fields and spaces. Affects and emotions are part and parcel of this process, shaping migrants' family and mobility trajectories.

Transnational migration often leads to spatial and social class immobility, as unveiled in a few cases in the volume. Asuncion Fresnoza-Flot remarks that some Filipino women who married Belgian or Dutch men became tied to the realm of home in their receiving countries, due to their husband's disapproval of their labor market engagement. By moving to a different country in their new roles as wives and mothers, some became deprived of basic spatial mobility due to not possessing a driver's license. This mobility and immobility entanglement coincides with these women's social class mobility in their natal country. There their marriage and transnational migration allowed them to attain the ideal Filipino womanhood, thereby increasing their respectability. Another example of tangled mobility and stasis can be found in the chapter by Liu-Farrer, which illustrates how emotions and intimate relationships can drive people to move to or settle in Asia or Europe. In this chapter, she shares stories of Asian migrants who settled in a country where they found self-fulfillment from family, legal, and professional points of view. This spatial immobility is often coupled with other forms of mobility, such as in sexual and social class terms. Liu-Farrer's findings confirm what "intimate mobilities" (Groes and Fernandez 2018) mean, and show their connection with stasis at some points in migrants' life trajectories.

Furthermore, mobility and stasis can be a shared experience between two or more individuals, either between migrants or between migrants and non-migrants. The chapter by Celero uncovers how working Filipino mothers' migration to Japan becomes tangled with the spatial and social class immobility of their stay-behind Japanese-Filipino children. When the latter migrated to Japan, they experienced legal mobility thanks to Japan's immigration and citizenship policies that emphasize one's biological link to a Japanese parent. This mobility takes place while their mothers experience legal and social class immobility. Another chapter, the one by Marilla, demonstrates that settlement in one country after migration can be tangled with spatial mobility of objects. She observes that Vietnamese migrants in couple with Belgians exchange objects transnationally with their natal families in Vietnam throughout the migration process. Objects follow where the migrants are, and when they reach their destination place, they move within the realm of home or from this place to public places where migrants engage in social activities or work. As they become spatially immobile, objects decay, but they remain temporally mobile in the memories and emotions of the owners.

In addition, spatial mobility can tangle with sexual immobility. In Tran's chapter, the migration of queer Vietnamese in Japan intersects with their sexualities and social class mobility. Their transnational spatial mobility is tangled with their immobility in terms of expression of their sexual identities in Japan, where they do not fit the image of a "desirable" figure in ethnicized, racialized, and classed queer dating sites. Their return migration to Vietnam, where they finally settle, allows them to regain a sense of respectability, as they become "desirable" potential partners in Vietnamese' sexual fields due to their past transnational migration to Japan. Therefore, their spatial immobility becomes twisted with what Farrer, in his chapter, calls "sexual mobility." Drawing from his long ethnography in Shanghai, Farrer reveals that migrants (transnational or translocal) move not only across spaces but also within and across social and sexual fields. During their movement and stasis, migrants may experience upward or downward sexual mobility. For instance, white Western men enjoyed upward sexual mobility during the period between 1998 and the early 2000s in Shanghai's transnational sexual field, whereas their white Western women counterparts underwent downward sexual mobility. This situation had changed by the 2010s, when rich Mainland Chinese men called "fuerdai" (the rich second generation) replaced both white Western and overseas Chinese men as "desirable" partners in this sexual field. Farrer remarks that sex, money, and status tangle in sexual fields, and that spatial mobility can become coupled with either sexual mobility or immobility.

Conclusion

The present volume draws on the mobility literature and Asian migration scholarship, as well as building on recent developments in transnational migration into, within, and out of Asia. Through the lens of tangled mobilities, it does not merely display different combinations of motivations or the messiness of entwined mobilities, but provides fresh perspectives on transnational migration phenomena in conceptual, empirical, and analytical terms.

From a conceptual point of view, the volume's focus on entanglements avoids adopting the dichotomic approach "mobility versus stasis" observed by Glick Schiller and Salazar (2013) in early mobility scholarship. It puts to the fore the relational aspects of mobilities. These aspects concern the plural, compounded motivations of migration, the interweaving social spheres, and the entwining of places, affects, and personhood. The various chapters demonstrate that different motivations (economic, existential, familial) become entangled in the migration of all migrants. Regardless of where migrants come from, where they go to, and how they articulate their initial motivations, their migration experiences and outcomes are affected by the simultaneous unfolding of their mobility trajectories in different fields. Migration, in other words, is "tangled mobilities," and viewing it as such is an effective starting point for understanding the power dynamics causing and resulting from it. Another relational aspect of mobilities highlighted in this volume is the interweaving of different social spheres (public, private, reproductive, and productive), which is due to the structuring power of state policies over migrants and their children's lives. This finding highlights the porosity of the socially constructed divides between social spheres (Fresnoza-Flot 2018; Lan 2008). Alongside these intertwined spheres is the entanglement of the often invisible dimensions of migration, including self-making and feelings of belonging. By paying attention to the complex emotions that shape, accompany, and stem from migration, this volume unveils the affective universe of individual migrants and their families. It lays bare the reality that people embark on the migratory journey with various aspirations and desires that are innately human.

Empirically speaking, through its case studies showing the recent developments in Asian transnational migrations, the volume diversifies the literature on mobilities that has, to date, mostly seen empirical examples from Western societies. The cases examined confirm previous observations that migration is multifaceted, and its patterns can overlap each other (e.g., Piper and Roces 2003). In most recent and emergent migration destinations in Asia where migration policy is nearly always presented in the utilitarian discourse, migrants are primarily considered as labor, whether productive or reproductive; or, more politely, as "human resources" or "global talents" (Liu-Farrer, forthcoming). By emphasizing complex migratory motives, the volume carries to policymakers the message that one cannot separate the manpower from the personhood of individual migrants.

In terms of analytical value, the volume's lens of tangled mobilities leads to a different approach to migration, as it focuses on entanglements and their processes at different levels of analysis (micro, meso, macro). Instead of fixing its analytical regard on only one or two forms of mobility, it takes into account the interrelatedness among mobility forms. This approach brings out the nuances, subtleties, and complexities of individuals' migration experiences, thereby avoiding an oversimplified and linear portrayal of their life trajectories. Drawing on qualitative case studies focusing on the micro level of human life, the volume shows the influence of intersecting categories of difference (e.g., gender, social class, sexuality, and age) on the occurrence of tangled mobilities in migrants' translocal and transnational social spaces. These observations challenge the conventional views that tend to associate lifestyle and existential migrations with the North-North or North-South mobilities of the middle-class and wealthy migrants, and equate economically driven migration to working-class labor migrants from the Global South. It also reveals the entanglement of different elements, components, and forms of mobilities as a factor in making migration outcomes unpredictable. In addition, by embracing an inclusive stance, the volume uncovers how heterosexual and LGBTQ migrants experience the sexual fields in their social spaces, (re)define themselves as they undergo (im)mobility in these fields, and gain new subjectivities during this process.

The different crisscrossing trajectories analyzed in this volume offer possible research topics for the study of tangled mobilities. First, the temporality of entanglement needs to be further incorporated in the analysis of migration. In the context of the COVID-19 pandemic, it is worth investigating how this pandemic disentangles or further complicates the intertwined (im)mobilities that migrants and their families experience. There is an urgent need to conceptualize stasis in this context and to revisit the degree to which it is linked to mobility, including the different social, economic, and political stakes it entails. Second, to understand the entanglement of elements, components, and forms of mobilities, it is crucial to design innovative methodological approaches appropriate to this intellectual enterprise. The volume highlights the usefulness of qualitative methodologies in this regard, leaving open the question of novel methodologies suitable for dealing with ongoing societal changes and challenges. Because mobility is an "assemblage" (Salazar 2019), the most effective methodologies for capturing its complexities will probably turn out to be assemblages too.

Asuncion Fresnoza-Flot is a tenured Associate Researcher of the Belgian National Fund for Scientific Research (F.R.S.-FNRS) and a Senior Lecturer (*maîtresse de conférence*) at the Laboratory of Anthropology of Contemporary Worlds (LAMC) at the Université libre de Bruxelles (ULB) in Belgium. Her recent works include the co-edited volumes *Mobile Childhoods in Filipino Transnational Families: Migrant Children with Similar Roots in Different Routes* (with Itaru Nagasaka, 2015) and *International Marriages and Marital Citizenship: Southeast Asian Women on the Move* (with Gwenola Ricordeau, 2017). Her other publications deal with transnational family dynamics, conjugal mixedness, and intergenerational transmission, as well as marriage and divorce involving Filipino and Thai migrants in selected European countries. Her ongoing research focuses on the contextual mobility of Belgian-Asian couples within their cross-border social spaces.

Gracia Liu-Farrer is Professor of Sociology at the Graduate School of Asia-Pacific Studies, and Director of the Institute of Asian Migrations, Waseda University, Japan. Her research examines immigrants' economic, social, and political practices in Japan, and the spatial and social mobility of students and professional migrants in Asia and Europe. She is the co-editor of the *Routledge Handbook of Asian Migration* (with Brenda Yeoh, 2018), and the author of *Labour Migration from China to Japan: International Students, Transnational Migrants* (Routledge, 2011) and *Immigrant Japan: Mobility and Belonging in an Ethno-nationalist Society* (Cornell University Press, 2020). Her ORCID is: 0000-0003-3241-8703.

REFERENCES

Asis, Maruja. 2006. "The Philippines' Culture of Migration." Blog. Migration Policy Institute. Retrieved 14 July 2021 from https://www.migrationpolicy.org/article/philippines-culture-migration.

Asis, Maruja, Seori Choi, Chang Won Lee, Hsiao-Ta Jeng, and Jung-Che Chang. 2019. "The Philippines-Korea and Philippines-Taiwan Migration Corridors: A Comparison of Recruitment Systems and Their Outcomes." *Asian and Pacific Migration Journal* 28(4): 469–76.

Asis, Maruja, Nicola Piper, and Parvati Raghuram. 2010. "International Migration and Development in Asia: Exploring Knowledge Frameworks." *International Migration* 48(3): 76–106.

——. 2019. "From Asia to the World: 'Regional' Contributions to Global Migration Research." *Revue europeenne des Migrations internationales* 35(1): 13–37.

Basch, Linda G., Nina Glick Schiller, and Cristina Szanton Blanc. 1995. *Nations Unbound: Transnational Projects, Postcolonial Predicaments, and Deterritorialised Nation-States.* Amsterdam: Gordon and Breach.

Bauder, Harald. 2003. "'Brain Abuse,' or the Devaluation of Immigrant Labour in Canada." *Antipode* 35(4): 699–717.

Benson, Michaela, and Karen O'Reilly. 2009. "Migration and the Search for a Better Way of Life: A Critical Exploration of Lifestyle Migration." *The Sociological Review* 57(4): 608-25.

Borch, Signe. 2017. "In 'No Man's Land': The Im/mobility of Serb NGO Workers in Kosovo." *Social Identities* 23(4): 478-92.

Canzler, Weert, Vincent Kaufmann, and Sven Kesselring, eds. 2008. *Tracing Mobilities: Towards a Cosmopolitan Perspective*. Farnham: Ashgate.

Chu, Julie Y. 2010. *Cosmologies of Credit: Transnational Mobility and the Politics of Destination in China*. Durham, NC: Duke University Press.

Coates, Jamie. 2018. "The Cultural and Economic Logics of Migration." In *Routledge Handbook of Asian Migrations*, ed. Gracia Liu-Farrer and Brenda S. Yeoh, 162-72. London: Routledge.

Constable, Nicole. 2003. *Romance on a Global Stage: Pen Pals, Virtual Ethnography, and "Mail Order" Marriages*. Berkeley: University of California Press.

———. 2010. "Introduction: Cross-Border Marriages, Gendered Mobility, and Global Hypergamy." In *Cross-Border Marriages: Gender and Mobility in Transnational Asia*, ed. Nicole Constable, 1-16. Philadelphia: University of Pennsylvania Press.

Crenshaw, Kimberlé. 1989. "Demarginalizing the Intersection of Race and Sex: A Black Feminist Critique of Antidiscrimination Doctrine, Feminist Theory and Antiracist Politics." *The University of Chicago Legal Forum. Feminism in the Law: Theory, Practice and Criticism*, 139-67.

Cresswell, Tim. 2006. *On the Move: Mobility in the Modern Western World*. New York: Routledge.

Darwin, Charles. 1872. *The Origin of Species by Means of Natural Selection, or the Preservation of Favoured Races in the Struggle for Life*, 6th edn. London: John Murray.

Debnár, Miloš. 2016. *Migration, Whiteness, and Cosmopolitanism: Europeans in Japan*. New York: Palgrave Macmillan.

De Hart, Betty, Wibo M. van Rossum, and Iris Sportel. 2013. "Law in the Everyday Lives of Transnational Families: An Introduction." *Oñati Socio-Legal Series* 3(6): 991-1003.

Douglass, Mike. 2010. "Globalizing the Household in East Asia." *The Whitehead Journal of Diplomacy and International Relations* 11: 63-78.

Farrer, James. 2010. "A Foreign Adventurer's Paradise? Interracial Sexuality and Alien Sexual Capital in Reform Era Shanghai." *Sexualities* 13(1): 69-95.

———. 2019. *International Migrants in China's Global City: The New Shanghailanders*. London: Routledge.

Fresnoza-Flot, Asuncion. 2012. "Security in Labor Migration in the Philippines: National Honor, Family Solidarity, and Migrants' Protection." In *Human Security: Securing East Asia's Future*, ed. Benny Teh Cheng Guan, 95-112. London: Springer.

———. 2018. "Raising Citizens in 'Mixed' Family Setting: Mothering Techniques of Filipino and Thai Migrants in Belgium." *Citizenship Studies* 22(3): 278-93.

———. 2022 forthcoming. "Gender Gaps in Migration Studies: Recent Developments and Prospects." In *Gender Equality in the Mirror: Reflecting on Power, Participation and Global Justice*, ed. Elisa Fornale. Leiden: Brill.

Fresnoza-Flot, Asuncion, and Gwénola Ricordeau, eds. 2017. *International Marriages and Marital Citizenship: Southeast Asian Women on the Move*. London: Routledge.

Fresnoza-Flot, Asuncion, and Kyoko Shinozaki. 2017. "Transnational Perspectives on Intersecting Experiences: Gender, Social Class and Generation among Southeast Asian Migrants and Their Families." *Journal of Ethnic and Migration Studies* 43(6): 867-84.

Frykman, Jonas, and Maja Povrzanović Frykman. 2016. *Sensitive Objects: Affect and Material Culture*. Lund: Nordic Academic Press.

Glick Schiller, Nina, and Noel B. Salazar. 2013. "Regimes of Mobility across the Globe." *Journal of Ethnic and Migration Studies* 39(2): 183-200.

Glodava, Mila, and Richard Onizuka. 1994. *Mail-Order Brides: Women for Sale*. Fort Collins, CO: Alaken.

Green, Paul. 2015. "Mobility Regimes in Practice: Later-life Westerners and Visa Runs in South-East Asia." *Mobilities* 10(5): 748-63.

Groes, Christian, and Nadine T. Fernandez, eds. 2018. *Intimate Mobilities: Sexual Economies, Marriage and Migration in a Disparate World*. New York: Berghahn Books.

Guzman, Manuel. 1997. "'Pa' la Escuelita con Mucho Cuida'o y por la Orillita': A Journey Through the Contested Terrains of the Nation and Sexual Orientation." In *Puerto Rican Jam: Rethinking Colonialism and Nationalism*, ed. Frances Negrón-Muntaner and Ramón Grosfoguel, 209-28. Minneapolis: University of Minnesota Press.

Hernes, Tor. 2008. *Understanding Organization as Process: Theory for a Tangled World*. London: Routledge.

Ho, Elaine Lynn-Ee. 2018. *Citizens in Motion: Emigration, Immigration, and Re-migration across China's Borders*. Stanford, CA: Stanford University Press.

Hochschild, Arlie Russell. 2000. "Global Care Chains and Emotional Surplus Value." In *Global Capitalism*, ed. Will Hutton and Anthony Giddens, 130-46. London: Jonathan Cape.

Hof, Helena. 2020. "Intersections of Race and Skills in European Migration to Asia: Between White Cultural Capital and 'Passive Whiteness.'" *Ethnic and Racial Studies* 44(11): 2113-34.

Ingold, Tim. 2008. "Bindings Against Boundaries: Entanglements of Life in an Open World." *Environment and Planning A* 40(8): 1796-810.

———. 2011. *Being Alive: Essays on Movement, Knowledge and Description*. Abingdon: Routledge.

IOM (International Organization for Migration). 2020. *World Migration Report 2020*. Geneva.

Kakihara, Masao, and Carsten Sørensen. 2001. "Expanding the 'Mobility' Concept." *ACM SIG Group Bulletin* 22(3): 33-37.

Kandel, William, and Douglas S. Massey. 2002. "The Culture of Mexican Migration: A Theoretical and Empirical Analysis." *Social Forces* 80(3): 981-1004.

Kawashima, Kumiko. 2010. "Japanese Working Holiday Makers in Australia and their Relationship to the Japanese Labour Market: Before and After." *Asian Studies Review* 34(3): 267-86.

———. 2018. "Longer-Term Consequences of 'Youth' Migration: Japanese Temporary Migrants in China and the Life Course." *Journal of Intercultural Studies* 39(6): 658–72.

Kowner, Rotem, and Walter Demel. 2012. *Race and Racism in Modern East Asia: Western and Eastern Constructions*. Leiden: Brill.

Lan, Pei-Chia. 2008. "New Global Politics of Reproductive Labor: Gendered Labor and Marriage Migration." *Sociology Compass* 2(6): 1801–15.

Lapanun, Patcharin. 2012. "It's Not Just About Money: Transnational Marriages of Isan Women." *Journal of Mekong Societies* 8(3): 1–28.

Ley, David. 2011. *Millionaire Migrants: Trans-Pacific Life Lines* (Vol. 97). Hoboken: John Wiley & Sons.

Liu-Farrer, Gracia. 2016. "Migration as Class-based Consumption: The Emigration of the Rich in Contemporary China." *China Quarterly* 224: 499–518.

———. 2020. *Immigrant Japan: Mobility and Belonging in an Ethno-nationalist Society*. Ithaca, NY: Cornell University Press.

———. 2022. "Japan's Immigration in the Heisei Era: Population, Policy and the Ethno-nationalist Dilemma." In *Japan in the Heisei Era (1989–2019*, ed. Noriko Murai, Jeff Kingston, and Tina Burret, 140–52. London: Routledge.

Liu-Farrer, Gracia, and An Huy Tran. 2019. "Bridging the Institutional Gaps: International Education as a Migration Industry." *International Migration* 57(3): 235–49.

Liu-Farrer, Gracia, and Brenda S. Yeoh. 2018. "Asian Migrations and Mobilities: Continuities, Conceptualisations and Controversies." In *Routledge Handbook of Asian Migrations*, ed. Gracia Liu-Farrer and Brenda S. Yeoh, 1–18. London: Routledge.

Liu-Farrer, Gracia, Brenda S. Yeoh, and Michiel Baas. 2021. "Social Construction of Skill: An Analytical Approach Toward the Question of Skill in Cross-Border Labour Mobilities." *Journal of Ethnic and Migration Studies* 47(10): 2237–51.

Madison, Greg. 2006. "Existential Migration." *Existential Analysis: Journal of the Society for Existential Analysis* 17(2): 238–60.

Mahdavi, Pardis. 2016. *Crossing the Gulf: Love and Family in Migrant Lives*. Stanford, CA: Stanford University Press.

Massumi, Brian. 1995. "The Autonomy of Affect." *Cultural Critique* 3: 83–109.

Nohl, Arnd-Michael, Karin Schittenhelm, Oliver Schmidtke, and Anja Weiß. 2014. *Work in Transition: Cultural Capital and Highly Skilled Migrants' Passages into the Labour Market*. Toronto: University of Toronto Press.

Noret, Joël, ed. 2020. *Social Im/mobilities in Africa: Ethnographic Approaches*. New York: Berghahn Books.

Ong, Aihwa. 1992. "Limits to Cultural Accumulation: Chinese Capitalists on the American Pacific Rim." *Annals of the New York Academy of Sciences* 645(1): 125–43.

Ono, Mayumi. 2010. "Long-Stay Tourism: Elderly Japanese Tourists in the Cameron Highlands, Malaysia." *Senri Ethnological Studies* 76: 95–110.

Ortiga, Yasmin. 2017. *Emigration, Employability and Higher Education in the Philippines*. Abingdon: Routledge.

Palmer, Wayne. 2016. *Indonesia's Overseas Labour Migration Programme, 1969–2010*, Vol. 307. Leiden: Brill.

Parreñas, Rhacel Salazar. 2012. "The Reproductive Labour of Migrant Workers." *Global Networks* 12(2): 269–75.

Parreñas, Rhacel Salazar, Rachel Silvey, Maria Cecilia Hwang, and Carolyn Areum Choi. 2019. "Serial Labor Migration: Precarity and Itinerancy among Filipino and Indonesian Domestic Workers." *International Migration Review* 53(4): 1230–58.

Paul, Anju Mary. 2017. *Multinational Maids: Stepwise Migration in a Global Labor Market*. Cambridge: Cambridge University Press.

Piper, Nicola, and Mina Roces, eds. 2003. *Wife or Worker? Asian Women and Migration*. Lanham, MD: Rowman & Littlefield.

Piper, Nicola, Stuart Rosewarne, and Matt Withers. 2017. "Migrant Precarity in Asia: 'Networks of Labour Activism' for a Rights-based Governance of Migration." *Development and Change* 48(5): 1089–110.

Rodriguez, Robyn Magalit. 2010. *Migrants for Export: How the Philippine State Brokers Labor to the World*. Minneapolis: University of Minnesota Press.

Salazar, Noel B. 2010. "Towards an Anthropology of Cultural Mobilities." *Crossings: Journal of Migration & Culture* 1(1): 53–68.

———. 2019. "Mobility." *REMHU: Revista Interdisciplinar da Mobilidade Humana* 27(57): 13–24.

Saxenian, AnnaLee. 2005. "From Brain Drain to Brain Circulation: Transnational Communities and Regional Upgrading in India and China." *Studies in Comparative International Development* 40(2): 35–61.

Scuzzarello, Sarah. 2020. "Practising Privilege: How Settling in Thailand Enables Older Western Migrants to Enact Privilege Over Local People." *Journal of Ethnic and Migration Studies* 46(8): 1606–28.

Sheller, Mimi, and John Urry. 2006. "The New Mobilities Paradigm." *Environment and Planning A* 38(2): 207–26.

Statham, Paul, Sarah Scuzzarello, Sirijit Sunanta, and Alexander Trupp. 2020. "Globalising Thailand through Gendered 'Both-Ways' Migration Pathways with 'the West': Cross-Border Connections between People, States, and Places." *Journal of Ethnic and Migration Studies* 46(8): 1513–42.

Suksomboon, Panitee. 2007. "Remittances and 'Social Remittances': Their Impact on Cross-cultural Marriage and Social Transformation." *IIAS Newsletter* 45: 6.

Thai, Hung Cam. 2014. *Insufficient Funds: The Culture of Money in Low-Wage Transnational Families*. Stanford, CA: Stanford University Press.

Thomas, William, and Florian Znaniecki. 1918. *The Polish Peasant in Europe and America: Monograph of an Immigrant Group*, Volume 1: Primary Group Organization. Boston, MA: Richard G. Badger, The Gorham Press.

Thrift, Nigel. 2008. *Non-Representational Theory: Space, Politics, Affect*. London: Routledge.

Tsoukas, Haridimos, and Robert Chia. 2002. "On Organizational Becoming: Rethinking Organizational Change." *Organization Science* 13(5): 567–99.

Tsuda, Takeyuki Gaku. 2018. "Japanese Brazilians in Japan and Conceptions of Homeland." In *Routledge Handbook of Asian Migrations*, ed. Gracia Liu-Farrer and Brenda S. Yeoh, 103–13. London: Routledge.

UNSD (United Nations Statistics Division). 2021. "Geographic Regions." https://unstats.un.org/unsd/methodology/m49/.

Walsh, Katie. 2007. "'It Got Very Debauched, Very Dubai!': Heterosexual Intimacy amongst Single British Expatriates." *Social & Cultural Geography* 8(4): 507–33.

Waters, Johanna L. 2008. *Education, Migration, and Cultural Capital in the Chinese Diaspora*. Amherst, NY: Cambria Press.

———. 2018. "*In Anticipation*: Educational (Im)Mobilities, Structural Disadvantage, and Young People's Futures." *Journal of Intercultural Studies* 39(6): 673–87.

Whittaker, Andrea. 2018. "Conceptualising Asian Medical Travel as Medical Migrations." In *Routledge Handbook of Asian Migrations*, ed. Gracia Liu-Farrer and Brenda S. Yeoh, 114–27. London: Routledge.

Xiang, Biao. 2013. "Return and the Reordering of Transnational Mobility in Asia." In *Return: Nationalizing Transnational Mobility in Asia*, ed. Biao Xiang, Brenda S. Yeoh, and Mika Toyota, 1–20. Durham, NC: Duke University Press.

Xiang, Biao, and Johan Lindquist. 2014. "Migration Infrastructure." *International Migration Review* 48: 122–48.

CHAPTER 1

Sexual Mobility, Migration, and Sexual Fields

James Farrer

Sexual Mobility and Sexual Fields

Many migrants experience what I call *sexual mobility*, or changes in their sexual status, sexual opportunities, and even sexual interests during migration. Some people migrate for sexual reasons, such as pursuing sexual variety or more available partners (Paquin 2014; Statham et al. 2020), making a living from sex work (Agustín 2006), engaging in extramarital affairs (Liu-Farrer 2010), finding a more accommodating context to live as a sexual minority (Carrillo 2018), or accompanying a partner with an expatriate assignment (Cangià 2018). These could all be described as "sexual migrants" (Carrillo 2018). While sexual migration can be a useful term, it places a great emphasis on sexual (or conjugal) motives, which often become entangled with a multitude of other considerations. Even moves officially recognized as "marriage migration" frequently involve a mix of motives, including material comfort, social status, and ease of mobility (Groes and Fernandez 2018). On the other hand, sexuality may also emerge as an important element of migration stories, even when it would not be reported as a primary motive or an incentive for mobility. For example, economic migrants may move for a job, with unforeseen consequences for their intimate lives (including marriage or divorce, and a gain or loss of sexual opportunities). Refugees and asylum seekers are not likely thinking of sex when they leave home, yet sexual violence or a lack of sexual intimacy may become critical issues in their journeys.¹ These are not "sexual migrants" in the usual sense, but mobility has consequences for their sexual and intimate lives. Sexual mobility is thus a broader concept than sexual migration, capturing experiences of eroticism independent of accounts of motive or desires. The sexual mobility concept also avoids the trap of "methodological conjugalism" or the tendency to privilege marriage-like relations and diminish the importance of sexual interests and interactions that are not conjugal. Sexual mobility also differs from the accounts of "intimate mobilities," or "the intimization of mobility," a concept that highlights the processes that facilitate mobility based upon intimate relationships (e.g., spousal and adoption visas) (Groes and Fernandez 2018: 2). Sexual mobility, as I define it, concerns the relationship between geographic mobility and a larger social field in which sexual desires and sexualities are experienced and defined. Linking to the discussions of tangled mobilities in this volume, the concept of sexual mobility shows how geographic mobility organized around movement in one social field (e.g., career mobility or educational mobility) becomes inadvertently entangled in mobility in other fields, in this case, sexuality. Different forms of mobility—economic, social, educational, sexual—are entangled in ways that actors cannot easily foresee, because linkages across social fields (e.g., the impact of career mobility on dating opportunities) are often unexpected by actors within them.

My concept of sexual mobility rests on the idea of a sexual field, represented in a growing body of research explaining how sexual life is organized at the social level (Martin and George 2006; Green 2008, 2014; Farrer 2010; Leschziner and Green 2013).² This conceptualization of sexuality as a field is itself loosely based upon the ideas of Bourdieu, with ancillary concepts such as "sexual capital" (the resources that provide sexual status within a field) and "sexual habitus" (the engrained dispositions that govern sexual action) adapted from Bourdieu's broader opus (Bourdieu and Waquant 1992; Green 2008). A sexual field is constituted by relations among differentially desirable and differently empowered actors in a sexual scene, determining what forms of desire and action are legitimate, who has the power of sexual initiative and refusal, and what is conventionally at stake in sexual interactions. In short, a sexual field is a socially constructed account of the rules of the "sexual game," in which some players have the power to set the rules to their advantage, while others may follow or contest these rules. There are multiple geographically and socially bounded sexual fields, ranging from mainstream heterosexual dating scenes to minority sexual subcultures, each operating according to different rules (Martin and George 2006; Green 2008).

Migrants typically experience sexual mobility as an unexpected consequence of exiting one sexual field and entering another, finding themselves in new "sexual games" in which they may feel unexpectedly disadvantages or (more rarely) advantaged. They may either find partners more easily, and find their sexual status enhanced, or they may experience greater difficulty, and thus have a diminished or lowered sexual status. They may adjust their sexual preferences and strategies to fit the new situation, or may even withdraw from the field altogether (Farrer 2010; Farrer and Dale 2014). Even for migrants not actively seeking partners or partnered sex, sexual fields provide a sense of status that may become an essential element of self-esteem, self-efficacy, or gender identity. Tracing sexual mobility, therefore, is less about establishing the motives of migrants than about investigating the nature of the sexual fields in which migrants are embedded and re-embedded, a process that may transform motives and reshape desires. Sexual mobility is not limited to migrants moving across borders but may also involve the mobilities of fields themselves. This can involve, for example, the advent of transnational sexual scenes, such as commercial sex work or nightlife subcultures, in emerging global cities (Farrer 1999, 2019: 136–37; Groes-Green 2013; Groes 2018). Thus, such sexual mobility may impact people who experience little geographic mobility but find themselves interacting with migrants from other places in new transnational fields that emerge in their cities. Sexual mobility is, therefore, mobility within or across sexual fields, and is related to, but not equivalent to, geographic mobility.

The goal of this chapter, in short, is to lay out the implications of this concept of sexual mobility for studies of migration, and to describe the tangled nature of sexual mobility—not only entanglements between sexual life and migration but between sexual and the other types of social fields that migrants move across. In doing this, I rely upon my two decades of qualitative research on sexuality and sexual mobilities in Shanghai, the cosmopolitan business center of China (Farrer 1999, 2002, 2007, 2008, 2010, 2011, 2013, 2016, 2019; Farrer and Dale 2014; Farrer and Field 2015). To supplement and extend this analysis, I also refer to studies published in other contexts. While my previous publications on Shanghai sexual scenes are detailed ethnographic case studies, the goal here is primarily conceptual, to show how the concepts of sexual mobility and sexual fields can contribute to migration studies more broadly.

Sexual Mobility as a Framework for Studying Migration

Looking at social life in terms of fields raises several empirical and theoretical questions.[3] The most general one is about the emergence of autonomous fields of sexuality with their own rule makers, arbiters of merit, and field-specific resources that are, to some extent, independent of those in other fields. It is not self-evident that sexuality constitutes a field, given that sexual relations and interests are implicit and entrenched in all forms of social interactions, whether in the arts or politics, or family life. Existing studies of sexual fields have demonstrated that the concept is useful in some sexual contexts, with the most typical examples being gay nightlife scenes. Still, it is not evident that all sexual interactions can be conceptualized as fields (see Green 2014).[4] Sexual spaces become organized as fields only as part of a process of differentiation, and by disembedding sexual and erotic interests from other areas of life. It is a process in which actors become collectively oriented toward a range of affective and corporal interactions that are then judged by relatively autonomous criteria (Green 2008). In general, sexuality in premodern societies seems deeply embedded in other social relationships—notably the political, family, and economic spheres—and thus the idea of a field of sexual activities that operates relatively autonomously from dynastic politics and economic interests seems quintessentially modern and Western (see Giddens 1992). This may not be the case, however. The worlds of medieval romance in Europe, India, and Japan offer examples of cultures of erotic interaction that were distinct from the dynastic and reproductive sexual norms of the age (Reddy 2012). The late Ming world of relationships between male literati and educated courtesans—based on an idealized concept of romantic feelings (*qing*)—might be considered another type of premodern, or early modern, sexual field (Zurndorfer 2011). Sexual fields are specific historical constructs, to be sure, but they are not unique to our era, and certainly not to the West. For migration studies, it is important to first consider the conditions for the establishment of distinct sexual fields in both sending and receiving regions, and to then see how migrants experience mobility within and across them. Some such sexual fields are transnational in their structure and may involve sexual interactions among partners with extreme inequality in resources.

A second general question about sexual fields is the issue of stratification within the field, or the unequal distribution of resources, power, and authority. This structuration of the field is often expressed in sociological research by the term "sexual capital," or sometimes "erotic capital" (Gonzales and Rolison 2005; Green 2008, 2014; Hakim 2011). Sexual capital refers to the resources, competencies, and endowments of a person that provide status as sexual agents within a field (Gonzales and Rolison 2005; Martin and George 2006; Farrer 2010). The concept of sexual capital implies not only an unequal distribution of sexual resources (or desirability and status) but possibly skewed rules of the game that benefit some types of actors over others. For the researcher, it may be difficult to discover how the rules are established within a sexual field, but it is usually possible to ask who benefits from these rules, and to observe how others may contest or attempt to subvert them. For example, race is a central component of sexual status in mainstream American sexual fields. Gonzales and Rolison (2005) show that, regardless of income, white men in the United States enjoy higher levels of sexual capital than black men, black women, and white women, allowing them more sexual opportunities and more latitude for sexual experimentation. In an analysis of the sexual popularity of white men in Japan—at a time when Japan was rich and many Japanese women earned more than their Western lovers—Kelsky (2001) argues that the whiteness and culture of Western men were "hegemonic constitutive elements" of the freedom and modernity that Japanese women longed for in general (ibid.: 148). Certainly, a key question for sexual mobilities involves repositioning migrants in gendered and racialized sexual hierarchies as they enter new sexual fields. These may intersect with other forms of stratification—economic, cultural—in contradictory ways.

A third empirical question is about the spatial and social boundaries of fields, a central issue for studies of sexual mobility experienced in migration. Sexual fields seem to be demarcated quite narrowly in some studies, such as a single type of gay bar in some ethnographic case studies (e.g., Green 2008), or much more broadly in actors' shared recognition of sexual rules, actors, and goals on a dating website. There are sexual fields that cross multiple national borders or transnational sexual fields (Farrer and Dale 2014). Clearly, in the latter cases, the boundaries of a field may be vague. Still, experiences of boundary crossing remain central for a study of sexual mobilities. We should ask what happens when migrants enter a new sexual field, how they become aware of new norms, actors, and standards of desire, and how they may seek to modify or challenge the rules of the game. Sexual fields exist at various scales—local, national, and transnational—and may be embedded loosely within each other (Jackson 2009). Mobility within a transnational field, such as one loosely constituted by gay sexual scenes in Asian cities, still involves adjustment to national and local variations in the larger transnational field.

A fourth question, especially relevant to the study of sexual mobilities, involves socialization into the field. The relational approach of field theory has the advantage of highlighting how notions of desirability and appropriate forms of desire are constructed within the sexual field as opposed to being "naturally" given outside of it. In the case of migrants, people may be entering new sexual fields and thus acquiring new forms of "erotic habitus" (Green 2008) and the sexual dispositions of actors peculiar to that field, including specific preferences, styles of interaction, and ways of self-presentation. Therefore, one consequence of migration may be a great deal of uneasiness with sexual mobility (Farrer 2010) and resistance to accepting a subordinate or marginal role (Farrer and Dale 2014). Migrants, however, may also find acquired sexual habitus to be empowering and liberating (Ding and Ho 2013).

The fifth focus of empirical research is the convertibility of sexual capital. The generic conception of "fields" allows that one form of "capital" may be convertible into another (cultural into economic capital being the classic example from Bourdieu: see Bourdieu and Waquant 1992). Capital conversions in the sexual field may go in both directions, and both may be construed as a type of sexual agency. Forms of cultural capital—nationality, education, language ability—may be actualized as sexual capital (or sex appeal). Sexual capital may be converted to economic capital, not only through transactional sex but also through various intimate exchanges (Ding and Ho 2013; Groes-Green 2013; Groes 2018; Priscitelli 2018). Capital conversions—from sexual to economic and social capital—transform the sexual field into a lattice of connections and opportunities for some migrants, a space that not only motivates but enables mobility. These lattices of opportunity may be created not only for migrants but for people who come into contact with migrants in emerging transnational sexual fields. I have used the concept of mobility lattice to describe how transnational social fields—such as a specialized culinary field—provide resources for the careers and geographic mobilities of migrants (Farrer 2019, 2020). Sexual fields may also be mobility lattices for some migrants, providing capital conversion and further mobility possibilities.

Finally, the central questions for migration studies involve the mobility within and across sexual fields that accompanies geographic mobility. Migrants not only move in space but within and across social fields. These may include employment, cultural, and—the focus here—sexual fields. Geographical mobility may be facilitated by the transnational structure of a field, such as the highly structured economic fields of corporate employment, or it may involve migrants crossing the boundaries of fields and losing field-specific capital (such as recognition of professional credentials) in a new context (Erel 2010). Sexual mobilities are analogous, but given that transnational sexual fields are generally less institutionalized and more localized than cross-border economic fields, migrants are likely to experience sexual mobility as a move *across* sexual fields, not within them, and thus experience abrupt shifts (often a loss) in sexual status. These six types of generic questions underlie the discussion that follows. I use my own and other scholars' research of sexuality to show how sexual fields shape the experience of migrants, how migrants are socialized into sexual fields, and how migrants exercise agency in the field.

Migrants in Emerging Sexual Fields: Producing a Transnational Sexual Field in Shanghai

Sexual mobilities are tied to the emergence of new sexual fields. One emergent sexual field in which migrants (albeit often second-generation migrants or the children of migrants) played a significant role was the development of urban dating culture in American cities in the late nineteenth and early twentieth century. Working-class "ethnic" men and women participated in a new culture of premarital sociability and intimacy that became a culture of "going out" or "dating" in US cities (Bailey 1989). This replaced the previous culture of "courting," which was centered in domestic spaces. While some types of migrants were marginalized within this emerging national sexual field (especially people of color or non-heterosexual youth), many migrants, including many "ethnic" women, found dance halls, amusement parks, and cinemas to be arenas for integration into urban American society (Peiss 1985). Young ethnic women living in crowded tenements in cities such as New York were pioneers of some of these practices as they were generally excluded from the courting culture that required a specialized space in the home (the parlor) to meet men. The new dating practices formed a heterosexual sexual field in which young people gained autonomy from their parents. This new national sexual field empowered youth over adults, and men over women. Young men (who spent money on dates) became the arbiters of what was to be done on dates, while women were expected to hold the lines on sexual intimacy (while still becoming progressively intimate with their "dates"). The second-generation European migrants who participated in this dating culture became "Americanized" (and "whitened"), because dating not only structured a national sexual field but a new national youth culture based on both heterosexual intimacy and reconfigured racial boundaries (Peiss 1985; Bailey 1989).

In my fieldwork in China in the 1990s, I documented the emergence of a similar national field of youth sexual culture in the post-Mao era. It was a space where, as in the United States a century earlier, young people gained partial autonomy from their parents by engaging in intimate behaviors in contexts outside the home—including, from the early 1980s onward, social dance halls in which young men and women practiced premarital intimacy (Farrer 2002; Farrer and Field 2015). The role of international migrants in creating this new sexual field was negligible at first. This field emerged in an indigenous process of liberalizing sexual mores, which swept China after the "reform and opening" policies of 1978 (Pan 1993; Evans 1997; Farrer 2002). Beginning in the 1980s, and spreading and deepening in the 1990s, a widespread "romantic revolution" in China extended a new legitimacy to premarital sexual intimacy as long as relationships were based on romantic "feelings." Race was not salient but urban and rural status were clear markers in this field (Farrer 2007). Although foreign migrants were barely visible in urban China until the late 1990s, images of foreign sexuality and foreign ideas of sexuality did play a role in these cultural developments (Farrer 1999). The popular narrative of "sexual opening up" (*xingkaifang*) implies an opening up of China to foreign sexual ideas (Farrer 2002). Farquhar (2002) describes a "newly eroticized public landscape" in 1980s China, which included images of sexualized foreign bodies and tales of foreign sexual prowess. However, these images were always in contrast with an image of the Chinese themselves. The latter was presented as relatively chaste and earnestly focused on marriage.

Through the mid-1990s, international migrants, especially men, who tried to participate in the Chinese dating scene—regional or local Chinese sexual fields—generally found that these rules applied to them also. Dating, especially if involving sexual intercourse, was linked to expectations of marriage; and this mainstream Chinese sexual field was not configured flexibly for foreigners who tried to enter it (Farrer 2019). Nathan, an American who eventually married a Chinese woman, described the strict enforcement of local cultural norms that foreign men faced when dating Chinese women in Beijing in the 1980s:

> Actually, I wasn't all that interested in Chinese women. I didn't find them all that attractive at first. And it was really not possible to date Chinese women. I also saw how things went with my American friends, and I thought it was way too much trouble to go through all that to be with a Chinese girl. It was illegal for a Chinese person to come to stay with you in a hotel or in any of the places foreigners stayed. For instance, once I went away for two weeks, and I lent my apartment to this American guy. When I got back, he wasn't there. And I asked what happened to him. He said that the police came in when he was there with his girlfriend. They asked if they were married, and when they found out they weren't, they took them into the police station and gave them a scolding. It was so traumatic that a week later, he proposed to marry her. (2002 interview)

In this context, short-term affairs were perilous for the Chinese, particularly for women who faced strict community scrutiny about premarital sex, in addition to state paranoia about Chinese socializing with foreigners. Many dating couples were rushed into marriage by authorities and relatives. Many Western migrant men I interviewed described not only alienation from the norms and practices in this Chinese sexual field but aversion to the young women embedded in it. This finding is in keeping with the idea that "desire" is also shaped by socialization into the field, and is not merely a pregiven, individual predilection.

When interviewing Nathan, I was surprised at his account of not being "interested" in Chinese women in the 1980s in Beijing. By the time of our interview in 2002, expatriate men had created their own transnational sexual field inside China, and they had begun inviting Chinese, especially young women, to participate in it. Nathan and his friends were eager participants. As I have written in a monograph on Western migrants in Shanghai, expatriates can be characterized as "power migrants," or migrants with the resources to transform the societies they move into, including the urban nightscape (Farrer 2019: 198). This power extends to producing and reshaping sexual fields. Western migrants in Shanghai, and Chinese business people trying to appeal to them, began transforming Shanghai nightscapes in earnest in the 1990s, creating spaces that became sites of a new transnational sexual field in which the rules of mainstream Chinese society did not apply. Bars and discos attracted Chinese with glamorous images of foreign eroticism, and became spaces where Chinese youth could engage in actual erotic encounters with foreign visitors (Farrer 1999). With the increasing numbers of foreign residents and tourists in the late 1990s, Shanghai's nightlife districts developed into full-fledged ethnosexual frontier zones in which Western expatriate professionals rubbed shoulders with Shanghainese white collars and Hong Kong entrepreneurs, as well as many female Chinese sex workers (Farrer 2011; Farrer and Field 2015).

These spaces operated according to Western rules—or more specifically, the rules of white male expatriates living in Asia. Asian women were expected to be sexually interested in white men, and white men in Asian women. Marriage was indeed possible in some cases, but most relationships were short-term flings while others evolved into compensated dating. The age gaps between expatriate men and their local girlfriends or lovers were often much greater than would be expected back "home" in Europe or North America. Both Asian men and white women reported feeling marginalized in these sexual scenes, whereas the Chinese women who participated reported a sense of release from the norms and expectations of the dominant Chinese dating scene (Farrer 2008, 2010, 2011, 2013, 2019; Farrer and Dale 2104; Farrer and Field 2015). This was a sexual field that flourished in Shanghai at the height of direct Western investment and expatriate managers' mobility into this city in the late 1990s and early 2000s. As described in the next section, these racialized power relations and the participants' relative statuses would shift rapidly after the financial crisis of 2008.

There is no doubt that migrants played a substantial role in creating the transnational sexual field in Shanghai. However, it is important to note that there were parallel local, national, and transnational sexual fields developing in the city. For example, throughout the 1990s, vast numbers of ballroom dance halls formed a sexual scene for middle-aged married Shanghainese, with their sexual hierarchies and standards of interaction. At the top of the sexual hierarchy were good dancers, a type of field-specific sexual capital. Non-Shanghainese (rural-to-urban) migrants were marginalized in these dance halls, no matter how young or attractive they were. This was a *local* sexual field with a strong Shanghainese nativist bias, in which international migrants played no role (See Farrer 2002; Farrer and Field 2015). The dominant premarital dating culture of Shanghai, in contrast, was mainly a *national* sexual field with a moral tone set by official state media, and with similar rules of interaction across other Chinese cities (though rural-to-urban migrants were largely excluded). The interethnic sexual field described above was quite marginal at the national level. However, it was part of a transnational sexual scene that extended to other Asian cities such as Hong Kong, Singapore, and Taipei, where these affluent migrants also worked and played according to similar field-specific rules.

Gendered Experiences of the Sexual Mobility: Adjusting to the Transnational Field in Shanghai

Migrants collectively shape emerging sexual fields in some cases, but individually they are shaped by them. As journalist Ted Fishman wrote in his book *China Inc.*:

> Sex is one of the allures of Shanghai ... Here, the middle-aged overseas Chinese can find willing youth, burly German mechanics can find little girls who simply don't exist at home, and nerdy Western engineers can find girls so hot their friends at home would laugh. (Fishman 2005: 29)

Fishman attributes most of the sex appeal of elite migrant men in Shanghai to the easy convertibility of economic capital into sexual capital, giving middle-aged men with money access to young and beautiful women. This quote also points to the unexpected nature of this good fortune for many male migrants. It also shows how sexual fields are racialized and gendered, and how men and women, even with the same ethnic and racial background, may experience radically different forms of sexual mobility in migration.

In my research in Shanghai in the late 1990s and through the 2000s, many men described experiencing much more interest from women in Shanghai than they experienced back home. Theirs was an experience of upward sexual mobility. Whiteness was a component of sexual capital for some men, including those who actually had only modest incomes but were seen as desirable by women because of their race and nationality (Farrer 2010). This sexual scene also attracted many internal Chinese migrants. Shanghai was considered to be a city for young, single women to develop a more individualized sexual persona and to explore their sexual options in a freer context (Pei 2011). Moreover, foreign men did not associate migrant women's migrant status with the stigma of "provincialism," unlike many urban Shanghainese men. Some young (rural-to-urban/*waidi*) migrant women thus also experienced a type of upward sexual mobility when entering this emergent transnational sexual field. These women's geographic and economic mobility into the city thus became entangled with their sexual mobility in the spaces where they played (and sometimes worked).

The transnational sexual field that emerged in the 1990s involved a new type of casual sexual interaction for many Chinese, including "pick-ups" in the bars and clubs (and later, online dating). The rules of interaction in this sexual field were associated with the spaces in which they occurred. Nightclubs, in particular, were a context in which relationships were defined by their casual, spontaneous, and playful characteristics. As one American man explained:

> That is one of the reasons that I really prefer to meet girls in the nightclubs, because out in the clubbing scene it is really about "play." I think that term really encompasses what people mean in China by going out. If a girl is out in a club, she knows that it is just play, and she won't expect to develop a long-term relationship with anyone she meets there. (2005 interview)

The conventional understanding of the nightlife scene as being about "play" meant that Chinese women understood that a sexual encounter could be just "playing around" or "one-night love." The conventional definitions of these social spaces thus shaped the relationships that were considered "normal" within this sexual field.

Some men played in this sexual field for years, some compulsively. When I asked Carl, a 40-year-old single white American, if he got tired of dating a different woman nearly every week, he replied sarcastically, "What? Get tired of having sex with hot 21-year-old girls? Nooo ... ." For him, as for many men, the visceral excitement associated with new sex partners required no explanation, nor did the attractions of women in their early twenties. All men would want the same thing if they were honest, he said. In many cases, however, migrants remarked that this field had altered their behaviors and tastes, causing them to form new nightlife habits and adopting new standards of desirable partners (e.g., only focusing on Chinese women, a racialized preference some derisively labeled "yellow fever").

An elevated sexual status was not limited to white male migrants. Ethnic Chinese men from abroad, especially Chinese-American men, were at the top of the sexual hierarchy in many respects, because not only could they participate in the transnational sexual field of casual play with multiple partners, but they were regarded by women as more fit also for the domestic Chinese sexual field centered on dating and marriage. Chinese-American men reported feeling like "kings of the candy shop" in Chinese cities. Chinese-American women, however, experienced downward sexual mobility, and were even labeled unwanted "leftover" women (Wang 2017). Their status as educated, foreign, and "independent" (a frequent self-description) did not readily convert to sexual capital in either the domestic or transnational sexual fields they experienced in Shanghai.

White Western women also reported downward sexual mobility when they arrived in Shanghai, especially during years in which white Western men seemed to be at the height of their sexual status (roughly 1998–2008 by most informant accounts). Many Western male migrants who participated in this sexual scene during this period reported reduced interest in "foreign" (white) women. As one 33-year-old African-American explained, "I typically don't date foreign women. Just because I've dated foreign [white] girls before in the US, and again you want to experience what China has to offer."

Expatriate women engaged in many strategies to avoid desexualization in a sexual field in which they felt marginalized. Some reported becoming more sexually aggressive and more sexually adventurous. Many informants ascribed this sexual "wildness" to the lack of ethics and morals in the Shanghai expat dating scene. They felt that expats had a view that they were "on vacation" and thus not beholden to the rules "at home." This is a view common to other expatriate subcultures, such as the one studied in Dubai by Walsh (2007), in which women also face a field constituted by short-term relationships. Similar to the experiences of expatriate women in the Gulf, a Chinese-Canadian informant stated about Shanghai: "Back home, I would be considered promiscuous, but here I think it's completely normal." This, in turn, leads to women (and men) being more sexually open, active, and experimental than they would in their home country (Farrer and Dale 2014).

In short, elite migrants experienced sexual mobility when moving to Shanghai, but in opposite directions. White and Asian men from developed countries generally described a rise in their sexual status, while women with the same backgrounds experienced a drop. Both types of migrants described adjusting to the new "rules of the game" of a largely unfamiliar sexual field in which short-term relations were a norm, and compensated dating was also much more common than where they were from. They developed a new sexual habitus, including new preferences in partners, new forms of self-presentation, and new patterns of interaction. Many Chinese locals, especially women, also joined this transnational sexual scene, developing a new sexual habitus focused on short-term interactions and a newfound indifference to chastity and marriage (or even marital status), which were still concerns in the mainstream domestic sexual field.

The sexual field is thus not only a space of mobility but also of socialization that differs by gender. Participation in the field provides not only sexual opportunities but sexual meanings. As Fligstein and McAdam (2012) write in their book *A Theory of Fields*, "strategic action in fields turns on a complicated blend of material and 'existential' considerations" (3). In sexual fields, these existential considerations extend to the moral nature of casual sex and the morality of sexual transactions (e.g., giving "taxi money" to casual female partners). Participation in new sexual fields involves, for example, learning new tactics of seduction but also new moral economies of sexual exchange or ways for understanding and legitimating the exchange of resources in sexual relationships (Priscitelli 2018; Groes 2018). Sexual mobilities are thus formative of new sexual subjectivities and new forms of sexual agency, and not only a question of rising and falling sexual status.

Shifting Entanglements and Capital Conversions: Sexual Agency in Transnational Sexual Fields

Relationships among players in a sexual field are not stable over time and may be contested, especially by new emergent elites. As Ho and Tsang's (2000) research on interracial gay relationships in Hong Kong shows, racialized sexual hierarchies can change significantly in a short time, depending on shifts in economic and cultural power (such as the handover of Hong Kong to China in 1997). Similarly, Hoang (2015) sees a decline in white male clients' status, and a rise in the status of Asian clients in the sexual scenes in Vietnam. In some cases, the changing distribution of resources in the economic field may influence the distribution and locus of resources in the sexual field. In other cases, new groups of actors may emerge. Both phenomena happened in the transnational sexual field dominated by white male expatriates for a brief period in urban China in the late 1990s and early 2000s. By the late 2000s, Chinese men were not only much wealthier and savvier in the ways of these sexual scenes, but they were also able to reconfigure interactions to their advantage. Even the nightclubbing spaces of Shanghai were redesigned according to Chinese modes of sociability.

In those spaces, groups of acquaintances partied together at fixed tables served with expensive drinks. Such new "VIP" clubbing spaces left few opportunities for (foreign) migrant interlopers to engage in sexual pick-ups, even if they could afford to visit the clubs. By the 2010s, Mainland Chinese "*fuerdai*" (second generation rich) were the new "kings in the candy shop," and not overseas Chinese or white foreign men. They were able to use their economic capital to reinvent the "rules of the game" within these transnational leisure spaces (Farrer and Field 2015; Field and Farrer 2018).

At the same time that these *fuerdai* Chinese men saw their sexual capital appreciating—along with their economic capital—a new group of Chinese women were also entering this sexual field, some of whom had studied abroad and returned to China with advanced degrees and/or well-paid employment. Often labeled "returnees" (*haigui*), most of these women primarily sought their partners in the mainstream national sexual field that was undergoing rapid transformations (To 2020). However, according to many informants, this domestic sexual field was becoming increasingly patriarchal and dominated by considerations of men's access to real estate (a marital apartment) and women's youth and beauty (see Davis and Friedman 2014). Women beyond their late twenties and women with advanced degrees were actually at a disadvantage in the mainstream national sexual field, and hence labeled "leftover women" (*shengnü*). Some of them, therefore, sought alternative opportunities in the transnational sexual field, looking for foreign white or overseas Chinese men, not primarily for sexual experimentation (though some did: Farrer 2013), but as an escape from a patriarchal domestic sexual field (Zurndorfer 2018; To 2020). In these interactions, which increasingly began online, the women emphasized their expectations that men should be reliable partners with economic resources and marriage orientation, and thus challenged the primacy of "play" in the expatriate dating scene described above.

Here we see not only how economic and sexual status become entangled, but also how moving "laterally" into new sexual fields may be a way of *avoiding* entanglements of one sort, even though new ones might emerge. For Shanghai divorcees, rural migrants, and highly educated "leftover women," movement into the transnational field can itself be a form of agency in which sexual stigmas salient in the national field—a rural background, higher education, or divorced status, all a type of negative sexual capital—can be avoided or reduced, and forms of positive sexual capital—international experience, foreign language ability—can be utilized (Clark 2001; Farrer 2008; Zurndorfer 2018; To 2020). For these women, participating in a transnational sexual field could be a form of sexual agency in which they sought relief from the patriarchal demands of the mainstream Chinese marriage market (To 2020). It was, of course, questionable whether romance with foreign men offered a reliable break from entanglements with patriarchy in general. Still, it offered a break from some expectations of Chinese courtship and marriage, such as a traditionally filial relationship to a husband's mother.[5] Participating in one type of sexual field (the transnational one) reduced entanglements, such as social expectations and stigmas, that limited action in another (the national one).

A sexual field is also a place where new forms of entanglement—between sex, money, and status—may be actively sought. "Entanglement" can here be understood as capital conversion. For example, we also see many marginalized women and men using their sexual capital as a convertible resource in emerging transnational sexual fields. In Mozambique, for example, young local women dating rich white migrants in the capital city pursue both short-term monetary gains and long-term relationships in a bid to win respect in the local society (Groes-Green 2013; Groes 2018). Brazilian women and Cuban men seek both material aid and relationships from their lovers from developed countries (Priscitelli 2018; Simoni 2018). In Thailand, marriage migrants pursue status and security through the exchange of sexual attention and caregiving (Statham et al. 2020). In urbanizing China, we also see the convertibility of migrant women's sexual capital through various forms of sex work (Ding and Ho 2013). In all these examples, women cultivate erotic and emotional capacities to enhance their well-being, produce income, and win respect in the local community (Groes-Green 2013; Groes 2018). As Ding and Ho (2013) write, "sexual capital involves the capacity for sexual expression and developing a new relationship with oneself, and has emotional significance, in addition to its potential for acquiring social and economic capital" (43). Through sexual mobility, sexual capital is converted not only to economic capital but also to social capital in the form of respect, status, and relationships.

In many cases, however, powerful actors in the sexual field may also oppose the convertibility of sexual capital, especially for marginal, working-class, and female migrants. Many governments, including China, criminalize prostitution or do not recognize sex workers as legitimate migrants (Agustín 2006). Government agencies question applications for spousal visas that seem based on sexual exchange rather than a normative middle-class ideal of emotional (and class) compatibility (Maskens 2018). Even nightclubs shape their spaces to make it difficult for women to achieve mobility in the sexual field, either through policing sex work or by creating exclusive VIP spaces to bar ordinary clubbers from accessing privileged elites (Field and Farrer 2018; Mears 2020). In particular, the criminalization of sexual exchanges also produces especially negative outcomes for female migrants (Agustín 2006; Ding and Ho 2013).

Conclusions: Sexual Mobilities and Entangled Mobilities

An "intimate turn," "affective turn," or "sexual turn" is increasingly well established in migration studies, producing multiple conferences, special issues, and edited volumes (e.g., Mai and King 2009; Groes and Fernandez 2018; Statham et al. 2020), as well as this one. Much of this research insightfully focuses on the interior lives of migrants and the micro-social organization of sexual intimacy. Other studies focus on the institutional (especially governmental) and discursive organization of intimate or erotic experiences, such as Nicole Constable's (2003) "cartographies of desire" concept. What the sexual mobilities perspective advanced here offers is a meso-social analysis of intimacy, desire, and sexuality. It moves away from the methodological individualism implied in many studies. Based on the concept of sexual fields, this approach sensitizes us to the social organization of sexual identities, opportunities, and desires at multiple geographic scales—local, national, and transnational—while emphasizing that sexual life is inherently social and not individual in organization. Migrants may come into contact with multiple sexual fields and have multiple and discordant experiences of sexual mobility. Based on the idea of sexual fields, the sexual mobility perspective offers particular insights on the entanglement of sexual mobility with mobility in other social fields through the mechanism of capital conversion.

Based on my partial review of this growing research literature, a few important trends could be emphasized through this lens. One is the role of migrants in the creation of new urban sexual fields. We can see the emergence of a transnational sexual field in Carrillo's (2018) study of gay male migrants from Mexico to the United States, and in my studies of how migrants helped contribute to the creation of a sexual field in Shanghai. The latter study emphasizes how non-migrant "locals" come to experience sexual mobility within these emergent transnational spaces (Farrer 2019: 136-37). We can also see this type of emergent sexual field in the case of Mozambican women who participate in the creation of a transnational sexual field through their interactions with white men in Maputo (Groes-Green 2013; Groes 2018). Sexual mobility in this sense is about the dynamics or emergence of the field as much as it is about the mobility of migrants within it, and a historical and sociological analysis of the field itself becomes central to understanding these migrant experiences.

One obvious contribution of field theory is the emphasis on sexual inequality—or unequal access to sexual opportunities and status—and the struggles of migrants coping with sexual marginalization and downward sexual mobility. We see this, for example, in Ahmad's (2009) study of the desexualization, "deprivation," and "melancholia" experienced by male Pakistani labor migrants to Europe. It is also in Pande's (2017) study of the sexual marginalization and emasculation experienced by migrant Bangladeshi men in South Africa and their strategies for coping. By contrast, Liu-Farrer (2004) shows how Chinese migrants deal with their marginalization in the dominant sexual fields in Japan by creating an alternative sexual space in the ethnic dance party circuit. We must also attend to the "resistance of the powerful," or how dominant actors endeavor to exclude migrants from sexual fields, as we can observe in the way Japanese men stigmatized the entry of Korean and Chinese men into the gay sexual field in Shinjuku Nichome in Tokyo (Baudinette 2016). These types of inequalities and barriers mean that for many, perhaps most, migrants from the Global South, sexual mobility is downward, as they find themselves marginalized in sexual fields in unfamiliar metropolitan environments.

Finally, my concept of sexual mobility offers accounts of sexual subjectivity and sexual agency for migrants that might be useful for revising a purely instrumental notion of sexual exchange. Much of the focus on discussions of "sexual capital" has been about the convertibility—especially the conversion of sexual capital to economic capital in "transactional" sexual relationships. However, beyond instrumental conceptions of sexual exchange, the agency of actors in the sexual field also involves projects of self-improvement and self-shaping as ways of navigating the field. There is also much to be gained from investigating the "existential" or moral investments of migrants in their positions in the field and their acquisition of new forms of sexual habitus that are transformative of sexual subjectivity. Interactions within a sexual field involve strategic and instrumental action, but the interesting questions are often about how the field shapes both the *ends* and the *means* of sexual interactions through sexual socialization.

James Farrer is Professor of Sociology at Sophia University in Tokyo. His research has focused on cities in East Asia, including ethnographic studies of sexuality, nightlife, expatriates, and foodways. He now leads a project on gastronomy in a Tokyo neighborhood in which he documents the place-making activities of small business people (www.nishiogiology.org) and a group project on the global spread of Japanese cuisine (www.global-japanese-cuisine.org). His publications include *International Migrants in China's Global City: The New Shanghailanders*; *Shanghai Nightscapes: A Nocturnal Biography of a Global City* (with Andrew Field); *Globalization and Asian Cuisines: Transnational Networks and Contact Zones*; and *Opening Up: Youth Sex Culture and Market Reform in Shanghai*. He has published over one hundred journal articles, book chapters, and articles in general media. Originally from Tennessee, after studying at the University of Chicago he moved to Japan, where he has now lived for over twenty years.

NOTES

1. For example, in her master's research conducted in Sweden, Hu (2016) found that a lack of sexual intimacy was a burning issue for male asylum seekers from Syria and other countries.
2. See Bourdieu and Waquant (1992), Fligstein and McAdam (2012), and Martin (2003) for general background on field theory. The concept of field developed in sexual fields research borrows primarily from Bourdieu, but some studies, mine in particular, also borrow from the approach of Fligstein and McAdam (2012), particularly their emphasis on the "existential meanings" that actors acquire from acting in fields.
3. This conception of the historicity of fields of action is based on Fligstein and McAdam (2012).
4. Wacquant (2014) presents a broad critique of the idea of sexual fields, arguing that sexuality is not an autonomous field. Wacquant's view of field theory, however, relies very narrowly on Bourdieu's original texts, and ignores the emergent autonomy of sexual fields demonstrated in actual case studies.
5. As To (2020) points out, women do expect to maintain filial relations with their own mothers in marriage. However, I have observed among informants that by marrying a foreigner they may easily opt to have a more distant or a more egalitarian relationship with the "foreign" mother-in-law. This allows women to disengage from what has traditionally been the most stressful relationship for married Chinese women, that with the husband's mother (Farrer 2019: 205).

REFERENCES

Agustín, Laura. 2006. "The Disappearing of a Migration Category: Migrants Who Sell Sex." *Journal of Ethnic and Migration Studies* 32(1): 29–47.

Ahmad, Ali Nobil. 2009. "Bodies that (Don't) Matter: Desire, Eroticism and Melancholia in Pakistani Labour Migration." *Mobilities* 4(3): 309–27.

Bailey, Beth L. 1989. *From Front Porch to Back Seat: Courtship in Twentieth-Century America.* Baltimore, MD: JHU Press.

Baudinette, Thomas. 2016. "Ethnosexual Frontiers in Queer Tokyo: The Production of Racialised Desire in Japan." *Japan Forum* 28(4): 465–85.

Bourdieu, Pierre, and Loïc J. D. Wacquant. 1992. *An Invitation to Reflexive Sociology.* Chicago, IL: University of Chicago Press.

Cangià, Flavia. 2018. "Precarity, Imagination, and the Mobile Life of the 'Trailing Spouse.'" *Ethos* 46(1): 8–26.

Carrillo, Héctor. 2018. *Pathways of Desire: The Sexual Migration of Mexican Gay Men.* Chicago: University of Chicago Press.
Clark, Constance D. 2001. "Foreign Marriage 'Tradition' and the Politics of Border Crossings." In *China Urban: Ethnographies of Contemporary Culture,* ed. Nancy N. Chen et al., 104–22. Durham, NC: Duke University Press.
Constable, Nicole. 2003. *Romance on a Global Stage: Pen Pals, Virtual Ethnography, and "Mail Order" Marriages.* Berkeley: University of California Press.
Davis, Deborah S., and Sara L. Friedman, eds. 2014. *Wives, Husbands, and Lovers: Marriage and Sexuality in Hong Kong, Taiwan, and Urban China.* Stanford, CA: Stanford University Press.
Ding, Yu, and Petula Sik Ying Ho. 2013. "Sex Work in China's Pearl River Delta: Accumulating Sexual Capital as a Life-Advancement Strategy." *Sexualities* 16(1-2): 43–60.
Erel, Umut. 2010. "Migrating Cultural Capital: Bourdieu in Migration Studies." *Sociology* 44(4): 642–60.
Evans, Harriet. 1997. *Women and Sexuality in China: Dominant Discourses of Female Sexuality and Gender since 1949.* Cambridge: Polity Press.
Farrer, James. 1999. "Disco Super-Culture: Consuming Foreign Sex in the Chinese Disco." *Sexualities* 2(2): 147–66.
———. 2002. *Opening Up: Youth Sex Culture and Market Reform in Shanghai.* Chicago, IL: University of Chicago Press.
———. 2007. "Sexual Citizenship and the Politics of Sexual Storytelling among Chinese Youth." In *Sex and Sexuality in China,* ed. Elaine Jefferys, 110–31. London: Routledge.
———. 2008. "From 'Passports' to 'Joint Ventures': Intermarriage between Chinese Nationals and Western Expatriates Residing in Shanghai." *Asian Studies Review* 32(1): 7–29.
———. 2010. "A Foreign Adventurer's Paradise? Interracial Sexuality and Alien Sexual Capital in Reform Era Shanghai." *Sexualities* 13(1): 69–95.
———. 2011. "Global Nightscapes in Shanghai as Ethnosexual Contact Zones." *Journal of Ethnic and Migration Studies* 37(5): 747–64.
———. 2013. "Good Stories: Chinese Women's International Love Stories as Collective Sexual Story Making." *Sexualities* 16(1-2): 12–29.
———. 2016. "Foreign-*f* Females: Debating Women's Transnational Sexualities in China." In *Introducing the New Sexuality Studies,* 3rd edn, ed. Nancy L. Fischer and Steven Seidman, 636–46. London: Routledge.
———. 2019. *International Migrants in China's Global City: The New Shanghailanders.* London: Routledge.
———. 2020. "From Cooks to Chefs: Skilled Migrants in a Globalising Culinary Field." *Journal of Ethnic and Migration Studies,* 1–17. DOI:10.1080/1369183X.2020.1731990
Farrer, James, and Sonja Dale. 2014. "Sexless in Shanghai: Gendered Mobility Strategies in a Transnational Sexual Field." In *Sexual Fields: Toward a Sociology of Collective Sexual Life,* ed. Adam Isaiah Green, 143–70. Chicago, IL: University of Chicago Press.
Farrer, James, and Andrew David Field. 2015. *Shanghai Nightscapes: A Nocturnal Biography of a Global City.* Chicago, IL: University of Chicago Press.

Field, Andrew David, and James Farrer. 2018. "China's Party Kings: Shanghai Club Cultures and Status Consumption, 1920s-2010s." In *Polarized Cities: Portraits of the Rich and Poor in Urban China*, ed. Dorothy J. Solinger, 127-48. Lanham, MD: Rowman & Littlefield.

Fishman, Ted C. 2005. *China, Inc.: How the Rise of the Next Superpower Challenges America and the World*. New York: Scribner.

Fligstein, Neil, and Doug McAdam. 2012. *A Theory of Fields*. Oxford: Oxford University Press.

Giddens, Anthony. 1992. *The Transformation of Intimacy: Sexuality, Love and Eroticism in Modern Societies*. Oxford: Polity Press.

Gonzales, Alicia M., and Gary Rolison. 2005. "Social Oppression and Attitudes toward Sexual Practices." *Journal of Black Studies* 35(6): 715-29.

Green, Adam Isaiah. 2008. "The Social Organization of Desire: The Sexual Fields Approach." *Sociological Theory* 26: 25-50.

———, ed. 2014. *Sexual Fields: Toward a Sociology of Collective Sexual Life*. Chicago, IL: University of Chicago Press.

Groes-Green, Christian. 2013. "'To Put Men in a Bottle': Eroticism, Kinship, Female Power, and Transactional Sex in Maputo, Mozambique." *American Ethnologist* 40(1): 102-17.

Groes, Christian. 2018. "Mobility through Sexual Economy: Exchanging Sexual Capital for Respectability in Mozambican Women's Marriage Migration to Europe." In *Intimate Mobilities: Sexual Economies, Marriage and Migration in a Disparate World*, ed. Christian Groes and Nadine T. Fernandez, 158-84. New York: Berghahn Books.

Groes, Christian, and Nadine T. Fernandez. 2018. "Introduction: Intimate Mobilities and Mobile Intimacies." In *Intimate Mobilities: Sexual Economies, Marriage and Migration in a Disparate World*, ed. Christian Groes and Nadine T. Fernandez, 1-27. New York: Berghahn Books.

Hakim, Catherine. 2011. *Erotic Capital: The Power of Attraction in the Boardroom and the Bedroom*. New York: Basic Books.

Ho, Petula Sik Ying, and Adolf Kat Tat Tsang. 2000. "Negotiating Anal Intercourse in Inter-Racial Gay Relationships in Hong Kong." *Sexualities* 3(3): 299-323.

Hoang, Kimberly Kay. 2015. *Dealing in Desire: Asian Ascendancy, Western Decline, and the Hidden Currencies of Global Sex Work*. Oakland: University of California Press.

Hu, Yajun. 2016. "Making Sense of Everyday Waiting: 'Integration' of Syrian Asylum Seekers in Sweden." Master's thesis. Graduate Program in Global Studies. Sophia University, Tokyo.

Jackson, Peter A. 2009. "Capitalism and Global Queering: National Markets, Parallels among Sexual Cultures, and Multiple Queer Modernities." *GLQ: A Journal of Lesbian and Gay Studies* 15(3): 357-95.

Kelsky, Karen. 2001. *Women on the Verge: Japanese Women, Western Dreams*. Durham, NC: Duke University Press.

Leschziner, Vanina, and Adam Isaiah Green. 2013. "Thinking About Food and Sex: Deliberate Cognition in the Routine Practices of a Field." *Sociological Theory* 31(2): 116-44.

Liu-Farrer, Gracia. 2004. "The Chinese Social Dance Party in Tokyo: Identity and Status in an Immigrant Leisure Subculture." *Journal of Contemporary Ethnography* 33(6): 651-74.

———. 2010. "The Absent Spouses: Gender, Sex, Race and the Extramarital Sexuality among Chinese Migrants in Japan." *Sexualities* 13(1): 97-121.

Mai, Nicola, and Russell King. 2009. "Love, Sexuality and Migration: Mapping the Issue(s)." *Mobilities* 4(3): 295-307.

Martin, John Levi. 2003. "What Is Field Theory?" *American Journal of Sociology* 109(1): 1-49.

Martin, John Levi, and Matt George. 2006. "Theories of Sexual Stratification: Toward an Analytics of the Sexual Field and a Theory of Sexual Capital." *Sociological Theory* 24(2): 107-32.

Maskens, Maïté. 2018. "Screening for Romance and Compatibility in the Brussels Civil Registrar Office: Practical Norms of Bureacratic Feminism." In *Intimate Mobilities: Sexual Economies, Marriage and Migration in a Disparate World*, ed. Christian Groes and Nadine T. Fernandez, 100-30. New York: Berghahn Books.

Mears, Ashley. 2020. *Very Important People: Status and Beauty in the Global Party Circuit*. Princeton, NJ: Princeton University Press.

Pan, Suiming. 1993. "A Sex Revolution in Current China." *Journal of Psychology and Human Sexuality* 6(2): 1-14.

Pande, Amrita. 2017. "Mobile Masculinities: Migrant Bangladeshi Men in South Africa." *Gender & Society* 31(3): 383-406.

Paquin, Jamie. 2014. "Should I Stay or Should I Go? Racial Sexual Preferences and Migration in Japan." In *Queering Migrations Towards, From, and Beyond Asia*, ed. Hugo Córdova Quero, Joseph N. Goh, and Michael Sepidoza Campos, 21-39. New York: Palgrave Macmillan.

Pei, Yuxin. 2011. "Multiple Sexual Relationships as a New Lifestyle: Young Women's Sexuality in Contemporary Shanghai." *Women's Studies International Forum* 34(5): 401-10.

Peiss, Kathy Lee. 1985. *Cheap Amusements: Working Women and Leisure in New York City, 1880 to 1920*. Philadelphia, PA: Temple University Press.

Priscitelli, Adriana. 2018. "From Programas to Help and Marriage: Transnational Sexual, Economic and Affective Exchanges among Brazilian Women." In *Intimate Mobilities: Sexual Economies, Marriage and Migration in a Disparate World*, ed. Christian Groes and Nadine T. Fernandez, 212-70. New York: Berghahn Books.

Reddy, William M. 2012. *The Making of Romantic Love: Longing and Sexuality in Europe, South Asia, and Japan, 900–1200 CE*. Chicago: University of Chicago Press.

Simoni, Valerio. 2018. "True Love and Cunning Love: Negotiating Intimacy, Deception and Belonging in Touristic Cuba." In *Intimate Mobilities: Sexual Economies, Marriage and Migration in a Disparate World*, ed. Groes and Nadine T. Fernandez, 240-70. New York: Berghahn Books.

Statham, Paul, Sarah Scuzzarello, Sirijit Sunanta, and Alexander Trupp. 2020. "Globalising Thailand through Gendered 'Both-Ways' Migration Pathways with 'the West': Cross-Border Connections between People, States, and Places." *Journal of Ethnic and Migration Studies* 46(8): 1513–42.

To, Sandy. 2020. "Caveats and Criteria: Intercultural Courtships of Shengnü ('Leftover Women') and Western Men in Urban China." *Families, Relationships and Societies* 10(3): 447–62. DOI:10.1332/204674320X15885850741253

Wacquant, Loïc. 2014. "Putting Habitus in its Place: Rejoinder to the Symposium." *Body & Society* 20(2): 118–39.

Walsh, Katie. 2007. "'It Got Very Debauched, Very Dubai!' Heterosexual Intimacy amongst Single British Expatriates." *Social and Cultural Geography* 8(4): 507–33.

Wang, Leslie K. 2017. "'Leftover Women' and 'Kings of the Candy Shop': Gendering Chinese American Ancestral Homeland Migration to China." *American Behavioral Scientist* 61(10): 1172–91.

Zurndorfer, Harriet. 2011. "Prostitutes and Courtesans in the Confucian Moral Universe of Late Ming China (1550–1644)." *International Review of Social History* 56(S19): 197–216.

———. 2018. "Escape from the Country: The Gender Politics of Chinese Women in Pursuit of Transnational Romance." *Gender, Place & Culture* 25(4): 489–506.

CHAPTER 2

Cycles of Irregularity
The Intergenerational Impacts of Trafficking Policies on Migrant Families

Pardis Mahdavi

Nadia, who had turned twenty-three just three days before I met her in 2013, was born and raised in the United Arab Emirates (UAE). Yet, she has never had Emirati or, for that matter, any other form of legal citizenship. For the first fourteen years of her life, she lived with her mother and five other women in makeshift housing near the Dubai Creek. Nadia's mother had migrated from India to seek domestic work in Dubai in the late 1980s. During her time working for a local family, she became pregnant and gave birth to Nadia. Although unaware of the details, Nadia was told by her mother that she had been fired when her employers discovered her pregnancy. For the first few years of Nadia's life, her mother worked informally as a domestic worker for several other Indian families. However, with housing costs rising and the cost of sustaining her daughter increasing, she decided to enter sex work when Nadia was roughly seven years old in order to supplement her income. Nadia recalled her mother being "honest" with her about the nature of her employment, and said that her mother's work never embarrassed her.

One day in 2004, when Nadia was fourteen years old, her mother was arrested in a brothel raid and deported to India after six weeks of detention. Nadia's requests to see her mother were denied, and she was taken to a local orphanage outside of Dubai. The mother's attempts to be with her daughter also failed. The situation worsened when Nadia discovered her condition of statelessness, which would prohibit her from traveling to India to be reunited with her mother. The circumstances of the mother's deportation also prevented her from returning to the UAE to see her daughter. Distraught, stateless, and parentless, Nadia remained in the orphanage for several years. After turning nineteen, Nadia decided to run away in the hope that she could find employment, save money, and eventually find a way to move to India. Through several contacts with her friends, Nadia managed to reach neighboring Oman. Finding work there was not easy, however, because she was stateless and lacked formal training. After a few months of working informally—first as a nanny, then a waitress, and then a bartender—Nadia faced the same challenges in making ends meet as her mother had before her. Tired of working odd jobs, she contacted some friends of her mother's and was able to find work as a dancer at a local establishment back in Dubai. She has been working in the sex industry for the past four years and continues to work to save money in order to find a way to reunite with her mother.

I met Lucinda one warm Wednesday afternoon when I visited an informal women's shelter at the Philippines Embassy. One of the Filipino labor attachés had been kind enough to allow me to visit the women in this shelter on occasion to talk to them about their experiences, and the reasons for them being sheltered. Most of the women were in their twenties, and had migrated to Kuwait as domestic workers. When things went wrong with their employers, such as abuse, inadequate wages, or in some cases both, the women absconded and ran away to the shelter. A few had ended up there due to abuses that had occurred outside the workplace, which had rendered them illegal. A few had even been sent to the embassy by their employers when they were found to be pregnant; in most of those cases, the embassy did their best to send them home before the baby was born.

I had just sat down to talk to a woman covered in knife wounds when a very young girl walked up and sat down across the table from me, eyeing the three muffins that another of the women had brought me. I slid the plate over to her, and she devoured one quickly. I was surprised to see a little girl in the shelter, as usually the children were sent to the orphanage. "Oh, you met Lucinda?" asked Ellie, the woman I had come to speak to. I nodded and stretched my hand out to shake Lucinda's while introducing myself. She turned away and faced the window. I asked Ellie if I should leave as I had the feeling I was making Lucinda uncomfortable. "Don't leave, please," Lucinda interjected. "I want you to interview me, hear my story," she said, trading seats with Ellie, who stood up and started brushing Lucinda's hair. Lucinda took another muffin from my plate and began telling me her story.

Lucinda told me that she thought she was nine years old, though her mother, who was also living in the shelter, had told her that she had lost track of the years. When I asked Ellie and Lucinda if I could speak to

Lucinda's mother, they shrugged their shoulders. I insisted that I needed Lucinda's mother's permission to talk to her, so she ran downstairs, had her sign the consent form, and returned. Ellie leaned over the balcony to ask Lucinda's mother if she wanted to be interviewed by me, but she did not answer. Lucinda returned quickly, and she and Ellie resumed her story. They were both speaking quickly, and I struggled to keep up but was able to piece together the details from the various stories they told. It turned out that Lucinda's mother, Marissa, had become pregnant after a year of employment as a domestic worker in Kuwait. Instead of turning her in to the police, Marissa's sponsor told her that she would be welcome to have the child at their home but that both mother and child would then be rendered illegal. They explained to her that children born out of wedlock could sometimes be separated from their mothers, who could then be detained and often deported. Afraid of this consequence, Marissa gave birth at home (with the assistance of her employer's sister), but from that point on neither Marissa nor Lucinda left the house out of fear of being caught by the police. Knowing that Lucinda was stateless, Marissa was terrified her daughter would be taken away from her. When it came time to renew her visa and contract, Marissa was afraid to do so, worrying that the authorities would find out about Lucinda, and arrest her.

As soon as Lucinda was old enough to help around the house, she did so, and was rewarded with sweets from her mother's employer. When Lucinda turned seven, however, Marissa's employer began withholding her wages. The children Marissa took care of also grew increasingly aggressive and would often tease and hurt Lucinda. Afraid to go to the authorities, Marissa worked for two years without pay, while Lucinda suffered from increased bullying. At one point, Lucinda was locked in the dryer by the two young boys who were Marissa's charges. Another time, Lucinda recalled that the boys took turns throwing shoes at her. When Marissa tried to stand up for her daughter, her employer became very angry and started to hit Marissa. One afternoon her employer came home and poured boiling water on Marissa's legs, complaining that Marissa had not prepared food for the children that was to their liking. The next morning Marissa and Lucinda packed their things and decided to take their chances by running away to the Philippines Embassy. They were placed in the informal shelter while their cases were examined. For nine years, Lucinda had managed to be incorporated into the home of her mother's employer—but now that had ended, and she indicated extreme fear of what would happen next.

Both Lucinda and Nadia were able to stay and find employment in the informal economy in the Gulf Cooperation Council (GCC). Although neither of them had been able to obtain citizenship, they had both circumvented laws about their presence in Kuwait and the UAE through informal channels, thus manifesting the perverse (in that it is illegal but works) aspect of integration. Their living and working situations point to an example of legally produced illegality, in which both young women were living and working illegally in the host country, not because they had done anything illegal, but because the contours of the immigration and labor laws do not take into account the possibilities or circumstances of their birth. In addition, the incongruence between home and host country laws further restricted these women's movements, keeping them simultaneously stateless and immobile.

Intergenerational Irregular (Im)Migration

This chapter highlights the intergenerational impacts of irregular migration, which is contoured and often produced by flawed policies to address gendered migration and citizenship. I draw on in-depth fieldwork with migrant women and the children of migrant women in two migrant-receiving countries in the GCC—Kuwait and the UAE. The stories of young people such as Nadia and Lucinda show how challenges with family reunification and with sending and receiving states reproduce inequality and irregular employment. Laws pertaining or responding to hypersexualized moral panic around human trafficking, labor laws, and citizenship regulations affect migrants and their kin, leading to not only the production but also the reproduction of irregularity across generations.

Gendered migration, wherein women migrate with as much if not more frequency than men (Parreñas 2001; Hondangeu-Sotelo 2003; Constable 2014; Boris and Parreñas 2010; Michel 2011) has been increasing globally for over three decades, and many migrant women have given birth to children at some point during their migratory journeys. While some scholars have focused on the effect of absentee parents on the lives of children left behind (Parreñas 2005; Yeoh and Lam 2007; Suzuki 2015a), others have focused on the challenges that migrant women themselves face (Parreñas 2001; Parreñas 2005; Lan 2008; Pratt 2012). Pratt (2012) and Suzuki (2015a) have engaged the question of what happens when these women are reunited with their children, either upon returning to the home country or in the host country. These studies, focused on how migration affects parenting, provide an important lens to examine the effects of parenting on migration as well as the experiences of children who remain in the home country while their mothers migrate abroad. In addition, fieldwork with the children of migrants—both in the host country and at home—shows how different migratory experiences can affect these children. This chapter will focus on the children who were born in the host countries of the UAE and Kuwait to migrant women who were working or had migrated irregularly.

It is interesting to note that thirty out of the thirty-five children I interviewed were also working informally in their home or host countries. These young people experience heightened feelings of liminality as they struggle to explore and express their subjectivities in countries where they do not always feel welcome. Their experiences highlight the tangled mobilities and the entanglement of issues of citizenship, law, and family.

Governments across the globe have expressed increasing frustration at the rising numbers of what are variously termed "illegal," "informal," or "irregular" migrants and immigrants. Globally, tensions exist between those understood as sending countries and those understood as receiving countries, as they struggle to negotiate ways to mitigate the undocumented flow of people across their borders. However, policymakers and individuals engaging in larger discourses about the woes of "illegal" or "irregular" migration frequently overlook the roles that national and international laws and policies play in producing situations wherein irregular migration or employment becomes the comparatively better—and sometimes only—option for social, economic, emotional, and physical mobility. To add to this, moral panic (Cohen 1972) about human trafficking and the ensuing policies also elide the lived experiences of migrants.

By looking at the disconnection between human trafficking and citizenship legislation on the one hand and the lived experiences of migrants on the other, the production of irregular migration and employment can be observed. Moreover, by exploring the lived experiences of migrants and their families, the lasting impacts of these policies in producing *cycles* of entangled irregular social mobility between generations are highlighted. The experiences examined in this chapter demonstrate the need to pay particular attention to the vulnerabilities and precarity that children of irregular migrant women face as results of the challenges and exclusions their mothers faced. These vulnerable and precarious conditions can be directly linked to their (or their mother's) migratory or employment status—statuses often produced by policies disconnected from lived experiences.

Many of the migrants whose experiences are analyzed in this chapter operate in grey areas alongside an ever-shifting continuum of legal/illegal, licit/illicit, and formal/informal economies and statuses. Illegality is not a quality that adheres to human beings as a defining feature of their humanness; instead, it is a status produced by states and immigration policies through efforts to contour a limited notion of the rights-bearing subject (Anderson, Sharma, and Wright 2009; De Genova 2002; Luibhéid 2013). As Garcés-Mascareñas (2010: 83) astutely argues, illegality must be explained "from within ... the context of immigration policy itself and the contradictions besetting the nation-state with regard to labor demands." By deploying intimacy as an overarching framework for analyzing inter-Asian migrations, the works on intimate labor by Friedman (2010), Parreñas (2005), and Boris and Parreñas (2010) broaden Garcés-Mascareñas's analytical scope by showing how illegality is produced across a broad swath of intimate and care-based labors to include both those that are openly remunerated (as in the case of domestic and sex workers) and those framed by the non-commodified rhetoric of familial obligation and intimacy. Immigration policies, as Anderson (2009) notes, produce particular kinds of people by molding them into migrants, workers, and familial dependants; and these molds also shape the forms of illegality that are made to attach to those statuses through the effects of immigration policies (Willen 2007).

Illegality may emerge from the barriers erected by migration categories (such as the distinction between worker and wife, or the legal incompatibility of worker and mother) from the way these categories interact with temporal restrictions designed to limit migrants' presence in and impact on the host society, and from long-standing relationships of mutual dependence between legal/licit economies and illicit or informal sectors. Scholars such as Kim (2015), Yeoh and Chee (2015), Suzuki (2015b), and Faier (2009) demonstrate in fine detail how the realm of the illicit is produced and bolstered by formal laws, legal categories, and migration paradigms, with particular attention to the historical and national specificities of how migrant illegality is constructed. If illegality is a mirror image of legality in a given time and place (Garcés-Mascareñas 2010), then its defining features and contours will be shaped by the immigration regimes specific to particular nation-states and international norms in that historical moment (De Genova 2002: 424). At the same time, however, the intergenerational cycles of irregularity within migration that I describe also display some shared trends with respect to how illegality is produced across the region, including its terms and configurations, and the consequences it generates for migrants forced to live within the "confines of legality" (De Genova and Peutz 2010; Garcés-Mascareñas 2010; Willen 2007).

By looking at the entangled intergenerational impacts of irregular migration, I aim to make an assessment of how illegality is produced by state investments in limiting what have been called "migration pathway switching" (Friedman and Mahdavi 2015; Yeoh and Chee 2015), especially with regard to the fluidity of relationships and practices of intimate life captured under the realm of human trafficking. Not only do migrants move between formal and informal sectors of the economy, but some also seek to switch their status from temporary foreign worker to permanent spouse of a citizen with rights to residency and ultimately citizenship. The "wife or worker" and "mother or worker" paradigms interrogated in the works of Constable (2014), Hsia (2015), Yeoh and Chee (2015), and Friedman (2015) reflect state desires to fix migrants in a single status, and restrict access to employment and residency rights. A migrant domestic worker on a temporary visa may become illegal by becoming pregnant or marrying a citizen, acts that establish claims to permanency and belonging, and are thus rendered illegitimate by her original migration status. Farmer (2004) has written extensively about the phenomenon of "structural violence," and has extended his analysis to discuss what he calls "cycles" of structural violence. Structural violence, as defined by Farmer (2004) and Galtung (1969) many decades before, refers to embedded structural inequalities (such as racism, sexism, and age discrimination) that have an adverse effect on the quality of life and health of certain populations. When Farmer writes about cycles of structural violence, he is pointing to the ways in which inequality and discrimination become reproduced and compounded within certain populations. He describes people as being caught in "cycles" wherein one type of discrimination builds on another and reinforces inequality, which can be passed down through generations. While in previous work I have argued that the inequalities migrants face in the Gulf take on forms of structural violence (Mahdavi 2011), here I aim to build on Farmer's analysis to highlight the production of cycles of *irregularity* experienced by migrant women and their children.

Research Methods

This section draws on ethnographic research conducted in Kuwait City, Dubai, and Abu Dhabi between 2008 and 2014. Fieldwork began in the UAE with domestic workers, sex workers, care providers, and service workers. This then led me to interviews with state officials and embassy personnel in the UAE and also in the United States. During this period, I made annual extended field trips to the Gulf for periods ranging from one to three months. I interviewed 213 female intimate laborers (including care workers, domestic workers, sex workers, and service workers in the beauty industry), 89 state and embassy officials, and 57 male migrant workers; I also interviewed 14 stateless children of varying ages, and 33 employers. The fieldwork also entailed participant observation at detention centers, hospitals, orphanages, shelters, and informal shelters at embassies. In addition, I conducted media analyses of articles appearing in the GCC and in the US about migrant labor in the Middle East. Finally, I supplemented the ethnographic fieldwork with a review of policies on human trafficking, domestic work, migration, and the *kefala*—a guest worker program that governs all laws pertaining to guest workers in the Gulf, and citizenship transfer laws. I have continued with online fieldwork since 2014.

Dubai, the UAE, and Kuwait in Perspective

The extremely large foreign population (estimates show that 80 percent of the UAE population are guest workers; in Dubai this number jumps to 92 percent) and the heavy dependency on foreign migrant workers have created serious problems for the UAE. Dubai is widely cited as a place with deep labor rights violations and gender inequality. Those who work on these problems confront a significant lack of data regarding actual numbers and the demographic makeup of migrants in the region. Though the statistics on the number of female migrants in particular, and the industries into which they migrate, suffer from a lack of accuracy and transparency, current statistical estimates show a dramatic increase in the number of female migrants in the last three decades. It is believed that "50 to 75 percent of the legal migrants leaving Indonesia, the Philippines, and Sri Lanka are women, most of them hoping to earn money as domestic workers in the Middle East and other parts of Asia" (Varia 2007: 4). Middle East migration scholar Ray Jureidini (2009: 76) has observed that there are over six hundred thousand domestic workers — and possibly more if undocumented migrants are considered — in the UAE. In Sabban's (2002: 1) in-depth study of female labor in the UAE, she notes that "domestics in the UAE represent the largest and fastest growing workforce in the UAE," with, on average, over three hundred visas per day granted to domestic workers. In general (albeit using her annual figures from 2000), the majority of domestic workers and sex workers—and it is worth repeating that spheres of intimate labor are not mutually exclusive, and indeed women do often move between spheres—migrate from India (6,730), Indonesia (11,543), Sri Lanka (7,588), and the Philippines (6,856), though increasing numbers of women are also migrating from Ethiopia, Eritrea, Nigeria, and Pakistan. Tables 2.1 and 2.2 below present the more updated population estimates of migrants to the UAE and Kuwait in 2019. Overall, migrants made up the majority of the population of both countries—approximately 88 percent in the UAE and 72 percent in Kuwait (IOM 2020).

In my field site, I found that certain structural factors, most notably those introduced by the *kefala* system, create unique forms of legal

Table 2.1. International Migrant Population in Kuwait and the UAE, 2019.

Country	International Migrant Population	Migrant Population as a Share of Total	Females among International Migrants
Kuwait	3,034.8 (thousands)	72.1 percent	33.6 percent
UAE	8,587.3 (thousands)	87.9 percent	26.3 percent

Table 2.2. Top Five Sending Countries to Host Country—Female Migrant Stock, 2019.

Kuwait	UAE
1. India—331,645	1. India—792,877
2. Egypt—173,236	2. Egypt—293,730
3. Pakistan—93,552	3. Pakistan—218,153
4. Indonesia—86,372	4. Indonesia—202,404
5. Bangladesh—61,658	5. Bangladesh—140,954

vulnerability for the UAE and Kuwait migrant workers. Female migrants in many parts of the world face challenges such as coping with abusive employers, working illegally with limited rights, and working unregulated hours with very little recourse if they are abused or if their pay is withheld. The conditions outlined by the *kefala* system in the Gulf countries, however, make the experience of intimate laborers somewhat unique. Under UAE and Kuwaiti labor laws, domestic workers are required to abide by the *kefala* system, and their residence in the country is dependent on their sponsor or *kafeel*, who is also their employer. They are dependent entirely on this person not only for residence but also for assistance in accessing services, such as health care. More problematic aspects of the General Provisions section of the 1980 UAE labor law, which structures the lived experiences of migration, includes Article 3, which states that "the provisions of this law shall not apply to the following categories ... domestic servants employed in private households, and the like ... farming and grazing workers," and Article 72, in which seafarers are added to the list of migrant workers not protected by any labor laws. Thus, while domestic workers must abide by *kefala* procedures, they are not protected by any labor laws. They, like other migrant workers, are also unable to participate in labor unions due to the UAE law banning the creation of such organizations.

In 2017 and 2018, many GCC countries, including Kuwait and the UAE, made progress on reforming *kefala*. While neighboring countries such as Qatar and Bahrain abolished the *kefala* system outright,[1] the UAE made significant revisions, including defining work hours and the scope of work for certain migrants, and standardizing work contracts. However, as the organization Migrants' Rights (2018) notes below:

> GCC countries have made notable progress in granting migrant workers more rights and protections. However, domestic workers are generally not included under standard labor laws in the Gulf, the justification being that they work in private homes and should be treated differently

than laborers in the public sphere. Even when legislation is drafted specifically for domestic workers, it does not offer the same protections granted to laborers in other industries.[2]

In Kuwait, in 2018, migrant domestic workers from the Philippines organized to get the Department of Labor and Employment (DOLE) in the Philippines to issue a total ban on sending migrant Filipina domestic workers to Kuwait after reports of abuse in the nation-state rose to new heights.[3] As of the writing of this chapter, however, overseas Filipina workers (OFWs) were continuing to migrate to Kuwait to work in homes.

Migrant workers are frequently subject to two levels of policing and disciplining, with these levels often suffering from incongruence. The first level involves state laws as outlined above, including labor laws (or the lack thereof), as well as the sponsorship or *kefala* system. The second level of discipline comes from the *kafeels* or sponsors themselves, who often do not abide by state laws. *Kafeels* can range from large corporations down to private employers in the home. While there are laws against retaining passports and not providing days off, and rules outlining the humanitarian treatment of workers, many sponsors take it upon themselves to discipline their employees. Many employees do not agitate for their wages or report abuse out of fear of deportation or detention, which allows these employers to continue to violate migrant workers' rights, resulting in trafficking-like experiences.

It is important to highlight that all workers in Dubai and Kuwait are migrants and not immigrants, in that they do not have the possibility of attaining residency or citizenship in the UAE or Kuwait, as naturalization is very difficult. Naturalization is only permitted through marriage to an Emirati citizen; even then, it can only take place after at least three years *and* if it has been announced by the ministry that the spouse is permitted citizenship. In some cases, it is possible to attain citizenship if the following criteria are met:

> Article 6: May be granted [to] any Arab who is a Muslim if they [have] resided continuously and legally in the United Arab Emirates for no less than seven years, and have a legitimate way of living, have a good character and [have] not [been] convicted of a crime involving dishonesty [or] immorality.

> Article 7: May be granted [to] any person who is a Muslim if they [have] resided continuously and legally in the United Arab Emirates since 1940 or earlier, and [have] maintained [their] residency there, and have a legitimate way of living, have a good character, [and have] not [been] convicted of a crime involving dishonesty [or] immorality, and [are] good in Arabic. (UAE 1972)

Thus, we see that attaining citizenship is subject to ethnicity and religion, as well as to living in a way deemed (usually by the ministry) as "honest and moral." How the ministry and immigrant institution define "moral" is operationalized to exclude migrant women from this moral status (see Ahmad 2012).

UAE laws regarding pregnancy outside of marriage and abortion further complicate the situation for many workers. While female domestic workers in particular do not have rights or access to women's health or family planning services, their pregnancy can be cause for immediate termination of their contract and their subsequent deportation. In accordance with Islamic law, abortion is strictly prohibited unless it is to save the life of the mother, or if the baby will be born with serious genetic defects and likely will not survive. The UAE government is quite clear on its stance toward pregnant women, as shown by its website:

> It is of utmost importance for a woman to be married if pregnant in the U.A.E. At the hospital when you go for your first check-up, you will need to show an original marriage certificate along with copies of your passport and visa. If you are unmarried and pregnant, you should either get married or expatriate. Unmarried expectant mothers should return to their home countries for the delivery. Moreover, abortions in Dubai are illegal unless there are medical complications, and the abortion is sanctioned by the hospital.

Pregnancy outside of marriage is not permitted. Although migrant women who become pregnant while in the UAE are encouraged to return to their home countries to deliver their children, if they cannot finance their own return travel then they may be held in detention. Some women do not wish to return to their home countries for reasons including fear of family stigma, fear of returning without money to pay back their family or their own debts, or a general preference to remain in the UAE. In these cases, the women become immediately undocumented and their children are placed in a precarious position.

Disconnected: Law and Lived Experience

Human trafficking and discriminatory citizenship policies create situations of frustrating precarity, tightening the contours of migration and migratory employment possibilities in the formal or regulated sphere. Rather than alleviating challenges for states (as discussed above) or migrants, trafficking policies function to increase bureaucracy while decreasing safe avenues for migration and work. Migrants have responded by employing creativity and

Table 2.3. Contractual Sterilization Laws in Other Gulf Cooperation Council Countries.

	Saudi Arabia	Qatar	Oman	Kuwait	UAE
Male Guardianship System[1]	✓	✓	✓	✓	✓
Coercion in Population Control[2]	✗	✗	✗	✗	✗
Ban on Gender Discrimination in the Workplace	✓	✗	✗	✗	✗
Women May Directly Transmit Citizenship to their Children[3]	✗	✗	✗	✗	✗
Women Must Obtain Male Guardian Permission to Travel	✓	✓	✓	✗	✓
Prohibition of Forced or Compulsory Labor	✓[4]	✓[5]	✓[6]	✓[7]	✓[4]

Notes:
1. Under the male guardianship system, a man controls a woman's life from her birth until her death. Every woman must have a male guardian, normally a father or husband, but in some cases a brother or even a son, who has the power to make a range of critical decisions on her behalf. The system is nuanced, and different in each country (USDS 2020).
2. The US Department of State (USDS) has not recorded any reports of coerced abortion or involuntary sterilization in the country in 2019 (ibid.).
3. Children derive citizenship only from the father (ibid.).
4. The law prohibits forced or compulsory labor, but the government did not effectively enforce the law. Forced labor occurred, especially among migrant workers—notably domestic servants (ibid.).
5. The government made efforts to prevent and eliminate forced labor, although the restrictive sponsorship system left some migrant workers vulnerable to exploitation (ibid.).
6. The law prohibits all forced or compulsory labor, but the law explicitly excludes domestic workers (ibid.).
7. The law prohibits and criminally sanctions forced or compulsory labor "except in cases specified by law for national emergency and with just remuneration." The law allows for forced prison labor as a punishment for expressing certain political views, and in cases of seafarers who breach discipline (ibid.).

turning to irregular modes of migration and employment. These alternative employment and migratory spheres offer comparatively safer and more lucrative options for many of my interlocutors, such as Meskit and Alia, introduced below.

Meskit's migrant trajectory from working as domestic labor in the formal sphere of the service industry to working in the informal economy of the sex industry and living as an "illegal alien" in Dubai was similar to at least seven other women with whom I spoke. After her father died, Meskit's mother and siblings were left in high debt in her home country Ethiopia. Worried about her family's future, she decided to ask her friends about possible avenues of migration to the Gulf. After announcing her decision to her mother and siblings and receiving their blessing, Meskit approached a friend of hers who advised a shortcut for her to get to Dubai more easily. In recent years, the Ethiopian government—in response to "moral panic" (Cohen 1972) about human trafficking—has passed a series of measures designed to regulate the flow of Ethiopians migrating for work, particularly to the Middle East (De Regt 2010). The state has imposed rules on licensing for recruiters, and has been working toward a system of employee training (similar to that in the Philippines) and contract monitoring. This increased bureaucracy has resulted in many women looking for other ways to leave Ethiopia, ways that are seen as simpler and faster routes for securing transnational employment.

Meskit's friend put her in touch with an illegal recruiter who asked for a high fee, equivalent to US$2,000, to secure Meskit's passage to Dubai (via boat through the Comoros Islands) and to draw up a contract for her to work as a domestic worker. Meskit never saw the contract, but she was told she would be met by another recruiter upon her arrival in Dubai.

When she arrived in Dubai after a long journey, she was met by a recruiter and then taken to the home of her new employers, a Lebanese family who had moved to Dubai a few years before. The family took her passport and the few personal belongings that Meskit had brought with her, but then never gave them back. To this day, she is working to retrieve her passport so that she can find legal employment and return to Ethiopia someday soon. During the six months that Meskit worked for this family, she had suffered beatings from her madam (the female employer and head of the household) and sexual harassment from the male head of the household and his son. Made to work up to eighteen hours a day, the family often locked Meskit in the house when they left, without providing dinner on most weeknights. "But I don't know where to go. I'm an illegal lady, coming illegally, so I'm not going to the embassy or police. But where to go?" she asked rhetorically. When she complained, she would be beaten, and the male head of household would make further advances toward her, making sexual threats that he would rape her one night while she was asleep.

Meskit was very afraid of these threats, so one afternoon she ran away from the apartment where she had been sequestered for the previous six months without pay. She jumped from the window of her room on the third story of the building, injuring her right leg badly; but instead of going to the hospital or police, Meskit decided to go to the church that she had been permitted to attend once a month. "I know other Ethiopians at the church; I know if I can get there, I can get help," she said. However, she did not know her way around town, and her injured leg severely restricted her mobility. After a few days of living on the street, she met a young Emirati man who wanted to help her. After a few weeks Meskit became romantically involved with this man and eventually became pregnant. The man was very happy to hear that she was pregnant and showered her with gifts and attention. He also promised to get her a legal visa and to be her sponsor and potentially her husband. Meskit was overjoyed, and during this period converted to Islam and became very involved at the local mosque that her Emirati boyfriend attended. After their son was born, however, things changed. The young man, who had not yet succeeded in retrieving her working papers or passport, suddenly became agitated with Meskit and ordered her to leave the house with the baby. He told her his family had heard about their situation and did not approve of his decision to continue living with Meskit in the future. He gave her some money for childrearing and sent her away. Although Meskit did not know it at the time, her son was undocumented because the boy's father had never acknowledged paternity. If caught, Meskit would likely be deported and separated from her son, who could possibly remain stateless in the UAE if the law suspected him of having Emirati paternity.

Meskit and her son moved in with some of her friends from the mosque while she tried to look for possible jobs to earn enough money to pay off the fines she had incurred by overstaying her visa, and to procure an outpass—a blank passport that allows migrants to exit with amnesty but does not confer citizenship—to return to Ethiopia with her son. Due to the lack of legal working papers, Meskit began by working in a restaurant in the Ethiopian neighborhood in town. After a few months working at this job, however, she stopped getting paid. One evening she met a group of women at the restaurant who worked as sex workers in a bar called Fantasi. After they told her what her earning potential could be, she decided to join them that evening. This marked the beginning of Meskit's work in the informal economy of sex work. After a few months working at the bar, Meskit was arrested one night on a raid. She was put in jail for three weeks and not permitted to see her son, who was still at the home of her friends with whom she had been living.

Alia's story was similar to those of Lucinda and Meskit. However, she had remained incorporated informally in Kuwait for twenty-seven years. Alia had been born to an unwed Indian domestic worker who had decided to give birth at the hospital in Kuwait City. As happens in many instances, Alia's mother was sent to jail, while Alia remained at the hospital and was cared for by the nurses and hospital staff. It was one of the nurses who had named Alia (after her aunt), and she was the one to tell Alia the very limited details she knew about the circumstances of her birth. At first the nurses would take Alia to the prison to be nursed by her mother. However, after six months, it was discovered that Alia's mother was no longer in jail and nowhere to be found. The hospital staff did not know if she had been deported or had voluntarily returned to India. Alia's father was unknown, and at the time it was difficult to send children in her circumstance to the orphanage (as the Emir had not yet passed a decree to allow for the transfer of stateless children). Without any clear place to send the child, the nurses ended up raising Alia in the hospital.

"I lived in the hospital until I was seven years old," Alia recalled. "But I helped out the nurses, the ones who would give me candies and treats. I would help them, I would go do things for them, pick up their laundry, get them medicines, get them lunch, and they helped me too." But the nurses would also tell Alia that she needed to leave the hospital, perhaps even go to school. "It was hard though, I was a little girl, and all I knew was life in the hospital," she said. "I didn't want to leave because I had become attached to the nurses, but at the same time, I did want to have a home."

One day an Indian couple came to the hospital for fertility services. When they met Alia, they asked the nurses if they could take her home. They promised to take good care of her and give her a good life. At the time, adoption in Kuwait was not common, nor were there any laws regulating the process of child adoption. Today, Kuwaiti citizens may adopt, but non-citizens, such as the couple who informally adopted Alia, are not permitted to do so, and even citizens may not adopt *Bidoon* (Arabic for "without"; i.e., the stateless). Alia remembered that the nurses felt conflicted about allowing Alia to go with the couple. "They kept asking me, 'Do you want to go with them?' And they told me that if I didn't want to go, I didn't have to, and I could stay." Alia was unsure of what to do, but the Indian couple came to visit her every day for one week, bringing her presents, clothes, and sweets. After a week of getting to know them, Alia told the nurses she would like to go and have a home. They told her she was welcome to come back to the hospital anytime, and said their goodbyes.

Alia lived with this couple for the next ten years. Although she was stateless, they arranged for her to go to the Indian school after teaching her to read and write. She did not fully understand the implications of her lack of citizenship until the Indian couple's work permits had expired and they were preparing to go back to India. "They had often gone in the summers, but one of them would stay behind with me. Whenever they traveled, someone stayed with me, or I was sent to stay with friends. I didn't understand what it all meant until I was seventeen and they told me they were leaving for good," Alia said. When Alia asked if she could go to India with them, they explained to her that she would have to stay in Kuwait because she did not have a passport.

Alia was unsure of what to do next or where to go. "In those days, I cried a lot, even cried myself to sleep most nights," she said. One day, three weeks before the Indian couple was scheduled to return home, some friends of theirs came over for a visit. These friends had two children, ages two and three, and the wife was pregnant with a third child. Upon hearing about Alia's situation, the wife offered Alia a room and full board if she would agree to work for the family as a nanny and housekeeper. Alia agreed and has been living with this family for the past ten years. She is now twenty-seven years old and has never left Kuwait's borders. While she is aware of her statelessness and that her working for an employer is technically illegal, she narrates her situation in terms of familial incorporation. "It's true I am working here for the family, but it's also like I'm one of the family, so perhaps it's not work. Also, Kuwait is my home, the only home I have ever known, so I feel happy to stay here," she explained.

As these stories show, migrants may end up moving, working, or living outside of the formal contours of the "legal" economy for a variety of reasons. For many of my interlocutors, it was a combination of having to employ creativity in the face of ever-changing and harsh laws about migration, employment (*kefala* in the UAE made it difficult for Filipinas' to work as entertainers), and citizenship, as well as a desire to mobilize their intimate lives. Someone like Meskit chose—from amongst a series of limited options—to migrate irregularly, because formal migratory routes were not available to her due to the anti-trafficking legislature seeking to restrict the out-migration of women in particular. Beginning the journey in an irregular fashion, once she arrived at her destination it became increasingly preferable for her to choose not just irregular migration, but irregular or informal employment as well. Both Alia and Meskit chose the space of the informal economy because it afforded them more freedoms, rights and empowerment, and also allowed them to fulfill their intimate lives. Both women were able to make a living and support themselves through working irregularly. While formal, legal work options had been closed off to them due to changing laws about gendered migration, informal work became the comparatively desirable option.

Many of my interlocutors do, however, experience some vulnerability in the spaces of irregular migration or the informal economy, and their intimate lives reflect this vulnerability most presciently. This new intergenerational aspect of irregular migration and employment does bear some reflection, as it is an unfortunate by-product of new economic realities of gendered migrations across Asia. Children of migrants, such as Alia, Nadia, and Lucinda, are, in a sense, born into a situation of irregularity. Produced by laws about gendered employment as well as citizenship, their situations and lives seem somewhat bleak. Many of these migrants' children with whom I have spoken have grown up legally stateless, though they have found ways to survive; however, most of them now work in the informal economy where they face many challenges.

It is important to recognize at least three aspects of irregular migration, employment, and status that are often eclipsed by policies that do not consider the migrants' lived experience. The first is that irregularity is most often produced by policies seeking to curb (gendered) migration and citizenship, as can be seen in the cases of the women introduced above. The second is that irregular migration or working status can be seen and experienced as a better, more lucrative and empowering strategy, and one that can afford migrants with limited mobility many options for economic, social, class, physical, and intimate mobilities. Finally, it is important to highlight that while living, moving, and working irregularly might be produced and may be seen as the comparatively desirable option (and for the children of migrants, often the only option), there are vulnerabilities that migrants are exposed to when living and moving in these spaces. These include the possibility of arrest and/or deportation—what De Genova (2002) has termed "deportability"—as well as precarious living and working situations wherein migrants are regularly abused, not paid their wages, and always subject to difficult working conditions. Unfortunately, policies responding to moral panic about human trafficking do not recognize the lived realities of gendered migration in the twenty-first century. The very same policies designed to "help" or "protect" migrants are actively producing increased irregular migration and employment, which is then reproducing its impact on the next generation of migrants born abroad.

Cycles of Irregularity—Conclusion

As the cases of migrant women and their children introduced here show, irregular migration, often produced by discriminatory and ill-informed policies, has the effect of ensnaring migrant women in cycles of irregularity, wherein they have to enter various forms of irregular migration and employment in order to survive. Weak policies have also generated long-term effects that go beyond the lifespan of one migrant, spilling into the next generations, whose lives are conditioned by the lack of citizenship status and the tangled intergenerational immobility. There currently exists a new generation of young people who are facing challenges that may not have been foreseen by policymakers seeking to respond to global policies such as those embodied in anti-trafficking legislation.

While policies continue to remain disconnected from lived experience, and migrant subjectivity continues to be challenged, the very real vulnerabilities of the next generation—people like Alia, Nadia, and Lucinda—remain eclipsed. It is important to recognize the intimate lives of migrants and their kin in order to have a more robust understanding of how gendered migration operates and is contoured within the transnational migrant economy. Without recognizing the precarity produced in the lives of migrants, and then their children, policies will continue to produce more challenges rather than alleviating the obstacles faced by increasingly vulnerable populations. These policies, while possibly well intentioned, reproduce not only cycles of structural violence but also precarity and irregularity, as they challenge migrants' subjectivities and intimate lives across borders and generations.

Pardis Mahdavi, PhD, is currently Dean of Social Sciences and Director of the School for Social Transformation at Arizona State University. Before coming to Arizona, she was Acting Dean of the Korbel School of International Studies at the University of Denver (2017-19), after spending eleven years at Pomona College (2006-17), where she latterly served as Professor and Chair of Anthropology and Director of the Pacific Basin Institute, as well as Dean of Women. Her research interests include gendered labor, human trafficking, migration, sexuality, human rights, transnational feminism, and public health in the context of changing global and political structures. She has published four single-authored books and one edited volume, in addition to numerous journal and news articles. She has been a Fellow at the Social Sciences Research Council, the American Council on Learned Societies, Google Ideas, and the Woodrow Wilson International Center for Scholars. In 2018 she was appointed by Colorado Governor John Hickenlooper and reappointed by Governor Jared Polis to serve on the Colorado Commission on Higher Education.

NOTES

1. For more on the phenomenon of moral panic, please see Cohen's (1972) work *Moral Panic and Folk Devils*.
2. For more information, please see Migrant Rights 2017, "Migration in the Gulf: 2016 in Review."
3. For more information, please see Everist 2018, "Working for Labor Laws to Protect Domestic Workers in the Gulf."

REFERENCES

Ahmad, Attiya. 2012. "Cosmopolitan Islam in a Diasporic Space: Foreign Resident Muslim Women's *Halaqa* in the Arabian Peninsula." In *Islamic Reform in South Asia*, ed. Filippo Osella and Caroline Osella, 421-44. Cambridge: Cambridge University Press.

Anderson, Bridget. 2009. "What's in a Name? Immigration Controls and Subjectivities: The Case of Au Pairs and Domestic Worker Visa Holders in the UK." *Subjectivity* 29(1): 407–24.

Anderson, Bridget, Nandita Sharma, and Cynthia Wright. 2009. "Why No Borders?" *Refuge: Canada's Journal on Refugees* 26(2): 5–18.

Boris, Eileen, and Rhacel Salazar Parreñas, eds. 2010. *Intimate Labors: Cultures, Technologies, and the Politics of Care.* Stanford, CA: Stanford University Press.

Cohen, Stanley. 1972. *Moral Panics and Folk Devils.* London: MacGibbon and Kee.

Constable, Nicole. 2014. *Born out of Place: Migrant Mothers and the Politics of International Labor.* Berkeley: University of California Press.

De Genova, Nicholas P. 2002. "Migrant 'Illegality' and Deportability in Everyday Life." *Annual Review of Anthropology* 31(1): 419–47.

De Genova, Nicolas P., and Natalie Peutz, eds. 2010. *The Deportation Regime: Sovereignty, Space, and the Freedom of Movement.* Durham, NC: Duke University Press.

De Regt, Marina. 2010. "Ways to Come, Ways to Leave: Gender, Mobility, and Il/legality among Ethiopian Domestic Workers in Yemen." *Gender & Society* 24(2): 237–60.

Everist, Audrey. 2018. "Working for Labor Laws to Protect Domestic Workers in the Gulf." *The Global Observatory.* Retrieved 15 September 2020 from https://theglobalobservatory.org/.

Faier, Lieba. 2009. *Intimate Encounters: Filipina Women and the Remaking of Rural Japan.* Berkeley: University of California Press.

Farmer, Paul. 2004. "An Anthropology of Structural Violence." *Current Anthropology* 45(3): 305–25.

Friedman, Sara L. 2010. "Determining 'Truth' at the Border: Immigration Interviews, Chinese Marital Migrants, and Taiwan's Sovereignty Dilemmas." *Citizenship Studies* 14(2): 167–83.

———. 2015. "Regulating Cross-Border Intimacy: Authenticity Paradigms and the Specter of Illegality among Chinese Marital Immigrants to Taiwan." In *Migrant Encounters: Intimate Labor, the State, and Mobility across Asia,* ed. Pardis Mahdavi and Sara L. Friedman, 206–30. Philadelphia: University of Pennsylvania Press.

Friedman, Sara L., and Pardis Mahdavi, eds. 2015. *Migrant Encounters: Intimate Labor, the State, and Mobility across Asia.* Philadelphia: University of Pennsylvania Press.

Galtung, Johan. 1969. "Violence, Peace, and Peace Research." *Journal of Peace Research* 6(3): 167–91.

Garcés-Mascareñas, Blanca. 2010. "Legal Production of Illegality in a Comparative Perspective: The Cases of Malaysia and Spain." *Asia Europe Journal* 8(1): 77–89.

Hondagneu-Sotelo, Pierette, ed. 2003. *Gender and U.S. Contemporary Trends.* Berkeley: University of California Press.

Hsia, Hsiao-Chuan. 2015. "Reproduction Crisis, Illegality, and Migrant Women under Captialist Globalization: The Case of Taiwan." In *Migrant Encounters: Intimate Labor, the State, and Mobility across Asia,* ed. Pardis Mahdavi and Sara L. Friedman, 160–83. Philadelphia: University of Pennsylvania Press.

International Organization for Migration (IOM). 2020. "World Migration Report 2020." Retrieved 15 September 2020 from https://publications.iom.int/books/world-migration-report-2020.
Jureidini, Ray. 2009. "In the Shadows of Family Life: Toward a History of Domestic Service in Lebanon." *Journal of Middle East Women's Studies* 5(3): 74–101.
Kim, Hyun Mee. 2015. "Intimacies and Remittances: The Material Bases for Love and Intimate Labor between Korean Men and their Foreign Spouses in South Korea." In *Migrant Encounters: Intimate Labor, the State, and Mobility across Asia*, ed. Pardis Mahdavi and Sara L. Friedman, 25–45. Philadelphia: University of Pennsylvania Press.
Lan, Pei-Chia. 2008. "Migrant Women's Bodies as Boundary Markers: Reproductive Crisis and Sexual Control in the Ethnic Frontiers of Taiwan." *Signs* 33(4): 833–61.
Luibhéid, Eithne. 2013. *Pregnant on Arrival: Making the Illegal Immigrant*. Minneapolis: University of Minnesota Press.
Mahdavi, Pardis. 2011. *Gridlock: Labor, Migration, and Human Trafficking in Dubai*. Stanford, CA: Stanford University Press.
———. 2016. *Crossing the Gulf: Love and Family in Migrant Lives*. Stanford, CA: Stanford University Press.
Michel, Sonya, ed. 2011. *Women, Migration, and the Work of Care: The United States in Comparative Perspective*. Washington, DC: Woodrow Wilson International Center for Scholars.
Migrant Rights. 2017. "Migration in the Gulf: 2016 in Review." 2017. Retrieved 15 September 2020 from https://www.migrant-rights.org/2017/01/migration-in-the-gulf-2016-in-review/.
Parreñas, Rachel Salazar. 2001. *Servants of Globalization: Women, Migration and Domestic Work*. Stanford, CA: Stanford University Press.
———. 2005. *Children of Global Migration: Transnational Families and Gendered Woes*. Stanford, CA: Stanford University Press.
Pratt, Geraldine. 2012. *Families Apart: Migrant Mothers and the Conflicts of Labor and Love*. Minneapolis: University of Minnesota Press.
Sabban, Rima. 2002. "United Arab Emirates: Migrant Women in the United Arab Emirates. The Case of Female Domestic Workers." Gender Promotion Program Working Paper No. 10. Geneva: International Labor Office.
Suzuki, Nobue. 2015a. "Suspended Mobilities: Japanese-Filipino Children, Family Regimes, and Postcolonial Plurality." In *Mobile Childhoods in Filipino Transnational Families: Migrant Children with Similar Roots in Different Routes*, ed. Itaru Nagasaka and Asuncion Fresnoza-Flot, 222–46. New York: Palgrave Macmillan.
———. 2015b. "Troubling Jus Sanguinis: The State, Law, and Citizenships of Japanese-Filipino Youth in Japan." In *Migrant Encounters: Intimate Labor, the State, and Mobility across Asia*, ed. Pardis Mahdavi and Sara L. Friedman, 113–33. Philadelphia: University of Pennsylvania Press.
United Arab Emirates Federal Law No. 17 for 1972 Concerning Nationality and Passports: Retrieved 22 March 2022 from https://www.refworld.org/pdfid/3fba182d0.pdf.

United States Department of State Country Reports on Human Rights Practices: United Arab Emirates 2020. Retrieved 22 March 2022 from https://www.state.gov/reports/2020-country-reports-on-human-rights-practices/united-arab-emirates/

Varia, Nisha. 2007. *Globalization Comes Home: Protecting Migrant Domestic Workers' Rights.* Washington, DC: Human Rights Watch.

Willen, Sarah S. 2007. "Toward a Critical Phenomenology of 'Illegality': State Power, Criminalization, and Abjectivity among Undocumented Migrant Workers in Tel Aviv, Israel." *International Migration* 45(3): 8–38.

Yeoh, Brenda S. A., and Heng Leng Chee. 2015. "Migrant Wives, Migrant Workers, and the Negotiation of (Il)legality in Singapore." In *Migrant Encounters: Intimate Labor, the State, and Mobility across Asia*, ed. Pardis Mahdavi and Sara L. Friedman, 184–205. Philadelphia: University of Pennsylvania Press.

Yeoh, Brenda S. A., and Theodora Lam. 2007. "The Costs of (Im)mobility: Children Left Behind and Children Who Migrate with a Parent." In *Perspectives on Gender and Migration* 5(4): 120–49. Bangkok: United Nations Economic and Social Commission for Asia and the Pacific.

CHAPTER
3

Mobile Homes, Mobile Objects
Materiality and Mobility of Vietnamese-Belgian Couples

Angelie Marilla

Introduction

One afternoon during the summer of 2019, I met with Thiên[1] in the coffee shop in Ho Chi Minh City that she ran with her husband Jean. We shared a hot tea that she had carefully laid on a handmade coaster, and for about four hours she candidly shared her experiences of being a wife to a Belgian in Vietnam. At one point, Thiên playfully talked about their sofa and Jean's furniture taste. The next day, Jean revealed that he had been listening to our conversation on the surveillance camera of their coffee shop while he was at home on that same sofa. He then told his migration story and that of the sofa—and why, whether Thiên found it beautiful or not, it stayed in the living room.

Thiên and Jean's comments about the furniture present for us the world of mixed couples through the lens of material culture where this exploratory study stems from—the possibility of locating the lived experiences of couples through the everyday objects in their homes. Home is the central part of the daily life of most people, even in mobility. The idea of "home" is often described as the dynamic attachment to a place, experiences, emotions, and relationships (Boccagni 2017). Home is also a contested and processual space of belonging that makes conjugal mixedness an interesting, fittingly illustrative analytical case. This concept of mixedness is drawn from Collet (2012), who treats conjugal mixedness "not only [as] a question of different cultures but one of conformity or deviance with regard to social norms" (71). Mixed couples are mostly mobile, and differ not only in terms of origin but also in their lifestyle and habitus. They, therefore, have to negotiate their diverse cultural backgrounds in the aesthetic of their homes.

Ethnography of Home Objects

This study is *ethnographic* in nature, *object-based* and *multi-sited*. The findings discussed in this chapter are informed by ongoing fieldwork in Belgium and Vietnam. The empirical data was gathered from the beginning of March 2019, and sporadically conducted throughout the year in Brussels, Wallonia, and Flanders. The Vietnam fieldwork covered Hanoi and Ho Chi Minh City. For this chapter, ten Belgian-Vietnamese couples have been interviewed.

This study is a domestic ethnography focusing on materialities such as interior decors and objects in the present, past, and aspirational homes. The research is done through the researcher's home visits and home stays. Whenever the home is not accessible, interviews are held in Vietnamese restaurants, coffee shops, cultural organizations, and workspaces, which are also important sites of everyday routines and life environments of research participants. Informants were initially recruited through the Embassy of Belgium in Hanoi, associations in Ho Chi Minh City and Brussels, and informal contacts—and then through snowballing.

As the study attempts to situate the representations and construction of home in material and multi-sensorial ways, the methodology of this research is guided by a participatory visual technique like photo/image elicitation and, most critically, object-based interviews. Photo-elicitation is a classic approach in ethnography that uses photographs to prompt responses during interviews (Harper 1998), while object interviews incorporate objects in the process of interviews (Woodward 2020). Initially, participants are asked to draw the floor plan, structure, or spaces within their homes. They are also instructed to bring objects with them, or to use the things they carry on a daily basis. Likewise, they are asked to take photographs of home objects and decorations, as well as of the spaces where they are located. They also imagine and visualize objects that are available or aspirational, and speak about them. In this approach, objects become active participants in the interviews, as this study closely follows the biography and agency of objects—from how they are made, collected, used, bought, sold, or given away, how they travel and cross-national boundaries, how they get to spaces in the house like the living room, how they map the domestic space—to the meanings and values the couple give to them, or the individual meanings they impute to these objects.

Finally, following objects is also a central part of "multi-sited ethnography" (Marcus 1995) to comparatively and fully account for the lived experiences of Vietnamese-Belgian couples "here and there" on transnational and translocal levels (Faist 2004). The inquiry is then not confined to those who move but also acknowledges their sedentary counterpart. Accounts of stay-behind families in their past and present homes, and the consequent flow of objects between these two social spaces (Belgium and Vietnam), are also crucial. This mobility of objects between two countries are contextual and material indices of transnational activities such as the presence of carried, sent, and received objects in their homes.

Agency of Objects and Materiality of the Home

The twenty-first century marked the proliferation of studies of migration using transnational perspectives. It witnessed paradigmatic shifts as "the focus moved from migration to the migrants and from transnationalism to transnationals" (Dunn 2010). While this embodied transnationalism leans toward an agency-oriented approach, the study of migration remains confined to the understanding of the mobility of people, and overlooks other sources of agency. Veering away from the conventional focus on migrants alone, this study intends to diversify perspectives on migration studies by looking at how objects narrate the biographies and experiences of migrants.

As the study shifts to human-object interaction, it addresses and redresses consumer culture by appropriating mass-produced objects into meaningful relationships of people and things through the ways they are used. Consumption in this perspective decommodifies and humanizes objects (Kopytoff 1986; Miller 1995, 1998, 2001, 2009). This perspective is closer to that of Gell (1998) and his concept of distributed agency of art objects, existing independently of the volition of the artist. The mobility and agency of these objects, as he contends, is not mere aesthetics but social agents, suggestive of what Appadurai (1986) prominently phrases as the "social life of things." Appadurai, in his more recent writing, has advanced this idea—which has come to be a preoccupation among new materialists— arguing that objects are not just "actants" (Latour 2005) but "mediants" with specific materialities that foreground forms of socialities (Appadurai 2015: 228). To employ this idea into the study of home objects means veering away from the abstraction of home as a symbol, and redirecting the emphasis to the mutually constitutive entanglement of people and things. This agentive tendency of objects clearly withdraws from the idea that commodities are dead material, purportedly fetishized and alienate people, as the usual reductive and materialistic perspectives suggest. Instead, people's relationship with things could reflect social meanings and relationships. As Inglis (2005) illustrates with the example of a person's relationship with a car, "turning to see if the car is 'all right' is perhaps associated with pride in ownership or fear of reprimand from the traffic authorities. If the former, then the behavior is connected to the pride in material objects that predominates in a highly consumerist society; if the latter, then it is connected to a characteristic aspect of the culture of social modernity, namely the bureaucratization of everyday life" (ibid.: 25).

To locate the agency of objects, this study is informed by and anchored to the anthropological and sociological literature of material culture and home. The diverse literature on the materiality of the home has its roots in the work of Bourdieu (1970) on the Kabyle house. He observes how dwelling places hint a structured worldview, and this will later appear to be crucial in his concept of "habitus" (1977). This seminal work opens up the space of the house as an interesting site of inquiry, gives rise to the conceptual differentiation between "house" and "home,"[2] and ushers into academic discussion the more affective and social performative aspect of domesticity and consumption (Ardener 1981; Douglas 1991; Humphrey 1988; Jackson and Moores 2014; Morgan 1881; Putnam and Newton 1990; Stea 1995; Tucker 1994; Wilk 1989).

Home objects[3] as an anthropological topic starts to be more concrete and visible in the popular works of Miller (1995, 1998, 2001, 2009; see also Cieraad 1999; Daniels 2010; Gregson 2007). Miller's writings on the materiality of the home (and chapters from scholars' writings on home ethnography) focus on how people make objects and space home-like through furnishing, decoration, renovation, and consumption practices, and also reflect biographies, identities, relationships, and social class in the United Kingdom. Hurdley (2006, 2007, 2015, 2016) has also consistently published on how and why people display objects in their homes through her case study on mantelpieces in British homes—the same field site as Miller's. Other works on home objects not only look closely at objects on display but also consider objects that are out of sight, stored in the attic/garage or hidden away in boxes or drawers, like the writings of Newell (2014, 2019) on the US domestic space, and Woodward (2015) on that in the UK.

Studies on the relationship between home objects and couples are rather scant. One exception is the book by Kaufmann (1998) entitled *Dirty*

Linen: Couples and their Laundry. As the title suggests, this study introduces a material perspective into the study of everyday domestic life of couples in France. However, focusing on the democratization of family life and depicting laundry as a domestic chore, Kaufmann, as might be expected, illustrates the role of the washing machine and dirty clothes in a performative manner rather than focusing more on the everyday materiality in couples' lives, making the object secondary to his inquiry. The earlier article of Bloch (1995) is rather more materially relevant, as his inquiry looks closely at material practices of Zafimaniry couples in Madagascar, and how they transform their houses over time—such as how wood carvings are incorporated in the different stages of a couple's life. As the family progresses, like the birth of the first child, the house is redecorated and renovated. It becomes increasingly stable, concrete, and decorative, reflecting the couple's changing roles as the family matures. My study leans toward this treatment of objects, but it focuses on their roles in the mobile homes of mixed couples.

My ongoing inquiry into mobile objects attempts to incorporate migration into the study of objects, and objects into the study of migration. While anthropologists and sociologists started to pay closer attention to home objects in the past decades, as seen in the previous discussion, the focus on home objects is a recent interest in migration studies. What has been written so far is a theoretical and methodological toolkit that advances the concept of home as a core subject in migration studies, as seen in the work of Boccagni (2017) who reintroduces home through the prism of mobility, where home is rendered as dynamic, mutable, relational, contextual, experiential, portable, and reproducible, both in material and experiential ways. To capture this processual component of the home experience more clearly, he coins the term "homing" to categorically embody the ongoingness of the social experience of people in mobility. Adopting this theoretical perspective, *mobile objects* in this chapter are conceived as material consequences of the mobility of people and their search for homes. This emphasis on mobility stems from the need to fix fluidity in the homing process that circumscribes around remembrance, belonging, and aspirations, "the origins (roots) and their evolving life milieus (routes)" (Boccagni 2017, cited in Marilla 2020: 118).

I will extend this homing perspective in the next section by discussing the different attributes of these mobile objects based on empirical data. The experience of mixed couples reveals that the typology of mobile objects is not just confined to spatial mobility but also has a *temporal* dimension. As objects move from one space and/or time context to another, the objects create their own social lives and biographies. These movements also lead to a *flow of meanings*, often as the consequence of the change in the life course of the couple, or as home objects become available to different cultural audiences or "interpretive communities" (Fish 1980).

Spatial Mobility of Objects

How objects travel from one space to another has an intensified role in the decision-making process between what couples bring or keep and what they discard. This spatial mobility, as might be expected, pertains to *objects crossing borders* within a transnational frame—for example, how they move from Vietnam to Belgium and vice versa—and the consequent transnational relationships of these material movements to both the receiving and the sending communities. However, based on my ethnography of the home, movements of things within the more micro-level perspective are equally relevant but not usually acknowledged, such as the mobility of home objects from the private space to a public space and movements within the domestic space.

Objects Crossing Borders

Jean had been living in Ho Chi Minh City for five years following the success of his business venture that he originally started through his visits in the Mekong Delta in 2015, which is where he met his wife, Thiên. When he moved to Vietnam, he carried along with him only two suitcases. After living in five different countries as a businessman, he describes himself as someone who lives out of a suitcase and is readily open to moving. While he can pack light as he moves, he reveals that he always makes sure he can ship his sofa, which has been with him for twenty years in three different countries. He confides: "I made furniture in Indonesia in 2000. I was a furniture builder. My furniture has followed me from Jepara to Dubai to here [Ho Chi Minh City]." Thiên, on the other hand, has never lived outside of Vietnam but takes occasional short business trips to Belgium or France during winter months. She shares that she let her husband choose the stuff to put in their house, even though she does not like his choices. She says, laughingly:

> I don't want to take you to our house, it's ugly. It's not presentable. I let him decide for the house. He brought a wooden sofa set and a modern table that don't fit together. The house is also empty and bare without any color. I don't bring my friends there; we meet in the coffee shop.

Jean admits that he does not have the time to tidy up:

> I rented a house, and about three years ago the owner doubled the rent, so I moved since that time. I did this and that, then broke my leg. I really don't have time to do it. I still have boxes everywhere. It's still a big mess.

The experience of Jean and Thiên offers a layered understanding of the domestic life of spatially mobile mixed couples that likewise echoes their social lives. It illustrates how couples negotiate decorating—who decides what objects get to be displayed, and the way they are arranged. First, the spatial movement of the objects reflects the biography of the migrant. The way the object travels records the movement of the migrant as well as peeking into his past life and past homes. Hence, the spatial mobility of the owner is tangled with that of the objects in his/her home. The migrant invests emotions and care into the object. Its migratory history, therefore, awards it the right of a personal heirloom, to be installed in the key space of the home such as the living room, regardless of the displeasure of the partner, other members of the household, or guests. Citing Mauss, Newell (2019) reminds us that precious things form the magic that "speaks, attaches itself to its possessor, which contains its soul" (129; translated, original in French).

Second, at first glance, the person in mobility decides on the home furnishings, and the decision is not necessarily out of a gender-based domestic routine. However, Jean rents the house and monitors the shop through the surveillance camera, even if Thiên is the one managing it full time. This situation discloses that conjugal decisions can be linked to economic and power relations. Furthermore, the remark of distaste by Thiên reverses the scenario and circles back on how women are supposedly responsible for ensuring that the interior of the home is beautiful and tidy. It is this sense of frustration, and not necessarily because the home is private, that inhibits Thiên from opening her doors to visitors. In this case, objects and how they are arranged inhabit the intersection of the personal and the social. Certain ordering of objects creates binaries—organized vs. messy, beautiful vs. ugly—reminiscent of the classic writing of Douglas (1991) on how social life is organized into binaries of order vs. disorder, good vs. bad, pure vs. impure. These categories are structural issues that compel Thiên to close the doors of their home from the public gaze.

Moreover, this is aligned with certain gender expectations in Vietnam as reflected by the popular proverb "Đàn ông xây nhà, đàn bà xây tổ ấm" (men build the house, women build the home), which often comes out as a response when Vietnamese informants are asked about the idea of house and home. In Southeast Asian societies, proverbs and metaphors are especially important rhetorical devices for expressing the roles of men and women (for example, see Fresnoza-Flot 2020). The metaphor of the woman as the homemaker is material and performative, as homeliness is also attributed to coziness and warmth, a form of mothering of space. The ethnographic data of Brickell (2013) also corroborates that this proverbial utterance of home in contemporary Vietnam is "often assumed as natural and self-evident in its inscription of gendered difference, despite the changes in the social spaces that women frequent" (217). This is despite the economic reforms since the Đổi Mới in 1986 that account for the urbanization of and expanding migration into Ho Chi Minh City, where 450 out of the 650 registered Belgians reside (2019 statistics from the Embassy of Belgium in Hanoi). As King and Wilder (2003) add, these broader economic and societal shifts "tend to be qualified by a baseline gender system that continues to root a nostalgic vision of femininity to the domestic, despite changing macro-economic circumstances" (cited in Brickell 2013: 212).

Objects crossing borders also reflect transnational connections. During my fieldwork in Hanoi in 2019, a grandfather asked me to bring a set of story books written in Vietnamese for his granddaughter, Marie. The books were lovingly received by the family who live in Brussels, and the books are now displayed on a small shelf in the corner of the living room of their apartment. Thuy, the mother, who has lived in Belgium for almost a decade, says that Marie's weekends are mainly devoted to learning Vietnamese culture and language through a cultural organization where she also meets, mingles and shares her books with other children of Vietnamese or other mixed couples. Thuy also makes sure that Marie talks to her family back in Vietnam through video calls. When I visited Thuy's parents' home in Hanoi, several framed photographs of Marie were noticeably displayed around the house; their presence appears to be a way for them to negotiate her absence. The grandparents spoke about how Marie was very beautiful, with beautiful hair, beautiful skin and beautiful eyes. Her photographs are enmeshed with the aesthetic of the house, the pride of the family, and are material evidence of the mobility of the status of the stay-behind family. This attests that mobility does not only concern those who migrate but also involves their sedentary counterparts, the stay-behind families in their past homes. As Barber (2017) relates to and borrows the idea of Thai (2011) during her fieldwork among second-generation Việt Kiều (overseas Vietnamese) in the UK, she describes this generation's strategies—like learning the language and return visits[4] to Vietnam—as "magnified moments of ethnic authentification" among second-generation Vietnamese (Barber 2017: 2). What she missed, however, is the role of gift circulation in magnifying those moments of building and maintaining ethnic authenticity. The flow of objects within the social space linking Belgium and Vietnam are crucial not only in preserving kinship ties but also in reinforcing these ties and ethnic identities. Likewise, the *Tết* (Vietnamese new year) is an important period when objects circulate all the more, which for some of my informants is considered as homecoming.

Aside from considering the sedentary human counterpart, mobility of objects is also about accounting for immobile objects. The objects that move and cross borders are entangled with the objects that remain immovable and stay-behind. As Julien shares:

> I wanted to decorate my house with books, put up a library because I enjoy reading as a hobby. Almost everything on the TV, in the bookstore, is in Vietnamese language, but I am unable to bring my books because of restrictions and censorship in Vietnam. I also left my CD collection that I collected when I was younger. I left it in Belgium and entrusted it to my son. I just have my old iPhone, I use it for music.

This manifests "regimes of mobility" (Schiller and Salazar 2013) where nation-states impose barriers to justify their emigration and immigration policies. On the one hand, these strategies of inclusion and exclusion are not limited to the question of *who* crosses state borders but also *what* is permitted or not allowed to move, making (im)mobility of objects contained by the larger Vietnamese state policies. On the other hand, seen from a micro-level perspective, (im)mobility of objects impacts migrants' emotions and ways of feeling at home, making the mobility of objects across frontiers equally important as mobility of people. Here, objects transform into memorialized items and provide a glimpse into past homes while reflecting on social experiences in the present home. However, while the object remains immobile, its social life continues, like a stay-behind family or a child who is likewise entrusted for care.

Mobility of Home Objects from Private Spaces to (Semi-)public Spaces

Based on my observation during frequent visits to a number of Vietnamese restaurants in Belgium,[5] restaurants are extensions of the home and hospitality, or as home-like social spaces often frequented or owned by some mixed couples. In a restaurant owned by Mai and Phillipe, a reproduction of the infamous Tô Ngọc Vân's *Thiếu nữ bên hoa huệ* (young woman with lily, 1943) is hanging on the restaurant's wall with a bright yellow spotlight underneath, rendering a bright glow on the subject of the painting—a lady with her white lilies and wearing a white *ao dai*. The mobile trajectory of the painting is rather striking. As a wedding gift, it traveled from Hanoi to Saigon, and then journeyed to Belgium and lived in various rental apartments before moving to their newly bought house, following the success of the restaurant. Now, it hangs in the restaurant, making the object available in a semi-public space.

My research into the painting linked me to the larger Vietnamese history and the French connection. Tô Ngọc Vân was schooled in the French academia, *Ecole des Beaux-Arts d'Indochine* in the twentieth century, and painted the *Thiếu nữ bên hoa huệ* (young woman with lily) in 1943. An art historian verifies:

> These paintings [the works of Tô Ngọc Vân] reflect the artist's academic training in composition and color harmony. The abundance of bright hues and flowers makes the pictures cheerful and decorative. Unlike other portraits, however, the women's features are not drawn realistically but are sketched with minimum detail. If the artist had models, he subordinated their individuality to their surroundings, presenting them as mere decorative motifs set against a floral background. (Taylor 1997: 15)

The image, through its long history of mobility, continues to inhabit different spaces and is not just locked away in the confines of the Ho Chi Minh City Museum of Fine Arts—a moment when historical art objects become everyday objects. While this is another art-historical-anthropological topic of concern, what is equally impressive is the liveliness and vibrancy of the painting as an everyday object that further activates the image's energy, dynamism, and social life. Here, the painting, as Gell (1998) contends, like Cézanne's Mont Sainte-Victoire [1902], is "a *process*, a movement of *duree*, rather than as a 'thing'" (244, emphasis in original). This flow of the image is then attached to the trajectory of the object itself, and also reflective of the changing milieus in the life of the couple as narrated through the movement of the object itself in an accessible visual form. It is the biography of the object and that of the couple that enables the painting to be available to the gaze of different interpretive communities in a public space.

Aside from commercial spaces, the workspace is also an extension of the home. The placement of objects on the office table and on shelves are ways of homing. Hurdley (2015)[6] paraphrases this as ways of "making home, identity and belonging in a workplace." For example, David, a Belgian man in this study, owns a vintage ceramic teacup that he had taken out of their kitchen to his workplace. He jokingly said that he had to receive consent from Ahn, his wife, to bring it to work. The cup is now displayed on his office table alongside a golden *maneki-neko*, a common motored cat waving in good fortune, which is a staple in Asian households and stores. Bình, a Vietnamese colleague of David, also owns a *maneki-neko*, which sits on his home desk. He captures it in a photo and fondly sends it to his work colleagues, saying "it gives me company," during the Covid-19 quarantine in Belgium. When David was asked what meanings the teacup and *maneki-neko* had for him, he explained that as the desks all look the same in his corporate office in Belgium, these items from home make his desk unique and different from the rest, so he can easily spot it. They also become subjects that can spark a conversation with people that come to his desk—and, as he candidly added, it is a way to introduce his wife. Here, the objects act both as performance for the self and others, making the office table a site of identities and social encounters. The office table is thus transformed into a personalized space that invokes a feeling of intimacy and lays out familial status and an image of how life is organized within a network of relations.

Objects' Mobility within the Home

How objects are socialized to occupy certain spaces and how they move within the confines of the home is another aspect of spatial mobility of objects on the micro level. Pierre shared that his possessions in the house moved a lot when Nga moved in with him. As a young couple, they cannot afford to change the interior completely, and Nga has opted to rearrange objects instead. Nga had added a makeshift altar placed in picture frames that she had put on a coffee table. These impermanent fixtures express the couple's mobility on a temporal and spatial level, as they want to buy a house of their own in the future, but in the meantime they are opting for more mobile, less expensive home decors that they can readily buy from IKEA. On the one hand, Nga intends to feel at home in her new place by reorganizing the interior. Often, the main reason given for the propensity to rearrange the domestic interior relates to feelings of newness or difference, or the need for dynamism in the space (Garvey 2001). Pierre, on the other hand, feels disoriented by these movements that consequently become a source of conflict between them. He narrated that in the beginning he did not mind Nga redecorating the house. However, as things get moved, he starts to feel lost in his own home as he even needs to ask Nga even for the wine opener, which had formerly been housed in his mini bar but was later moved to the kitchen drawer. As Nga became more familiar with the place, Pierre felt more unfamiliar, caused by the movement of objects. Pierre's experience can be explained by Warnier (2006)'s theory that the bodily schema is integrated into the arrangement of the domestic space, and a change of location of a given piece of furniture means relearning motor algorithms to search for objects in their new locations (187). In this sense, objects operate within a system and are socialized to occupy their own social spaces where rules are followed, like storing them according to certain spaces designated for them. This also points to the question of routine.

Giddens (1991) postulates that orientations toward aspects of the object world are an early involvement with routine, and these symbolic residues will be carried into later life (cited in Garvey 2001: 54).

Some couples, to avoid conflict and negotiate difference, may label some objects as personal rather than conjugal, or create their personal spaces within the house:

> Thiên: We have two TVs. He watches with loud sound so I wait until he sleeps so I can watch in peace and stay up late. He also always looks at the news about terrorism, fighting and something like that. Me, I only like something soft and sweet like love songs, sweet music, love stories, and romantic movies.
>
> Jean: No, because I also like cars and speed, about mechanical stuff. It's missing a little bit here [Vietnam]. So I just watch movies about these stuffs. I also watch news in French, English. I watch on TV5 in French, CNN, Discovery, NatGeo.

Frictions between previous lifestyles and current conflations of taste are rather apparent in this empirical example, displaying tensions around how couples negotiate differences. The consequence may be a nuanced sense of "personal" versus "conjugal" space in the home, or a unique experience of couples' ways of belonging and senses of homeliness. The relationship of people and things, whether these objects move from one space to another or stay put in the fixed spaces they occupy, are glimpses of how these couples negotiate their differences in their everyday domestic lives. As Beck and Beck-Gernsheim (1995) describe, individualization, democracy, and chaos are the norm in a couple's life in modern society.

The Temporal Dimension: Objects' Ongoingness and Decay

Aside from the flows of objects in different spatial contexts, mobility of objects is also rooted in time and memory. Sarah, whose father is Vietnamese and whose mother is Belgian, shows me a photo that she captured and posted on her social media with the caption *"décoration familiale, detail"* (family decoration, detail). In the photo is an image of a golden Buddha, with cracked paint and showing visible signs of deterioration, which sits on a vintage cabinet with intricate designs. While looking at the photograph, Sarah recalls her life when she was still living with her parents through the objects in the picture:

> My dad got a Buddha, it was an old one and [he] painted it gold because gold is shiny, [and] it means prosperity. He usually repaints the decorations in gold, even the cabinet. There are a lot of objects

> in the house that are Vietnamese. When my friends come, they say our house looks like a Chinese restaurant. I remember, we moved into the house in Wallonia when I was five. I remember growing up we [always] went to a special shop to buy the decorations for the house. I can't remember where but I remember it was a special one that we go to during weekends where my dad buys stuff. I am not sure if it's an antique shop, Asian shop or a *brocante* (flea market).

Sarah continues, and remembers her father's migration story through the biography of objects:

> My dad came to France during the 1970s. He was studying there together with his brother. During the war, my grandfather cannot send money anymore, and so my dad didn't continue his studies and started working until he moved to Belgium and met my mom. He waited to come back to Vietnam. After about thirty years, my dad came back to Vietnam. They [the parents] now go to Saigon—I mean Ho Chi Minh City—every year, and they bring back new decorations from Vietnam each time. And so the house is filled with Vietnamese stuff.

Sarah remembers her past home as lived experience through objects. The statue of Buddha and the cabinet also reflect the object's changing ownership and materiality, as her father, the new owner and caretaker of these old objects, transforms and repaints them to ascribe a sense of newness to them. Here, objects are not reduced to dead materiality but are instead viewed as dynamic and ongoing. They age, move across time, and are transformed and recontextualized in their changing life milieus. This is congruent with how circulation transforms secondhand things: "Rather than merely having cultural biographies, secondhand things are reconfigured through *their shifts between different social contexts in a process that here is understood as a form of growing*" (Appelgren and Bohlin 2015: 143, emphasis added). In addition, as Ingold convinces:

> Far from being the inanimate stuff typically envisioned by modern thought, materials in this original sense are the active constituents of a world-in-formation. Wherever life is going on, they are relentlessly *on the move—flowing, scraping, mixing and mutating*. The existence of all living organisms is caught up in this ceaseless respiratory and metabolic interchange between their bodily substances and the fluxes of the medium. Without it, they could not survive. (Ingold 2007: 11, emphasis added)

Here, the object is not frozen in time devoid of its ephemeral quality but instead assumes a sense of "vitality" (Bennet 2010). But like the stay-behind objects, the life course, the liveliness, and the ongoingness of things endure, not necessarily because they are mended, reused, or renovated, but because they age, break down over time, and decay.

Moreover, the time dimension in the object's mobility also relates to the life course of the couple (recall Nga's makeshift altar). As the couple move from one place to another or advance the stage of their relationship—from living together as a young couple, to marriage, to building a family—home decorations move and change as well. For example, the house of Thuy and Paul in Brussels became more decorated with Vietnamese objects the moment Marie was born. Some objects that Thuy hid away in boxes, like the traditional umbrella made out of bamboo, which was only used in performances during the *Tết*, is now displayed near the mantelpiece. Here, Thuy introduces her partner and/or kids to her past home, culture, and lifestyle as she relives her gender expectation as the homemaker (*đàn bà xây tô ấm*) through mothering of the home space.

Flow of Meanings and Material-Social Relations

Meaning-making is a cultural experience. The transfer and translation of objects in space and time also means an ongoing construction of meaning. For example, the image of Buddha and domestic shrines is a specific cultural object at the center of Vietnamese households. Apart from these objects being a spiritual center of the home, and thus symbolic, the materiality of religious objects in the home makes them status markers that are "semiotically interpreted or manipulated as indices of social status" (Riggins 2013: 42). For example, the statue of *Thổ Công*, lord of the soil and the ground, and a strong symbol of settlement, is often found in houses of middle-class families in Vietnam, and in some established Vietnamese places in Belgium. It only exists, however, in the homes of Vietnamese families who have been living in Belgium for a very long time. The presence of this object in the home signifies permanency and high status in the migratory chain. While statues such as that of *Thổ Công* are only found in some of the migrants' homes, what is more common in the homes of my informants, especially those with children, is an altar to honor ancestors. The altar[7] typically includes framed photographs of family members who have passed away, alongside incense and vase(s) for flowers, and some offerings of food and tea. Ancestor worship has an important place in Vietnamese families, including mixed-race couples. The altar is a specific cultural object at the center of a Vietnamese household, but is an alien material to the Belgian partner. In some cases, they are reduced to secular and mundane objects, perceived by the Belgian partner as mere decoration and aesthetic of the house, and devoid of its symbolic meaning as a spiritual object. Hence, a multitude of meanings can arise at different levels, traversing through different subjectivities and demographic biographies—like the meaning that Sarah (Belgian, second-generation Vietnamese, mixed) attaches to Buddha and the altar may be particularly distinct from that of her father (Vietnamese migrant, first-generation) and her mother (Belgian).[8]

Meanings here are contingent upon and co-constructed by different interpretive communities. It is important to note that interpretive communities do not consist merely of audiences but, as in the sense Fish (1980) developed the concept, it pertains to anyone to whom cultural objects are available for interpretation—that is, from the production of the object to its consumption. This meaningful interaction between people and objects makes people active producers of meaning rather than passive consumers. For home objects, meanings are diversified as the objects move across and between spaces, and as the home becomes available for public gaze where it enters into a duality as a private and public space. Usually, the living and dining rooms are public spaces that display heirlooms available for potential scrutiny and judgment by visitors. For instance, Thuy displays, in a glass cupboard, a set of ceramic teacups that she received from her departed grandma that she reserves for very special occasions and guests; in her words, "it is rarely used so as to be preserved and taken care of." In Newell's (2014) study on hoarding, these heirlooms on display are also "'durables' [that] tend to have a provenance in the established capital that allows for the maintenance of stable kin relations, or even in some cases enforces it for the sake of holding the wealth intact" (202). Newell calls these objects "kin-objects":

> While in consumption theory possessions are typically thought of as "extensions of the self" under the control of their master (Belk 1988), it is worth considering the reverse possibility, in which the spirits of things also get a hold of us and refuse to let go. It is in this sense that these objects assert their claim to "belonging" as members of the household, even when sequestered out of the space of sociality ... Things thus have agency not merely in the Latourian sense of resisting our efforts at cultural mastery but also in the sense that they engage us socially, obligating us to treat them in specific ways. (Newell 2014: 196)

Like the story of Jean's sofa at the beginning of this chapter, Thuy's teacups demand a territorial claim in the house, seeking to be accommodated and cared for as members of the household. The relationships of Jean and Thuy with their objects, and their actions toward them, are an act of hospitality (Newell 2019). Objects, in turn, have the ability to reciprocate, like Bình's *maneki-neko* offering him company during the quarantine. This agency of animate and humanlike qualities of objects and their sociability are concrete entanglements of people and things, and of the meanings and relationships that organize the mobile social lives of people and objects.

Conclusion

The trajectories of objects are routes into understanding forms of tangled (im)mobilities that lead to insights on how (im)mobile social lives are organized, reflecting relationships and ambiguities in the everyday domestic lives of mixed couples. They negotiate and perform their identities in the confines of their own homes. The home objects that they own and value reveal their own trajectories, and their personal experiences in their past and present homes, as well as their future aspirations. This process of home-making, a complex act of belonging to "a basic sense of home, is informed by the home cultures that people bring from the past—[for example,] the ways of using domestic space, the meanings and functions of domestic objects and the implicit views of what a 'proper home' should look like" (Boccagni 2017: 54). Boccagni adds that "migrants' present home experience is interdependent with the past one(s), as recollected through home-related objects and rituals" (ibid.: 78). This dynamic process of homing, as this chapter suggests, reveals the entanglements of peoples and things; how in the process of human mobility, immobile and mobile objects are entangled and how these mobilities result in entanglements of temporalities, and change meanings in the spaces that these objects occupy.

The material component of the home is under analyzed, even if the lives of people and the lives of things are enmeshed in everyday life. The analysis of the entanglements of peoples and things moves the object out of inertia and brings it active qualities as a vibrant matter (Bennett 2010). Objects possess agency (Gell 1998) and do not just reflect meaning. They compel people to act in certain ways and endow them with care, hospitality, and territoriality as members of the household (Newell 2014, 2019). The migratory trajectory of the objects all the more assert this belongingness as the emblem of the trajectory of their owner, making them worthy of their visual performance and display in the public space of the household. This dynamic relationship between people and objects allows us to appreciate and understand the non-verbalized, the visual, material, sensual, and embodied, consequently offering a methodological possibility of an object-based ethnography where we can let the objects speak and narrate the stories of people.

While trajectories of people and things overlap, entanglements of mobilities and immobilities of objects are also apparent. For people on the move, people lose and take things along the way, stirring memories of loss and hopes through what they are able and allowed to bring, and what they needed to leave behind. These objects of remembrance not only speak about their past homes, their connections and relationships with their stay-behind families and stay-behind possessions, but also account for the homeliness in their present homes.

As objects move, their meanings change in relation to their changing temporal and spatial contexts. They are invested with meanings that emerge through association and usage that also vary with regard to the relationship people have with objects across contexts. This flow of the object in time and space ascribes a sense of ongoingness to the object, because the object is entangled with people's biographies and changing life milieus. This makes the home objects dynamic, mutable, relational, experiential, and contextual, as the overall idea of homing suggests.

These entanglements and complexities in the home experience are materially expressed in things that reproduce a couple's past and present tastes and lifestyles, resulting in appropriation and symbolic boundaries within the home, transnational connections, and the gendering of space. Home objects also become material indices of ethnicity, gender, cultural practices, and social status. As objects narrate these identities, they are moved out of their inanimate fixedness and rigidities, and transformed into moving, animate, agentive entities that activate their meaningful social lives.

Acknowledgments

I acknowledge the guidance, thoroughness, and valuable comments of my supervisor, Dr. Asuncion Fresnoza-Flot. I also appreciate the questions and comments from my colleagues in the Laboratoire d'Anthropologie des Mondes Contemporains (LAMC) and the Center for East Asian Studies (EASt) whose feedback has been incorporated in this chapter. Most specially, thanks to the couples and their families who generously shared their time, experiences, and opened their homes to this research.

Funding

This ongoing research project is currently funded by the Belgian National Fund for Scientific Research (FNRS), from October 2020 to September 2024. It also received a two-year funding (February 2019 – September 2020) from the Université libre de Bruxelles (ULB)-ARC through Dr. Asuncion Fresnoza-Flot's project *Contextual Mobility in Europe-Southeast Asia Social Spaces: Belgian-Vietnamese and Belgian-Laotian Couples in Focus*.

Angelie Marilla is a PhD candidate at the Laboratory of Anthropology of Contemporary Worlds (LAMC), Université libre de Bruxelles (ULB) in Belgium, where she is currently working on her doctoral thesis on materiality, mobility, and conjugal mixedness. She completed with honors her master's in Cultural Sociology at Masarykova Univerzita in the Czech Republic through the Erasmus Mundus program. Her research interests and works traverse along lines of visual anthropology, cultural sociology, history, material culture, migration, and Southeast Asian studies. Her doctoral research project was initially funded by the ULB-ARC project on Belgian-Asian couples and is currently funded by the Belgian National Fund for Scientific Research (F.R.S.-FNRS).

NOTES

1. Pseudonyms have been used to ensure the anonymity of research participants.
2. The lengthy literature on the distinction between house and home is recently revisited and well detailed in the essay of Samanai and Lenhard (2019), which often delineates the idea of "houses as normative, widely reproduced, and often material forms, while homes center around the subjective feelings of belonging and dwelling" (13).
3. Home objects are also labeled as domestic objects in the literature. However, the term "domestic object" is not used interchangeably with "home object" in this chapter. I refer to these objects as home objects to emphasize the concept of "home," which is crucial to migration studies. This is also to avoid some confusion on categorization when one talks about domestic objects. For example, Riggins (2013), in his article on the home as an ephemeral art project, attempts to fit domestic objects into categories (refer to Kannike and Laviolette 2013: 40–42). I find that loosely casting home objects into categories is problematic. Based on my fieldwork, home objects are dynamic, fluid, and mutable (in this chapter, I refer to them as "mobile" objects) and cannot be readily catalogued or classified. For example, as the life course of the couple changes or advances, meanings and uses of objects could change simultaneously, and hence cannot be strictly cast into rigid categories. Categories could also overlap, and/or objects could be refused for categorization.
4. It can be represented and linked to the 2008 song "Hello Vietnam" (original in French, *Bonjour Vietnam*, released earlier in 2006), a popular *Việt Kiều* song sang by Quynh Anh, a Belgian-Vietnamese singer in Belgium. The song is about the longing for "homeland."
5. Based on my survey, there are over a hundred Vietnamese restaurants in Belgium, signifying that there have been thriving Vietnamese communities in the three regions of Belgium—around thirty-four in Wallonia, twenty-one in Flanders and about fifty-one concentrated in Brussels (data mapped through Google Maps as of June 2020).
6. Also listen to BBC radio episode "Land Ownership, Home at Work," 5 December 2015, https://www.bbc.co.uk/sounds/play/b06r5y7b, last accessed on 4 March 2020.

7. Anchored on the belief that the dead people were buried in the ground but that their souls live, *"tử tuất quy thổ, cốt nhục têu, hạ âm vi gia thổ, kỳ phí phát duỏng u' thượng vi chiêu minh"* (Vu and Nguyen 2019: 162).
8. An ongoing fieldwork; my home visit to Sarah's parents' house in Wallonia is hampered by the Covid-19 pandemic, making it a challenge to do ethnography of the home and its materiality, where home visits and object interviews are crucial, as this contact is a complete sensory experience (as discussed elsewhere in this chapter).

REFERENCES

Appadurai, Arjun, ed. 1986. *The Social Life of Things: Commodities in Cultural Perspective.* New York: Cambridge University Press.

———. 2015. "Mediants, Materiality, Normativity." *Public Culture* 27(2): 221–37.

Appelgren, Staffan, and Anna Bohlin. 2015. "Growing in Motion: The Circulation of Used Things on Second-Hand Markets." *Culture Unbound* 7(1): 143–68.

Ardener, Shirley, ed. 1981. *Women and Space: Ground Rules and Social Maps.* London: Croom Helm.

Barber, Tamsin. 2017. "Achieving Ethnic Authenticity through 'Return' Visits to Vietnam: Paradoxes of Class and Gender among the British-Born Vietnamese." *Journal of Ethnic and Migration Studies* 43(6): 919–36.

Beck, Ulrich, and Elisabeth Beck-Gernsheim. 1995. *Normal Chaos of Love.* Cambridge: Polity Press.

Belk, Russell W. 1988. 'Possessions and the Extended Self'. *Journal of Consume Research* 15(2): 139–68.

Bennett, Jane. 2010. *Vibrant Matter: A Political Ecology of Things.* Durham, NC: Duke University Press.

Bloch, Maurice. 1995. "The Resurrection of the House amongst the Zafimaniry of Madagascar." In *About the House: Lévi-Strauss and Beyond*, ed. Janet Carsten and Stephen Hugh-Jones, 69–83. Cambridge: Cambridge University Press.

Boccagni, Paolo. 2017. *Migration and the Search for Home: Mapping Domestic Space in Migrants' Everyday Lives.* New York: Palgrave Macmillan.

Bourdieu, Pierre. 1970. "The Berber House or the World Reversed." *Social Science Information* 9(2): 151–70.

———. 1977. *Outline of a Theory of Practice.* New York: Cambridge University Press.

Brickell, Katherine. 2013. "Towards Geographies of Speech: Proverbial Utterances of Home in Contemporary Vietnam." *Transactions of the Institute of British Geographers* 38(2): 207–20.

Cieraad, Irene. 1999. *At home: An Anthropology of Domestic Space.* Syracuse, NY: Syracuse University Press.

Collet, Beate. 2012. "Mixed Couples in France: Statistical Facts, Definitions and Social Reality." *Revista De Sociologia* 97(1): 61–77.

Daniels, Inge. 2010. *The Japanese House: Material Culture in the Modern Home.* London: Bloomsbury Academic.

Douglas, Mary. 1991. "The Idea of a Home: A Kind of Space." *Social Research* 58(1): 287-307.

Dunn, Kevin. 2010. "Embodied Transnationalism: Bodies in Transnational Spaces." *Population, Space and Place* 16(1): 1-9.

Faist, Thomas. 2004. "Towards a Political Sociology of Transnationalization: The State of the Art in Migration Research." *European Journal of Sociology* 45(3): 331-66.

Fish, Stanley Eugene. 1980. *Is There a Text in This Class?: The Authority of Interpretive Communities*. Cambridge, MA: Harvard University Press.

Fresnoza-Flot, Asuncion. 2020. "'Men are Butterflies, Women are Hindlimbs of an Elephant': Thai Women's Gendered Being in Transnational Spaces." *Gender, Place & Culture* 28(5): 1-22.

Garvey, Pauline. 2001. "Organized Disorder: Moving Furniture in Norwegian Homes." In *Home Possessions: Material Culture Behind Closed Doors*, ed. Daniel Miller, 47-68. Oxford: Berg Publishers.

Gell, Alfred. 1998. *Art and Agency: An Anthropological Theory*. Oxford: Clarendon Press.

Giddens, Anthony. 1991. *Modernity and Self-Identity: Self and Society in the Late Modern Age*. Stanford, CA: Stanford University Press.

Gregson, Nicky. 2007. *Living with Things: Ridding, Accommodation, Dwelling*. Wantage, UK: Sean Kingston Publishing.

Harper, Douglas. 1998. "An Argument for Visual Sociology." In *Image-Based Research: A Sourcebook for Qualitative Research*, ed. Jon Prosser, 24-41. London: Falmer Press.

Humphrey, Caroline. 1988. "No Place Like Home: The Neglect of Architecture." *Anthropology Today* 4(1): 16-18.

Hurdley, Rachel. 2006. "Dismantling Mantelpieces: Narrating Identities and Materializing Culture in the Home." *Sociology* 40(4): 717-33.

———. 2007. "Objecting Relations: The Problem of the Gift." *The Sociological Review* 55(1): 124-43.

———. 2015. "Pretty Pants and Office Pants: Making Home, Identity and Belonging in a Workplace." In *Intimacies, Critical Consumption and Diverse Economies*, ed. Emma Casey and Yvette Taylor, 173-96. London: Palgrave Macmillan.

———. 2016. "Everyday Life." In *The SAGE Handbook of Cultural Sociology*, ed. David Inglis and Anna-Mari Almila, 372-89. London: SAGE Publications.

Inglis, David. 2005. *Culture and Everyday Life*. London: Routledge.

Ingold, Tim. 2007. "Materials Against Materiality." *Archaeological Dialogues* 14(1): 1-16.

Jackson, Stevi, and Shaun Moores, eds. 2014 (1st edition). *The Politics of Domestic Consumption: Critical Readings*. London: Routledge.

Kannike, Anu, and Patrick Laviolette, eds. 2013. *Things in Culture, Culture in Things*. Tartu, Estonia: University of Tartu Press.

Kaufmann, Jean-Claude. 1998. *Dirty Linen: Couples as Seen Through their Laundry*, trans. Helen Alfrey. London: Middlesex University Press.

King, Victor T., and William D. Wilder. 2003. *The Modern Anthropology of South-East Asia: An Introduction* (Vol. 1). London: Routledge Curzon.

Kopytoff, Igor. 1986. "The Cultural Biography of Things: Commoditization as Process." In *The Social Life of Things: Commodities in Cultural Perspective*, ed. Arjun Appadurai, 64–92. Cambridge: Cambridge University Press.
Latour, Bruno. 2005. *Reassembling the Social: An Introduction to Actor-Network Theory*. Oxford: Oxford University Press.
Marcus, George E. 1995. "Ethnography in/of the World System: The Emergence of Multi-sited Ethnography." *Annual Review of Anthropology* 24(1): 95–117.
———. 2020. "Book Review: Migration and the Search for Home: Mapping Domestic Space in Migrants' Everyday Lives." *Cultural Sociology* 14(1): 117–19.
Miller, Daniel. 1995. "Consumption and Commodities." *Annual Review of Anthropology* 24(1): 141–61.
———. 1998. *Material Cultures: Why Some Things Matter*. London: University College Press.
———. 2001. *Home Possessions: Material Culture behind Closed Doors*. London: Berg.
———. 2009. *The Comfort of Things*. London: Polity Press.
Morgan, Lewis Henry. 1881. *Houses and House-Life of the American Aborigines*. Washington: US Government Printing Office.
Newell, Sasha. 2014. "The Matter of the Unfetish: Hoarding and the Spirit of Possessions." *HAU: Journal of Ethnographic Theory* 4(3): 185–213.
———. 2019. "L'Hospitalité des *Hoarders*. Accumulations et Relations dans l'Espace domestique aux États-Unis." *L'Homme* 3–4(231–32): 111–34.
Putnam, Tim, and Charles Newton, eds. 1990. *Household Choices*. London: Futures Publications.
Riggins, Stephen Harold. 2013. "The Natural Order is Decay: The Home as an Ephemeral Art Project." In *Things in Culture, Culture in Things*, ed. Anu Kannike and Patrick Laviolette, 36–54. Tartu, Estonia: University of Tartu Press.
Samanani, Farhan, and Johannes Lenhard. 2019. "House and Home." *The Cambridge Encyclopedia of Anthropology*, 1–18. doi:10.29164/19home.
Schiller, Nina Glick, and Noel B. Salazar. 2013. "Regimes of Mobility across the Globe." *Journal of Ethnic and Migration Studies* 39(2): 183–200.
Stea, David. 1995. "House and Home: Identity, Dichotomy, or Dialectic?" In *The Home: Words, Interpretations, Meanings, and Environments*, ed. David N. Benjamin, David Stea, and Eje Aren, 181–201. London: Avebury.
Taylor, Nora. 1997. "Orientalism/Occidentalism: The Founding of the Ecole des Beaux-Arts d'Indochine and the Politics of Painting in Colonial Việt Nam, 1925–1945." *Crossroads: An Interdisciplinary Journal of Southeast Asian Studies* (11)2: 1–33.
Thai, Hung Cam. 2011. "Homeland Visits: Transnational Magnified Moments among Low-Wage Immigrant Men." In *At the Earth of Work and Family: Engaging the Ideas of Arlie Russell Hochschild*, ed. Anita Ilta Garey and Karen V. Hansen, 250–61. New Brunswick, NJ: Rutgers University Press.
Tucker, Aviezer. 1994. "In Search for Home." *Journal of Applied Philosophy* 11(2): 181–87.
Van, Vu Hong, and Nguyen Trong Long. 2019. "Ancestor Worship Belief in the Spiritual Life of Vietnamese People." *Journal of Philosophy* 7(4): 160–66.

Warnier, Jean-Pierre. 2006. "Inside and Outside"; In *Handbook of Material Culture*, ed. Chris Tilley, Webb Keane, Susanne Kuechler, Mike Rowlands, and Patricia Spyer, 186–96. London: SAGE Publications.

Wilk, Richard R. 1989. "Decision Making and Resource Flows within the Household: Beyond the Black Box." In *The Household Economy: Reconsidering the Domestic Mode of Production*, ed. Richard R. Wild, 23–52. Boulder, CO: Westview Press.

Woodward, Sophie. 2015. "The Hidden Lives of Domestic Things: Accumulations in Cupboards, Lofts, and Shelves." In *Intimacies, Critical Consumption and Diverse Economies*, ed. Emma Casey and Yvette Taylor, 216–31. London: Palgrave Macmillan.

———. 2020. *Material Methods: Researching and Thinking with Things*. London: SAGE Publications.

CHAPTER
4

Tangled Intergenerational Mobilities
Maternal Migration and Japanese-Filipino Children in Japan

Fiona-Katharina Seiger

Introduction

In this chapter, I explore the tangledness of Filipino women's migration projects with their Japanese-Filipino children's experiences of migrating to Japan. Born to Filipino mothers and Japanese fathers, the children spoken about in this chapter were primarily raised in the Philippines, before moving to Japan. In most cases, they were raised by their mothers and maternal families, in the absence of their biological fathers. Frequently, they never met their fathers before arriving in Japan, and even upon migration, in-person meetings remain scarce or never occur. Having partly grown up in the Philippines, these children are part of a larger population of 1.5-generation migrants from the Philippines in Japan. However, they move together with their mothers instead of following their parent to the destination country with some delay, as is the case for numerous other migrant Filipino and Japanese-Filipino minors (see Takahata and Hara 2015; Suzuki 2015). Also, they are part of a recent cohort of migrants from the Philippines who enter Japan to either launch the process of (re)claiming Japanese nationality or, in some cases, making use of their Japanese passports.

Yet, the mothers' migration is geared toward the labor market. It is recruiters and labor brokers who enable this spatial mobility by selecting, training and dispatching the mothers to companies in Japan. While the type of job depends on the broker and their networks, owners of Japan-based caregiving facilities for the elderly have shown the greatest interest in employing foreign workers. All the migrant mothers interviewed were indeed deployed to Japan as caregivers. In the process, they accumulated debts, which they had to pay off over the period of their contract, usually lasting three years.

This creates a system of brokerage relying on laws geared at family unification to enable migration for work, exclusively for women with young children of Japanese fathers. Most of these women, who were called "entertainers" or "talents," have a prior history of migration to Japan, where they had first met the fathers of their children. The current in-tandem migration of Filipino women and their Japanese-Filipino children to Japan is thus a continuation of the mothers' first travels to the country, and, as previously, the women are directed to highly feminized, ill-paid jobs.

Philippine-based brokers have tapped into discourses of human rights and charity to market their support in securing employment in Japan for adult applicants, in addition to Japanese nationality for children of Japanese fathers. However, these services are only available to those mother-and-child families who can provide clear evidence of the child's biological relationship with a Japanese national. The more complicated cases are not considered commercially viable, and are therefore frequently refuted.

This more recent migration to Japan started when Japan's nationality law amendment came into force in January 2009. For a decade now, an increasing number of mothers and their children have shown interest in acquiring Japanese citizenship and migrating overseas. The mothers usually enter Japan with a long-term residence visa, which remains dependent on their children's legal status in Japan. As their legal guardians, the mothers receive such "guardian of a Japanese national" visas if their children are Japanese citizens or if the children have long-term residency rights as offspring of a Japanese citizen.

The case of Japanese-Filipino children and their mothers presents an intriguing instance of family migration, as the resettlement from the Philippines to Japan is conditioned upon the children's Japanese descent and their young age. Often thrust into mobility against their will, migrant Japanese-Filipino children and youth are faced with important changes affecting familial relationships and care arrangements, their schooling and plans for academic pursuits, as well as the challenge of building relationships with peers in a new cultural and linguistic environment.

As the editors write in the introductory chapter, tangled im/mobilities exist alongside or result in interacting or overlapping forms of stasis and movement. In this chapter, I show how Japanese-Filipino children's routes to Japan remain tied to their mother's past migratory projects, and are embedded in regimes of mobility that require their displacement to enable their mother's current migratory endeavors. This tangled intergenerational mobility frequently leads to emotional hardships, including sentiments of loss and sacrifice for a "better life," which in the literature have largely been explored in the context of long-distance mothering. While the case of migrant Japanese-Filipino children highlights the salience of unequal power relations within the family in migration decision-making processes (see Celero in this volume), the disruptive experiences of migration are come to terms with through the prisms of "good motherhood" and notions of "good childhoods."

Migrant Motherhoods and Childhoods

Literature theorizing the nexus of migration and mother-child relationships has furthered nuanced understanding of how women in migration contest, negotiate, reproduce, and expand narratives of "good motherhood." Mainly focusing on migrant mothers away from home, this body of research has highlighted structural constraints, such as gender norms and regimes of mobility, as scaffolds within which experiences of transnational mothering unfold (Fresnoza-Flot 2009; Horton 2009; Parreñas 2005). Contextually specific gendered expectations of "good motherhood" provide the normative frame through which transnational practices of mothering are gauged and come to terms with. In the Philippine context, notions of "good mothering" are couched in the ideal of the Filipino family, denoting a heterosexual married couple with their biological children. Lived realities of prolonged spatial separation following overseas migration, especially where the mother is physically absent, have made it difficult for family members to conform to this ideal. Notably, mothers away from home have frequently taken on both breadwinning and nurturing roles, feeling the pressure to live up to being a "good mother" (see Fresnoza-Flot 2009). Parreñas (2005) points out the central and often detrimental role played by patriarchal family norms for mothers in migration and their "left-behind" children in coping with prolonged separation. Horton (2009), however, warns of observing the intersections of migration, mothering, and "global childhood" merely through the prism of gender constructs and ideologies, as this too often reduces the distress experienced by children to "a reactionary response to mothers' troubling of the patriarchal gender norms that structure the family" (31). Global inequalities and rigid immigration policies create many of the constraints leading to long-term, long-distance parenting, and coproduce the various forms of coping with it. Indeed, research has shown that mobility regimes[1] and legal status bear upon mothering practices. Based on the research of Filipino migrants in France, Fresnoza-Flot (2009) explores how migration status influences transnational mothering practices, whereby prolonged separation due to a lack of documentation and the ensuing immobility are offset by more intense communication and gift-giving practices. Similarly, Horton (2009) draws attention to the importance of gift-giving in the absence of co-presence, as these gifts become proxies for parental love, reassuring the children of the continuity of parental care but also justifying parental absence. The ubiquitous connectivity of "polymedia environments" has enabled mothers away from home and their children to live in ambient co-presence with both positive and negative emotional consequences (Madianou 2016). Parent-child separation, Horton (2009) concludes, is a "symptom of the injustice of the global division of labor" (22), and highlights the embeddedness of individual emotional hardship in structures that engender the "sociopolitical inequality [that] shapes individual affect and produces specific patterns of social suffering" (37). "Regimes of mobility" (Glick Schiller and Salazar 2013) give shape to mothering practices where physical proximity is not an option, demonstrating how (im)mobility across borders is tangled with intimate practices. An understanding of practices of mothering and emotional tensions in mother-child relationships following migration must therefore be explored not only with regard to culturally contextual norms of "good motherhood," but also against the backdrop of social, economic, and political inequalities and structures producing both mobility and stillness.

Migration and (im)mobility shape childhoods too. In their edited volume *Mobile Childhoods in Filipino Transnational Families*, Nagasaka and Fresnoza-Flot (2015) present a collection of essays that analyze how spatial mobility has shaped the lives of 1.5-generation Filipino migrants in different contexts. The chapters of the volume clearly show that children are not the passive bystanders they are often assumed to be. Indeed, the study of children's geographies has aimed to destabilize the imaginary of children as adults in-the-making, implicitly denying their agency as social beings (Holt and Holloway 2006). Children in transnational migration are important social actors too, who are "involved in the construction of their own social lives, the lives of those around them, and of the societies in which they live" (Prout and James 1997: 8).

The case of Japanese-Filipino children arriving in Japan together with their mothers provides the opportunity to look into how children deal with leaving behind their friends, extended family, and in some cases their siblings, to transition into a new sociocultural environment. In the process, their mobility is tangled with that of their mothers, and embedded in legal structures that make this in-tandem migration both possible and necessary. Mothering practices develop around a situation wherein mothers become de facto single parents (as they leave behind their extended social network) who need to balance child care and full-time work in a country where single mothers and their children are at a high risk of plummeting into poverty.[2] Moreover, as indicated above, some women have to leave behind their non-Japanese children,[3] placing upon them the challenges of simultaneous physical co-presence and remote mothering, and bearing the potential for ruptures, guilt, and jealousy among siblings. A central question following the disruption of leaving behind family, friends, and familiar environments is thus how mothers and children come to terms with apparent contradictions of resettlement for a "better life" and the distress it causes. Considering that ideals of motherhood place the responsibility for delivering emotional care upon the female parent, how do migrant mothers justify their decisions to migrate when faced with the emotional strain their children experience? How do their children respond? In what follows, I explore the emotional, generational, material, and legal tangledness of this in-tandem migration of Filipino mothers and their Japanese-Filipino children to Japan.

Methodology

This chapter is based on fieldwork conducted in 2015 and 2016 in the Kansai area of Japan. I formally interviewed two dozen Japanese-Filipino beneficiaries of educational support initiatives, who were aged between nine and twenty-one at the time. I initially concentrated on conducting participant observation before complementing my observations and informal chats with in-depth interviews and focus group discussions with Japanese-Filipino children and their mothers. The data presented here focuses on the stories told by a group of five mothers and thirteen children and teenagers who arrived in the same area of the Kansai region within the span of a few years, starting in 2010. Many had been recruited through the same broker in the Philippines and had ended up living and working in close proximity of one another. I met my participants through volunteering for an educational support group organized by a schoolteacher and members of the local Catholic Church. While the data collected and the ensuing analysis contribute to stitching the larger picture of mother-child relationships and migration-decision negotiations in the case of recent migration from the Philippines to Japan, the situatedness of the data and the specific networks of support available to this group of people make a generalization difficult. Nevertheless, because these migrant women and children share conditions with other migrant families, this chapter contributes to a nuanced picture of the different outcomes that similar structural constraints can produce.

Reasons for Returning to Japan

As earlier studies (Asis 2002; Horton 2009) have shown, the desire to financially and materially provide for the family often features prominently in decision-making processes regarding labor mobility. Globally traveling media images of middle-class lifestyles, too, have fed into parents' endeavors to provide their offspring with such "good childhoods" via overseas employment (Horton 2008). Migrant mothers who arrived in Japan together with their Japanese-Filipino children commonly assert that they decided to migrate to secure both their and their children's livelihood and to provide the children with an education. Adult respondents often underline the necessity of their move—namely, to escape low-paid and precarious employment that made it hard for them and their children to live a "better life" if they remained in the Philippines. The women I spoke to all had different jobs with low or unpredictable income before emigrating from their hometowns. Two had been members of a nongovernmental organization (NGO) in Manila, where one had found work as a beautician via the NGO's livelihood project, another worked in a restaurant at a shopping mall, another owned a small *sari-sari* store,[4] another was as a massage therapist before departing for Japan, and another was a health worker at her *barangay* (district). The following are answers given by migrant mothers when asked how they felt about their current situation, compared to the early days after their arrival.

> Cheryl: For me it's okay. If I were still in the Philippines, I probably wouldn't have a comfortable life. We probably wouldn't have anything to eat because I wouldn't have any other job. Where would I get a job if I didn't even finish studying? How will I get a decent job? I'd probably be a laundry woman. That's what I also told my children. If we were in the Philippines, we probably wouldn't have this life. But of course, our situation is still difficult because our children grew up seeing our difficulties.
> Sara: She's right.

Amy: We don't have a choice. We need to survive it. We need to survive it for the future of our children, and of course, we also have families in the Philippines.
Sara: Especially in my case, because I'm the only one earning in my family. My older sister died, my older brother died, and our youngest. They left their children with my mom and dad. They're the ones taking care of them. I'm the one who ...
Interviewer: Supports?
Sara: Yes. My younger sibling can't. He has this thing here [he is sick].
Interviewer: Do you think that [it] would have been impossible or less likely in the Philippines [for the children to have a good future, get their citizenship, and finish their studies]?
Amy: Yes, it's hard in the Philippines. It's impossible because we don't have a permanent job. Even if it's difficult here, even if work is hard, by the end of every month, we have our salary. We'll be able to support their needs.
Interviewer: So, when you think of the decision to come to Japan, when you think about it now, [would] you take the same decision again?
Amy: Yes. We'd still take the risk because we have no choice. But if there was a better job in the Philippines, we probably wouldn't have left.
Maricris: We don't have a choice, right? We really don't.

These women underlined the urgency of having had to seek employment overseas, culminating into a justification of their move as the only real option. Economic vulnerability features prominently in decisions to work abroad (Asis 2002), as do the material and symbolic gains that international migration and overseas employment engender (Aguilar 2014: 75). Read against the backdrop of what Kelly (2007) has described as a sense of "stickiness in the class structure" (17), decisions to leave are also expressions of frustration with the limited social mobility and the futility of aspirations to move up in the class strata. Suffering from tangled social and spatial immobilities, their desires to cross borders are thus intertwined with desires to evade stuckness. Overseas employment is perceived as an opportunity to introduce movement and change into one's life. These sentiments, often expressed, of wanting a "better life" for oneself and one's family, are widely shared by those embarking on journeys to labor overseas (see Kelly 2007; Aguilar 2014; Asis 2002; Parreñas 2005).[5]

Unemployment or underemployment, socioeconomic inequality, and immobility have fueled the Philippine labor export industry with workers. Organized and mobilized across borders by the state and placement agencies, labor migration follows gendered morals of who ought to be recruited into what kinds of jobs (Fresnoza-Flot and Shinozaki 2017: 868), with women often performing reproductive work as nurses, caregivers, domestic helpers, nannies, or hostesses (Suzuki 2000). If the choice to seek one's fulfillment of middle-class aspirations overseas (or mere sustenance) is embedded in structural inequalities, so are the ramifications of these choices, including the configuration and reconfiguration of families.

Indeed, the current migration of women and children follows from an earlier migration of Filipina women into Japan's nightlife industry. Most migrant mothers entering Japan as caregivers today had previously worked in Japan as "talents," where they had met the fathers of their children. Their short-term visas did not allow for an extended stay in Japan. Thus, despite their pregnancies, most women opted to return and give birth in their home countries, where their children were then raised. With the births of the children remaining unrecognized by their fathers, and thereby unregistered with the Japanese authorities, neither women nor children gained access to legal status in Japan. The biological fathers frequently absented themselves—personally, emotionally, and financially—from raising their offspring. Consequently, numerous mothers of Japanese-Filipino children decided to take the opportunity of earning an income in Japan, and entrusting brokers with the task of securing their children's Japanese citizenship.

The latter is a promise made to prospective migrant workers by organizations registered as foundations of non-profits in the Philippines, specializing on the brokerage of people of Japanese descent. Having set up recruitment programs specifically for mothers of Japanese-Filipinos, these organizations cater to the mothers' desires to secure their children's formal citizenship in Japan, thereby facilitating the mothers' own rights to abode and engage in paid employment in the country. This "passport consciousness" (Faier 2009) expresses the mothers' knowledge of cross-border mobility as a marker of privilege and a means to gain greater agency in a world where immigration regimes constrain the lives and prospects of those immobilized across borders by their documents. Japanese immigration and residency policies, in particular, have rendered Filipino migrant women's pathways to long-term residency dependent on marrying or giving birth to a Japanese citizen (Parreñas 2011: 179).[6]

Reconfigurations of Family Life

Arriving in Japan, mothers and children leave behind their network of support provided by extended family and friends. Cheryl, a mother of two, describes her youngest son's loneliness when they first arrived:

> My youngest was just twelve years old when we arrived. Our house was bare. Just like they said, it didn't have anything. No radio, no

TV. ... Monday to Sunday, I wasn't home. My kid was left alone at home for one to two weeks. He didn't have anyone to talk to because he was alone. He just waited. He was crying when I got home. "Mama, I want to go home to the Philippines." I felt sorry for him. I told him, let's go to 7-eleven. Let's buy *oden* [Japanese winter dish]. The first one he ate was an egg oden. So, every day when I got home, he says "Mama, let's go to 7-eleven. Let's buy *oden*." I felt like crying. He said "Mama, we don't even have a computer to talk to them [the family]." ... I was crying while he was sleeping. I said to myself, "Lord, we can do this. I know we can do this." Then when he started going to school, that was the time he was kind of okay.

Hiromi, aged fourteen, recounts that she felt scared when she first had to stay home all by herself during her mother's nightshift:

At first, I wasn't used to the arrangement, because [in the Philippines] I lived with my cousins ... That's why when I got here, it was so quiet. Very unlike our home in the Philippines, which was always noisy. Here, it was just my mother and me. I'm a Mama's girl. I'm not used to my Mom being away all the time. That's why if she has *shigoto* [work]; if she has work or something, I have the house to myself. It gets scary sometimes. ... Around fifth grade. That's why, uhm, there's a night shift. They leave at 4 PM, they get back at 9 AM the next day. That's why ... good thing our neighbor is also a Filipino. She let me stay at her place. But still, it was very difficult. Eventually, I got used to it. I can sleep alone now.

Upon resettlement into Japan, migrant children need to get used to new caregiving arrangements. Although all the mothers interviewed had been working in the Philippines before their migration, they had mostly worked during daytime and had had the support of extended family. Once in Japan, the women cope with the demands of their jobs by sharing childcare duties. This situation is in part engineered by brokers who "market" their female labor force to prospective employers as one that relies on the community to both do the job and take care of the children. During a visit I made to one foundation based in the south of Metro Manila, the managing director related to me that they recommended employers to arrange for housing and work shifts in a way that enables the women to take turns in watching over each other's children, especially so during night shifts.

Employers rely on and exploit their female workers' social capital in recruitment and staffing processes. The brokers' interest in Filipino women as workers, not mothers, is moreover exemplified by the limitations placed upon bringing all their children with them, including those from relationships with non-Japanese partners. Sachi, a Japanese-Filipino girl who had resettled to Japan only a few months before our interview, had two younger siblings of a different father who had to remain in the care of their grandparents in the southern Philippines: "My Mom wanted [my siblings] to come here. ... When we went to the airport and said our goodbyes, my mommy cried because we'll miss them." Similarly, a mother of two relates her feelings of guilt for having had to leave her non-Japanese child behind:

> Amy: I was supposed to come here with my other child, my second child; we both have visas. All three of us were supposed to [come] here to Japan.
> Interviewer: You were supposed to [come] here all together?
> Amy: But the agency told us it wasn't allowed. My second child didn't make it to the school cutoff;[7] that's why he wasn't allowed. I told them even if he didn't make it to the (cut)off, it's okay because he has a visa, so I can bring him with me. They told me I couldn't. I would have to feed him. I told them I was the one who was going to feed him. I was the one who was going to pay for it. They said, "No." Then I said, "I'll tell our boss." They said, "Even if you tell the boss, we still won't allow it." Why wouldn't they allow me? I left the Philippines feeling bad because they didn't allow my other child.

These instances illustrate a highly practical approach to labor recruitment into caregiving facilities for the elderly, whereby "useful" children are included in the migratory process while others are considered potential burdens whose presence might become a financial strain. In this migration process, Japanese-Filipino children's legal status in Japan (as citizens or long-term residents) allows their mothers to gain legal status as their primary carers, and to thereby qualify as documented migrant workers for brokers and employers. It is considered that children of non-Japanese fathers, however, are less likely to be "useful" to Japan in the long-term but may instead burden their mothers financially and with increased caring duties. Ironically, the organizations involved in facilitating the migration of Japanese-Filipinos and their mothers to Japan are frequently registered as foundations and non-profits, tapping into discourses of charity and rights. As with migrant women separated from all of their children, this system takes advantage of the political, social, and economic inequalities that render some families more vulnerable to structural violence than others.

The tangled intergenerational cross-border migration of Filipino mothers and their Japanese-Filipino children is coproduced by desires for better lives, and the laws governing immigration and settlement, as well as intermediary organizations brokering employment and mobility.

Concerns over Being a "Good Mother"

> Maricris: When we first arrived, my child said, "Mama, are we going to live here?" Yes. "How come we only have a bed and a pillow?" Let's put up with it for now. "How come we don't have things?" That's what she said when we got here. She said, "How come it's different in the Philippines?" [I said,] "Just be patient, it's just our first time here." We really didn't have anything.

Tied to their employer by debt and the hope of obtaining Japanese citizenship for their children, the families have little choice but to make do with their poor working and living conditions. Upon arrival, the initial arranged-for quarters in Kansai area proved disillusioning. In recounting these events, the women sound apologetic and guilty for having failed to fulfill their promises to their children of a comfortable life.

> Amy: [My son] really didn't want to [come to Japan]. Especially when we just arrived. The house was so bare. The only thing that was in our house was used diaper. When you open the cabinet, it was there. That was the only thing in our house. When we arrived, I didn't sleep for one night. I just cleaned the house. I cleaned up a small bit then I let the kid sleep. Then I cleaned the entire room. When we arrived, we didn't have food. They just gave us *onigiri* [rice ball]. My son didn't know what that was. He said "Mama, I thought [when] we went to Japan, we'd have a better life?" They just gave us …
> Cheryl: Bread.
> Amy: One *onigiri*. What bread? No, *onigiri*! My son wasn't familiar with it. We also didn't have anything to drink. One member of the staff told our boss to buy us drinks, but he said, "No. Drink from the faucet." We didn't have a choice. We were walking at 11 pm. We were a big group that arrived, and we all went to 7-eleven since it was the nearest. We bought food for the kids.

Recounting the emotional impact of their initial arrival in Kansai on them and their children, the women's narratives show the tanglement of mobility, decision-making power, and the negotiation of responsibility, guilt, and sacrifice. The sentiments of deferral of happiness and the acceptance of hardship and pain resound dominant Catholic cultural mores that produce particular subjectivities of *migranthood* and motherhood. In the Philippines, the journeys of Overseas Filipino Workers (OFWs) are celebrated as heroic acts, whereby these "modern-day heroes" are "transnational economic agents trained to internalize and deploy modes of ethical docility toward what is promoted as the martyric pursuit of both spiritual and economic ends" (Bautista 2015: 426). This migrant "hero-martyr" overlaps with ideals of motherhood in the centrality of their sacrificial nature. In the predominantly Catholic Philippines, cultural conceptualizations of "mothering" draw from a strong devotion to the Virgin Mary that set expectations of women for "qualities such as kindness, piety, obedience, care, and virtue—essentially a sacrificial being who puts God's will above her own needs" (Soriano, Lim, and Rivera-Sanchez 2015: 4). In their moral presentation of self, migrant mothers thus often feel the need to aspire to the qualities of the Marian persona (ibid.: 5).

The suspension of happiness and the acceptance of hardship are thus part of a cultural repertoire of available strategies for coming to terms with the unplanned for, the emotional strain, and the challenges engendered by overseas migration. Migrant aspirations and the coming to terms with the consequences of spatial mobility thus need to be understood against the backdrop of the Philippine political-economy, discourses of sacrifice and martyrdom defining ideals of motherhood and migranthood, and the personal migratory and familial histories that precede the ongoing cross-border mobility of Filipino women and their Japanese-Filipino children.

The decision to take up overseas employment is frequently juxtaposed with the pain of material deprivation to justify the unsettling consequences of migration as necessary for survival. Having thrust their children into cross-border mobility—often against their will—mothers deal with their sense of guilt by reasserting the initial reason why they left the Philippines to reconcile their choices with ideals of "good motherhood." Public narratives of "good mothering" do not always mesh well with parenting practices in mobility (Åkesson, Carling, and Drotbohm 2012: 238). Ideal motherhood often implies a range of duties, including the prioritization of their children's emotional and educational needs, whereby the "intensive mothering" ideal of the late twentieth century places tremendous emotional demands and financial pressures on women, who are expected to put their children's needs above their own (Soriano et al. 2015). As a consequence, women working full time—whether migrants or not, poor mothers, or women otherwise unable to fulfill these responsibilities—often feel guilt for what they perceive as failures as a parent. Carling, Menjívar, and Schmalzbauer (2012) write that "[home-away] mothers often express feelings of hopelessness, distress and guilt about 'abandoning' their children ... even if their migration was prompted by a sense of obligation to provide their children with education, food, clothing and a lifestyle they could not otherwise have afforded" (194).

Asis (2002) writes that notions of the "good mother" (92) are redefined by women migrants away from home as they reposition themselves from being primarily nurturers to being providers. However, in this case of physically co-present mothering in single-parent families, migrant mothers attempt to fulfill both roles. Asked how they managed to balance work and their duties as a parent, my respondents describe particular mothering activities, all of which emphasized their abilities to provide material and emotional well-being, despite their intense work schedules and their tiredness.

> Cheryl: When I'm working at night, I always call my kids. I check on them. How are you? Did you eat? Do you have food? They're grown up, so I know they can manage. When I arrive home, since they're boys, they didn't do the laundry. When I come from work, I see heaps of laundry. They're boys, so they don't know how to clean. They don't want to clean. So even if I'm tired, as a mother, I'll do it. Even if I lecture them, nothing. That's the role of a parent. So, the moment you go to bed, you immediately fall asleep. Then when it's *yasumi* [off-day], we have time to get together and chat.

> Maricris: When I have money, I go out with my kid to bond. But my daughter doesn't want to. ... But when I'm home, I cook for her, and then we bond. We talk. Then when I'm trying to be sweet to her, she doesn't like it. I try to be the sweet parent because she's the grouchy type. She says "Mama, don't hug me." Then I tell her someday she'll crave my hugs. If I don't hug her, she's the one who hugs me. I tell her, look, now you're the one who wants to hug. When she hugs me, I hug her back. We chat too. I ask her about school. Then when she's on the cell phone, I ask what are you doing? Then she tells me.

> Amy: Until now I still feed him by hand, even [though] he's grown up. If we're having fish, I take out the bones and I feed him by hand. He's the youngest. He's sweet. So even [now] he's all grown up, he tells me "Mama, carry me on your lap." No, I can't. I don't think I can because you're too big now. It should be you carrying me.

These statements illustrate their efforts to conform to the image of a "good mother"—taking the time to be physically present to provide food, to make sure their children are clothed, and to give emotional support— are efforts to fulfill expectations of traditional mothering (Uy-Tioco 2007: 255). Not being able to do so results in "a sense of loss and the guilt of not being a 'good' mother" (ibid). Reflecting upon how their past and present migrations have affected their children, my respondents continue to elaborate on their concern:

> Cheryl: We always think about the discrimination experienced by our children. It's okay with us parents if we're discriminated against. We can take it. But we always think about what our children experience. That's what we're worried about. It's nice that they're able to interact with a lot of people, but discrimination can't be avoided.

> Maricris: If we had gone back to Japan to get a different kind of work, if we worked in the clubs, our children would get bullied. [Our boss said that] it's also hard to take care of a child when you're drunk. It's better to be a caregiver instead.

The latter statement can be read as a response to the "disciplining discourses within their host society," slotting Filipino women into one of the two "wife or whore" categories (Suzuki 2000: 432). The statement follows a retrospective account of their previous jobs as "talents," which are described as comparatively easy and better paid. By forgoing such an opportunity, Cheryl and Maricris show that they are keeping their children's best interests at heart,[8] while still demonstrating an awareness of local ideals of appropriate femininity.

While these accounts strengthen the idea that gendered ideals of parenthood shape mothering practices as well as performances of motherhood, they need to be contrasted with the broader research conducted among groups of Filipino migrant mothers and their children, children who have grown up in Japan, or children who joined their parent in Japan after years of separation. As mentioned above, my participants' accounts contribute to a larger body of studies on how mothers and their children experience and deal with migration from the Philippines to Japan. Suzuki (2015), for instance, demonstrates that migrant Japanese-Filipino youth often suffer emotionally from their mothers' indifference toward them and their exploitation as additional sources of labor and income upon arriving in Japan (223). Also, the data I collected from interviews with Japanese-Filipinos and their mothers during my doctoral research reveals instances of conflict that provide further nuances to the accounts above.[9]

Migrant Children Coming to Terms with Moving to a New Place

In November 2015, I attended a multicultural festival in the Kansai area, where a group of Japanese-Filipino migrant children gave a dance performance. Having assembled in front of the stage after the festival, we strolled from the park where the event was being held to the nearest Starbucks, together with a friend and fellow researcher. While walking, the group of six children—five girls and one boy, aged eleven to fifteen—engaged in excited conversation, switching between Japanese and Tagalog as they spoke. At Starbucks, the children got Frappuccinos as their reward for their performance at the festival. One of the girls, Hiromi, told me this was the only drink her mother allowed her to have because of its low coffee content.

As we sat, we spoke about the differences they had noticed between life in Japan and that in the Philippines. One girl mentioned that she had been excited about the prospect of seeing snow at first, but this had worn off quickly as she got annoyed with the cold. The others nodded and expressed agreement. Hideo, the only boy in the group, told me he would prefer returning to the Philippines. Two of the girls, Hiromi and Yuki, concurred. They believed life was more fun in the Philippines, and mentioned that schools organized a "prom" night after grade four, whereas no such thing existed in Japan. Yuki reiterated this sentiment during a later interview in which she described the school in Japan as "haggard." They expressed envy of their friends in the Philippines, but their friends envied them too; according to Hiromi and Yuki, their friends would say, "Wow, you're in Japan, that's so cool!" But they would reply, "No, it's not like that."

As our conversation continued, they asked me if I wanted to return to Europe, to which I replied that I was still undecided. Yuki then advised me to remain in Japan. As I pointed out the contradiction between her fondness of the Philippines on the one hand and her insistence on Japan being the better choice on the other, she replied: "It is better to stay in Japan, for work and for the future." Hiromi then further explained: "My mother said, what do you want to do in the Philippines? There is nothing you can do there. Japan is better for the future." During a focus group discussion a few months after our first meeting, the same two girls reiterated why they needed to resettle in Japan:

> Hiromi: If I stay in the Philippines, I'll have nothing to eat. If I [come] here, I can eat, but I'm alone. I'm happy when I'm in the Philippines, but I'll get hungry.
> Yuki: It's hard to find work in the Philippines.

Both girls accepted the plans their mothers had made for them, and believed that suspending their wishes was in their best interest, relying on their mothers' knowledge of the "adult world." Despite having had to resettle in Japan to enable their mothers' employment there, most of the Japanese-Filipino children and youths (ages nine to twenty-one) I spoke to had not wanted to leave the Philippines. A volunteer, while introducing me to the educational support group they were running, told me that most children they worked with had not wanted to leave their homes in the Philippines. "The parents don't care about the children's opinions. The children tell me so," she says. "But luckily, many of them end up making friends here." This illustrates that in these decision-making processes "children rarely appear to be consulted and are often excluded. ... It is generally the adult family members who take the decision for the children to migrate and who organize their travel documents, which reflects the unbalanced 'power-geometry' in many migrant families" (Nagasaka and Fresnoza-Flot 2015: 25).

It is thus noteworthy that, in their narratives, the young migrants I spoke to did not paint their mothers as indifferent to their wishes but instead tried to rationalize their mothers' decisions and their roles in the entire migration project. Migrating for the sake of the family "runs through the script of migrants, men and women alike" (Asis 2002: 74). Considering that their mothers migrated to Japan not only to improve their economic situation but also often that of their other children who had to remain in the Philippines, as well as their extended family, it is unsurprising that the children, too, see migration as the "natural thing to do" (ibid.: 77), and their role in it as a necessary sacrifice.

In her study of undocumented Salvadorian migrant women in the United States and their families, Horton (2009) observes that children separated from their migrant mothers frequently offer to shoulder the adult burden in an attempt to reunify the family in one place, and challenge their mothers' rational explanations for their departure ("to provide for the family") by offering to contribute to the family income as well. My young respondents, too, seem to try taking the weight off of their mothers' shoulders, albeit not by challenging the decision to migrate, but by accepting and reiterating their justifications for resettling in Japan.

Repeated conversations over the period of a year showed that the children spoke inconsistently about their experiences of having to leave family and friends to live elsewhere. During our group interview, the children trivialized their move by declaring they were indifferent about leaving the Philippines, with one girl even being excited and exclaiming she had expected to see real *anime* figures running around Japan's streets: "If our Mom says so, we'll do it," Hiromi declared. Yet, when I asked for a description of their initial experiences in Japan, one of my respondents teared up, and another one expressed continued sadness over living apart from her grandparents and siblings. Akiko and Sarah, two young women aged twenty and twenty-one whom I met and spoke to during a gathering, told me about their involuntary move to Japan four years earlier. Akiko's sister had had to quit college to work in a factory in Japan, and Sarah said she felt "taken out of her structure" when she had to leave her hometown in the Philippines. Both seemed resigned about the possibilities that migration to Japan opened: "For us here it's not so much about what we want to do, but what we can do," said Sarah, reiterating her lack of decision-making power.

Francisco-Menchavez (2018) warns against casting children affected by parental migration into emotional stasis, as they too are able to develop "an emotional grammar during sustained separation" (9), or as in this case, in migration. The children's feelings about being in Japan may thus seem contradictory at times, but as such reflect a process of coming to terms with the many conflicting feelings the experience indeed involves, including their willingness to recognize their mothers' good intentions. "Children deeply understand what is at stake for their migrant mothers abroad. They sympathize with the sacrifice their mothers make as they work their fingers to the bone, staying abroad for an indefinite amount of time" (ibid.). This sentiment of sympathy and understanding frequently leads to labor of care in the form of reciprocation that Francisco-Menchavez coins *"sukli,"* a concept "deeply linked to the Filipino cultural value of *'utang ng loob,'* [which] can be loosely translated to 'reciprocation' in the context of family obligation" (ibid.: 1; also see Celero in this volume).

Hideo's mother, Amy, recounts her joy over earning her son's recognition for her hard work:

> When he was in junior high school, they had this thing wherein they will work for two days in the place where we work. He saw other helpers like us working. When I arrived home, he told me, "Mama, your work is really hard. Why don't you stop and look for an easier work?" He saw for himself, so he was the one who told his older brother. Of course, I don't mention things like that when we talk to relatives in the Philippines. I always call my son [the one left in the Philippines]. It's difficult because he's a guy. I don't want him to hang out with the wrong crowd. Even if my sister's there in the Philippines, it's different when I'm the one taking care of him. My son [in Japan] tells him, "This is Mom's work here."

By acknowledging his mother's hard work and showing concern over her well-being, Hideo engages in emotional labor. His mother Amy subsequently expresses her desire for her second son, who had to remain in the Philippines, to do the same by not hanging out "with the wrong crowd." The acknowledgment of their mother's sacrifices, and the readiness to endorse her decisions, are a way of caring that children develop as they resettle and live with their mothers in Japan.

Conclusion

The spatial mobilities of Filipino mothers and their Japanese-Filipino children are tangled on numerous levels: emotional, structural, temporal, generational, and material. Their case shows that both the mothers' and children's ways of coming to terms with the emotional dimensions of their migration are interconnected with wider economic, social, and political structures and processes. The mothers' and the children's mobilities are codependent processes, whereby the children enable their mothers' migration without having any real decision-making power. Remaining dependent on their mothers as caregivers throughout the process, the latter expressed feelings of guilt for having put their children through emotional distress.

Spatial mobility entailed profound changes in family structure and in overseas employment, and, at least in the beginning, failed to deliver on its promise for "better lives." The affective responses to these emotional hardships entailed by cross-border mobility are frequently expressed through powerful ideals of motherhood and the trope of the migrant martyr-hero. Similarly informed by notions of sacrifice and debt, children and youth who are recruited into these migratory enterprises, despite their wishes, rationalize the decisions taken for them and often support their mothers' decisions.

The motives and routes to migration are manifold and entangled; the mothers are effectively labor migrants, while the children are crossing borders as Japanese citizens or to claim their Japanese citizenship. Both migration for work and migration for rights are motivated by aspirations to better lives and greater opportunities. Intermediary actors facilitate the entrance into Japan by exploiting these desires, the demands of the Japanese labor market, and migration regimes that hamper the mobility of those with the least capital—social, cultural, or financial.

The mothers' migration to Japan for work, which outside of my group of respondents also occurs among Japanese-Filipinos of working age, bears striking parallels to the migration of Filipino women into Japan's adult entertainment industry decades ago. Recruited to work for Japanese clubs, pubs, and bars, Filipino migrant "entertainers" were saddled with debt and found themselves performing reproductive and care labor, as many do today in their roles as caregivers. Similar brokerage practices linger, as do notions that Filipino workers require monitoring.[10] Here, present spatial mobilities tangle with past ones, and result in the continuity of exploitative practices.

This temporal tangledness is accompanied by legal and material tangledness. Women and children depend on intermediaries' and employers' support in securing the family's legal status (where children are not yet Japanese citizens) and their subsistence in Japan via employment. Employers and brokers are dependent on the migrant workers fulfilling their tasks. Brokers work for profit, and employers require affordable labor. Bringing these families to Japan on visas that are not employment bound bears the risk of "losing" workers, should they find more attractive work opportunities. Thus, the support of local managers in securing the children's Japanese citizenship is tied to their mothers' compliance to their employer.

The recent migration of Japanese-Filipino children with their mothers to Japan feeds off similar social, economic, and gendered inequalities, as did the initial arrival of young Filipino "entertainers" in the past (Ogaya 2020).

It thus remains to be seen whether this form of tangled spatial mobility will lead yet again to the reproduction of such inequalities, or whether the families' aspirations for upward social mobility will come to fruition in their country of destination.

Fiona-Katharina Seiger is a migration expert who has worked with women, children, and youth in Japan and the Philippines. Her intellectual project centers on the politics of belonging in a world in flux, to which she now adds a burgeoning interest in urban spaces and in qualitative research involving "the digital." Her education and research career have taken her to Vienna, Paris, Kyoto, Tokyo, Manila, Singapore, and Antwerp, and she is now with Erasmus University, Rotterdam (EUR). Prior to embarking on her PhD, she worked for a nongovernmental organization based in Manila catering to migrant returnees from Japan and their children; this experience laid the groundwork for her ensuing research projects. She holds a PhD in Sociology (National University of Singapore, 2014) with a thesis on Japanese-Filipino children born from migration between the two countries. At the center of her doctoral research stood an exploration of the material dimensions of ethnic identity constructions and identity claims. Her post-doctoral research (Kyoto University CSEAS, 2015–16) builds upon her doctoral work by exploring how identity constructions and claims change in migration, as people cross into different sociocultural and political contexts. Fiona-Katharina joined the Department of Public Policy and Sociology at EUR in September 2019, where she is exploring narratives of Europe from outside the continent, as part of the H2020 project PERCEPTIONS. She is also always looking for different ways of publishing research; since March 2020, Fiona-Katharina produces "The Migration Podcast."

NOTES

1. Mobility regimes denote "a constellation of policies, cultural norms and networks that condition, constrain or facilitate migration" (Xiang 2007: 3).
2. Single-mother households in Japan, or "fatherless families" as they are called in the Surveys by the Ministry of Health and Welfare, are especially vulnerable to poverty, as over 50 percent of all single-parent (mostly single-mother) families in Japan live with an income that sets them below the poverty line (http://www.japantimes.co.jp/news/2015/11/07/business/no-relief-sight-japans-poor-single-parent-families/, last accessed 31 January 2022). On average, the salaries reportedly earned by my respondents were between 150,000 and 180,000 yen a month (70,000–85,000 PhP or 1,300–1,600 USD) before deductions, for rent, utilities, the payback of their debt, and money remitted home. After all deductions, the women

I talked to were left with only about 20,000–70,000 yen (approx. 170–600 USD) a month for their and their children's needs.
3. Meaning, their children with non-Japanese partners. Only the offspring of a Japanese parent qualify for either a long-term visa and/or Japanese citizenship.
4. A small neighborhood shop where one can buy a variety of products for everyday use. *Sari-sari* means "variety."
5. Migration is also regarded as a "rite of passage" (Aguilar 2014), showing the interconnectedness of geographical and social mobility, as well as personhood, in the process.
6. A small number of caregivers and prospective nurses have reached Japan under the Japan–Philippine Economic Partnership Agreement (JPEPA). More recently, the Japanese government under Prime Minister Abe decided to allow the recruitment of domestic helpers from abroad, but limited to Tokyo and Osaka, two "special zones" (Venzon and Suruga 2017).
7. Amy refers to age fifteen, when compulsory education ends and when entry examination for senior high school needs to be taken.
8. The group of people I worked with are not representative in this respect, as Filipino migrant women in Japan frequently go back to work in nightclubs. But nightclubs do not guarantee a steady income. A volunteer at a support group tells me that many women were laid off when the economy was bad as fewer customers were spending their money on these types of entertainment. Caregivers on the other hand are always very much in demand in this hyper aging society.
9. One such story revolved around Felix. Now in his mid-twenties, his resident mother petitioned Felix to Japan when he was seventeen to increase the family income by finding a job. Several verbal fights with his mother led the then-teenager to move in with friends instead, and chart out his own livelihood project over time, resulting in circular migration between the greater Tokyo metropolitan area and Metro Manila. Over the years, our communication often touched upon Felix's feelings of alienation from his mother and his disagreements with her priorities and lifestyle—notably, her addiction to gambling and her and her husband's alleged physical violence toward Felix's younger half-siblings.
10. Ogaya (2020: 8) writes that owners and managers of care facilities are mostly men who remember Filipino women as entertainers who are exploitable and who need to be monitored. She quotes one of her respondents claiming that women who used to work as entertainers had to be under managerial control, as they have the habit of deceiving their customers.

REFERENCES

Aguilar, Filomeno V. 2014. *Migration Revolution: Philippine Nationhood and Class Relations in a Globalized Age*. Honolulu: University of Hawaii Press.
Åkesson, Lisa, Jørgen Carling, and Heike Drotbohm. 2012. "Mobility, Moralities and Motherhood: Navigating the Contingencies of Cape Verdean Lives." *Journal of Ethnic and Migration Studies* 38(2): 237–60.

Asis, Maruja. 2002. "From the Life Stories of Filipino Women: Personal and Family Agendas in Migration." *Asian and Pacific Migration Journal* 11(1): 67-93.
Bautista, Julius. 2015. "Export-Quality Martyrs: Roman Catholicism and Transnational Labor in the Philippines." *Cultural Anthropology* 30(3): 424-47. https://doi.org/10.14506/ca30.3.04.
Carling, Jørgen, Cecilia Menjívar, and Leah Schmalzbauer. 2012. "Central Themes in the Study of Transnational Parenthood." *Journal of Ethnic and Migration Studies* 38(2): 191-217.
Faier, Lieba. 2009. *Intimate Encounters: Filipina Women and the Remaking of Rural Japan*. Berkeley: University of California Press.
Francisco-Menchavez, Valerie. 2018. "Sukli: Uneven Exchanges of Care Work of Children Left Behind in Filipino Transnational Families." *Children's Geographies* 16(6): 604-15.
Fresnoza-Flot, Asuncion. 2009. "Migration Status and Transnational Mothering: The Case of Filipino Migrants in France." *Global Networks* 9(2): 252-70.
Fresnoza-Flot, Asuncion, and Itaru Nagasaka. 2015. "Conceptualizing Childhoods in Transnational Families: The 'Mobile Childhoods' Lens." In *Mobile Childhoods in Filipino Transnational Families: Migrant Children with Similar Roots in Different Routes*, ed. Itaru Nagasaka and Asuncion Fresnoza-Flot, 23-41. Basingstoke: Palgrave MacMillan.
Fresnoza-Flot, Asuncion, and Kyoko Shinozaki. 2017. "Transnational Perspectives on Intersecting Experiences: Gender, Social Class and Generation among Southeast Asian Migrants and their Families." *Journal of Ethnic and Migration Studies* 43(6): 867-84.
Glick Schiller, Nina, and Noel B. Salazar. 2013. "Regimes of Mobility across the Globe." *Journal of Ethnic and Migration Studies* 39(2): 183-200.
Holt, Louise, and Sarah L. Holloway. 2006. "Editorial: Theorising Other Childhoods in a Globalised World." *Children's Geographies* 4(2): 135-42.
Horton, Sarah. 2008. "Consuming Childhood: 'Lost' and 'Ideal' Childhoods as a Motivation for Migration." *Anthropological Quarterly* 81(4): 925-43.
———. 2009. "A Mother's Heart is Weighed Down with Stones: A Phenomenological Approach to the Experience of Transnational Motherhood." *Culture, Medicine, and Psychiatry* 33(1): 21-40.
Kelly, Philip. 2007. *Filipino Migration, Transnationalism and Class Identity*. Singapore: Asia Research Institute Working Paper Series No. 90.
Madianou, Mirca. 2016. "Ambient Co-Presence: Transnational Family Practices in Polymedia Environments." *Global Networks* 16(2): 183-201.
Nagasaka, Itaru, and Asuncion Fresnoza-Flot. 2015. *Mobile Childhoods in Filipino Transnational Families: Migrant Children with Similar Roots in Different Routes*. Basingstoke: Palgrave MacMillan.
Ogaya, Chiho. 2020. "Intergenerational Exploitation of Filipino Women and their Japanese Filipino Children: 'Born out of Place' Babies as New Cheap Labor in Japan." *Critical Sociology*: 1-13. doi: 10.1177/0896920520935626.
———. 2005. *Children of Global Migration: Transnational Families and Gendered Woes*. Stanford, CA: Stanford University Press.

———. 2011. *Illicit Flirtations: Labour, Migration, and Sex Trafficking in Tokyo*. Stanford, CA: Stanford University Press.

James, A., and A. Prout (eds). 1997. *Constructing and Reconstructing Childhood: Contemporary Issues in the Sociological Study of Childhood* (2nd ed.). London: Routledge. https://doi.org/10.4324/9780203362600.

Soriano, Cheryll Ruth R., Sun Sun Lim, and Milagros Rivera-Sanchez. 2015. "The Virgin Mary with a Mobile Phone: Ideologies of Mothering and Technology Consumption in Philippine Television Advertisements." *Communication, Culture and Critique* 8(1): 1–19.

Suzuki, Nobue. 2000. "Women Imagined, Women Imaging: Representations of Filipinas in Japan since the 1980s." *US–Japan Women's Journal [English Supplement]* 19: 142–75.

———. 2015. "Suspended Mobilities: Japanese-Filipino Children, Family Regimes, and Postcolonial Plurality." In *Mobile Childhoods in Filipino Transnational Families*, edited by Itaru Nagasaka and Asuncion Fresnoza-Flot, 222–46. Basingstoke: Palgrave Macmillan.

Takahata, Sachi, and Megumi Hara. 2015. "Japan as a Land of Settlement or a Stepping Stone for 1.5-Generation Filipinos." In *Mobile Childhoods in Filipino Transnational Families*, ed. Itaru Nagasaka and Asuncion Fresnoza-Flot, 117–47. Basingstoke: Palgrave Macmillan.

Uy-Tioco, Cecilia. 2007. "Overseas Filipino Workers and Text Messaging: Reinventing Transnational Mothering." *Continuum* 21(2): 253–65.

Venzon, Cliff, and Tsubasa Suruga. 2017. "Filipino Housekeepers' Japan Dream." *Nikkei Asian Review*. Retrieved 29 November 2020 from https://asia.nikkei.com/Business/Japan-dreams.

Xiang Biao. 2007. "A New Mobility Regime in the Making: What Does a Mobile China Mean to the World?" *Global Governance* 10: 1–19.

CHAPTER
5

Emotions, Places, and Mobilities
The Affective Drives of the Migration and Settlement Aspirations among Highly Educated Migrants

Gracia Liu-Farrer

The increasingly globalized education and labor markets offer people more opportunities to move, and, at the same time, also enhance highly educated individuals' expectations of career development through geographic mobility (Hof 2019). The question is then: given the increased opportunities, how do people decide where and when to move, and where and when to settle down? What matters in their migratory decision-making? Existing research has offered many explanations about highly educated people's geographic mobility or emplacement. These motivations range from assessing the benefit of migration in terms of economic and career development (Beaverstock 2005; Millar and Salt 2008), the opportunities and constraints of destination countries' institutional characteristics, employment systems (Oishi 2012; Liu-Farrer 2020; Tseng 2020), and lifestyle choices (Ho 2011; Marinelli 2011), to combined motivations of "romance, adventure and quality of life" (Favell et al. 2011: 24). Moreover, studies show that life stages influence the choice of migration or emplacement. The young and single are more willing to move because of the lure of adventure and the desire to build a career. The middle-aged with families have to deliberate on a range of factors, from spouses' careers to children's education (Ryan and Mulholland 2014).

While these studies provide great insights into individuals' migratory decisions, they lean toward more instrumental motives to explain their mobilities. This chapter aims to examine migration decisions through an affective lens. Migration, by moving people from one environment to another, and separating them from one set of social relationships and inserting them into another, invariably creates emotional consequences. Although often implicit in the analysis, relatively few studies have examined emotions as forces in driving migration. This scarcity has to do with the difficult task of singling out an emotional dimension in the complex reasons that constitute motives for action. The most common approach to investigate affective drives of migration is quantitative. Using survey data, researchers can detect the significance of affective effect in each migration decision after controlling other variables (Ivlevs 2015). This study employs a qualitative approach to trace the logic of migration and emplacement aspirations through individuals' narratives. It does not seek to untangle the different dimensions of decision-making, or to show the unique effect of emotions. Instead, it sees affects as a consequence of the entanglement of different mobilities. Migration, a form of spatial mobility by moving people from one place to another, simultaneously brings about other forms of mobilities, such as: social—the relative social positions in the society; legal—the change of legal status in different countries and the residential security connected to it; and sexual—whether one becomes more sexually marketable or not. These various forms of mobilities, being tangled and unevenly accomplished, result in different emotions toward the place. In turn, these different emotions serve as driving forces for different migratory decisions—either onward movement or settlement.

This study takes as its premise that migration is essentially a decision made about places. Therefore, it examines migrants' articulations of feelings about places and how such sentiments are used as justifications for their migratory decisions and destination choices. Drawing on interviews with university-educated international migrants in Germany and Japan, this chapter shows that positive and negative emotions operate differently. It is often negative emotions about the place or their life in that place that compel the desire to move, despite instrumental rationality. The interviews also reveal that love relationships play a central role in adult migrants' migratory decisions. Moreover, places themselves are capable of engendering migrants' emotional responses toward them. This is because their natural and built environment and historically developed sociocultural and institutional practices can structure intimate and social relations, and thereby condition migrants' experiences within these places.

Affective Drive for Migration

Migration is a form of social action. Like any type of social action, it can be rational because it consciously pursues a goal or value, or be affectively determined, as a result of current emotional states; and as Weber (1978) argues, a social action seldom takes only one form or the other (28). The discussion of the motivation for migration is dominated by concerns of economic rationality during most of the twentieth century. With the "emotional turn" (Bondi, Davidson, and Smith 2016) that took place in human geography and cultural studies in the early twenty-first century, migration studies have increasingly brought in the affective lens to examine the conditions involved in people's geographic mobilities.

One strand of literature highlights the emotional underpinning of migration aspiration. Carling and Schewel (2018) point out that while migration aspiration is commonly conceptualized as a comparison of places, it is also a culturally defined project and a matter of personhood or identity. The desire to move is, therefore, a highly emotional matter. From Chu (2010)'s anxious young Fujianese woman sitting on her suitcase in an empty apartment waiting to go overseas to Fong (2011)'s Chinese students in Dalian longing for studying abroad in "paradise"—preferably a developed anglophone country, affects, such as anxiety and hopefulness, illustrate the desiring subjects in anticipation of migration. Spatial mobility itself also has intrinsic value. Waters, Brooks, and Pimlott-Wilson (2011) show that notions of fun, enjoyment, and the pursuit of happiness abroad, rather than rational strategies around education, feature strongly in young British students' aspirations to study overseas.

Places themselves are imbued with affects. Choices of destinations are driven by the "affective possibilities" (Conradson and Latham 2007) of the places, especially global cities or Eurocities (Favell 2008). Conradson and Latham's study shows that many of New Zealand's temporary migrants flocked to London because of the city's "affective promises." The fantasy of Shanghai being a "chic" and "magical" city, and an exotic place reminiscing New York and Berlin fifty years ago, is as much a reason for the "Shanghai Rush" as the economic opportunities it offered to Taiwanese businessmen (Tseng 2011). Sometimes, the country as a whole can be a desired destination for migration. Japan, for example, attracts young migrants who grew up with anime and video games. The desire to migrate to Japan was so strong that some would "have stepped over (their) own mother to get out here" (Liu-Farrer 2020: 85).

One field that has explored the affective dimension of migration is happiness studies. Happiness research aims to examine the affective effect of migration quantitatively. In an attempt to understand people's reasons for residential mobility, Nowok et al. (2013) found that migration is usually preceded by a period when individuals experience a significant decline in happiness for a variety of reasons. However, findings regarding whether one achieves happiness after the migration are not consistent. While the Nowok et al. study carried out in the United Kingdom shows that residential mobility brings a boost in happiness, studies about internal migration in China and Thailand indicated that rural migrant workers reported lower happiness after moving into urban areas (Knight and Gunatilaka 2010; De Jong, Chamratrithirong, and Tran 2002). Among international migrants, research finds that a lack of life satisfaction is also associated with a desire to emigrate internationally (Ivlevs 2015). A more comprehensive economic study that involves countries in different world regions shows a nonlinear relationship between happiness and migration tendency, and directions are different between countries with higher happiness scores and those with lower scores. Among countries where the general population reports a relatively lower degree of happiness, the lower the country's happiness score, the higher the emigration rate. In happier countries, the higher the country's happiness score, the higher the emigration rate (Polgreen and Simpson 2011).

Affects are also an important drive for return migration. In Thomson's (2005) historic research of returned British migrants from Australia, immigrants are driven home by the feeling of "homesickness" and their longing "for people and places" and "ways of life" in the home country (118). Among the contemporary Chinese migrants in Japan, the frustration from social marginalization and status loss, and the nagging sense of discomfort of "being under other people's roof" propel some Chinese migrants in Japan to return to their home country (Liu-Farrer 2011). At the same time, the emotional ties to their parents or kin pull people back to their places of origin. Baldassar (2015)'s study about Italian migrant living in Australia, but with aging parents back in their home country, shows that the feeling of guilt operates in such a transnational family context, entailing a moral obligation to return. Similarly, the singleton Chinese students overseas feel the emotional and moral obligation entailed in the notion of filial piety, and see their eventual return to take care of their elderly parents as an inevitable part of the future plan (Liu-Farrer 2014).

Finally, affects not only drive people away but also keep people in place. This affective relationship with places has been discussed in the literature on place-belongingness—a personal and intimate feeling of being at home in a place (Antonsich 2010). Migration is essentially a form of "displacement" or "deterritorialization." Places provide the physical as well as social spaces that can facilitate or disrupt the anchoring of one's belonging. The places immigrants feel attached to vary on geographic scales, from one's apartment (Walsh 2006) and the neighborhood (Ehrkamp 2005) to the nation-state itself (Ho 2006, 2009).

This study builds on this developing scholarship on the affective dimension of migration by qualitatively examining how emotions can lead to varying migratory decisions among highly educated migrants—the most mobile individuals that many countries compete to attract and retain. In particular, by approaching these migrants' migration decisions in the place they have already migrated to, the study aims to clarify how different aspects of places engender varied emotions, and how such emotions might play a role in a migrant's migratory decisions.

Data, Methods, and Labeling

This chapter draws on interview data that I collected from highly educated migrants in Japan and Germany between 2015 and 2019. This project aims to understand these migrants' career mobilities in a global labor market and how they experience national employment systems and sociocultural life in both these countries. Although the fieldwork has been conducted in two different receiving contexts, instead of comparing the effects of specific places on people's migration, it focuses on examining how emotions matter to immigrants' migratory decisions in either location, and on how different places elicit different emotional responses. The Japan part of the data includes interviews with thirty-five individuals—fourteen women, and twenty-one men. The majority of them were aged between twenty-four and forty, with one who was forty-nine, at the time of interview. Among them, ten were Chinese, and the rest were mostly from Europe, North and South America, Africa, and Oceania. The German data includes twenty-five interviews conducted between 2017 and 2019—twelve women and thirteen men. Five of them came from other European Union countries, and the rest were from non-EU or non-European countries, such as India, Bangladesh, Brazil, China and Taiwan, and the Middle East. The majority of them were in their mid-twenties to early forties, but one was a retired medical doctor in his sixties.

Emotions were not originally planned as a research focus. As highly skilled migrants have relatively fewer institutional constraints and more resources to be mobile, the discussions about their migratory trajectories and career mobilities began to touch upon the affective aspects of places— be they workplaces, cities, or countries. In their narratives, it became clear to me that for these mobile migrants, the choice of place depended not only on the economic and professional opportunities it could provide, but also on how they *felt* about it or their life in it.

In this chapter, I use both "affect" and "emotion" in the text. Psychologists and cultural studies researchers consider affect to be a broader conceptual category than emotion. Emotions are seen as intense and temporary, and often culturally specific, such as anger, jealousy, and happiness. At the same time, affect can be more nebulous, and as simple as feeling good or bad (Russell 2003). Moreover, affect theory sees affects as "forces—visceral forces beneath, alongside, or generally other than conscious-knowing, vital forces insisting beyond emotion—that can serve to drive us toward movement, toward thought and extension" (Gregg and Seigworth 2010: 1). I thus choose to use "affective motive" to express this research's objectives while emotions are used in the analysis to describe the specific feelings about places that my subjects expressed.

Negative and Positive Emotions in the Migration Decision-Making

Practical and emotional reasons are often both present and entangled in their narratives of migration decisions. When does either become more dominant in one's migration decision? At least from this study, it shows that negative feelings about a place—feelings of unhappiness—are often more potent in one's leaving decision, even though it might not be rational by the individual judgment. Positive feelings about a place, in comparison, exercise less pulling effect.

Boris is an engineer from Russia. His account of his multinational mobility trajectory illustrates such different degrees of influence by positive and negative emotions. He had been working for a big energy company in North Rhein Westphalia (NRW) in Germany for three years when I interviewed him. He lived in Düsseldorf with his wife. Boris first worked for a Norwegian firm in Russia upon graduating from university. Two years into his job, he had an opportunity to move from Russia to its Norwegian headquarters. Three years later, he obtained the permanent residency and so went back to Russia and married his girlfriend, Natasha. The young couple commuted between Russia and Norway in the first six months of their marriage because Natasha had a job in Russia that she liked. Also, she did not like Norway when she visited, and did not want to move there to live.

Soon, the company decided to move some of their production to Malaysia and looked for engineers who were willing to be stationed there. Boris discussed the opportunity with his wife, and they decided that, although the salary for working in Malaysia would be lower than what he was making in Norway, many of their expenses would be covered by the company. In addition, Malaysia was much cheaper to live in, and so they would eventually save money. They were also lured by the warm weather, the possibility of speaking English (a language his wife was capable of), and a new environment. They moved, and quickly became absorbed into the expatriate community of the city. Natasha also enrolled herself in a Master of Business Administration program. They managed to make friends through such activities.

After staying in Malaysia for nearly two years, Boris faced a choice. Norwegian permanent residency stipulated that the maximum a resident could remain overseas without losing their residency was two years. Being a national from a non-EU country, that would mean his losing access to Europe, so he decided to move back to Norway even though he was enjoying his life in Malaysia. "My wife didn't want to move, but she said 'I will support you ... if you really think it's important.'" Boris gave up his position, left the company, and went back to Norway with his wife.

The second time in Norway turned out to be a painful experience. Through a connection of one of his former colleagues, Boris started to work at a consulting firm in Oslo. The majority of the employees were Norwegian. "The Norwegians were reserved, so it was difficult to build friendships. In particular, my wife was unhappy. She couldn't speak the language, had no friends, and initially also had some trouble with her legal status because she had never really lived in Norway before leaving for Malaysia." Natasha started to talk about going back to Russia, but Boris was not willing to. He decided to look for jobs in other European countries. He was interviewed for four of them, two of which were in Germany. He accepted the job in Düsseldorf although, in his own words, this move was an irrational choice—because by the time they decided to leave the country, Boris had become eligible to apply for Norwegian citizenship, which would have given him much more freedom for residential mobility than his Russian passport. Nevertheless, the move to Germany turned out well. He commented:

> The money was good, and they took care of us really well. We got all the immigration papers within a week. My wife was super happy. When we moved here and she saw the prices, she said, "Look, it's cheaper to live here." So it was a boost of energy for her, and she was dragging me in terms of emotion. She wasn't happy in Norway, so that was that.

When I talked to Boris in a meeting room in the sleek, modern, high-tech office compound where he worked, he said that he had comfortably settled in Germany and into his new job. Being "comfortable" was not the ideal state for Boris, he confessed, because he liked excitement and challenge, especially in terms of work. However, Natasha was happy in Düsseldorf because she had made friends and started working. He was also happy with his life, and because of this contentment, he was not actively seeking other jobs. Boris still received recruiters' phone calls and put his profile out, but he was conservative about moving. Unless an exceedingly good opportunity came up, he said, he would stay put.

From Boris's narratives of his journey through different countries, one can see that instrumental and affective reasons tangled in his migration decision. However, depending on the nature of their emotions, he gave different priorities to instrumental and affective reasons. For example, when his Norwegian permanent residency was expiring, which would mean losing his access to Europe, he decided to leave Malaysia, even though both he and his wife were happy living there. At that moment, the instrumental reason, a European residency, was prioritized. The positive feelings brought by their expat life in Malaysia were not a strong enough pull to keep them there, even though leaving Malaysia also meant leaving the cushy job in this multinational firm. Later, when both he and his wife became unhappy in Norway, he sought jobs in other countries, despite soon being eligible for Norwegian citizenship—a legal status that would have brought him much more freedom than his Russian passport. When he finally moved to Düsseldorf, they became happy and content again. Because of this positive attachment to the place, they were more or less prepared to settle. Now, the only possibility for them to leave is if a great exciting opportunity came along—an instrumental reason yet again.

One might argue that Boris was among more privileged migrants whose skill was in great demand. He was in the EU region where the labor market was more integrated, and therefore enjoyed a better prospect for onward migration. He could afford to be more footloose when negative emotions arose. However, negative emotion-driven migration was also observed in Japan, even though it frequently meant returning to the home country. In an earlier study, I encountered in China a young man named Jing. Originally from Inner Mongolia, Jing went to Japan as an international student in 1998. Upon graduation, he started to work in a small city as an engineer for a company that manufactured car parts. He worked long hours and had a long commute, usually left home at 7 A.M. and returned at 11 P.M. The salaries were good, but he had no girlfriend nor time to look for one. To make things worse, his relationship with his neighbor soured over a parking space—the neighbor sometimes parked his car in the spot designated for Jing. This stressful lifestyle, compounded by the lack of a partner and a bad relationship with his neighbor, resulted in an intense feeling of loneliness.

> It was such an unbearable feeling. After all, from the day he is born, a person needs to communicate with people daily. Every day, if there is something unpleasant, you can talk to your friends, your loved ones. [But in Japan] I sometimes did not dare to speak. Because if you spoke

[about unpleasant experiences] with parents, they couldn't help you but would worry ... I thought I had better go back to China.

After some searching, Jing found a job at a Japanese company in Shanghai. When I interviewed him in China, he was married and expecting a child. Although he was financially worse off than he had been in Japan, his life was much happier.[1]

Tangled Emotions: The Centrality of Intimate Relationship

Both Boris's and Jing's stories bring out another characteristic of the affective drive for migration: the centrality of an intimate relationship. On the one hand, sex and love relationships themselves are potent drives in the migration process.[2] The potency of a love relationship provides a strong pull for people to leave a place, and it could just as quickly encourage someone to stay put (Farrer 2019; Liu-Farrer 2020). On the other hand, people's emotions in a relationship tend to tangle with those of their intimate others. Boris's statement about his wife "dragging" him in terms of emotions signals that his feelings were strongly connected to those of his wife. In the end, whether to move or to stay is a collective decision made by the couple, a finding that is also presented by other studies about highly skilled migrants (Ryan and Mulholland 2014).

Both Maria and Lingling followed their hearts. Originally from Latvia, Maria arrived in Japan aged twenty, enrolling at a Japanese university as an exchange student. She ended up staying, and finished a bachelor's as well as a master's degree. Speaking fluent Japanese and English, and three other European languages, she was employed by a prestigious Japanese firm. After working there for four years, she met a man from Australia who was in Japan on short-term assignments. After over a year of a long-distance relationship, she decided to leave Japan for Australia because it would be harder for him, who did not speak Japanese, to find a job in Japan than for her to continue her career in Australia, where her firm also had branches.

Lingling, a 36-year-old Chinese woman, was an engineer when I interviewed her. She had graduated from a master's program in engineering in the UK and then stayed on to work in London. As a foreign woman in an occupation dominated by English men, and working at places that often had no toilets for women, she went through a lot of hardship. She succeeded in gaining trust, attaining promotions, and earning a good salary. By her tenth year in the UK, at the age of thirty-three, she had become a branch manager in a multinational company, leading a team of English men who were mostly older than her. She then met a man who would be her future husband, a German, and faced a decision. Lingling loved London. During the interview, she talked about how she enjoyed the abundant nightlife, colorful cultural events, and multiethnic and open social environment in this global city. She had also been in romantic relationships with different men, so her love life was not a total void. After she had met her husband-to-be, she spent several years traveling back and forth between the UK and Germany. Nonetheless, after they decided to marry, she left bustling London for Germany. The presence of a romantic relationship, therefore, exerted a strong enough emotional drive to pull her out of a place she was attached to and was making a successful career in. After moving to Germany, she and her husband chose a small town in which to build a house, where she would also have a garden to plant flowers. "That's what I do now after work—planting flowers and watching the same crime series on TV on Sunday evenings." Though this could not be more different from her former urban lifestyle, she felt satisfied with such a peaceful domestic life.

In contrast to Lingling and Maria, Carlos's decision to settle down had to do with finding his partner in Japan. Carlos was a gay man from a South American country. He had always wanted to leave his home country because of his resentment toward its corrupt political regime. He spent the first five years of his postgraduate life in the United States as a language teacher, teaching Spanish. When his contract ended, he went back home and worked for a multinational foreign language education provider. Not wanting to stay in his home country, he looked for open positions his company advertised, and applied for several of them. Japan was just one of the choices. Not having been to Asia previously, he decided to try it out. While in Japan, he met his partner Takashi. By the time I talked to him, he had already been in Japan for fifteen years and had not long before obtained permanent residency and bought an apartment. Reflecting on his migratory decisions, Carlos emphasized that although the decision to come to Japan was out of the desire to escape his home country's political environment, having Takashi in his life helped solidify his decision to settle in Japan.

Place and Affects

Migration aspiration is essentially a comparison of places (Carling and Schewel 2018). The place is not only a labor market where migrants can find better economic opportunities but it is also where affects and what matters to affects, such as intimate relationships, are engendered and structured. In recent social sciences, place, to be differentiated from space, is seen as constructed by human activities and as an intricate web of relations perceived by subjects (Massey 1994). However, a place is both a network of relations and a physical thing. The place is a geographic location where nature and climate all play a part in conditioning one's activities. It is also historical, with settled cultural patterns and institutionalized practices shaping the manner in which social and intimate relationships can be formed and performed. Places consequently affect people's experiences and impact on their emotions. In the sections below, I explore how places engender affective responses to them, both by structuring intimate and social relationships and through their more general physical, social, institutional, and political environment.

Structuring Relations

Emotions are embodied experiences and can be internal responses to stimuli created in interpersonal relationships (Boccagni and Baldassar 2015: 74). Places, with their historically cultivated social and cultural patterns, sometimes dictate what kinds of relationships are possible and how they are constructed and performed, and thereby trigger emotional responses. This section focuses on two broad types of relationships: intimate/romantic relationships and more general social/friendship relationships.

Intimate Relations

The characteristics of the place influence the possibilities as well as the patterns of intimacy. Research finds that postcolonial racial hierarchy, localized status stratification, and global inequality that organize the socioeconomic landscapes in each place affect one's chances in the sexual field as well (see also Farrer and Tran in this volume). Legal and religious institutions in particular places also provide opportunities as well as constraints to specific demographic groups, and condition their sexual behavior. For example, in Shanghai, white women feel marginalized and undesirable in the sexual field they are involved in, and are thereby more inclined to leave (Farrer 2010). Dubai, on the other hand, attracts British women because, in contrast to the host country's restrictive moral codes and social environment regarding sexual practices, they have abundant sexual opportunities (Walsh 2007).

My fieldwork yields similar findings. Because I am a Chinese speaker, I was more likely to interact with Chinese migrants in Japan and Germany. In both countries, I have encountered unhappy and unsatisfied single heterosexual Chinese men. A sense of a lack of recognition of their masculinity frustrated them. Jun was a tall and stylishly dressed Chinese man I met at a global meet-up event in Düsseldorf. He had been in Germany for ten years, the first five as a student and the second five as an accountant in a German firm. He had recently purchased an apartment and a secondhand BMW car, but when talking about his emotional life, Jun was dissatisfied. He complained, referring to the women present at the event, "These women only want to date German guys. What do I not have? I have a house, a car, and a good job. I beat most of the people here [at this organized social event]. But no, they still chase after the German guys." I asked why. He said, after a pause, "Because I am ugly." "But you are not!" I said. "I don't understand," he replied, visibly agitated, "what they are looking for." He then talked about how in China he could get whomever he wanted with his *tiaojian* (resource conditions). However, while some single Chinese men I had encountered, such as Jing, returned to China to look for marriage partners, Jun was not ready to resort to that means yet. He was attracted to European girls. At the time of our meeting, he was working to improve his English so he could have the opportunity to move to other countries in Europe where he might have a better chance of finding a partner.

Places also structure migrants' intimate life and their migratory trajectories by conditioning their social life. In both countries where I conducted the fieldwork, the highly skilled migrants share the sentiment that it is hard to develop close friendships with the local residents—a phenomenon also documented in other studies on migrants' friendship networks (Butcher 2009; Scott 2007; Liu-Farrer 2012; Walsh 2014; Hof 2018). Instead, migrants are likely to cluster around co-ethnics (Liu-Farrer 2004, 2012). Among the highly skilled, friendships are often built with other foreigners through work, professional associations, or organized social activities (Ryan and Mulholland 2014; Liu-Farrer 2020). Romantic relationships between migrants from different nationalities frequently develop in such social contexts. When it is time to consider long-term plans, complex decisions around career potentials and linguistic and cultural adaptation will sometimes cause one party to become an onward migrant, as shown in the cases of both Maria and Lingling.

Social Relations

Aside from intimate relationships, the other crucial interpersonal relationship is social, as friendship, community life, and clubs feature importantly in mobile people's relationships with places (Plöger and Becker 2015; Ryan 2015, 2018; Frykman and Mozetič 2019). Whether there are social organizations and communities in a place is extremely important for skilled migrants' emotional well-being. For some migrants, social networks and a group of friends provide emotional comfort and keep negative feelings at bay, even when other aspects of their life might not be entirely satisfactory. It is often these social resources that tie them to the place.

Juan was a Taiwanese woman who had obtained her first master's degree in economics at a German university. She had moved to mainland China when her German boyfriend at the time was transferred there. After the relationship failed, she had to go back to Taiwan because her German visa had expired. Juan was not happy in Taiwan. Not only was she unsatisfied with her work, but she also perceived her return as a failure. She detested the feeling of failing, because she had always been considered inferior to her elder brother. He had been to an elite school and had become a high-earning doctor while she only managed to go to a second-tier college in Taiwan. It was to prove her worth that she decided to study abroad. Aside from her dissatisfaction with herself being in Taiwan, she also missed the social circle in Germany. Most of her friends were in Germany, particularly in Düsseldorf, where there was a big Asian community, and she had been involved in all kinds of social groups. She decided to apply for another master's program in Germany, and found her way back to Düsseldorf. When I interviewed her, she was working for a small family-trading firm near Düsseldorf. Juan had never been satisfied with her work life in Germany because most of the places she worked for had been small firms. When I asked why she loved to live in Germany, especially Düsseldorf, she said, "Look around. In this area (near the main train station), you don't even see Germans." Indeed, when we walked out of a Japanese restaurant on a Tuesday night, somebody from a group of young Asian and half-Asian people in the store next door called out her name. Juan said, "I go out almost six days a week, and I have to set a day to myself to spend alone every week."

While many social groups seem to center around shared ethnic origins or professions, recently many social organizations have emerged that cater to the emotional needs of the globally mobile community. I joined InterNations, one of such organizations, before I headed to Germany. My mailbox has been bombarded by all sorts of social events since I signed up, from cocktail parties to movie-going and philosophical discussions. I went for a Sunday hiking event. It was a cool and sunny late summer day. Over thirty people from more than ten countries gathered at a train station in suburban Düsseldorf. Those who arrived first introduced themselves, and immediately started friendly chats. Conversations continued throughout the over 20-km walk through the beautiful German woods. Many of the people who went on the hike had already met each other at other events. Indeed, two days later, I spotted a few familiar faces when I went to an InterNations evening gathering with over 350 people from seventy different countries attending.

Many globally mobile people join such organizations. I have encountered single people at these events who were there both socializing and looking for potential partners. Even though the latter goal might not be immediately satisfied, the fulfillment of the former quenches the hunger for conviviality and social intimacy. Anita, an Indian woman, explained: "People are social. Well, at least I am. I like such social gatherings. We make friends, build networks, and just have a good time. Yes, I want a family. I want kids. But it is not happening right now. I am quite happy living here because I have friends and many social activities."

It is important to note that looking for communities and participating in such social circles are themselves learned skills. Boris, the Russian engineer featured in the previous section, said migration itself was a process of learning how to deal with emotional needs. After a multinational migratory experience, he and his wife had learned to anticipate the post-migration emotional responses. He pointed out that the first three months after arriving in a new place is like a honeymoon. "You love everything. You go everywhere, like a tourist. And then after that, it comes another six months of the difficult period." It is difficult because migrants often have few social connections in the new environment, and find themselves isolated. "And I think that was the experience: I need to socialize. I need to network ... now. I don't need to wait for three months of honeymoon, [and] another six months of stress. I need to do it now." Although he did not join those organized activities himself upon coming to Germany, his wife signed herself up and participated in many social events. "She now knows how not to wait three months to let the stress period kick in. She immediately connects herself."

Affects and the Physical, Social and Institutional Environment

People's emotions in a place are not only affected by whether or not they can find intimate partners or a group of friends; the physical and social characteristics of the place itself can facilitate or inhibit people's attachment to a place. Indeed, sometimes it is the little physical details in one's environment that elicit positive feelings in people. Walsh (2012), for instance, described the case of a British woman from Newcastle who claimed she felt at home in Dubai because of the feelings invoked by the stretches of beach she walked on, the malls she went shopping in, and the morning sun shining through her bedroom window.

The general built environment and the sociocultural milieu in the place elicit affective responses among the skilled migrants I have interviewed in both Japan and Germany. For example, every migrant attached to Japan praises Japan's security and convenience, and the general civility that Japanese people display. In particular, migrants' narratives center around the specific localities they live in, especially the cities. For example, Tokyo is referred to as a global city that offers a charming and vibrant urban life. Contrary to common perceptions, Tokyo is also affordable, especially in terms of housing—a fact many migrants only realize after they have started living there (Liu-Farrer 2020). My respondents also liked to point out that there were cheap and healthy meals available at any time of the day. The efficient, affordable, and extensive public transportation system impressed all of them. Thus, even though many young skilled migrants complained about other aspects of their life—such as the lack of social interactions with Japanese people, or the irksome Japanese workplace culture—they chose to stay because of the affordability and the excitement of life in Tokyo.

Similarly, Sunil decided to stay in Germany after he moved to Berlin because he found Berlin more international and had a lively social scene. Sunil first came to Germany for a six-month internship in Munich in 2013. He had previously been working for two years in Mumbai for a large tech company. Bored with the sameness of his life in Mumbai, he wanted to go somewhere else and experience other things, which drove him to apply for paid internship programs "in countries he was interested in." These countries ranged from Cambodia to Chile, but also included Germany. That he ultimately came to Germany was merely because it was the first place where he got a suitable internship offer. After a difficult first two months, Sunil started to enjoy his life in Germany and decided to look for a job there. As he felt that there were not enough job opportunities in Munich, he broadened his search to other cities, mainly looking for jobs in Hamburg and Berlin, sending out over one hundred applications. After weekend trips to both Berlin and Hamburg, he decided on a company in Berlin. The job was satisfactory, but Sunil was more passionate about Berlin itself: not only were there many events and leisure opportunities, such as clubbing and sports, but Berlin also had a higher concentration of international people to whom he could easily relate. In particular, Sunil described the tech scene in Berlin as tightly knit. Everybody knew everybody else, which meant that he immediately heard about every new opening. In one way or the other, he was always considering changing jobs, because, according to him, the average "lifespan" of a job in his industry was two years, which made him, having now spent three years at his current company, "a dinosaur." Nonetheless, he did not consider moving to another country in Europe, as Berlin offered enough excitement and ample career opportunities.

Every place also has particular social landscapes shaped by both the localized historical, racial, and ethnic relations, and global power relations and structural inequalities. An individual's socioeconomic standing, racial and national background, gender, and age influence their social status in a given place. Geographic migration is often a process of identity disruption or remake, and, for many people from relatively less developed regions, entails a status drop or suspension. Sometimes, this status differential is reflected in the legal system's different treatments and the inability to transfer one's cultural capital in the labor market. A sense of marginalization and loss of social status foment resentment toward a place and can produce the urge for onward migration. Nohl et al.'s study (2014) describes how a man from North Africa was distressed by his experiences of discriminative treatments in German society. Even after he obtained German citizenship, he had trouble securing his father-in-law's visa to visit Germany. Fed up with his marginal status in Germany, he moved his family to Sweden, hoping that the treatment would be different there.

Finally, places themselves change, and one's affective ties to them also change. Mahir was the oldest interviewee in the project. He had been born and raised in Aleppo (Syria), had studied medicine in Cairo (Egypt), and had moved to Germany after graduation in the 1980s. He retired in 2015. His relationship with Germany changed over the nearly four decades he was in the country. When Mahir first arrived in Germany, he felt welcome because there was a severe shortage of medical staff. He developed his career and became a head surgeon in his local hospital. He obtained German citizenship in 1992, and made friends with local Germans through sports activities. However, things took an adverse turn in the last two decades. He sensed increasing racism in German society, even before the 2015 refugee crisis. He had been supporting refugees from Syria by providing translation services to the local refugee and immigration offices. Once, when he was volunteering, a public servant asked him about his nationality, and he replied, "German." The officer demanded to see his identification document. After examining the I.D., the officer still claimed that carrying a German I.D. did not make him "German." For Mahir, this was a traumatic experience. He had perceived himself as "German" up till that point. After that, he spoke about himself as a "naturalized Syrian." With the recent migration and refugee discourses, he felt a further distancing from Germany, a place he used to consider home. He still enjoyed his quiet life in a small town near Hamburg, but sometimes he "got sick of his life in Germany." When that feeling occurred, he would fly to Greece, to an island where his father-in-law lived.

Conclusion: Affects, Mobilities, and Places

Migration is a process contingent upon a wide range of conditions, from practical incentives to legal structures, and from predictable outcomes to serendipitous encounters. Migratory trajectories are also tangled with an individual's social mobilities and life courses, influenced by imperatives inherent in different mobility logics. This study has used the lens of emotions to investigate the complex causalities. It shows, first, that migration is essentially a choice of places. Migration results in varied feelings toward places, and such emotions as much as practical reasoning affect the further migration decision-making. Negative emotions often trump instrumental concerns, and act as a primary driver for leaving a place. The opposite is true for positive emotions toward a place. Though migrants tend to be conservative about leaving if they are content with the place, instrumental incentives can still pull a person out of the place. Second, this study highlights the centrality of intimate relationships in migratory decisions. Love relationships can pull migrants out of a place or keep them there. A partner's emotions also influence migration decisions because emotions often tangle within a relationship. Finally, this study demonstrates that places can engender affective responses to them and thereby influence people's migratory decisions. Places elicit different emotions because of their social and physical attributes, and the opportunities and constraints they present. In particular, they shape emotions by structuring the patterns and prospects of intimate relationships and social relationships.

This study was conducted in Germany and Japan, two countries located in markedly different geopolitical regions, with different sociocultural and institutional contexts. While the opportunities of migration might vary and directions of trajectories might differ for migrants in these two countries, the key findings of affective drives of migration and emplacement are observed in both countries. It affirms that wherever they are, migrants need intimacy, whether it is romantic or social; they desire recognitions, whether it is through their work or social circle; and they look for places that can provide existential security and at the same time fulfill these different emotional needs.

Gracia Liu-Farrer is Professor of Sociology at the Graduate School of Asia-Pacific Studies, and Director of the Institute of Asian Migrations, Waseda University, Japan. Her research examines immigrants' economic, social, and political practices in Japan, and the spatial and social mobility of students and professional migrants in Asia and Europe. She is the co-editor of the *Routledge Handbook of Asian Migration* (with Brenda Yeoh, 2018) and the author of *Labour Migration from China to Japan: International Students, Transnational Migrants* (Routledge, 2011) and *Immigrant Japan: Mobility and Belonging in an Ethno-nationalist Society* (Cornell University Press, 2020). Her ORCID is: 0000-0003-3241-8703.

NOTES

1. This story is documented in Liu-Farrer 2020: 116.
2. See, for example, Liu-Farrer 2010, and the special issue in *Mobilities* edited by Mai and King (2009).

REFERENCES

Antonsich, Marco. 2010. "Searching for Belonging: An Analytical Framework." *Geography Compass* 4(6): 644–59.

Baldassar, Loretta. 2015. "Guilty Feelings and the Guilt Trip: Emotions and Motivation in Migration and Transnational Caregiving." *Emotion, Space, and Society* 16: 81–89.

Beaverstock, Jonathan V. 2005. "Transnational Elites in the City: British Highly-Skilled Inter-Company Transferees in New York City's Financial District." *Journal of Ethnic and Migration Studies* 31(2): 245–68.

Boccagni, Paolo, and Loretta Baldassar. 2015. "Emotions on the Move: Mapping the Emergent Field of Emotion and Migration." *Emotion, Space, and Society* 16: 73–80.

Bondi, Liz, Joyce Davidson, and Mick Smith. 2016. "Introduction: Geography's 'Emotional Turn.'" In *Emotional Geographies*, ed. Joyce Davidson, Liz Bondi, and Mick Smith, 1–16. London: Routledge.

Butcher, Melissa. 2009. "Ties That Bind: The Strategic Use of Transnational Relationships in Demarcating Identity and Managing Difference." *Journal of Ethnic and Migration Studies* 35(8): 1353–71.

Carling, Jørgen, and Kerilyn Schewel. 2018. "Revisiting Aspiration and Ability in International Migration." *Journal of Ethnic and Migration Studies* 44(6): 945–63.

Chu, Julie Y. 2010 *Cosmologies of Credit: Transnational Mobility and the Politics of Destination in China*. Durham, NC: Duke University Press.

Conradson, David, and Alan Latham. 2007. "The Affective Possibilities of London: Antipodean Transnationals and the Overseas Experience." *Mobilities* 2(2): 231–54.

De Jong, Gordon F., Aphichat Chamratrithirong, and Quynh-Gian Tran. 2002. "For Better, for Worse: Life Satisfaction Consequences of Migration." *International Migration Review* 36(3): 838–63.

Ehrkamp, Patricia. 2005. "Placing Identities: Transnational Practices and Local Attachments of Turkish Immigrants in Germany." *Journal of Ethnic and Migration Studies* 31(2): 345–64.

Farrer, James. 2010. "A Foreign Adventurer's Paradise? Interracial Sexuality and Alien Sexual Capital in Reform Era Shanghai." *Sexualities* 13(1): 69–95.

———. 2019. *International Migrants in China's Global City: The New Shanghailanders*. London: Routledge.

Favell, Adrian. 2008. *Eurostars and Eurocities: Free Movement and Mobility in an Integrating Europe*. Hoboken, NJ: Wiley-Blackwell.

Favell, Adrian, Ettore Recchi, Theresa Kuhn, Janne Solgaard Jensen, and John Klein. 2011. "State of the Art Report." EUCROSS Working Paper 1. *EUCROSS*. Retrieved 4 December 2020 from http://www.eucross.eu/eucross/images/docs/eucross_d2_2_state_of_the_art.pdf

Fong, Vanessa L. 2011. *Paradise Redefined: Transnational Chinese Students and the Quest for Flexible Citizenship in the Developed World*. Stanford, CA: Stanford University Press.

Frykman, Maja Povrzanović, and Katarina Mozetič. 2019. "The Importance of Friends: Social Life Challenges for Foreign Physicians in Southern Sweden." *Community, Work & Family* 23(4): 385–400.

Gregg, Melissa, and Gregory J. Seigworth. 2010. *The Affect Theory Reader*. Durham, NC: Duke University Press.
Ho, Elaine Lynn-Ee. 2006. "Negotiating Belonging and Perceptions of Citizenship in a Transnational World: Singapore, a Cosmopolis?" *Social & Cultural Geography* 7(3): 385–401.
———. 2009. "Constituting Citizenship through the Emotions: Singaporean Transmigrants in London." *Annals of the Association of American Geographers* 99(4): 788–804.
———. 2011. "Migration Trajectories of 'Highly Skilled' Middling Transnationals: Singaporean Transmigrants in London." *Population, Space and Place* 17(1): 116–29.
Hof, Helena. 2018. "'Worklife Pathways' to Singapore and Japan: Gender and Racial Dynamics in Europeans' Mobility to Asia." *Social Science Japan Journal* 21(1): 45–65.
———. 2019. "The Eurostars Go Global: Young Europeans' Migration to Asia for Distinction and Alternative Life Paths." *Mobilities* 14(6): 923–39.
Ivlevs, Artjoms. 2015. "Happy Moves? Assessing the Link between Life Satisfaction and Emigration Intentions." *Kyklos* 68(3): 335–56.
Knight, John, and Ramani Gunatilaka. 2010. "Great Expectations? The Subjective Wellbeing of Rural-Urban Migrants in China." *World Development* 38(1): 113–24.
Liu-Farrer, Gracia. 2004. "The Chinese Social Dance Party in Tokyo: Identity and Status in an Immigrant Leisure Subculture." *Journal of Contemporary Ethnography* 33(6): 651–74.
———. 2010. "The Absent Spouses: Gender, Sex, Race and the Extramarital Sexuality among Chinese Migrants in Japan." *Sexualities* 13(1): 97–121.
———. 2011. *Labor Migration from China to Japan: International Students, Transnational Migrants*. London: Routledge.
———. 2012. "Becoming New Overseas Chinese: Transnational Practices and Identity Construction among the Chinese Migrants in Japan." In *Living Intersections: Transnational Migrant Identifications in Asia*, ed. Caroline Plüs and Chan Kwok-bun, 167–90. Dordrecht: Springer.
———. 2014. "Tied to the Family, Bound to the Labor Market: Understanding Chinese Student Mobility in Japan." In *The Emergence of International Dimensions in East Asian Higher Education*, ed. Akiyoshi Yonezawa, Yuto Kitamura, Arthur Meerman, and Kazuo Kuroda, 185–206. Dordrecht: Springer.
———. 2020. *Immigrant Japan: Mobility and Belonging in an Ethno-nationalist Society*. Ithaca, NY: Cornell University Press.
Mai, Nicola, and Russell King. 2009. "Love, Sexuality and Migration: Mapping the Issue(s)." *Mobilities* 4(3): 295–307.
Marinelli, Elisabetta. 2011. "Graduate Migration in Italy: Lifestyle or Necessity?" 51st Congress of the European Regional Science Association: "New Challenges for European Regions and Urban Areas in a Globalised World," Barcelona, Spain, 30 August – 3 September 2011. Retrieved 5 December 2020 from http://hdl.handle.net/10419/120333.
Massey, Doreen. 1994. "Double Articulation: A Place in the World." In *Displacements: Cultural Identities in Question*, ed. Angelika Bammer, 110–22. Bloomington: Indiana University Press.

Millar, Jane, and John Salt. 2008. "Portfolios of Mobility: The Movement of Expertise in Transnational Corporations in Two Sectors—Aerospace and Extractive Industries." *Global Networks* 8(1): 25–50.

Nohl, Arnd-Michael, Karin Schittenhelm, Oliver Schmidtke, and Anja Weiß. 2014. *Work in Transition: Cultural Capital and Highly Skilled Migrants' Passages into the Labour Market*. Toronto: University of Toronto Press.

Nowok, Beata, Martin Van Ham, Alan M. Findlay, and Vernon Gayle. 2013. "Does Migration Make You Happy? A Longitudinal Study of Internal Migration and Subjective Well-Being." *Environment and Planning A: Economy and Space* 45(4): 986–1002.

Oishi, Nana. 2012. "The Limits of Immigration Policies." *American Behavioral Scientist* 56(8): 1080–1100.

Plöger, Jörg, and Anna Becker. 2015. "Social Networks and Local Incorporation: Grounding High-Skilled Migrants in Two German Cities." *Journal of Ethnic and Migration Studies* 41(10): 1517–35.

Polgreen, Linnea A., and Nicole B. Simpson. 2011. "Happiness and International Migration." *Journal of Happiness Studies* 12(5): 819–40.

Russell, James. A. 2003. 'Core Affect and the Psychological Construction of Emotion'. *Psychological Review* 110(1): 145–72.

Ryan, Louise, and Jon Mulholland. 2014. "Trading Places: French Highly Skilled Migrants Negotiating Mobility and Emplacement in London." *Journal of Ethnic and Migration Studies* 40(4): 584–600.

———. 2015. "Friendship-Making: Exploring Network Formations through the Narratives of Irish Highly Qualified Migrants in Britain." *Journal of Ethnic and Migration Studies* 41(10): 1664–83.

———. 2018. "Differentiated Embedding: Polish Migrants in London Negotiating Belonging Over Time." *Journal of Ethnic and Migration Studies* 44(2): 233–51.

Scott, Sam. 2007. "The Community Morphology of Skilled Migration: The Changing Role of Voluntary and Community Organisations (VCOs) in the Grounding of British Migrant Identities in Paris (France)." *Geoforum* 38(4): 1105–29.

Thomson, Alistair. 2005. "My Wayward Heart: Homesickness, Longing and the Return of British Post-War Immigrants from Australia." In *Emigrant Homecomings: The Return Movement of Emigrants 1600–2000*, ed. Marjory Harper, 105–30. Manchester: Manchester University Press.

Tseng, Yen-Fen. 2011. "Shanghai Rush: Skilled Migrants in a Fantasy City." *Journal of Ethnic and Migration Studies* 37(5): 765–84.

———. 2020. "Becoming Global Talent? Taiwanese White-Collar Migrants in Japan." *Journal of Ethnic and Migration Studies* 47(2): 1–17. doi: 10.1080/1369183X.2020.1731986.

Walsh, Katie. 2006. "'Dad Says I'm Tied to a Shooting Star!' Grounding (Research On) British Expatriate Belonging." *Area* 38(3): 268–78.

———. 2007. "'It Got Very Debauched, Very Dubai!' Heterosexual Intimacy amongst Single British Expatriates." *Social & Cultural Geography* 8(4): 507–33.

———. 2012. "Emotion and Migration: British Transnationals in Dubai." *Environment and Planning D: Society and Space* 30(1): 43–59.

———. 2014. "British Transnational (Be)longing: Emplacement in the Life of Skilled Migrants in Dubai." In *Migrant Professionals in the City*, ed. Lars Meier, 232–49. London: Routledge.

Waters, Johanna, Rachel Brooks, and Helena Pimlott-Wilson. 2011. "Youthful Escapes? British Students, Overseas Education and the Pursuit of Happiness." *Social & Cultural Geography* 12(5): 455–69.

Weber, Max. 1978. "The Nature of Social Action." In *Weber: Selections in Translation*, ed. Walter Garrison Runciman, 7–32. Cambridge: Cambridge University Press.

CHAPTER 6

Affects, Aspirations, and the Transformation of Personhood
A Case of Japanese-Pakistani Marriages through a Generational Lens

Masako Kudo

Introduction

Drawing on longitudinal research among Japanese-Pakistani families, this chapter explores how the entanglements of affects and multifaceted aspirations shape and are shaped by their trajectories of family making. Through a generational lens, it illuminates how such entanglements entwine with children's mobility, and how entanglements forge and transform personhood across time and space.

Scholarly works on marriage migration have documented the challenges and struggles of couples across state frontiers. In Asian contexts, a pioneering study by Constable (2005) and subsequent endeavors have documented the complex dynamics involved in migrant spouses' socioeconomic positionings, agency, transnationalism, and citizenship. Another emerging area of research on marriage migration is the "emotional turn" (Liu-Farrer and Yeoh

2018: 10). Not only has increased attention been directed to the role that emotions play in mobility across state frontiers, but the burgeoning literature has highlighted how emotions are entangled with materiality (Andrikopoulos 2019; Bloch 2011; Groes and Fernandez 2018). This advance, particularly in the context of marriages between citizens from the Global North and Global South, expands the traditional understanding of the importance of economic gains for immigrant spouses from the Global South by incorporating affect and emotion in the formation and development of intimate ties. Cole and Groes capture the complex dynamics involved in the entanglement between affects and materiality through a framework of "affective circuits." Their term refers to social (re)formations that emerge from the myriad exchanges of goods, money, people, ideas, images, and emotions. They note that the transactions that constitute "affective circuits" often combine "material and emotive elements simultaneously such that love, obligation, and jealousy become entangled with the circulation of money, consumer goods, ideas, and information" (Cole and Groes 2016: 8).

Importantly, a wide range of actors that constitute affective circuits may also regulate and block flows of exchange, whereby migrants and their families negotiate and rework intimate ties and produce new forms of belonging and personhood (Cole and Groes 2016: 14–15). Their nuanced conceptualization of intimacy reveals the creative tension existing in kinship relationships. More recently, Andrikopoulos and Duyvendak (2020) have drawn attention not only to solidarity, reciprocity, and trust among kin but also to the exploitation and secrecy that unveil the dynamics and elasticity of kinship relations in the contexts of migration and mobility.

Building on this research, this chapter presents the complexity of Japanese-Pakistani family trajectories through an analysis of their evolving transactions across borders.[1] In so doing, I consider the interconnectedness or entanglement of geographical, temporal, social, intimate, educational, and class (im)mobilities (Fresnoza-Flot and Nagasaka 2015), which may bring unintended consequences to the lives of their children.

Further, this chapter approaches the complexity of transnational family making by examining the asymmetrical power and emotional friction within the family, which are shaped by the intersection of gender, generation, and larger social forces such as global inequalities. As feminist scholars have pointed out, the family is not a unitary entity (Yuval-Davis 1997). Observing how gender and other intersecting factors shaped asymmetric power relationships within the family and beyond, migration scholars have documented diverse ways in which immigrant wives struggled and responded to the inequalities and predicament that they faced both within the family and vis-à-vis nation-states (Faier 2009; N. Suzuki 2017; Yeoh, Chee, and Vu 2013). In this chapter, I illuminate the dynamics of transnational family making through a generational lens by focusing on the struggles and predicaments of Japanese wives and their children. The experiences of the citizen spouses and their children in South-North marriages are under-researched except for a few studies (López 2015; N. Suzuki 2015). Through the exploration, I investigate specific ways in which gender, class, and generation interact in this type of South-North marriage. By so doing, I unveil the complex entanglements between affects, aspirations, and different forms of mobilities, through which new forms of intimate relationships and personhood emerge.

Research Methodology and Participants

The data used in this chapter came from two sets of interviews from my multi-sited and longitudinal research following Japanese-Pakistani couples and their children. The first set of interviews, which I started to collect in 1998, were with forty Japanese wives. I also conducted participant observation at women's congregations at mosques and gatherings in more informal settings such as their homes. Regarding their educational backgrounds, one finished her education after secondary school at the age of fifteen, ten were high school educated, eleven continued their studies at vocational college, four at junior college [*tanki daigaku*], nine at university, and one completed a postgraduate degree. These data were not obtained in the remaining four cases. Twenty-eight husbands had started businesses by the early 2000s; twenty-seven were involved in used-car businesses.

The second set of interviews, conducted since 2016, involved thirty-five Japanese-Pakistani young adults between eighteen and thirty years old, of whom twenty-three were female. They came from twenty-four families, twelve of which I already knew from my previous research. In seven of the twenty-four families, couples were legally divorced in Japan, but the couple in one of the families maintained a de facto marriage while the husband married a second wife who joined him from abroad. In another family, the couple maintained their legal marriage in Japan while the husband married a second wife, who, after the wedding, continued to reside in Pakistan. In terms of nationality, the amendment of the Nationality Law in 1984 granted citizenship to children born to Japanese mothers and non-Japanese fathers. Three participants from the same family recently acquired citizenship in the UK, where they resided. The remaining thirty-two participants held Japanese nationality, twenty-two of whom have held no other nationality. Seven of the children once held Pakistani citizenship but renounced it, mainly for practical reasons—it is easier to cross national borders with a Japanese passport than a Pakistani passport.[2]

The children's migratory trajectories through high school graduation varied. Nine received education through high school solely in Japan. Of the remaining twenty-six respondents, ten studied both in Japan and other countries, including Pakistan. The other sixteen were mostly educated abroad—ten in Pakistan and six in other countries. At the time of their first interviews, eighteen were based in Japan, six in Pakistan, five in the UAE, four in the UK, one in Thailand, and one in New Zealand. In many cases, their countries of residence (and those of the Japanese women married to Pakistani men) changed during my study, reflecting the transnational nature of family making. In terms of the children's occupations, at the time of the last interviews, twenty were students, of whom fifteen were university students. Six were employed by private companies and engaged in non-manual jobs. Two were teachers, and one was a civil servant on a short-term contract. The remaining six had other occupations, including medical professions and fashion models. To maintain the anonymity of the research participants, I use pseudonyms,[3] and some personal data have been changed.

Japanese-Pakistani Marriages: A Union Tangled with Law, Economy, and Religion

The number of Japanese nationals marrying foreigners rose sharply during the 1980s, and this trend continued until 2006. While this period was marked by an increase in the number of Japanese men marrying women from less economically developed countries,[4] the same post-1980s statistics show a significant change in the patterns of Japanese women marrying foreign men (Ministry of Health, Labour and Welfare 2020). While Americans and Koreans continue to be a large proportion of the foreign spouses of Japanese women (79.1 percent in 1980 and 50.3 percent in 2000), the range of nationalities has become more diverse, reflecting, among other factors, an increased level of intimate encounters between Japanese women and male migrants seeking economic opportunities in Japan. The Japanese economy boomed in the late 1980s, and the 1985 Plaza Accord resulted in a sharp rise in the yen, which attracted a stream of unskilled labor from the Global South to fill Japanese industry's acute labor shortages. A significant migration trend during this period was a sharp increase in the entry of Pakistanis in the late 1980s. The then existing reciprocal visa exemption agreement between Japan and Pakistan was a major factor in this increase. Before the mutual agreement was suspended in 1989, Pakistani nationals could obtain short-term visas on entry to Japan. Pakistani migrants to Japan were predominantly male and hailed from the middle or lower-middle classes in cities such as Karachi and Lahore. The majority entered relatively low-skilled manual labor occupations in Japan, work that they would not normally undertake in Pakistan. With a few exceptions,[5] the Japanese government did not grant visas to what they deemed low-skilled or unskilled labor. Under such circumstances, marrying Japanese nationals offered Pakistani migrants one of the few options to continue to live and work in Japan.[6]

Young Pakistani men, however, did not move to Japan and marry Japanese citizens purely for economic reasons. My interviews with Japanese wives indicate that their husbands had come to Japan not only to make money but also to see different worlds or to escape from marriages arranged by their families. After arriving in Japan, Pakistani men met their prospective partners in workplaces, restaurants, in the street or other public spaces, and through the personal introduction of mutual friends and acquaintances.

Interviews with wives suggest two main motives for marrying Pakistani men. First, the women saw in their prospective husbands a new type of masculinity. Many women remarked that they were attracted to their prospective husbands because they look after their families in Pakistan, not only economically but also by being emotionally involved in family relationships. They presented these women with an alternative to typical Japanese husbands, who work long hours as the breadwinners, but without being much involved in family life. Second, by marrying Pakistani husbands, they saw the possibilities of being exposed to cultures and values that were novel to them. Pakistani men's complex motives for crossing national borders, and Japanese women's desires for alternative forms of partnership, were among the elements that led to their decisions to marry after their intimate encounters during the late 1980s and 1990s.

Japanese women and their Pakistani husbands had to overcome multiple barriers. First, Pakistani men's families had ambivalent attitudes toward them marrying Japanese women. On the one hand, some families opposed the marriages because, violating Pakistani norms, they were not arranged marriages. Also, families perceived Japanese women, raised in non-Islamic environments, as sexually loose, even immoral. On the other hand, sending a member of the family to the rich Global North offered an invaluable resource for the economic survival of the extended family. As a result, some families reluctantly accepted the marriage, although they were not entirely satisfied with the match. A Japanese wife, Sadia, who married in the early 1990s, shared:

> When I met my husband, Shahid, I was working in the apparel industry after graduating from a vocational college. I fell in love with Shahid but was not sure if I could cope with all the problems that I would face if I

married him. My parents were extremely worried. I decided to visit his family in Pakistan on my own (as Shahid was overstaying his visa and could not leave Japan) to see if I could build a family with him. When I met my father-in-law, I asked him if he would allow our marriage. He asked me in simple English if I liked Pakistan and whether I loved his son. I said yes and he allowed us to marry. At this time, Shahid's paternal grandfather was still alive, and he had all the power to decide who would marry whom within the family. Before Shahid left Pakistan for Japan, he had asked his grandfather if he could choose his marriage partner by himself, because he did not want his marriage arranged. His grandfather had given Shahid his permission. This is why his relatives could not object to his marriage openly, although many of them complained, asking why Shahid should marry somebody outside the family, let alone a foreign woman.

On her first visit to Pakistan, she brought *jahez* (dowry) in the form of money. Shahid's parents reciprocated with gifts that filled her suitcase on her way back to Japan. Interestingly, such traditional Pakistani marital transactions did not take place among most of my sample. Aisha, another Japanese wife, remarked that her husband's family must have been satisfied that he could get a visa to Japan by marrying her.

In many cases, Japanese wives also met with strong opposition from within their own families and friends, largely due to the negative image of "foreign workers" from other Asian countries. In the late 1980s, the number of male migrants who were apprehended for working illegally rose sharply. Pakistanis and Bangladeshis constituted a significant segment of that group. This led to a Japanese government crackdown, which has been repeated since then (E. Suzuki 2009: 80–85). The term "foreign workers" therefore conjured images of illegality in public discourse.

Pakistani migrants also suffered from racial discrimination. When I was visiting the home of a Japanese-Pakistani couple, the Japanese wife, Ameena, reported that her parents had fiercely objected to their marriage, so their marriage was almost like eloping. Their marriage had caused a serious family feud in Pakistan too as her husband had had a fiancée within his extended kin, although her husband-to-be's parents finally agreed to their marriage. Listening to our conversation, Ameena's husband, Naeem, added: "For us foreigners to economically survive in Japan, we have to do a dirty and physically strenuous job with lower wages than our Japanese workmates. In addition, we are discriminated against because of the color of [our] skin, while those from America and Europe are given a privileged status." Japanese women who married Pakistani migrants therefore risked being social pariahs and experiencing downward social mobility. The couples suffered discrimination in various aspects of their lives, including housing and work. Moreover, the opposition from wives' natal families meant a loss of practical and moral support in overcoming the structural inequalities the couples faced early in their marriages.

State control of binational marriages affected couples' lives adversely. Although a visa status for a foreign spouse ("Spouse or Child of Japanese National") was created in 1982, removing the overt form of gender inequality that had existed earlier, the new legal provision had its limitations (Kobayashi 2009).[7] For the purpose of preventing "sham marriages," immigration policies made it increasingly difficult for those who overstayed their visas to be granted a spousal visa.[8] Many of the women in my study recalled long and painful processes for obtaining a spousal visa for their Pakistani husbands, most of whom had overstayed and were working without permission at the time of marriage. While marriages between Japanese citizen men and women from the Global South are tolerated because they contribute to the reproduction of the nation-state in the face of a population decline, the legitimacy of citizen women marrying men from the Global South is scrutinized in a more negative light, because not only their migrant husbands but also the women and their children tended to be regarded as outside of the Japanese nation.[9]

State regulations over binational marriages affected couples' lives in another way. Japanese women had to become Muslim for foreign husbands to obtain a spousal visa. Couples must certify that they have been married in accordance with the laws of both countries. Pakistan, an Islamic republic, requires the submission of a religious marriage contract, *nikah nama*, under Muslim family laws.[10] Prior to signing this contract, most women in my sample converted to Islam because, according to the Muslim law of Pakistan, Muslim men can only marry Muslims or "people of the Book," meaning generally Christians and Jews.[11] This is why at the time of conversion many Japanese wives in my sample had considered themselves "paper Muslims," because they only converted to fulfill the legal requirements to register their marriages. At later stages of their lives, some underwent religious journeys, becoming practicing Muslims. Hence, as Fernandez (2013) points out, state intervention brought unintended consequences to the lives of binational couples.

Conversion to Islam had important implications in these women's lives. First, their conversions helped moralize the marriages in the eyes of Pakistani families, who saw wives from non-Islamic countries as morally inferior. This meant that Japanese wives were expected by their husbands, extended kin, and the moral community formed by the Pakistani diaspora in Japan and beyond, to conform to an ideal Muslim femininity. Second, the Islamic gatherings organized in Tokyo and surrounding areas formed a network of mutual assistance among Japanese women facing similar challenges marrying Pakistani men. Further, there was a tendency among Japanese wives who congregated at Islamic gatherings to develop their religious identities based on a discourse they identified as "true Islam." By "true Islam," the women meant the religious faith and practices that follow the scriptures of the Qur'an or the hadith,[12] not blindly following the culture of Pakistan. A discourse on true Islam allowed Japanese women to contest and negotiate the ideal Muslim femininity their husbands and in-laws expected. For example, one woman told me:

> Yesterday, when my husband and I were going out to see a Muslim couple, he wanted me to wear *shalwar qameez* (a long tunic and trousers worn in Pakistan). I refused his request, protesting that, according to the Qur'an, it is enough if I wear modest Western clothing that covers my arms and legs. My husband was not happy but could say no more.

As her narrative exemplifies, the women argued that their husbands' expectations were based on the culture of Pakistan rather than the teachings of true Islam. Further, building an identity as Muslims enabled them to draw a boundary between themselves as "Japanese Muslims" and non-Muslim Japanese society. Thus, becoming Muslim became a resource to craft their new subjectivities after marrying Pakistani migrants in Japan.

Creating Affective Circuits across Borders

The challenges couples faced in the early stages of marriage created "affective circuits" (Cole and Groes 2016) through which money, kin, and service (such as care) are exchanged across national borders. First, some couples relocated to Pakistan so that husbands who had overstayed their visas could arrange for spousal visas from there. Second, after the husband's legal status was stabilized, they could travel not only to Pakistan but also to other countries to expand their business opportunities. Pakistani men who married Japanese women often started their own businesses. The majority of Pakistani husbands in my sample started businesses exporting used cars to Pakistan, the UAE, Russia, Chile, and other countries. A shift from factory workers to transnational entrepreneurs was a way to overcome their marginality in the domestic labor market and continue remitting money to their extended families in Pakistan while providing for their families in Japan. The involvement of Japanese wives in newly established businesses was indispensable in several ways, including dealing with business documents in Japanese and applying for visas for husbands' male kin to join them in Japan so that they could help the family businesses or otherwise work and send remittances to extended families in Pakistan.

Wives' parents tended to soften attitudes as grandchildren appeared, even serving as guarantors for couples' businesses. Sana, a woman whose husband started a business, shared that he first resisted relying on her parents' help because he felt that it would undermine his male authority. She persuaded her husband to accept her parents' help as it was vital for him to establish his business. To overcome structural inequality within Japan, couples had to negotiate gender ideals and power balances when they mobilized assistance from wives' kin.

Third, care exchange across borders took place, marking an early stage in care trajectories (Kofman 2012). This took several different forms. For example, Shazia, a Japanese wife, relocated with her infant children to her husband's extended family in Pakistan partly because she could get child-care support, whereas in Japan she had no close kin to help. In some cases, a husband's female kin travelled to Japan to provide the short-term care couples needed, while in Japanese society it is more common that the wife's family provides care at the time of childbirth. The Japanese women I interviewed explained that because female kin from Pakistan could cook Pakistani food for their husbands, kin visits significantly reduced the chores wives had to perform after having a new child. Interestingly, care was not always provided by women. A Pakistani man I met during my research in Pakistan recalled travelling to Japan to look after the two children of his brother and his Japanese wife, who could not care for them. He remembered being unable to turn over in bed as both children wanted to hold his hands when they slept. This suggests that the sexual division of labor can be rearranged when kin cross borders.

As wives' parents in Japan aged, the next phase of care arrangements emerged. For example, a Japanese woman who relocated to Pakistan with her children—a move that I describe in the next section—returned to Japan for several months to care for her parents. This was only possible because she could leave her children in the care of the extended family in Pakistan (Kudo 2017). In the following sections, I investigate how the entanglements of affect and multifaceted aspirations that were observed early in marriage shifted as life cycles progressed, shaping the evolution of affective circuits across time and space.

The Emergence of Transnationally Split Families

When children reached school age, different circuit patterns emerged, with Japanese wives and their children migrating abroad while their Pakistani husbands remained in Japan to run businesses. Among the forty Japanese wives I interviewed, thirteen relocated to Pakistan with their children, among whom three relocated again to other countries at a later life stage.

One woman relocated from Japan to another country. In three other cases, the wives remained in Japan and sent the children to extended families in Pakistan. In the remaining twenty-three cases, families remained in Japan. The wives and children who moved to Pakistan usually joined their extended families, while those who migrated to other countries formed female-headed households. In the latter cases, destination countries included the UAE and New Zealand, where husbands had established business links to export used cars from Japan.

Multifaceted aspirations and desires triggered this type of transnationally split family. First, many of the women I interviewed emphasized that their husbands strongly wished their children to be raised in Islamic environments. What husbands meant by "Islamic education" was highly gendered, often synonymous with protecting their daughters' sexual purity. Saki, a Japanese wife, stated that her husband once told her that he had sleepless nights fearing that his five-year-old daughter would be negatively influenced in Japan, which he saw as sexually corrupt. Behind the husbands' strong desire to "protect their daughters" was the religio-cultural norm of *parda* (meaning "a curtain," referring to the sexual segregation practiced widely in South Asia), according to which females have to be separated both physically and symbolically (by wearing a veil) from unrelated males. This gender norm is integral to the notion of family honor. The norm of *parda* is most strictly adhered to by the lower-middle- and middle-class families in urban Pakistan, from where many of the husbands hail, as they try to differentiate their status from the lower strata of the society by doing so. Fatima, the daughter of a Japanese-Pakistani couple, was raised in Pakistan and shared that her paternal kin regarded her as morally superior to her female cousin who had been brought up in the United States, a country they considered sexually corrupt.

Second, splitting families between Japan and Pakistan had economic implications. If Japanese wives and children lived in Pakistan, families could maximize the economic gap between the Global North and Global South, and consequently raise the living standards of the extended families. Furthermore, couples could send their children to prestigious private schools in urban Pakistan that offer English-language education. In Japan, on the other hand, international schools were too costly for many of the couples. Investing in the education of the next generation reflected the aspirations of Pakistani men and their families to achieve upward social mobility.

When Japanese mothers and children relocated to a third country, the couples could combine used-car export businesses, giving their children English-language education, and, where possible, an Islamic education.[13] Japanese wives considered it easier to pursue their mothering roles in these countries, which had more amenable climates and better functioning infrastructures than Pakistan. The women could also be freed from the politics of the extended families in Pakistan. However, those who relocated to the UAE, the UK, or New Zealand faced challenges, including strict immigration controls and financial strains, which could prevent families from visiting each other as frequently as they wished. They could also suffer from a lack of child-care support, and possible discrimination against Asians and/or Muslims.

Dynamics of the Power Shaping Family Trajectories

Japanese women did not always share their husbands' desires to educate their children in Islamic environments, and it often took a long time for them to decide to relocate abroad, particularly to Pakistan, which was their most common destination. Power dynamics between couples shaped family migratory trajectories.

Most Japanese wives in my sample left their full-time jobs after they had children. Not only was this due to husbands' cultural-religious gender norms, but the change also reflected gender norms in Japan and the marginality of married Japanese women with young children in the mainstream labor market (Tamiya 2020). Whereas many wives became involved in their husbands' businesses, it did not necessarily empower women economically because it meant that wives would lose their economic autonomy vis-à-vis their husbands.

The second factor affecting family power dynamics was changes in a husband's visa status in Japan. Husbands in my sample, most of whom had already overstayed their visas at the time of their marriages, relied on their Japanese wives to obtain spousal visas. Most husbands managed to obtain permanent residency, and some even achieved Japanese citizenship. With the securing of their legal status in Japan as well as a decrease in their wives' economic power, power dynamics shifted from wives to husbands. Further, insufficient state welfare support for single mothers (Tamiya 2020) makes it difficult for women to divorce.[14]

Shifting power dynamics affect whether Japanese wives relocate to Pakistan. Kana, a Japanese wife who moved to Pakistan, remarked: "I came here as I had no other options." Having lived in Pakistan before (for her husband to obtain a visa from the Japanese Embassy in Pakistan), she knew of various challenges that she would have to face, but she acceded to her husband's strong desire to educate her children in Pakistan, mainly because she did not have sufficient economic means to support herself and her children if she were to divorce him. Her case illustrates an uneven distribution of power within the complex patterns of the power geometry of time-space compression (Kudo 2017). While some can initiate movements across national borders, others are not "in charge" of the process, despite much physical moving (Massey 1993: 61–63).

Not only did the power balance between couples shape their migratory trajectories, but geographical mobility across borders brought a new turn in power dynamics between couples. As Ong (1999: 20–21) and Liu-Farrer (2018: 134) point out, mobility across national boundaries may confine women to caring roles, reinforcing gender norms. After relocating to Pakistan or other countries, the Japanese women's roles became limited to caring for their families, and for children especially. The possibility of engaging in economic activities abroad was constrained by multiple factors, including women's immigration status in the destination country, the religio-cultural practice of women's seclusion (*parda*), and lack of language skills and social capital.

The position of Japanese wives within transnationally split families was, however, ambiguous, which indicates complex relationships between women's geographical mobility and empowerment (Liu-Farrer and Yeoh 2018: 5). On the one hand, to carry out everyday tasks related to maternal roles in Pakistan, Japanese women had to rely on male kin in extended families due to the women's seclusion, lack of linguistic skills, and knowledge about Pakistani society. Dependence on male kin further weakened their position within the household, where the power balance was already shaped by gender and seniority. On the other hand, wives could exert a degree of power because they came from the Global North. Women's positions within the household were partly determined by how much they and their husbands had contributed to the household economy (Kudo 2017). Hiromi, a Japanese wife, returned to Japan with her children to be reunited with her husband after struggling to settle in Pakistan. Her husband was not happy about her decision but finally agreed to raise their children in Japan because, among other reasons, her income, which she would earn by working in a local supermarket, would contribute significantly to remittances to Pakistan. She stated, "My daughters and I would have been sent back to Pakistan if my husband were economically successful." Her husband's business had been hit hard by the stagnating economy in Japan, while living costs in Pakistan were rising sharply. Hiromi's case illustrates the dynamics of patriarchal bargaining (Kandiyoti 1988), which shape the trajectories of transnationally split families.

Lodged in the changing power dynamics within the family, the Japanese women negotiated their and their children's positions by employing various mothering techniques (Fresnoza-Flot 2018). Some wives distanced themselves from relatives in Pakistan after they relocated there. A Japanese woman, Saima, who resided in Pakistan confided that she deliberately did not learn Urdu, a language her husband's family spoke, to avoid extended family politics. Her speaking only Japanese at home also allowed her children to maintain their ability to speak Japanese. Another Japanese wife, Naira, who sent her daughters to the extended family in Pakistan, remarked that she refused expensive gifts from her husband's kin to her daughters because she feared they might lead to expectations that they could arrange her daughters' marriages to cousins in Pakistan. Thus, some Japanese wives tried to keep their family life intact while sometimes blocking the flow of goods between kin.

Evolving Trajectories of Transnational Families

Educational Mobility

In the cases of the transnationally split families described earlier, the next phase of migratory trajectories began when the children moved to another location for tertiary education or to start a career. This created new dynamics in family migratory trajectories.

Many who had been raised abroad wished to study in an English-speaking country such as the UK or Canada. As the children of Japanese-Pakistani marriages held Japanese nationality, it was relatively easier for them to obtain student visas to the West than it was for their Pakistani national peers. The majority, however, ended up studying at a university that offered its courses in English, either in Japan or in other non-Western countries in Southeast Asia or Eastern Europe. Some who had been raised in Pakistan or the UAE chose branches of Western universities in those countries—in many cases, this was primarily due to financial and familial circumstances. The reasons were also gendered. Asked why she chose to study in Pakistan, Saera responded that her father had given her no choice. He did not want her to live in a foreign country on her own due to gender norms, but her brothers could do so.

Further, while economic constraints were a major reason behind their return to Japan, the move could not be explained entirely by individual rational choices taken in the context of economic inequalities. Family circumstances and emotions arising from them also shaped the choices of where to study and work. Basit's case illustrates this well. He was accepted at a university in the UK after finishing high school in Karachi. He changed his mind, however, and decided to study at a university in Japan instead. While it was partially because of the family's financial difficulties, he made this decision also because of the emotions invoked by childhood memories of care (Cole and Groes 2016: 8). He felt deeply indebted to his mother, who made sacrifices to raise him and his siblings in Pakistan despite difficult family politics and without much help from his father, who was mostly in Japan. He and his mother were unable to visit Japan for most of his teens largely due to family circumstances. The feelings of immobility caused frustration and resentment. Gender-based inequality within the family also influenced his decision to study in Japan because his mother and sisters could only move back to Japan if he went there. His educational mobility created a way to bring his mother and sisters back to Japan and to rebuild the family, which had been split across borders. His case suggests that holding Japanese citizenship and achieving English competency did not necessarily mean that the children headed to the West, which was the most obvious sign of upward social class mobility in postcolonial Pakistan. It exemplifies a complex entanglement between geographical (im)mobility and other forms of mobilities, such as educational and intimate.

Divorce and Polygamy

Over the last decade, an increase in divorce and polygamy added a new dimension to family trajectories. Overall patterns of divorce and polygamy among Muslim minorities are complex and diverse due to plural legal systems (Charsley and Liversage 2012; Qureshi 2016). The divorces and polygamy that I witnessed mainly fell into three patterns. In the first, the legally divorced couples cut their marriage ties altogether. In all such cases except for one, the Japanese wives took sole custody of their children, whereas in the other two patterns, the husbands appear to maintain, to varying degrees, their moral and economic involvement in the lives of the Japanese wives and children.

In the second pattern, Japanese-Pakistani couples were legally divorced in Japan but kept their religious marriage contracts, *nikah*. In some of those cases, the husband brought a second wife to Japan on a spousal visa, while also maintaining a de facto marriage relationship with his Japanese wife. In two cases, the second marriage occurred when the husband met another woman in a third country to which he had travelled for his used-car exporting business.

In the third pattern, the couple remained legally and religiously married in Japan but the husband took a second wife, either in Pakistan or in another country outside Japan, forming transnational polygamous families.[15] In one case, the second wife, a Pakistani, lived in Pakistan and cared for the husband's parents, suggesting the possibility that polygamy fills the needs of the extended family in Pakistan. Such cases indicate that polygamy occurs not necessarily as a traditional form of marriage in the sending country but as a new marriage practice to respond to transnational contexts (Charsley and Liversage 2012).

From the perspective of Japanese wives, how they respond to their polygamous arrangements differs, depending on individual circumstances. While some wives cut de facto marital ties with husbands who took second wives, others accepted polygamy for complex reasons. Although I have not collected sufficient data to present the complexity, informal conversations that I have had with Japanese wives suggest that shifting power dynamics lie behind accepting polygamy. In addition to the stabilization of a husband's legal status in Japan, the precarious situation of single mothers in Japan in terms of work, care, and welfare (Ezawa and Fujiwara 2005; Tamiya 2020) appear to discourage women from divorcing. Further, some women who shared their marital problems with me felt that because they had married Pakistani men, despite strong opposition from their Japanese families, the women should not rely on Japanese kin support in times of marital crisis. This sense of "self-responsibility" (*jiko sekinin*) can also hinder them from divorcing and reconstructing a new life in face of their husband's polygamy.

Transformation of Personhood: Children's Journeys

As examined above, the entanglements of different forms of mobilities shape the complex trajectories of family making. This leads to nurturing new forms of personhood among the children of Japanese-Pakistani marriages. The narrative of Hina, whose parents divorced, capture their journeys of self-making.

The Case of Hina

When I last interviewed her, Hina was in her early twenties and had lived in Japan her entire life, although she used to visit her father's extended family in a town in Punjab during school holidays until she was in her early teens. While she did not like staying with her large extended family in Pakistan because of the lack of privacy, when she returned to her quiet house in Japan she found herself missing the noise. Also, she was attracted to the beautiful *shalwar qameez* that she saw and wore in Pakistan. It still influences what she chooses to wear in Japan.

Her parents divorced when she was in her late teens. Before that, her father had controlled what she could wear, and he made sure that she did not mix with boys; meanwhile, her brothers lived in a "different world," with far greater freedom. She struggled to cope with the different cultural practices at home and in school, where she was the only Muslim. She felt it unreasonable that her father controlled her for the sake of maintaining his honor, and that it was unfair that only girls were expected to conform to the gender norms while boys were free to do anything.

As her mother took sole custody of the children after the divorce, she was freed from her father's control. This did not mean, however, that she departed from the world she had lived in. She experienced a sense of loss. When she saw her friend whose father was Pakistani, she understood the struggles her friend had to go through, and saw her past self in her friend. Her journey of self-searching started then. Although she used to distance herself from the Islamic values that her father had tried to impose upon her, she started to reflect on what Islam meant to her. She gradually developed her own interpretation of Islam, which became an important pillar around which to organize her life. She has never thought of marrying a Pakistani because from her experiences of her father and his friends she feels that Pakistani men would control their women. She thinks, however, she might marry a Muslim from a different ethnic background because she wants to share religious values with her husband. Her case demonstrates that reconfiguring herself as a Muslim continues after her parents' divorce.

Discussion and Conclusion

The trajectories of family making among Japanese-Pakistani families exhibit the entanglements of different forms of mobilities, involving diverse exchanges of emotions, money, gifts, and services such as care and labor, from which complex forms of global interconnectivity emerge. These entanglements reveal that separately conceptualized mobilities—economic, care, intimate, educational, and social class—crisscross the lives of migrants and their families. Findings from my longitudinal study can be summarized in three points.

First, entangled affects and multifaceted aspirations shape and are shaped by the trajectories of family making. Intimate encounters between Pakistani men and Japanese women involve not only the men's material aspirations, but also their desires to broaden their life-horizons, and to experience alternative forms of love outside Pakistani society. Japanese women's hopes for alternative conjugal relationships also shape their intimate encounters. Couples' struggles to overcome the challenges they meet early in marriage lead to a subsequent stage of geographical movements between the Global North and Global South. Formations of transnationally split families are shaped by multiple aspirations, hopes, and ambitions embraced by the couples and their family members. Those forces are not only economic, but social and cultural. Notably, raising children in "an Islamic environment" in Pakistan means accumulating moral currency, particularly by protecting the sexual purity of daughters. Economic gains have to be carefully blended with moral capital to maintain the status of the kin group within Pakistan and its diasporic communities, and to move upward in their cultural cosmologies (Chu 2010, quoted in Cole and Groes 2016: 25). Thus, Pakistan can be a moral magnet that draws to it child-rearing Japanese-Pakistani couples. This moral force combines with other hopes and desires to create a reverse movement by Japanese wives and their children from the Global North to the Global South. Many, however, move back again to Japan after child-rearing, suggesting a link between geographical and temporal mobilities that shapes the ongoing processes of family trajectories through the life course. Educational mobility initiated by the children is also shaped by entanglements between their multiple aspirations and emotions.

Second, as the life course progresses, affective circuits involve much wider networks of kin, creating a complex social web connecting the Global North and Global South. This complexity calls for a need to avoid methodological conjugalism, which narrowly focuses on the relationships of heterosexual and monogamous marital ties, and sees the normative forms of marriage as the natural end of a migratory path from the Global South to the Global North (Groes and Fernandez 2018: 13–14). Further, my research finds that individuals become emplaced differently in social networks of kin across borders. Family members negotiate their positions and try to control the flow of exchange as life progresses (Cole and Groes 2016: 14–15). Family members do not always share goals or aspirations. Power dynamics, shaped by structural inequalities connected to gender, nationality, and class, add to the complexity of the mechanisms through which their migratory trajectories evolve. The affective circuits expand as husbands seek business opportunities on a global scale. This, in some cases, brings new intimate encounters, resulting in divorce or polygamy, inviting a complex mix of emotions, conflicts, and desires across generations.

Third, the entanglements of different forms of mobilities create and transform personhood for the next generation. Basit's case illustrates that his sense of obligation to his mother was nurtured through his experiences of transnationally split families where mother and children moved from the Global North to the Global South. This process forged a form of personhood, which cannot be explained as an autonomous individual pursing his own interests. Rather, it was a "node in systems of relationships defined by mutual assistance and asymmetrical exchanges" (Cole and Groes 2016: 11). This, in turn, triggered the next move in the family trajectory through which he, his mother, and siblings "returned" to Japan. His case demonstrates the centrality of emotions in shaping migration trajectories (Skrbiš 2008; Charsley 2013), pointing to the need to go beyond the push-pull framework, which privileges economic aspirations, and to capture complex entanglements of mobilities from an intergenerational perspective.

One final point is that Hina's case unveils the dynamic process of self-making that accompanies the trajectory of family (un)making. Affective circuits were blocked when her mother divorced her father, resulting in a disruption in her father's desire to raise her as an ideal Muslim woman. This does not mean, however, that her struggles to negotiate her religious self and femininity have ended. Rather, the separation from her father created an opportunity to reforge her personhood and develop a new orientation for her marriage partner. Her journey reveals the importance of bringing non-normative intimate patterns into perspectives (Constable 2018) that further our understanding of the diverse forms of entanglements from which new forms of personhood emerge. As her case shows, a "failed marriage," an apparent disruption in affective circuits, can invigorate the flow in a creative and unexpected way through which the next generation of Japanese-Pakistani marriages continue their journeys of self-making, and navigate intimate realms on the global stage.

Acknowledgments

My foremost thanks go to the participants in my research who shared their experiences and feelings about being members of transnational families. I am also grateful to Asuncion Fresnoza-Flot and Gracia Liu-Farrer who made insightful comments on an earlier version of this chapter. This work was supported by JSPS KAKENHI Grant Numbers JP23251006, JP16K03244, and JP20H05828.

Masako Kudo is a Professor of Cultural Anthropology at the College of Tourism, Rikkyo University, Japan. She has conducted longitudinal and multi-sited research among Muslim migrants and their families that are based in Japan and the UK. She is the co-author of *Marriage Migration in Asia: Emerging Minorities at the Frontiers of Nation-States* (NUS Press and Kyoto University Press, 2016) and *Rethinking Representations of Asian Women: Changes, Continuity, and Everyday Life* (Palgrave Macmillan, 2015), and has authored jointly and singly other publications.

NOTES

1. In this chapter, I use the term "border" to mean geographical borders controlled by nation-states.
2. I do not know whether the remaining three of the thirty-two children with Japanese nationality had (or once had) Pakistani nationality. Japanese nationality law, in principle, prohibits dual nationalities. According to the Ministry of Justice, those with multiple nationalities are required to choose their nationality "by a certain time limit." For details, see Ministry of Justice 2021.
3. As for the names of the Japanese women married to Pakistani migrants, they mainly used their Muslim names when interacting with each other in the networks of Japanese Muslim women. Thus, the pseudonyms I use for them in this chapter are Muslim names except for the cases in which the women used their Japanese names.
4. In Japan, international marriages constituted 0.9 percent of all marriages in 1980. This figure rose during the subsequent two decades and peaked in 2006 at 6.1 percent (Ministry of Health, Labour and Welfare 2020). In this peak year, 80 percent of international marriages were between Japanese men and foreign women.
5. The exceptions include Japanese descendants, particularly from Brazil and Peru, and those who work on intern programs (Douglass and Roberts 2000; Shindo 2014). In December 2018, the Diet passed a bill that formally opened its doors to foreign blue-collar workers for the first time.
6. The number of residency visas issued to Pakistanis under the visa category of "Spouse or Child of Japanese National" rose from 112 in 1984 to 1,630 in 2000 (Japan Immigration Association 1985–2001). My research strongly indicates that, during the 1990s, many spousal visas were converted to permanent resident visas. In June 2020, those registered under "Spouse of Japanese National" and "Permanent Resident" visa categories accounted for 32 percent of the 18,296 Pakistani residents in Japan (Ministry of Justice 2020).
7. According to Kobayashi, before 1982, when legal provisions for spousal visas were created, a foreign husband was required to provide proof of his ability to earn enough income to support his family, even if his Japanese wife was able to do so. A foreign wife, by contrast, had little trouble gaining permission to stay in Japan as a dependent of her Japanese spouse. Behind this discriminatory requirement was the state's gender-biased assumption that men provide for the family while women care for the family. This also implied that a foreign wife was expected to contribute to the nation through child bearing in the domestic sphere (Kobayashi 2009).
8. As marriage migration has become one of the few remaining doors for citizens of the Global South to enter the Global North, states have begun imposing stricter control on cross-border marriages (Fresnoza-Flot and Ricordeau 2017). State scrutiny and control are entwined with the idea that marriage and the family are core institutions for reproducing nation-states and good citizens (Moret, Andrikopoulos, and Dahinden 2019: 6).
9. Women from the Global South who marry Japanese men are by no means free from social stigmatization or the "international policing of women"—i.e., state

restrictions by both sending and receiving countries of marriage-migrant women (Fresnoza-Flot and Ricordeau 2017: 8–10).
10. For a discussion of complex interactions between modern state law and Islamic law in Pakistan, see Menski 1997.
11. While the majority of the women in my sample converted to Islam at the time of marriage, there were a few exceptions. One woman had already embraced Islam by the time she met her husband. Another woman came from a Christian family, but converted to Islam because she wanted to follow the same religion as her husband.
12. The hadith is the authoritative record of the Prophet Muhammad's exemplary speeches and actions.
13. When Japanese women and their children relocated to Western countries, they mobilized the Muslim/Pakistani diasporic networks in building their lives.
14. The social security system, which presupposes male breadwinner households, has produced a high level of insecurity among unmarried and divorced mothers, who together constitute the vast majority of single mothers in Japan (Tamiya 2020). The situation of Japanese women contrasts with the cases of transnationally married Turkish women in Denmark who can sustain themselves economically after divorce because of easier access to education, the labor market, and the welfare support provided by the state (Liversage 2012: 153–55).
15. There are also cases in which the husband was already married in Pakistan when he married a Japanese woman in Japan. Some Japanese wives were aware of the fact—but others were not.

REFERENCES

Andrikopoulos, Apostolos. 2019. "Love, Money and Papers in the Affective Circuits of Cross-border Marriages: Beyond the 'Sham'/'Genuine' Dichotomy." *Journal of Ethnic and Migration Studies* 47(2): 343-60 DOI: 10.1080/1369183X.2019.1625129.

Andrikopoulos, Apostolos, and Jan Willem Duyvendak. 2020. "Migration, Mobility and the Dynamics of Kinship: New Barriers, New Assemblages." *Ethnography* 21(3): 299–318.

Bloch, Alexia. 2011. "Intimate Circuits: Modernity, Migration and Marriage among Post-Soviet Women in Turkey." *Global Networks* 11(4): 502–21.

Charsley, Katherine. 2013. *Transnational Pakistani Connections: Marrying "Back Home."* New York: Routledge.

Charsley, Katharine, and Anika Liversage. 2012. "Transforming Polygamy: Migration, Transnationalism and Multiple Marriages among Muslim Minorities." *Global Networks* 13(1): 60–78.

Cole, Jennifer, and Christian Groes. 2016. "Introduction: Affective Circuits and Social Regeneration in African Migration." In *Affective Circuits: African Migrations to Europe and the Pursuit of Social Regeneration*, ed. Jennifer Cole and Christian Groes, 1–26. Chicago: The University of Chicago Press.

Constable, Nicole. 2005. *Cross-Border Marriages: Gender and Mobility in Transnational Asia*. Philadelphia: University of Pennsylvania Press.

———. 2018. "Temporary Intimacies, Incipient Transnationalism and Failed Cross-Border Marriages." In *Intimate Mobilities: Sexual Economies, Marriage and Migration in a Disparate World*, ed. Christian Groes and Nadine T. Fernandez, 52–73. New York: Berghahn Books.

Douglass, Mike, and Glenda S. Roberts. 2000. "Japan in a Global Age of Migration." In *Japan and Global Migration: Foreign Workers and the Advent of a Multicultural Society*, ed. Mike Douglass and Glenda S. Roberts, 3–37. Honolulu: University of Hawai'i Press.

Ezawa, Aya, and Chisa Fujiwara. 2005. "Lone Mothers and Welfare-to-Work Policies in Japan and the United States: Towards an Alternative Perspective." *Journal of Sociology and Social Welfare* 32(4): 41–63.

Faier, Lieba. 2009. *Intimate Encouters: Filipina Women and the Remaking of Rural Japan*. Los Angeles: University of California Press.

Fernandez, Nadine T. 2013. "Moral Boundaries and National Borders: Cuban Marriage Migration to Denmark." *Identities: Global Studies in Culture and Power* 20(3): 270–87.

Fresnoza-Flot, Asuncion. 2018. "Raising Citizens in 'Mixed' Family Setting: Mothering Techniques of Filipino and Thai Migrants in Belgium." *Citizenship Studies* 22(3): 278–93.

Fresnoza-Flot, Asuncion, and Itaru Nagasaka. 2015. "Conceptualizing Childhoods in Transnational Families: The 'Mobile Childhoods' Lens." In *Mobile Childhoods in Filipino Transnational Families: Migrant Children with Similar Roots in Different Routes*, ed. Itaru Nagasaka and Asuncion Fresnoza-Flot, 23–41. Basingstoke: Palgrave Macmillan.

Fresnoza-Flot, Asuncion, and Gwénola Ricordeau. 2017. "Introduction: International Marriages of Southeast Asian Women through the Lens of Citizenship." In *International Marriages and Marital Citizenship: Southeast Asian Women on the Move*, ed. Asuncion Fresnoza-Flot and Gwénola Ricordeau, 1–21. New York: Routledge.

Groes, Christian, and Nadine T. Fernandez. 2018. "Intimate Mobilities and Mobile Intimacies." In *Intimate Mobilities: Sexual Economies, Marriage and Migration in a Disparate World*, ed. Christian Groes and Nadine T. Fernandez, 1–27. New York: Berghahn Books.

Japan Immigration Association. 1985–2001 editions. *Zairyū Gaikokujin Tōkei* [Statistics on foreigners registered in Japan]. Tokyo.

Kandiyoti, Deniz. 1988. "Bargaining with Patriarchy." *Gender and Society* 2(3): 274–90.

Kobayashi, Junko. 2009. "1982 Nen Nyūkoku Kanrihō no 'Haigūsha Biza' Shinsetsu wo Meguru Jendā no Kōsaku: 'Kokusai Kekkon wo Kangaeru Kai' no Taikōteki Undō wo Jirei toshite" [Complexity in gender factors in the enactment of the spouse visa in the Japanese 1982 Immigration Law: A case of counter action by the Association for Multicultural Families]. *Joseigaku* 17: 74–91.

Kofman, Eleonore. 2012. "Rethinking Care through Social Reproduction: Articulating Circuits of Migration." *Social Politics* 19(1): 142–62.

Kudo, Masako. 2017. "The Evolution of Transnational Families: Bi-national Marriages between Japanese Women and Pakistani Men." *Critical Asian Studies* 49(1): 18–37.

Liu-Farrer, Gracia. 2018. "From Asia with Money: The Emigration of the Wealthy." In *Routledge Handbook of Asian Migrations*, ed. Gracia Liu-Farrer and Brenda S. A. Yeoh, 128-37. New York: Routledge.

Liu-Farrer, Gracia, and Brenda S. A. Yeoh. 2018. "Introduction. Asian Migrations and Mobilities: Continuities, Conceptualisations and Controversies." In *Routledge Handbook of Asian Migrations*, ed. Gracia Liu-Farrer and Brenda S. A.Yeoh, 1-18. New York: Routledge.

Liversage, Anika. 2012. "Transnational Families Breaking Up: Divorce among Turkish Immigrants in Denmark." In *Transnational Marriage: New Perspectives from Europe and Beyond*, ed. Katharine Charsley, 145-60. New York: Routledge.

López, Jane Lilly. 2015. "'Impossible Families': Mixed-Citizenship Status Couples and the Law." *Law & Policy* 37(1-2): 93-118.

Massey, Doreen. 1993. "Power-geometry and a Progressive Sense of Place." In *Mapping the Futures: Local Cultures, Global Change*, ed. Jon Bird, Barry Curtis, Tim Putnam, George Robertson, and Lisa Tickner, 59-69. New York: Routledge.

Menski, Werner F. 1997. "South Asian Muslim Law Today: An Overview." *Sharqīyāt: Journal of the Dutch Association for Middle Eastern and Islamic Studies* 9(1): 16-36. Retrieved 9 September 2020 from https://eprints.soas.ac.uk/10149/.

Ministry of Health, Labour and Welfare. 2020. *Jinkō Dōtai Tōkei* [Vital statistics of Japan]. Tokyo: Health, Labour and Welfare Statistics Association. Retrieved 31 August 2020 from https://www.e-stat.go.jp/dbview?sid=0003411850.

Ministry of Justice. 2020. *Zairyū gaikokujin tōkei* [Statistics on foreigners registered in Japan]. Retrieved 15 August 2021 from https://www.e-stat.go.jp/stat-search/files?page=1&layout=datalist&toukei=00250012&tstat=000001018034&cycle=1&year=20200&month=12040606&tclass1=000001060399.

———. 2021. *Choice of Nationality*. Retrieved 2 August 2021 from http://www.moj.go.jp/EN/MINJI/minji06.html.

Moret, Joëlle, Apostolos Andrikopoulos, and Janine Dahinden. 2019. "Contesting Categories: Cross-border Marriages from the Perspectives of the State, Spouses and Researchers." *Journal of Ethnic and Migration Studies* 47(2): 325-42. DOI: 10.1080/1369183X.2019.1625124.

Ong, Aihwa. 1999. *Flexible Citizenship: The Cultural Logics of Transnationality*. Durham, NC: Duke University Press.

Qureshi, Kaveri. 2016. *Marital Breakdown among British Asians: Conjugality, Legal Pluralism and New Kinship*. London: Palgrave Macmillan. DOI: 10.1057/978-1-137-570 47-5.

Shindo, Reiko. 2014. "The Category Mismatch and Struggles over Citizenship in Japan." In *Routledge Handbook of Global Citizenship Studies*, ed. Engin F. Isin and Peter Nyers, 376-87. London: Routledge.

Skrbiš, Zlatko. 2008. "Transnational Families: Theorising Migration, Emotions and Belonging." *Journal of Intercultural Studies* 29(3): 231-46.

Suzuki, Eriko. 2009. *Nihon de Hataraku Hiseiki Taizaisha: Karera wa "Konomashikunai Gaikokujin Rōdōsha" nanoka?* [Irregular migrants working in Japan: Are they "undesirable foreign workers"?]. Tokyo: Akashi Shoten.

Suzuki, Nobue. 2015. "Suspended Mobilities: Japanese-Filipino Children, Family Regimes, and Postcolonial Plurality." In *Mobile Childhoods in Filipino Transnational Families: Migrant Children with Similar Roots in Different Routes*, ed. Itaru Nagasaka and Asuncion Fresnoza-Flot, 222–46. Basingstoke: Palgrave Macmillan.

———. 2017. "Postcolonial Desires, Partial Citizenship, and Transnational 'Un-mothers': Contexts and Lives of Filipina Marriage Migrants in Japan." In *International Marriages and Marital Citizenship: Southeast Asian Women on the Move*, ed. Asuncion Fresnoza-Flot and Gwénola Ricordeau, 121–39. New York: Routledge.

Tamiya, Yuko. 2020. "Lone Mother Households and Poverty in Japan: New Social Risks, the Social Security System and Labour Market." In *Routledge Handbook of East Asian Gender Studies*, ed. Jieyu Liu and Junko Yamashita, 253–66. New York: Routledge.

Yeoh, Brenda S. A., Heng Leng Chee, and Thi Kieu Dung Vu. 2013. "Commercially Arranged Marriage and the Negotiation of Citizenship Rights among Vietnamese Marriage Migrants in Multiracial Singapore." *Asian Ethnicity* 14(2): 139–56.

Yuval-Davis, Nira. 1997. "Women, Citizenship and Difference." *Feminist Review* 57: 4–27.

CHAPTER

7

Intergenerational Intimacies and Mobilities in Transnational Families
The Experiences of Japanese-Filipino Children

Jocelyn O. Celero

Introduction

This chapter is concerned with the role of children growing up in transnational families, families that are formed through bi/international marriage, whose members are geographically separated and employ strategies to sustain households and relationships in two or more societies. These strategies reflect how families adapt to the rapidly changing world (Chakraborty and Thambiah 2018: 584). While the phenomena of international marriages and transnational families are nothing new, research on the relational lives of children born of such marriages and families remain limited (Findlay et al. 2015). Taking into account this lacuna, the present chapter interrogates how children in transnational families manage intergenerational intimacies and mobilities across space and time. It uses the empirical case of Japanese-Filipino children born to international marriage families whose childhood and family life experiences involve moving between the economic, social, and cultural contexts of Japan and the

Philippines. Some of these children are partly raised in the Philippines before moving to Japan by the age of eighteen to reunite with migrant parents, thereby developing bifocal understandings of childhood, familyhood, and kinship. While raised in a transnational family, they become exposed to ambivalences in family relationships resulting from shifting and unequal socioeconomic and cultural conditions between Japan and the Philippines. The different historical and structural characteristics in both societies influence their mobility and immobility as part of "doing" family across borders.

Before proceeding to the im/mobilities of Japanese-Filipinos, it is necessary to define mobility and immobility as utilized in this chapter. The concept of mobility is about "people's movement as well as the connected flux of materialities, money, ideas, images, knowledge and technologies, and the way such diverse mobilities are restricted, facilitated or understood" (Groes and Fernandez 2018: 4). It pertains to the multiple forms of spatial or geographical migration intersecting with other types of movement (intimate, legal, and social) that bring about change in the meaning and practice (Salazar, Elliot and Norum 2017) of, in this case, nurturing intimate family ties. Intimate mobility occurs through relativizing (Bryceson and Vuorela 2002) or relational practices (Hordsworth 2013) in which families adjust the proximity and intensity of emotional connection with other members. Legal mobility, on the other hand, refers to changing one's citizenship and/or to other kinds of legal status, while social mobility refers to upward or downward movement of one's class position. In the context of this chapter, the interlocking spatial, intimate, legal, and social im/mobilities of Japanese-Filipinos are grounded in transnational family ties. The chapter focuses on Japanese-Filipinos' mobile and immobile subjectivities, referring not only to the different im/mobility routes, experiences, and motives, but also to their politics of mobility (Cresswell 1999, 2010) which, arising from the entanglement of their im/mobilities and those of their Filipino migrant (and Japanese) parents and extended kin, engenders power relations and contradictory effects on intergenerational ties.

The chapter begins with briefly reviewing the literature on transnational families in Asia to situate the lived experiences of Japanese-Filipino children, followed by clarifying the theoretical concepts such as care, intergenerational reciprocity, and children in transnational families. Next, it presents the research methods employed to gather data on the profile of Japanese-Filipino children according to the types of migration and mobility that they experience alongside their parents and extended kin. Third, it juxtaposes their im/mobilities to those of their Filipino and Japanese parents and Filipino kin to underscore their care work through performing familial roles. Fourth, it discusses the impact of their care labor on their understandings and views of intergenerational intimacies. The chapter ends with a discussion on the social impact of transnational migration and family arrangements in Japan and the Philippines, and the growing importance of children's perspectives on mobility and family migration research.

Japanese-Filipino Families as Transnational Families

Japanese-Filipinos are children born to Japanese and Filipino parents whose international marriage and transnational family formation peaked in Japan in the 1990s, following the inbound migration of thousands of women from the Philippines (Haines, Yamanaka, and Yamashita 2012; Jones and Shen 2008; Yamashita 2008). The Center for Japanese-Filipino Families (CJFF) records that about 340,000 Japanese-Filipino children who are now in their twenties have resided or are currently residing in either Japan or the Philippines, while the International Organization for Migration's (IOM) conservative estimate is somewhere between 100,000 and 200,000. These inconsistent statistics complicate issues that Japanese-Filipinos face with regard to familial and legal categorizations over the last two decades (Ito 2005; Suzuki 2010). In Japan, Japanese-Filipinos have multiple legal statuses. Some have Japanese citizenship, while others hold visas of either a child of a Japanese national or a child of a permanent resident. In the Philippines, on the other hand, they may be legally recognized as Filipino or dual national. Through Japanese citizenship as a resource for migration, more Japanese-Filipinos have been migrating to Japan in recent times. Regardless of how they are defined legally, Japanese-Filipinos' individual and family lives have been impacted by the historical, legal, sociocultural, and economic conditions in the two societies.

Normative ideals and expectations based on societal cultures influence how families carry out social reproductive activities such as child-rearing and socialization. In the Philippines, the family is a social institution in which family relationships—specifically those between spouses, as well as those between parents and children—are fundamental to the well-being of Filipinos (Asis 2000: 257). The pervasiveness of familism in the Philippines extols Filipinos' strong attachments to their extended families (Alampay 2014), and explains why both extended and nuclear families are considered as ideal family models. Interdependence between members occurs to carry out family practices and obligations across generations. As the postindustrial Filipino society transitions to a modern and diverse value system, however, the function of family has shifted toward prioritizing individual needs over collective welfare, and young people are increasingly making decisions on matters that directly affect them, such as education and relationships (Medina 2001: 276).

Meanwhile, integral to postwar Japan's rapid transformation into a modern industrialized democracy was its structural shift from traditional extended family to the nuclear, patriarchal system, dichotomizing the roles of fathers and mothers into breadwinners and caregivers, respectively (Holloway 2010: 196; Holloway and Nagase 2014: 62). Since the 1970s, Japan has also been a quarter of a century ahead of the rest of Asia in terms of fertility and population decline (Ochiai 1997), and these demographic challenges have had economic consequences for families across generations in general, and for women in particular. Despite the rising cost of sustaining a household, divorce, and a recent decline in the appeal of marriage, childcare and household production have remained in the hands of housewives/mothers (Holloway 2010: 96; Ochiai 2009: 74–75). Whether married or divorced, Filipino migrant mothers make no exception; they must deal with the costs of child care and the demands of family life in Japan.

Transnational living arrangement has become the strategy of Japanese-Filipino families to negotiate the prevailing ideals, expectations, and norms in the two societies. Thus, this chapter explores how Japanese-Filipinos navigate through normative conditions of family and kinship across borders. It looks into the relationship between their family life and multiple im/mobilities. The transnationality of Japanese-Filipinos, resulting from sporadic episodes of stay-behind childhood, parental absence, and temporal family reunions, can be classified into two major modes: split-to-reunited and circulating. The first of these, which is akin to the stay-behind family arrangement as an outcome of parental migration depicted in migration literature (Carling, Menjivar, and Schmalzbauer 2012; Parreñas 2005; Save the Children 2006; Zentgraf and Chinchilla 2012), will be the focus of the chapter. It occurs when Japanese-Filipinos experience immobility as stay-behind children in the Philippines, co-reside with Filipino extended kin, and become physically separated from, but eventually reunite with, Filipino (and Japanese) parents working in Japan.

The transnational strategies among Japanese-Filipino families vary in terms of resources for parenting and raising a family. Filipino migrant women's "mobile motherhood" (Ogaya 2015) results from the inadequate financial and cultural capital for parenting, and the anticipated difficulty of managing work and family life in Japan. First-time Filipino mothers decide to give birth in the Philippines where they have greater familiarity with and access to maternity, infant care, and other kinds of support from natal family. Working in Japan enables them to support their stay-behind children raised by their Filipino relatives. Some Filipino (and Japanese) parents also perceive the social environment in the Philippines as more conducive to their children's growth than that in Japan, where stories of children of immigrants experiencing bullying and discrimination abound.

Among divorced and/or single Filipino mothers, the difficulty of raising children alone forces those who cannot easily access social welfare provisions in Japan to send their children temporarily to the Philippines. Even dual-parent Japanese-Filipino families who neither live together nor establish familial bonds with Japanese extended kin struggle to access child-care support, and therefore choose to send their children to be raised in the Philippines. The period of separation from their children in the Philippines depends on the time Filipino women need to improve their socioeconomic situation in order to reunite with children in Japan.

The present study focuses on the transnational family relationships of Japanese-Filipino children that they maintain through multiple, intersecting im/mobilities. These intertwining spatial, legal, and social mobilities connect them to their Filipino and Japanese parents, as well as to extended kin who constitute their "circuits of intimacy and care" (Hondagneu-Sotelo and Avila 1997).

Conceptual Clarification: Care and Reciprocity among Children in Transnational Families

Transnational families are an outcome of global economic inequality, and reproduce new modes of dependence on a transnational division of labor (Schmalzbauer 2004: 1029; also in Yeoh, Huang, and Lam 2017: 312). Existing literature on transnational families in Asia can be summed up into three interrelated arguments (Lam et al. 2018; Yeoh et al. 2017; Yeoh et al. 2005). First, transnational families draw on ideological imaginaries of family, household, and kinship to sustain belonging despite physical absence. Second, they are realized through lived experiences, where varying degrees of intimacy are negotiated through new communication technologies and the time-structuring conditions, such as care work of existing migration regimes in Asia. Third, these families often assume transnational morphologies with the strategic intent, such as migrant parents overseas while children are stay-behind, or mobile children and stay-behind parents. Within this corpus of scholarship are three burgeoning strands that underscore children's social agency: children as educational migrants and family aspirational projects, children moving to counter marginal circumstances, and stay-behind children's role in negotiating parental migration and child-care arrangements. These trends indicate scholars' increasing attention to the "situated agency" (Choi, Yeoh, and Lam 2018) of children who are affected by migration processes beyond borders. Children's agency includes their generational resources of power, such as age and family position, to "influence, organize, coordinate, and control events that take place in their changing family worlds" (Alanen 2001: 21).

The current chapter departs from the predominantly adult-centric perspective on family migration and practices, through considering the voice and situated agency of children in transnational families as they participate in the exchange of practical, moral, emotional, personal, accommodation/co-residence, and economic support (Finch 1989: 9, as cited in Baldassar and Merla 2014: 12) between their parents and extended kin to ensure the collective well-being of the family. The chapter also takes a life course approach in examining how Japanese-Filipinos manage intergenerational intimacies across spaces and through time. In doing so, it underscores the dynamic relationship between historical and social structures framing migrant life course and individual biographies (Wingens et al. 2011: 2–3), and the role of migration as a continuous process, rather than a single event, through which children contribute to the life narratives of transnational families. It also emphasizes both the capabilities as well as limitations (at times powerlessness) of their action as children in relation to their parents and extended kin. Japanese-Filipino children's interlocking mobilities of different directions and motives are aimed at simultaneously extending and nucleating familial bonds.

The nurturance of intergenerational relations is undergirded by *utang na loob* (debt of gratitude), a Filipino emotional grammar that defines the function as well as the intensity of family connections. As a Filipino cultural logic of reciprocity and cooperation within families, it consists of two components: (1) the filial piety of children toward their parents, and (2) the "natural" duty of the family to care for its members (Asis et al. 1995: 159). Children's "ethic of reciprocity" in particular is evident in the ways they carry out filial duties and exhibit good behaviors toward their migrant parents (Alipio 2015, as cited in Menchavez 2018: 3) as means of repayment for the latter's upbringing and sacrifices. The emphasis of the current chapter is on the context upon which *utang na loob* informs, enables, and constrains Japanese-Filipinos' im/mobilities and care labor. The chapter further illustrates how the multiple im/mobilities of Japanese-Filipinos engender ideational shifts as they progress in their life course. Reflecting on the accumulated family experiences, memories, and emotions in relation to other members, they consciously regulate the nature and extent of *utang na loob* toward their caring kin in the Philippines and their parents in Japan. The next section discusses the methodology and profile of Japanese-Filipinos in this study.

Research Methods and Profile of Japanese-Filipino Families

Data for this paper is derived from semi-structured and in-depth interviews with seventy Japanese-Filipinos residing in Tokyo and Manila, from 2010 to the present, as part of my longitudinal study on intergenerational mobility of 1.5- and second-generation Japanese-Filipinos. I met them through personal and professional networks. I benefited most from interviewing Filipino mothers who then referred me to their children. Establishing rapport with Japanese-Filipino child respondents, I was introduced as "mom's friend" or as an "older sister." Apart from getting the consent of their mothers to participate in the study, interviews with children below eighteen years old were conducted in the presence of their mother, who would sometimes act as interpreter and/or fellow interviewer. Mothers took such interactions as opportunities to ask questions to their children. At the start of fieldwork in Tokyo, I also gained the trust of young interviewees easily by introducing myself as a PhD student at Waseda University, functioning as my symbolic capital because it is a reputable university.

Each interview lasted for about two to three hours using a mix of Filipino, English, and Japanese, depending on the participant's language ability and preference. Interviews were recorded with the permission of the respondents, fully transcribed, and translated into English. The interview questions focused on birth, childhood, family life, and relations of Japanese-Filipinos. They were assigned pseudonyms to maintain the anonymity of data. Doing this multi-sited fieldwork that has included face-to-face as well as online conversations over the last ten years, I have accumulated numerous life narratives from Japanese-Filipino children who have transitioned from different levels of education, training and employment, and have moved between Japan and the Philippines at various points of their individual and family lives. Pseudonyms were assigned to protect the identity of both the children and their parents, and to maintain the confidentiality of the interview data.

The narratives featured in this chapter illustrate Japanese-Filipinos' present emotions and reflexivity toward the intersecting im/mobilities in their relational lives. Their transnational migration can be analyzed by including their childhood and adolescent experiences from the vantage point of their current stage in their life course. Thirty-six of them were born in the Philippines, compared to thirty-three who were born in Japan, while only one was born in another country. This paper concentrates on the family experiences of thirty Japanese-Filipinos who moved from the Philippines to Japan.

The majority of my respondents belonged to the sixteen to twenty-five age bracket, and most of them were born in the 1990s. Japanese-Filipinos in this study hold different national memberships, which likewise shape their capacity to move between the two countries frequently. Of the seventy respondents, thirty-two are Japanese citizens, eighteen are Filipino, and twenty hold both Filipino and Japanese citizenships. This chapter is based on the recollections and experiences of Japanese-Filipinos who were stay-behind children in the Philippines before reuniting with their working mothers who had become permanent residents in Japan. At the time of the interviews with the children, their Filipino mothers were either married (thirty-one), remarried (seven), or single parents (seventeen divorced, five unmarried, and six widows), which variously shaped the development of intergenerational relationships—mainly between them and their Filipino mothers, but also with their extended kin in the Philippines, and Japanese fathers to some extent.

When Children Care: Japanese-Filipinos' Transnational Family Relations

This section examines the care labor of Japanese-Filipinos during the two phases of a split-to-reunited living arrangement of Japanese-Filipino families. It begins with the context of their spatial immobility as stay-behind children co-residing with Filipino extended kin, which entangles with the spatial and intimate im/mobilities of their Filipino and Japanese parents in the Philippines. Consequently, it details the entanglement between their multiple im/mobilities and the legal and social im/mobilities of their parents following a reunion in Japan.

First Phase: Multiple Immobilities of Children, Spatial Mobility of Extended Kin, Spatial and Intimate Im/mobilities of Parents

Children's stay-behind status depends on their parents' economic and legal status abroad, as well as the children's life stage. In my sample, twenty-seven of Japanese-Filipino children went to a grade school in the Philippines (until twelve years old), while nineteen of them remained in the Philippines to attend high school (until sixteen years old). Another ten children moved from the Philippines to Japan in the middle of grade school, while nine were taken to the Philippines from Japan to continue primary school, suggesting disruptions in child socialization and schooling due to family circumstances and parents' considerations of "conducive" environment for raising children properly.

As stay-behind children in the Philippines, Japanese-Filipinos go through childhood and socialization stages that require tremendous care exchange. Thus, in the first phase of their family arrangement, spatially immobile

Japanese-Filipinos "actively engage both in caring for and caring about family survival and maintenance" (Baldassar and Merla 2014: 12) through mediating transnational family relationships with their Japanese and Filipino parents, as well as Filipino extended kin in the Philippines.

Japanese-Filipino children deal with temporal, physical, and emotional distance (Bauzon 1999; Nuqui 2009; Satake 2004; Suzuki 2010) and presence of their Filipino (and Japanese) parents in their lives while growing up in the Philippines. Their Filipino mothers tend to take short vacation trips a few times a year, each lasting for several days or weeks, taking advantage of the homeland's geographical proximity and cheap flights from Japan. Materializing family obligations, their mother's visits include bringing *balikbayan* (returning migrant's) boxes and spending on excursion trips and homecoming parties. Through their hard-earned yen, Filipino mothers are able to rear an extended household in the Philippines due to the affordability of housing, education, and a middle-class lifestyle.

Japanese fathers, meanwhile—aside from visiting their child at the time of birth, and sending financial support and material goods—seldom come to the Philippines to spend time with children. For many Philippine-raised Japanese-Filipino children, having a Japanese father who resides and works in Japan for practically the entire year means dealing with his perennial absence and minimal involvement in child care. Japanese-Filipino children who neither see nor communicate with their Japanese father regularly due to the language barrier have the least intimacy. Irregular and minimal family visits have prevented them from establishing father-and-child bonds. Although the Filipino mother may mediate contact, some Japanese-Filipino children become frustrated over not attaining deep emotional closeness with their father.

Japanese-Filipino children's pain of absent father-child relations is comparable to never knowing their fathers at all. Indeed, Japanese-Filipino families have a lot more fathering deficit than other migrant families in the Philippines. Of the seventy respondents interviewed in Tokyo and Manila, six had never met their father, while five of them had only seen their father once when they were between three and eight years old. Eighteen of them had parents who had divorced while growing up either with their mother in Japan, or their extended kin caregivers in the Philippines (Celero 2016). Due to the lack of joint custody rights in Japan, the ties between the "departing" father and the "abandoned" child gradually become disjointed over time. The spatial immobility, entangled with the legal and social immobilities, of many Japanese-Filipino children who grew up in the Philippines without a father due to either marital breakup or lack of paternal recognition (Nuqui 2009; Seiger 2014; Suzuki 2010) impacts the pursuit of legal and other mobilities in the latter stages of their lives.

Compensating for the limited or constrained intimacy with parents are the Filipino extended kin—commonly grandmothers and aunts caring as "the other mothers" and uncles as "the other fathers" for Japanese-Filipino children. Filling the parental void, they serve as authoritative figures and siblings, providing love, guidance, and protection for the children from the pain and trauma of family disintegration. Some Japanese-Filipino children, meanwhile, facilitate the spatial mobility of their extended kin through convincing their parents that they co-reside with their relatives so that the latter can save on housing costs while the former eases relativizing or building affinity with their kin.

There are desirable outcomes of co-residence for Japanese-Filipino children. First, it acculturates them to Filipino values and outlook on intergenerational relations. Living together with caring relatives for a considerable time enables them to flexibly rework familial ties, like other stay-behind children in the Philippines (Hoang et al. 2015). As a sense of extended family is inculcated in them, Japanese-Filipino children learn to show filial respect, love, and obedience not only toward their co-residing kin but also to their physically distant mothers (and fathers). Second, they develop *utang na loob* as they appreciate the parenting role of their caring kin, and their own parents' hard work overseas through the remittances sent regularly. In turn, they manifest their "ethic of reciprocity" through displaying self-discipline and respect. Attributing power to their parents for their financial support, Yuki describes her mother as the "mother and father of the household," and the most powerful head of their family, despite being physically absent in their everyday life.

Living with extended kin may, however, expose Japanese-Filipino children to the negative features of familial relations in the Philippines. For instance, prolonged reliance of their relatives on their physically distant parents, as in the case of Yuta, a stay-behind child in Manila until the age of sixteen:

> My mom did not tell me to study hard. It grew on me because I witnessed everything in the Philippines ... all the poverty there. I realized I cannot help her if I do not finish school because I cannot get a good job. I will end up like my relatives. That is how it is in the Philippines. I picked that up as a kid.

Living in an extended household that two to three families share, some Japanese-Filipinos become aware of their relatives' economic dependence on their working parents in Japan, because they neither work abroad nor fend for themselves. Their unemployment serves as an everyday reminder of poverty etched in their memory as children. The economic reliance of Yuta's relatives on his mother made a lasting impression on him, motivating him to persevere with his studies in order to one day alleviate his mother's financial burdens.

Comparing Japan and the Philippines in their imaginary of social mobility, they begin to associate immobility in the Philippines with poverty and dependence, while migration to Japan is linked with social mobility and autonomy, evident in how their migrant parents provide more for the transnational household. Experiences of physical separation from and longing for their parents yield contradictory feelings toward their extended kin (appreciation for their caring kin but disdain for dependent relatives), and manifest power through influencing the subsequent family movement (Dreby 2007: 1062). As a United Nations Report on Social Costs of Migration (2013) reveals, Filipino stay-behind children tend to have ambivalent feelings about prolonged parental absence, which intensifies the desire for family togetherness. While their mothers battle guilt for leaving their responsibilities behind, children easily convince them to finally reunite in Japan.

Second Phase: Multiple Im/mobilities of Japanese-Filipinos, Legal and Social Im/mobilities of Filipino Parents in Japan

Many stay-behind Japanese-Filipino children eventually overcome sedentariness in the Philippines and move to Japan to reunite with their parents. A child's age at the time of migration accounts for diverse family desires and obligations. In my sample, twenty Japanese-Filipino children born and raised in the Philippines moved to Japan before the age of twelve to either start or resume grade school. The educational, legal, and social mobilities for Japanese-Filipinos are frequently entangled as their educational and career aspirations overlap with reinvigorating intimacies, not only with their parents and/or siblings after years of separation, but also with Japan from which they claim rights as Japanese citizens (Celero 2016; Seiger 2014) and fulfill their nostalgia toward their "other" homeland (Hara 2011).

The legal mobility of Japanese-Filipinos is determined by the prevailing immigration and citizenship regimes that give priority to a nuclear family and blood-based relations in Japan. First, moving to Japan to claim Japanese citizenship is based on their biological relationship to a Japanese parent, according to Japan's Nationality Law.[1] Second, lacking access to Japanese citizenship due to denied paternal recognition, other Japanese-Filipinos secure rights to live and work in Japan by being a child of their long-term and permanent resident Filipino parents.[2] Third, through marriage or remarriage, undocumented or overstaying Filipinos may obtain a spouse visa to legalize status and lead a family in Japan. Seven children in my study benefited from their mothers upon the latter's re/marriage, and were even adopted by their Japanese stepfathers. The last two structural conditions show that the change in the legal status of Filipino migrant mothers intertwines with the legal, intimate, and social mobilities of Japanese-Filipinos in Japan. Family intimacy shifts with their corporeal presence in the everyday life of their parents, who used to be physically distant from them. As they redefine their positions as a youth and sibling, their intimacy-building strategies of co-residence and breadwinning respond to the downward mobility of their parents.

The legal mobility of Japanese-Filipino children entangles with their intimate mobility desire to "nucleate" family relationships (Yeoh, Graham, and Boyle 2002). Factors such as their age at migration, and the period of separation, as well as their migrant parents' family resources, complicate the simplistic goal of physical co-presence in Japan. Many parent-child reunions are prone to drama and conflict due to incompatible familial expectations; the younger the Japanese-Filipino child, the less their capability to bargain for the conditions of the reunion, and the more excruciating the nucleating bonds can be.

Rika was a newborn when her parents took her to the Philippines in 1991 to be raised by her grandmother, aunts, and *yaya* (babysitter). When she was eight years old, her mother remarried and decided to take her back to Tokyo to live with her. Rika recalled:

> My mom took me back because she wanted us to become family. At first, I did not know I was going to move to Japan because they [grandmother and aunts] just sort of said, "Oh, you are going there for a long vacation. You have a newborn sister." I felt deceived. It was heartbreaking because I [had] lived with them for years ... it was really sad for me to leave like that.

Adjusting to a different social, cultural, and economic context, Japanese-Filipino children are not free from distress caused by sudden physical separation from their Filipino kin with whom they have formed a stronger emotional attachment. Forming emotional closeness initially displaces "uprooted" Japanese-Filipino children from a newfound family. As first-borns, however, they tend to get caught in newfound roles, such as older sibling and stepchild. Rika observed the change in her mother upon her sister's birth:

> I think my mom started becoming a mother when my stepsister was born and when I came into the family picture, I was already eight years old. It was hard [for her] to switch (between) taking care of a baby and a kid. I did get jealous at the time; maybe [I felt] that I wanted to move back to the Philippines at some point because there I was treated more like a kid—but here, I became a big sister with a responsibility to take

care of my siblings, changing nappies ... (Rika, reunited with mother at eight years old in Tokyo)

Remarriage improves the social mobility of some Filipino mothers, making them capable of redesigning spousal and familial bonds favorable for them and their children. Despite failing to build an emotional connection with their Japanese father's other children, the majority of my Japanese-Filipino interviewees were able to expand their constellation of care and affection with the inclusion of their stepparents and siblings into their nuclear family imaginary. Such effort is influenced by their *utang na loob* toward their mother, who worked toward their reunion and integrating them into the newly formed family.

Amidst their effort of "normalizing" parent-child relations, however, Japanese-Filipino children do not sever their emotional ties with kin carers in the Philippines. They continue to adhere to *utang na loob*, showing affection through mobile communication, sending gifts, and even paying visits together with their mother and siblings during holidays. Continuous communication through phone calls, Facebook, Viber, and Skype complements reliance on the affective bonds once felt with their caring grandmothers, aunts and uncles. The nurturance of the extended ties alleviates physical isolation, and emotional and mental stress, as well as other hardships associated with adjusting to the new familial setup.

Other children interpret their efforts toward co-residence as ensuring their parents' emotional well-being. Securing a home in Japan can be costly, and many Filipino immigrant women must ensure a stable economic status to afford physical togetherness with their children. Filipino migrant mothers have occupied a spectrum of economic status in Japan over the years. Some have become business owners (e.g., ethnic food shops, bars, and aesthetic centers), full-time caregivers or assistant language teachers, while others are part-time workers still dabbling in menial jobs to complement government social provisions.

Consequently, the "contradictory class mobility" (Parreñas 2005) of the first-generation Filipino migrants is evident in how not all of them can provide sufficient economic and cultural resources for the sociocultural adaptation of newcomer Japanese-Filipino children in Japan. While some Japanese-Filipino children are supported by their middle-class families in transitioning to Japanese school, others in lower-class families are inclined to delay or stop schooling. Some Filipino mothers opt for inviting the older child first, who can adapt faster and eventually assist their younger siblings. Apart from being more resilient to learning a new language and culture, older Japanese-Filipino children also tend to be the first to recognize when the family is confronting economic challenges.

Breadwinning is another strategy of Japanese-Filipino children to care for their families. As a salient feature in many households in Asia (Selin 2014), breadwinning has become an alternative form of headship in which older children may share or gain power in the family (Asis 2000: 263). Coinciding desires to revitalize nuclear family bonds and claim Japanese nationality is the need for Japanese-Filipinos to take on a breadwinning role to contribute to the social class mobility of their respective families.

While studying at a university in Manila, Hiromi was told by her mother to come to Japan in 2008 to help support their stay-behind family. Being the eldest child, she, at eighteen years old, came to Tokyo ahead of her four siblings. Within the first month of her arrival, she began to work as a restaurant crew, a job introduced by her mother's friend. She recalled how her sudden move affected her:

> My mom never told me I was going earlier [to Japan] ... I have always been the obedient child, 'yes Ma, yes Ma ...' When I arrived, I didn't like it, I wanted to go home. I honestly wanted to stay [in the Philippines] because seriously when you're eighteen, you just care about your studies and friends ... I cannot imagine being alone, living just with my mom. There, you will never experience working unless you're done with university. Here [in Japan], the youth start doing *arubaito* (part-time job) at a young age, right? Still, I couldn't accept that my mother asked me to work.

The inability to negotiate role expectations and youth life prior to migration often results in conflict between Japanese-Filipinos and their parents. Japanese-Filipinos would eventually learn that it is commonplace for the Japanese youth to engage in part-time work while studying, which is contrary to the typical experience of young Filipinos who are preoccupied solely with studies. At the time of the interview (2014–15), of thirteen Japanese-Filipino respondents in Tokyo, eleven worked as part-time convenience store staff or restaurant crew, one as an office clerk, and one an academic tutor. While it serves as Japanese youth's initiation rite to paid work, doing a part-time job for Japanese-Filipinos, in particular, is to support their family financially. Takaya et al. (2015) reveal that some Japanese-Filipinos tend to grow up in a household where the Japanese father is a blue-collar worker and the Filipino mother is a housewife or is also a blue-collar worker (71). Compared to Japanese and other non-Japanese households, the ratio of Filipino single-mother households depending on living subsidies is significantly higher.

Although breadwinning is not instantaneously commensurate with power-sharing in the transnational household, it does reinforce the children's *utang na loob* through the conscious pursuit of harmonious relations. Hiromi refused but eventually yielded to her mother after communicating with her aunt in Manila, with whom she has a closer relationship. Calling her almost every day during the first month, her aunt extended comfort and encouragement for her to be empathic toward her mother's situation as a single parent. Coming to terms with doing a part-time job (while studying) and adhering to the virtue of a "good child," Hiromi transitioned from being a full-time student in the Philippines to co-breadwinning in Japan in order to appease both her mother and her aunt.

There are also children who voluntarily embrace breadwinning roles. Such a decision can be influenced by a downward mobility of their parents owing to either sudden financial adversities or aging that has stifled their breadwinning capability. Others are driven to help their single mothers who have been struggling to make ends meet (Celero 2014; Yamagishi and Tolentino 2012). Familial love and sensitivity to the situation of one's parents are integral to Japanese-Filipinos' *utang na loob* that they learned while growing up in the Philippines. Ensuring the well-being of their parents by becoming a breadwinner may sometimes constrain them from prioritizing their personal goals. Satomi quit university and came to Japan at eighteen years old in 2009 in order to work and help her financially struggling father:

> When I was in the Philippines, I wanted to open a business, like retail, like Uniqlo ... but when I came here [to Japan], it changed; I now wanted to be an employee in a company ... If I am there [in the Philippines], if I cannot find one [job], I cannot do anything [to help my family]. We need to focus on helping our father for now. After he is done paying all his debt, that's the time we can focus on our own aspirations.

Satomi's father was one of those hit hard by the Lehman brothers shock in 2008, which led to the closure of his printing business and incurred him debt. When economic downturns engulf families, "the children feel the pinch first" (MacLellan 2011: 6), compelling them, especially those from bigger families, to commit to family obligations. Satomi has five siblings. In 2010, her sister, Ayane, also quit college to work in Japan. Working together for five days a week from 9:00 A.M. to 8:00 P.M. in a factory that cuts glass used as screen covers for cellular phones, they earn 170,000 yen a month each. Satomi has another part-time job at a nearby *izakaya* (Japanese bar) three days a week in which she earns 900 yen per hour. They send half of their combined monthly income to their mother and three younger siblings still studying in the Philippines.

As lower-class Japanese-Filipino families face socioeconomic hardships, some Japanese-Filipino children opt to delay education and other personal aspirations in order to assist their parents financially. Analyzing the relationship between the spatial segregation and social class location of immigrants in Japan, Fielding (2010: 105-8) reveals that Filipino migrants concentrated in the Kanto region can be identified in production and personal service sectors of Japan's occupational structure. As delayed education results in stunted acculturation process, some Japanese-Filipinos moving to Japan at an older age may end up in the same occupational niche that subjects their migrant parents and other Filipinos to ethnic discrimination.

Other Japanese-Filipinos downplay, however, their parents' loss of breadwinning capability, and perceive themselves to be better off than their unemployed kin and friends in the Philippines. Despite a sense of interdependence within the family, Japanese-Filipinos conceive of breadwinning as a family obligation of "dutiful children" (Oishi 2005: 115). Comparing the configurations of Japanese wife-Japanese husband, Japanese wife-Filipino husband, and Filipino wife-Filipino husband households, Takaya (2014) finds that Filipino wives married to Japanese husbands have the lowest rate of labor market participation. This trend suggests that dependence on a male breadwinner is the highest in dual-parent, nuclear families in Japan. Missing in this analysis, however, are the breadwinning contributions of Japanese-Filipinos of working age co-residing with their Filipino (and Japanese) parents. To augment the household income of their Filipino mothers (and Japanese fathers) taking on irregular and part-time jobs, Japanese-Filipino children share household expenses, and occasionally contribute to the remittances of their parents for the health-care needs of grandparents, education of stay-behind siblings or cousins, special occasions, and other necessities of close kin in the Philippines. While familial contingencies serve as opportunities for children to demonstrate a sense of responsibility (Orellana 2001), these also test the resilience of Japanese-Filipino children and their Filipino migrant parents in dealing with the long-term costs of keeping a transnational household.

Continuous breadwinning beyond borders has previously been known as an economic role for a Filipino migrant woman as head of a transnational family (Aguilar 2012; Yamagishi and Tolentino 2012 Faier 2008). Takahata's (2012) study on 1.5-generation Japanese-Filipino children in Shizuoka reveals, meanwhile, the tendency of some low-skilled Japanese-Filipino children to be "trapped" in a financial responsibility just like their Filipino migrant parents. As much as breadwinning denotes adherence to *utang na loob*, it likewise obscures the line between dependence and interdependence, altruism and responsibility, with which both Japanese-Filipinos and their mothers struggle in order to achieve the right balance.

Discussion

The maintenance of intergenerational affinities illustrates the interconnectedness of family obligations, individual desires, and negotiation of structural conditions in the lives of Japanese-Filipinos. As they engage in multiple mobilities across space and time, their perspectives on transnational family relations mature, prompting them to re-examine the meanings of *utang na loob* in relation to the different members of their "circuits of intimacy and care" (Hondagneu-Sotelo and Avila 1997).

Growing up while temporarily immobile in the Philippines facilitated the transmission of *utang na loob*, which positively benefited their Filipino (and Japanese) parents in Japan. Empathy toward their Filipino parents for their marginalized status in Japan also emerges from their own experiences of having precarious labor status as a part-timer, with meager income and limited social benefits. Others are sympathetic toward their parents whose health, job, or business had been severely affected by Japan's decades of economic recession, as they recalled reductions in remittances, in visits to the Philippines, and in frequency (or loss) of contact.

In settling *utang na loob*, Japanese-Filipinos reflect on the accumulated caring experiences and expectations of their family members, as well as the availability and responsiveness or attentiveness of their parents and kin to their needs in the past (Feeney 1999). They also recall the "normalcy" of transnational family arrangement based on the frequency of exchange of care, contact, and co-presence of their parents and caring kin during childhood. Due to physical abandonment, emotional and cultural dissonance, and lack of financial support from their Japanese father, it is no surprise that many Japanese-Filipino children expressed a mixture of anger, frustration, and indifference over denied paternal bonds, and the exclusion of their father from their family life. Yet, it is interesting how some children articulate *utang na loob* in terms of feelings of gratitude for their biological link to their Japanese father, captured by the statement, "I would not be Japanese without him."

In reciprocating care toward extended kin, Japanese-Filipino children redefine the bounds of family, having witnessed the co-dependence of some relatives in the Philippines. They sustain communication and send monetary support only to their kin carers who reared them, and helped them adjust to life in Japan. Settling emotional and moral debts affirms that care was received in the past, formed intimacy remained in one's memory, and is now being repaid.

With Japanese-Filipinos' conscious effort to recompense care to their close kin in the Philippines and the sacrifices of their parents in Japan, the chain of reciprocity between them may diminish but is less likely to end in the future. Depending on their economic status in Japan, some Filipino mothers interviewed may relieve Japanese-Filipino children of the obligation to extend support to their kin, while others are more likely to continue sending remittances through the contributions of their children. Some Japanese-Filipinos politicize reciprocity by confronting their Filipino parents when conditions such as economic abuse, prolonged dependence, and mismanaged transnational household violate or exploit *utang na loob*.

Although remittances promote interdependence among kin, Japanese-Filipinos realize over time that the conditions of *utang na loob* need to be redrawn through adjusting the intensity of connection toward parents and extended family. Many respondents in this study see their Filipino mother's migration as both a source of inspiration and a reminder of the economic failure of Filipino relatives as they sketch their own life aspirations.

While there is evidence suggesting shifts in ideational orientation among the current younger generation (Asis 2006: 261), as they increasingly become interested in their individualized ambitions over family life,[3] such outlook is mainly contingent on the socioeconomic status of one's family. Similarly, many Japanese-Filipinos may aspire to balance personal and family goals. However, as the previous section has shown, they may be compelled to focus on supporting their family when migrant parents face sudden downward mobility in Japan. Consequently, they give greater attention to the social, economic, and emotional well-being of parents in Japan following the reunion, than that of their kin carers in the Philippines. Fewer than half of Japanese-Filipino respondents in Tokyo revealed that they were willing to invite grandparents and relatives for a short visit, and only eleven out of seventy mothers were able to invite family members to work in Japan. While some are willing to pay occasional visits to their close relatives or to attend family gatherings in the Philippines, others gradually have a lowered level of interest in such temporary reunions because it pressures them to build affinity with distant kin.

Moreover, ideational change is evident in how Japanese-Filipinos recognize the contradictory function of *utang na loob* in their intergenerational ties. Whilst it drives intimate and social mobilities, it also restrains them. It undermines their affective capacity to manage coexisting conflict and solidarity, intimacy and obligation, as well as dependence and interdependence resulting from simultaneously extending and nucleating family relationships. Transnational migration may either weaken or strengthen familial ties; it may, thus, either resuscitate or rupture family bonds over the long haul.

Conclusion

This chapter has examined the transnationality of Japanese-Filipino families, focusing on the im/mobile subjectivities of Japanese-Filipino children to manage transnational household and intergenerational intimacies. To circumvent the challenges of organizing family life across borders, Japanese-Filipinos engender different kinds of im/mobility—spatial, legal, social, and intimate—that link their lives to those of their Filipino and Japanese parents, and Filipino extended kin. Their multiple im/mobilities of different routes, experiences, and motives may reinforce existing family norms and ideals, as well as divergent socioeconomic, cultural, and legal conditions between Japan and the Philippines.

The im/mobilities of Japanese-Filipinos entangling with those of their parents and extended kin denotes that these children actively participate in exchanging care and mutual support across borders. Their multiple immobilities facilitate Japanese-Filipinos' care labor, which engenders contradictory effects on intergenerational intimacies. In the Philippines, Japanese-Filipinos' immobilities interlock with im/mobilities of their kin carers and Filipino parents. Through co-residence, these children develop intimacy and positive behaviors toward their caring relatives as well as spatially distant parents. On the other hand, it also results in Japanese-Filipino children's exposure to the economic dependence of relatives. In Japan, Japanese-Filipinos' multiple mobilities are driven by their desire to nucleate family life through co-residence and breadwinning, which intertwine with the legal and social im/mobilities of Filipino migrant (and Japanese) parents. Co-residence may reinvigorate intimacy with parents, but it may also directly expose them to the "contradictory social mobility" and economic exclusion of Filipino migrants in Japanese society. Breadwinning may be a means for Japanese-Filipino children to contribute to the social mobility of transnational families, though it may also inhibit the pursuit of their own social mobility.

Japanese-Filipinos' family-maintenance strategies also bear social implications for both the Philippines and Japan as sending and receiving countries. As a host society, Japan still has ambivalent attitudes toward immigrant families, as its immigration, citizenship, and welfare regimes continue to be restrictive. Local government units, migrant support, and ethnic networks have taken the larger role of extending social and legal services to incorporate immigrant families into local communities (Celero 2018). As shown in the case of Japanese-Filipinos, the legal status may allow spatial mobility to Japan, but it does not always ensure upward social mobility. Meanwhile, the Philippines may have benefited from the remittance flows over the years; however, the government has yet to secure the social welfare of stay-behind families stereotyped as "middle class," or to enhance their capacity to support stay-behind children of Filipinos overseas. The case of Japanese-Filipino families suggests that prolonged economic dependence of the Filipino kin extends beyond the period of fostering Japanese-Filipino children.

Japanese-Filipinos contribute to the maintenance of intergenerational intimacies. At the same time, they consciously review their "circuits of intimacy and care" (Hondagneu-Sotelo and Avila 1997). Their im/mobilities are fundamentally tangled because they are embedded in multiple affective and social ties that are structured according to gender, age/generation, citizenship, and class. Second, their mobilities often entangle with the shifting social norms, structural opportunities, and constraints found in Japan and the Philippines. Third, the dynamics of transnational family life are fluid and in flux, constantly putting migrant families' resilience and agency to the test. While family relationships still matter in their lives, Japanese-Filipinos are often challenged on how to exchange intimacy and care with their aging Filipino (and Japanese) parents, as well as Filipino kin over time and across space. Analyzing their transnational family experiences from their voice and "situated agency" is integral to understanding the significance of intergenerational relations on their current and future life trajectories.

Jocelyn O. Celero is Associate Professor at the Asian Center, University of the Philippines Diliman where she teaches courses on Japanese economy, society, culture, and politics. She obtained her PhD in International Studies at Waseda University, Tokyo, in 2016. Her dissertation examined the transnational life trajectories of 1.5- and second-generation Japanese-Filipinos. She has published on the migration and transnationality of Filipino migrants and Japanese-Filipinos. Since 2019, she has been a research fellow/focal person for UP-CIFAL Philippines.

NOTES

1. Since amending Article 3 in 2008, Japan has been granting Japanese citizenship to children born out of wedlock from a foreign national mother on the condition that the child secures Japanese paternal recognition. In 2015 alone, Japan recognized 5,695 fatherless child applicants as Japanese nationals (Ministry of Justice 2015).
2. As of 2020, the number of Filipinos with long-term resident status (those legally permitted to stay, based on having children with Japanese citizenship) has reached 54,141, while the number of permanent residents has soared to 134,272 (Ministry of

Justice 2021). Many Filipino mothers interviewed in Tokyo were granted permanent and long-term residencies within five years after marriage and while they were on a spouse visa.
3. This result was based on the 2019 Deliotte Global Millenial Survey conducted with young adults aged 18–32 across forty-two countries, including Japan and the Philippines.

REFERENCES

Aguilar, Filomeno. 2012. "Differentiating Sedimented from Modular Transnationalism: The View from East Asia." *Asian and Pacific Migration Journal* 21(2): 149–71.

Alampay, Liane Peña. 2014. "Parenting in the Philippines." In *Parenting Across Cultures: Childrearing, Motherhood and Fatherhood in Non-Western Cultures*, ed. Helaine Selin, 105–21. Dordrecht: Springer Science & Business Media.

Alanen, Leena. 2001. "Childhood as Generational Condition: Children's Daily Lives in a Central Finland Town." In *Conceptualizing Child-Adult Relations*, ed. Leena Alanen and Berry Mayall, 129–43. London: Falmer Press.

Alipio, Cheryll. 2015. "Filipino Children and the Affective Economy of Saving and Being Saved: Remittances and Debts in Transnational Migrant Families." In *Transnational Labour Migration, Remittances and the Changing Family in Asia*, ed. Lan Anh Hoang and Brenda S. A. Yeoh, 227–54. Basingstoke: Palgrave Macmillan.

Asis, Maruja. 2000. "Imagining the Future of Migration and Families in Asia." *Asian and Pacific Migration Journal* 9(3): 255–72.

———. 2006. "Living with Migration: Experiences of Left-behind Children in the Philippines." *Asian Population Studies* 2(1): 45–67.

Asis, Maruja, Lita Domingo, John Knodel, and Kalyani Mehta. 1995. "Living Arrangements in Four Asian Countries: A Comparative Perspective." *Journal of Cross-Cultural Gerontology* 10(1–2): 145–62.

Baldassar, Loretta, and Laura Merla, eds. 2014. *Transnational Families, Migration and the Circulation of Care: Understanding, Mobility and Absence in Family Life*. London: Routledge.

Bauzon, Leslie. 1999. "Filipino-Japanese Marriages." *Philippines Studies* 47(2): 206–23.

Bryceson, Deborah, and Ulla Vuorela. 2002. *The Transnational Family: New European Frontiers and Global Networks*. Oxford: Berg.

Carling, Jorge, Cecilia Menjivar, and Leah Schmalzbauer. 2012. "Central Themes in the Study of Transnational Parenthood." *Journal of Ethnic and Migration Studies* 38(2): 191–217.

Celero, Jocelyn. 2014. "In Fulfillment of Motherhood: An Exploratory Study of Migrant Mothers on Welfare in Japan." *Journal on Global Social Welfare* 1(4): 179–89.

———. 2016. "Japanese-Filipinos' Transnational Pathways to Social Mobility: Education, Occupation and Life Aspirations." PhD dissertation, Waseda University, Tokyo.

———. 2018. "Bonds, Bridges and Links of Hope: Migrant Support Organizations (MSOs) as Agents of Social Integration of Japanese-Filipino Families." In *Thinking*

Beyond the State: Migration, Integration, and Citizenship in Japan and the Philippines, ed. Johanna Zulueta, 221–54. Manila: De La Salle University Publishing House.

Chakraborty, Kabita, and Shanthi Thambiah. 2018. "Children and Young People's Emotions of Migration across Asia." *Children's Geographies* 16(1): 1–8.

Choi, Susanne, Brenda Yeoh, and Theodora Lam. 2018. "Editorial Introduction: Situated Agency in the Context of Research on Children, Migration, and Family in Asia." *Population, Space and Place* 25(3): e2149.

Cresswell, Tim.1999. "Embodiment, Power and the Politics of Mobility: The Case of Female Tramps and Hobos." *Transactions of the Institute of British Geographers* 24(2): 175-92.

———. 2010. "Towards a Politics of Mobility." *Environment and Planning: Society and Space* 28(1): 17–31.

Dreby, Joana. 2007. "Children and Power in Mexican Transnational Families." *Journal of Marriage and Family* 69(4): 1050–64.

Faier, Lieba. 2008. "Runaway Stories: The Underground Micromovements of Filipina Oyomesan in Rural Japan." *Cultural Anthropology* 23(4): 630–59.

Feeney, Judith. 1999. "Adult Attachment, Emotional Control, and Marital Satisfaction." *Personal Relationships* 6(2): 169–85.

Fielding, Tony. 2010. "The Occupational and Geographical Locations of Transnational Immigrant Minorities in Japan." In *Global Movements in the Asia Pacific*, ed. Pookong Kee and HidetakaYoshimatsu, 93–122. Singapore: World Scientific.

Finch, Janet. 1989. *Family Obligations and Social Change*. Cambridge: Polity Press.

Findlay, Allan, David McCollum, Rory Coulter, and Vernon Gayle. 2015. "New Mobilities across the Life Course: A Framework for Analysing Demographically Linked Drivers of Migration." *Population, Space and Place* 21(4): 390–402.

Groes, Christian, and Nadine Fernandez, eds. 2018. *Intimate Mobilities: Sexual Economies, Marriage and Migration in a Disparate World*. New York: Berghahn Books.

Haines, David, Keiko Yamanaka, and Shinji Yamashita. 2012. *Wind over Water: Migration in an East Asian Context*, Vol. 2. New York: Berghahn Books.

Hara, Megumi. 2011. "Ekkyo suru Wakamono tachi, Bokyo suru Wakamono tachi: Shin-nikkei Firipin-jin no Seikatsuki karano Kosatsu" [Cross-border youth and desire for homecoming: Life history of new second generation Japanese-Filipinos]. *The Bulletin of Global Human Studies* 4: 5–25.

Hoang, Lan Anh, Theodora Lam, Brenda S. A. Yeoh, and Elspeth Graham. 2015. "Transnational Migration, Care Arrangements and Left-behind Children's Responses in Southeast Asia." *Children's Geographies* 13(5): 263–77.

Holloway, Susan. 2010. *Women and Family in Contemporary Japan*. Cambridge: Cambridge University Press.

Holloway, Susan, and Ayumi Nagase. 2014. "Child Rearing in Japan." In *Parenting Across Cultures*, ed. Helaine Selin, 59–76. Dordrecht: Springer.

Hondagneu-Sotelo, Pierette, and Ernestine Avila. 1997. "I'm Here, but I'm There: The Meanings of Latina Transnational Motherhood." *Gender & Society* 11(5): 548–71.

Hordsworth, Clare. 2013. *Family and Intimate Mobilities*. Basingstoke: Palgrave Macmillan.

Ito, Ruri. 2005. "Crafting Migrant Women's Citizenship in Japan: Taking 'Family' as a Vantage Point." *International Journal of Japanese Sociology* 14(1): 52-69.

Jones, Gavin, and Hsiu-hua Shen. 2008. "International Marriage in East and Southeast Asia: Trends and Research Emphases." *Citizenship Studies* 12(1): 9-25.

Lam, Theodora, Shirlena Huang, Brenda Yeoh, and Jocelyn Celero. 2018. "Children's Experiences and Perspectives." In *Routledge Handbook of Asian Migrations*, ed. Brenda S. A. Yeoh and Gracia Liu-Farrer, 250-63. Abington: Routledge.

MacLellan, Dawn Grimes. 2011. "'Kids These Days …': Globalization and the Shifting Discourse of Childhood in Japan." In *Japan in the Age of Globalization*, ed. Carin Holroyd and Ken Coates, 60-78. New York: Routledge Contemporary Japan Series 36.

Medina, Belen. 2001. *The Filipino Family*. Diliman: The University of the Philippines Press.

Menchavez, Valerie Francisco. 2018. "Sukli: Uneven Exchanges of Care Work of Children Left behind in Filipino Transnational Families." *Children's Geographies* 16(6): 604-15.

Ministry of Health, Labor, and Welfare. 2013. "Population Survey Yearly Report." Retrieved 24 May 2020 from http://www.mhlw.go.jp/english/wp/wp-hw7/dl/01e.pdf.

Ministry of Justice. 2015. "Kaisei Kokusekiho ni Tomonau Kokuseki Shutoku Todoke no Jokyo" [The situation of application of nationality acquisition after the Amendment of Nationality Law]. Retrieved 30 April 2020 from http://www.moj.go.jp/MINJI/MINJI41/minji174.html.

———. 2021. "Foreign Residents by Nationality." Retrieved 16 December 2021 from https://www.e-stat.go.jp/stat-search/files?page=1&layout=datalist&toukei=00250012&tstat=000001018034&cycle=1&year=20210&month=12040606&tclass1=000001060399&result_back=1&tclass2val=0.

Nuqui, Carmencita Gopez. 2009. "International Migration, Citizenship, Identities and Cultures: Japanese-Filipino Children in the Philippines." *Gender, Technology and Development* 12(3): 483-507.

Ochiai, Emiko. 1997. *The Japanese Family System in Transition: A Sociological Analysis of Family Change in Postwar Japan*. Tokyo: LTCB International Library Foundation.

———. 2009. "Care Diamonds and Welfare Regimes in East and South-East Asian Societies: Bridging Family and Welfare Sociology." *International Journal of Japanese Sociology* 18(1): 60-78.

Ogaya, Chiho. 2015. "When Mobile Motherhoods and Mobile Childhoods Converge: The Case of Filipino Youth and their Transmigrant Mothers in Toronto, Canada." In *Mobile Childhoods in Filipino Transnational Families: Migrant Children with Similar Roots in Different Routes*, ed. Asuncion Fresnoza-Flot and Itaru Nagasaka, 205-21. New York: Palgrave Macmillan.

Oishi, Nana. 2005. *Women in Motion*. Stanford, CA: Stanford University Press.

Orellana, Marjorie Faulstich. 2001. "The Work Kids Do: Mexican and Central American Immigrant Children's Contributions to Households and Schools in California." *Harvard Educational Review* 71(3): 366-90.

Parreñas, Rhacel Salazar. 2003. "The Care Crisis in the Philippines: Children and Transnational Families in the New Global Economy." In *Global Woman: Nannies,*

Maids, and Sex Workers in the New Economy, ed. Ehrenreich, Barbara, Arlie Russell Hochschild, and Shara Kay, 39–54. New York: Henry Holt and Company.

———. 2005. *Children of Global Migration: Transnational Families and Gendered Woes.* Stanford, CA: Stanford University Press.

Salazar, Noel, Alice Elliot, and Roger Norum. 2017. "Introduction." In *Studying Mobilities: Theoretical Notes and Methodological Queries,* ed. Noel Salazar, Alice Elliot, and Roger Norum, 1–24. New York: Berghahn Books.

Satake, Masaaki. 2004. "Filipina-Japanese Intermarriages: A Pathway to New Gender and Cross-Cultural Relations." *Asia Pacific Migration Journal* 13(4): 445–73.

Save the Children. 2006. "Left Behind, Left Out: The Impact on Children and Families of Mothers Migrating for Work Abroad." Sri Lanka.

Schmalzbauer, Leah. 2004. "Searching for Wages and Mothering from Afar: The Case of Honduran Transnational Families." *Journal of Marriage and Family* 66(5): 1317–31.

Seiger, Fiona Katherina. 2014. "Claiming Birthright: Japanese-Filipino Children and Mobilization of Descent." PhD dissertation, National University of Singapore.

Selin, Helaine. 2013. "Introduction.".*Parenting across Cultures: Childrearing, Motherhood and Fatherhood in Non-Western Cultures,* ed. Helaine Selin, 1–11. Dordrecht: Springer Science & Business Media.

Suzuki, Nobue. 2010. "Outlawed Children: Japanese-Filipino Children, Legal Defiance and Ambivalent Citizenships." *Pacific Affairs* 83(1): 31–50.

Takahara, Sachi. 2012. "The 1.5-Generation Filipinos in Japan: Youths Straddling between Education and Employment." *Journal of International Relations and Comparative Culture* 11(1): 291–302.

Takaya, Sachi. 2014. "Citizenship of Long-Term Migrant Filipino Women in Japan: Impacts of Positions in Japanese Families." XVIII ISA World Congress of Sociology, Yokohama, 13–19 July.

Takaya, Sachi, Yukiko Omagari, Naoto Higuchi, Itaru Kaji, and Nanako Inaba. 2015. "2010 nen kokusei chousa ni miru zainichi gaikokujin no shigoto [Jobs held by Japan's Foreign Residents: Views from the 2010 Census Data]." *Journal of Humanities and Social Sciences* 39: 37–56.

Wingens, Matthias, Helga de Valk, Michael Windzio, and Can Aybek. 2011. "Introduction." In *A Life-Course Perspective on Migration and Integration,* ed. Matthias Wingens, Michael Windzio, Helga de Valk, and Can Aybek, 1–26. Dordrecht: Springer Nature.

Yamagishi, Motoko, and Leny Tolentino. 2012. "The Meaning of Living in Poverty for Migrant Women and their Families." *Voices from Japan* 23(1): 25–27.

Yamashita, Shinji. 2008. "Transnational Migration in East Asia: Japan in Comparative Focus." *Senri Ethnological Reports.*

Yeoh, Brenda, Elspeth Graham, and Paul Boyle. 2002. "Migrations and Family Relations in the Asia Pacific Region." *Asian and Pacific Migration Journal* 11(1): 1–11.

Yeoh, Brenda, Shirlena Huang, and Theodora Lam. 2005. "Transnationalizing the 'Asian' Family: Imaginaries, Intimacies and Strategic Intents." *Global Networks* 5(4): 307–15.

———. 2017. "Transnational Family Dynamics in Asia." In *Handbook on Migration and Globalisation*, ed. Anna Triandafyllidou, 413–30. Cheltenham: Edward Elgar Publishing.

Zentgraf, Kristine, and Norma Stolz Chinchilla. 2012. "Transnational Family Separation: A Framework for Analysis." *Journal of Ethnic and Migration Studies* 38(2): 345–66.

CHAPTER
8

Truly Liberal and Immensely Oppressive?
The Experiences of Returned Queer Vietnamese Migrants from Japan

An Huy Tran

Introduction

It was a hot autumn afternoon when I met Dat for the first time in a small outdoor coffee shop in Hanoi. While the customers sitting next to our table grew tired sitting in the humid weather, our conversation lasted until the evening shift when the waitress came to ask whether we wanted our fourth drinks. Dat had a lot to share. He had known about his sexual orientation from early childhood but had hidden it from his family and friends, fearing being discriminated against. Dat wanted to "escape" from such a "source of oppression" in Vietnam after graduating from high school, and chose Japan as a place to migrate to:

> The image of Japan in my head at that time was very idealistic: safe, stable economic conditions. And I thought the view of Japanese people on LGBTQ[1] issues would be more open and tolerant than in other Asian countries ... So I hoped that I would be free from all the fears if I went to Japan.

After four years of studying in Japan, Dat "wanted to escape again," but this time from Japan. Upon coming back to Vietnam, he came out to his family and friends and openly embraced his identity and lifestyle as a gay man. Indeed, Dat was not the only one who decided to return to the place where he had initially run away from.

The movement of people across borders involves a wide range of social practices, through which migrants' motivations, desires, and expectations are constantly negotiated (Carling and Collins 2018). While economic and labor practices, education alternatives, political engagements and family-related issues have formed a large body of literature, the sexual dimension has historically been marginalized, and is still typically absent in the mainstream sociological studies of transnational migration (Carrillo 2017; Manalansan IV 2006). Some scholars have recently established the connections between migration and changing sexual practices, desires, and identities, but the typical and ideal migrant is still considered to be heterosexual (Luibhéid 2008). The experiences of non-heterosexual migrants, therefore, remain inadequately studied. In the few studies that investigate queer migration, sexual minority migrants' mobility trajectories are commonly presented as unidirectional. In particular, studies on global flows of queer migrants predominantly feature movements from "oppressive" destinations (mostly rural areas, in developing countries in the Global South) to more "progressive" ones (mostly urban areas, in developed countries in the Global North), where queer practices, identities, and subjectivities are enabled and realized (Carrillo and Fontdevila 2014). While migration trajectories and outcomes are complex and contingent on divergent factors, the reverse migration movements among non-heterosexual migrants have yet to receive sufficient attention.

This chapter aims to address these gaps by examining the experiences of returned queer Vietnamese migrants who used to live in Japan. It considers sexuality, in the forms of sexual subjectivities, desires, practices, and identities, as tangled in economic, education, or family-oriented issues to facilitate migrants' migration decision-making and (im)mobility trajectories. Lived experiences before, during, and after migration of queer migrants would be investigated to make sense of the negotiations and processes of return migration, in which sexuality emerges as an important feature. The chapter begins with a review of existing literature on sexualities, migration, and mobilities, followed by explanations of research design and methodology. Narratives of returned queer migrants who identify as gays and lesbians are then analyzed to unfold the ways in which these individuals negotiate their sexual, social, and spatial mobilities in tandem with relentlessly changing social landscapes and institutions in Vietnamese and Japanese societies. While the chapter acknowledges that there is a need to fully conceptualize sexuality in migration (Carrillo 2004), it does not advocate distinguishing sexually motivated migrations from other forms of mobility, but rather leans toward the concept of tangled mobilities (Fresnoza-Flot and Liu-Farrer, this volume) to understand the complexities of return migration among queer individuals. The chapter ends with a theoretical discussion, in which original observations are examined through a "sexual field" perspective (Green 2008, 2014, 2015). Inspired by Bourdieusian field theory and Goffman's analysis on situational presentation of self, a sexual field approach aims to explain desire, desirability, sexual practices, and the diverse power hierarchies involved in the process of negotiating sexualities in a contemporary collective sexual life. It assists our understanding of the ways in which queer former migrants negotiate their positions within different sexual fields through transnational migration between Vietnam and Japan. In addition, focusing the analytical lens on the spatial, sexual and social mobilities of returned queer migrants also questions common assumptions in international queer migration studies.

Sexualities and Queers on the Move

While sexual desires and identities have always been important factors that trigger relocations, conventional migration studies used to conceal them with motivations that were perceived to be more rational. It was not until the late 1990s that a sexual and emotional turn in migration studies emerged, acknowledging intimacies, sexualities, and romance to be "at the heart of the migration decision making and behaviors" (Mai and King 2009: 296). The emphasis on sexual motives deviates from strict economist interpretations of migration motivations, and suggests that migration processes are more complicated and tangled than have been recognized in the past. In order to make clear the connection between individuals' sexualities and migration, scholars have coined some specific terminologies. "Sexual migration," for example, refers to journeys that are motivated both directly and indirectly by sexual identities, desires or behaviors of those who migrate (Cantú 2009; Carrillo 2004; Luibhéid 2008). Examining queers' mobility trajectories in Australia, Gorman-Murray observes "queer migration," which "occurs when the needs or desires on non-heterosexual identities, practices and performances are implicated in the process of displacement" (Gorman-Murray 2009: 443).

Imaginaries of contrasting sexual cultures and landscapes are also crucial in inciting migration. Many queers have chosen international relocation to avoid discrimination and stigmas in the home countries, to navigate specific life events, or to facilitate identity developments (Lewis 2014). In this sense, migration decisions are not limited to the search for material and social advancement or involuntary displacement, but go beyond to highlight the multidimensionality of intimacy and pleasure-seeking migrant subjects (Manalansan IV 2006; Groes and Fernandez 2018). This perspective not only makes migration more humanized by giving significance to the pursuit of intimacies, emotions, and sexualities, but it also challenges the simplistic framing of migration's motivations and heterosexuality. Moreover, a focus on sexualities allows a deep understanding of migrants' social incorporation and the unfolding of social relations and structures of oppression, freedom, agencies, and hierarchies that contour migrants' negotiation of sexualities, identities, and collective belongings (Gorman-Murray 2007; Lewis and Naples 2014).

Other developments in migration studies that necessitate the need to consider sexualities in migration include the "transnational turn" and the "mobility turn." The transnational perspective developed in the early 1990s understands migration not as a permanent move from one country to another but rather a process taking place in social spaces that are constantly reworked and negotiated by migrants' simultaneous participation in multi-sited arenas (Basch, Schiller, and Blanc 1994; Levitt and Jaworsky 2007; Vertovec 2009). Migrants' previous ways of thinking about and practicing sexualities are not erased as they still actively maintain connections with families, loved ones, and communities back home. Transnational migration, therefore, involves the labor of negotiating with and making sense of new and old sexual behaviors and identities. It introduces migrants to more complex engagements with sexualities while simultaneously (re)imposing sexual constraints as a result of racial and social class discrimination, unsuitable working and living arrangements, and the surveillance of co-ethnic communities (Ahmad 2009; Cantú 2009; Hoang and Yeoh 2015).

Migration as a concept has been criticized for focusing too much on physical and spatial movements rather than on the interaction between actors, structures, and contexts (Groes and Fernandez 2018). Thus, the "mobility turn" advocates for the consideration of connected flux of human, materials, ideas, images, technologies and how such diverse mobilities are conditioned (Sheller and Urry 2006). Rather than seeing people crossing borders as a result of rational choices, the mobility approach incorporates journeys that are triggered by all sorts of motivation, including hopes, desires, images, symbols, and cultural practices. Hence, mobility scholars pay attention to the interconnections between divergent types of mobility to show that spatial and geographical movements are closely linked to intimacy, social structures, personal identities, status, and senses of belonging (Favell and Recchi 2011). Understanding mobility as being facilitated by and deeply entwined with gender, power, kinship, and sexuality, Groes and Fernandez conceptualize "intimate mobilities" as involving "all forms of mobility shaped, implied or facilitated by bodily, sexual, affective or reproductive intimacy," and thus encompassing other forms of mobility motivated by emotions, desires, or pleasures (2018: 1).

The sexual, transnational, and mobility turns have provided theoretical and methodological venture points for queer migration studies to explore how mobility can be tied to the pursuit of personal fulfillment among individuals of different sexual identities. Queer migration scholarship to date, however, tends to celebrate the post-migration sexual liberation or emancipation, and ignores the critical stances that migrants might have with the new environments. Furthermore, transnational queer migration literature has seen research depicting two specific patterns of movements. The first one focuses on the relocations from Asia and Latin America to the United States (Cantú 2009; Carillo and Fontdevila 2014; Hirano 2014). The second features journeys from Eastern Europe or the Middle East to Western Europe (Dhoest and Szulc 2016; Wimark 2016). Transnational queer migration is also commonly understood as unidirectional, stemming from the oppressive and backward Global South to the liberal and progressive Global North, where higher tolerance toward queerness and stronger legal protection for sexual minorities exist. This viewpoint not only disregards the variances in global queer movements but also reinforces the political dichotomies of East-West, North-South, and legacies of colonialism in migration studies. Besides, queer Asian migrants have mostly been examined in Western contexts, where structural factors such as white hostility and lingering colonialist aftereffects, degrading media representations, and hierarchies based on sex, gender, race, and class negatively impact their sexualities (Kong 2002; Han 2006; Hibbins 2005; Nguyen 2014). While there is a wide range of sexual ideologies and expressions in Asia, the ways in which queer Asian migrants negotiate their sexualities within Asian contexts have not been sufficiently studied. Consequently, queer migration studies have yet to fully engage with other areas of the world to deviate from the effects of US-centrism and Eurocentrism (Chiang and Wong 2017). As migrants' lives are curtailed by various social structures in both home and host societies, it is necessary to touch on how homosexuality is perceived in Japan and Vietnam in order to understand the ways in which queer Vietnamese migrants negotiate their sexuality and mobility trajectories in different phases of migration.

Queerness in Contemporary Japan and Vietnam

The perceptions of non-heterosexuality in Japan have diversely changed from early modern times to contemporary society. In premodern Japan, there was abundant material on homosexuality, and non-heterosexual love was socially accepted (or ignored) to a certain degree. Same-sex love during this time featured mostly male homosexuality in the forms of cross-gender homosexuality and cross-generation homosexuality (Lunsing 2001). After the Meiji period in the nineteenth century, however, Japan embarked on a program of Westernization, in which Western modernity and culture were major sources of influence on how non-heterosexuality was perceived. Homosexuality was then stigmatized and considered in a very negative light (McLelland, Suganuma, and Welker 2007). After World War II and during the American Occupation, Japanese perceptions of sexuality underwent further Western influences. Even though homosexuality was still regarded as a "taboo of urban society" in general public discourses, gay media started to proliferate. The Japanese gay media in the postwar era, however, heavily fetishized white Western bodies and Western gay culture, leading to the erasure of black and non-Japanese Asian bodies from the consciousness of Japanese gay subcultures (Mackintosh 2010; Suganuma 2012). By the late 1990s and early 2000s, there was a "gay boom" in Japanese culture due to increased flows of global queer consumerism and the emergence of queer subcultures in the country. Such a boom has not only given a greater voice to previously sidelined sexual minorities but has also widely disseminated a perception of a tolerant Japanese society toward queerness (McLelland 2005). However, this perception, circulated through certain media and cultural products, does not necessarily represent the lives of sexual minorities in Japanese society. There is thus a contradictory discourse on non-heterosexuality in Japan; although the country can be seen as queer-friendly via popular culture and a few governmental policies, queerness is still considered as something negative in the daily lives of most people (Dasgupta 2017; Kawasaka 2018).

In addition, despite the growing population of foreign residents in the country, it is often assumed that most of the discourses on sexual orientation and gender identification in Japan "concern only ethnically Japanese members of sexual minority groups" (Suganuma 2017: 248). A few scholars have pointed out that the label of "foreigner" might foster contrasting sexual connotations (Kazawa and Kawaguchi 2003; Paquin 2014). For example, while the Western-oriental gay lovers might find it easy to enjoy homosexual encounters in the country (Suganuma 2012; McLelland 2000; McLelland and Dasgupta 2005), foreigners of Asian descent might have different and even contradictory experiences (Baudinette 2016; Quero 2014). It is important to note that the majority of foreign migrants in Japan come from neighboring Asian countries (Liu-Farrer 2020), and there is therefore a need to further inquire into how queer Asian migrants negotiate their sexualities in Japanese society.

The last ten years have witnessed a rapid acceleration in the number of Vietnamese migrants in Japan. The transnational flow of migrants from Vietnam to Japan started to increase in the early 2010s, and by the end of 2019, Vietnamese have been the third largest group of foreign residents in Japan[2] (Ministry of Justice 2020). Although numerous Vietnamese express economic or educational rationales when they migrate to Japan (Liu-Farrer and Tran 2019), other motivations should not be downplayed. As Japanese culture has enjoyed remarkable popularity in Vietnam in the last decade, going to Japan is appealing not only for migrants seeking to accumulate their economic and cultural capital but also for those wishing to satisfy their cultural curiosity. Moreover, as cultural representations of sexualities have the ability to cast effects on migration decisions, the widespread images of the Japanese "gay boom" and a queer-tolerant Japan invite relocation consideration among Vietnamese sexual minorities.

Similar to Japan, the ways in which non-heterosexuality is perceived in Vietnam have gone through considerable changes. Despite of the fact that there has been no law that explicitly criminalizes homosexuality, several discriminatory regulations have existed. During the 1990s and early 2000s, it was common for the official media and public discourses to associate homosexuality as one of the "social evils,"[3] alongside crime, prostitution, gambling, and moral degradability. The Vietnamese Law of Marriage and Family in 2000 even forbade marriage between same-sex individuals. According to a report conducted in 2009 that covered more than five hundred press articles, the image of the LGBTQ community in Vietnam was negatively biased and represented (iSEE and AJC 2009). Consequently, the everyday life of sexual minorities in Vietnam used to be largely affected by homophobia and heterosexism across institutions such as the family, the science of sexuality in medicine and psychology, and the state (Khuat, Le, and Nguyen 2010; Newton 2017).

In recent years, however, the ways in which LGBTQ issues and rights are perceived in Vietnam have enjoyed a swift change thanks to constant advocacies by civil society organizations. In 2015, the Vietnamese LGBTQ movement achieved remarkable successes as the same-sex marriage ban was removed, and a passage of law was approved that allowed individuals who undergo gender reassignment surgery to register under their preferred gender. As the law changed, same-sex marriages mushroomed, and the LGBTQ community became more visible in daily life (Vu, Do, and Chu 2019). Nowadays, Pride parades happen frequently in big Vietnamese cities, many celebrities come out in public, and some popular reality shows[4] have become public platforms for LGBTQ awareness. Social media has also empowered more critical engagements with global and local LGBTQ rights and issues. The transformation of institutional and public discourses on non-heterosexuality in Vietnam indeed suggests the need to consider the experiences of queer people who live through such changes. Many individuals featured in this chapter are in such cases, as they negotiated their mobility trajectories (both spatially and socially) in accordance with the gradual changes in how queerness is perceived in Vietnam.

Methodological Approach

Aiming to uncover the tangling of sexual, spatial, and social mobilities conditioned by social contexts and structures, this chapter examines the experiences of return migration among homosexual Vietnamese migrants, and the ways in which they make sense of their trajectories. The chapter employs the life-history interview, which contemplates migrants' own encounters, subjectivities, and reflections over the life course. As a life-history interview accounts for respondents' shifting situational practices and identifications, the method attends to how migration, as a multifaceted reality, is imagined, desired, experienced, and negotiated with regards to temporal and spatial variances. Moreover, a life-history interview could reveal the emotional dimensions of social experiences, and therefore support the making sense of migrants' "sexual stories" where sexualities and migration are formed, challenged and (re)negotiated (Carpenter 2015; Plummer 1995). From an ethical perspective, a life-history interview enables a more balanced power dynamic between the researcher and the researched, because participants can actively shape the inquiry direction without having their experiences framed in the researcher's agenda and words.

The empirical data of this chapter derives from twelve interviews that I conducted in Vietnam in 2018 and 2019 with nine returned Vietnamese migrants. One of them identifies as a lesbian woman and the rest identify themselves as gay men. The respondents' ages ranged from the mid-twenties to late-thirties at the time of interviews, and they had lived in different parts of Japan for three to seventeen years before returning to Vietnam. I initially met two participants via the introductions of friends on Facebook, and then got to know the rest via snowballing. In qualitative interviews, the researcher's positionalities and identities in relation to those of participants could considerably affect the interviews' accesses and outcomes. Ryan (2015) describes such an encounter as a "qualitative dance" (5), in which factors such as race, ethnicity, gender and sexuality, class, and religion of both parties are "ingredients in a complex and active mix of identities." During the processes of recruiting and interviewing participants, my positionality as a Vietnamese researcher from a German university conducting research in both Japan and Vietnam, my research goals, and the different facets of my identity were revealed. Such practice aimed to create a "third positionality," which is neither an entire "insider" nor a complete "outsider" to the group of research participants, and is based on the characteristics and markers of identity that are actively managed in the research setting (Carling, Erdal, and Ezzati 2014). For instance, while I share a common ethnicity, nationality, and the experience of living in Japan with research participants, my social backgrounds and trajectories are different from theirs. Therefore, a third positionality could transcend the regularly assumed similarities between people from the same ethnicity or nationality.

Apart from such positionality, I actively offered participants information on my own sexual identities and experiences to foster open interactions and rapport, as well as to balance the power asymmetries between the researcher and the researched. It should be noted that while participants were open with me about their sexual identities, they were not necessarily "out" to the public. I therefore explicitly asked participants to choose interview settings in which they felt the most comfortable. While all interviews were conducted in Vietnamese, Japanese phrases and words were sometimes used by participants to refer to specific situations or terminologies. Interviews were recorded with the consensus of the participants, then transcribed and translated by me, using pseudonyms. In the upcoming sections, the chapter unfolds the tangle in participants' return migration processes chronologically, from choosing Japan as a migration destination, to living in Japan, and finally to returning to Vietnam.

Japan as an Alluring "Escape" Destination

There are three mainstream explanations for the drastic growth of the Vietnamese population in Japan. First, as a result of the growing investment flows from Japan to Vietnam, several Japanese firms have been opening branch offices in Vietnam. Going to Japan to either study or gain work experience is thus a strategy for many Vietnamese youths to compete in the labor market. Second, international education as a migration industry has enthusiastically channeled Vietnamese students to Japan with simplified procedures and low requirements (Liu-Farrer and Tran 2019). Last but not least, there is still a big wage gap between Vietnam and Japan, which allows migration brokers to advertise about the possibility of earning a salary three to four times higher if one chooses to migrate to Japan. These three reasons, however, are presented as instrumental and economic-oriented, and cannot fully explain why certain groups of Vietnamese migrants choose to migrate to Japan. The queer former migrants' narratives in this chapter indeed indicate that economic rationales, educational motivations and sexual imperatives tangle in the impulse of migration.

Dat, who was introduced earlier, recalled that one of his first exposures to homosexuality when growing up in Vietnam was from *Yaoi*, a Japanese manga sub-genre that predominantly features male homosexual love. The representations of sexuality in *Yaoi* manga and the genre's popularity gave Dat the impression that homosexuality was not only tolerated but also *Ninki* (popular) in Japan. Similarly, Thuy, a 24-year-old lesbian who studied in Japan for three years, thought that Japan was an alluring destination for the LGBTQ community after seeing pictures of Japanese Pride parades and LGBTQ-themed manga on the Internet. For both Dat and Thuy, the perception of an LGBTQ-friendly Japan stood in stark contrast with their pre-migration experiences. It should be noted that the participants in this chapter all started to be aware of their sexualities during the late 1990s and early 2000s, when homosexuality was still negatively characterized in Vietnamese society. Consequently, many of them report being exposed to homophobic attitudes and behaviors, and having to hide their true sexual identities. Dat, for instance, lived in constant fear of being discovered as gay during his teenage years: "At that time, I was scared, because of the domestic media. Whenever they mentioned about homosexuality, it would be about stealing, raping, and killing ... or *benh hoan* (perverts) ... or *quai go* (freaks)." Such media representations had indeed led to homophobic behaviors. Tai, an interpreter in his late thirties, described his experience during middle school and high school:

> I knew about my sexuality at a relatively early age ... And somebody might have known somehow, and then they teased me ... From then until when I was twenty years old and went to Japan, it had been very tough being different from others and having to *gong ganh* (hold up) in order to hide it.

The word *gong ganh* that Tai used refers to hiding one's true identities and complying with heteronormative expectations by performing heteronormative behaviors. It has a similar meaning to the Western notion of being "closeted," and suggests an extremely exhausting process. From Goffman's (1956) self-presentation perspective, non-heterosexual Vietnamese had to always carry out heteronormative gender performances in the "front stage" of their social interactions with others, and could only reveal themselves in the "backstage" where very few people can see. Migration, therefore, could be contemplated as a strategy for some Vietnamese queers to express their sexualities more freely without facing homophobic or heterosexist sentiments. Tai, for example, saw migration as an escape chance:

> I wanted to migrate because I wished to get away from Vietnamese society, from all the stuffiness, the closeness ... Sexuality was a matter at that time that urged me to find a new environment, to escape. So when I knew that I had got a scholarship to study in Japan, I went immediately without thinking twice.

The sexual dimension in migrants' social lives is not just bound to the migration decision-making process. Even if sex-related concerns do not motivate migration in the first place, they are still deliberately and strategically considered throughout the course of migration (Baas 2018; Carrillo 2004, 2017; Liu-Farrer 2010). After graduating from a university in Vietnam, Lam, a thirty-year-old IT (Information Technology) worker in Ho Chi Minh City, initially planned to enroll in a language school in Tokyo for only two years to improve his Japanese skills. Toward the end of his study, Lam's boyfriend in Vietnam cheated on him, and Lam decided not to return as previously intended. His stay in Tokyo eventually lasted for four more years, during which he obtained a master's degree and worked for a Japanese IT company. Although structural factors such as education and job opportunities inevitably mattered in conditioning Lam's trajectory, his sexuality contributed to the decision to stay longer.

In general, Japan is perceived to offer several advantages and, thus, an attractive migration destination for queer Vietnamese individuals. Together with the possibilities for economic and educational advancement, the perception of Japan as a liberal country with a high tolerance for sexual diversity plays a salient role in facilitating migration. The triggering effect for migration among the participants of this chapter is more potent when such an image of Japan was juxtaposed with the homophobic sentiments they had experienced in Vietnam in the past.

Truly Liberal? Negotiating Queer Sexualities in Japan

While queer migration literature often celebrates the post-migration sexual emancipation, it is not necessarily what most migrants experience. Migration could allow queer migrants' dreams of sexual freedom to be realized, but it can also bring about isolation or social exclusion. For instance, although migrants are more likely to socialize with their co-ethnics for practical reasons, ethnic communities could be a double-edged sword and curtail migrants' sexual identities and behaviors (Carrillo 2017). In contrast to the expectation to express his sexuality more freely after migrating, Dat still had to make excessive efforts to hide his sexual orientation in Japan. As the city where he studied was small, and people in the Vietnamese community there tended to know each other, Dat tried to avoid being "out" involuntarily with fellow Vietnamese who were "very fond of homophobic jokes." Indeed, he closeted himself for the whole four years that he studied in Japan, and paid extra attention to the ways he behaved in public to not appear too effeminate. After seeing many Japanese gay men consider getting married to women and having children, Dat realized that "(Japanese) people were not exposed that much to gender and sexual diversity." Disappointed with the situation, Dat wished to move to Tokyo (though he never did) because he imagined that amid the cold urban lifestyle of the capital "everybody just cares about their own stuff," which would make the city "a good hiding place." Dat's observation aligns with the fact that performances of heteronormativity are still expected among sexual minorities in Japan, and adhering to such fondness is a common daily strategy that many have to employ (Dasgupta 2017).

In addition to the conservative attitudes toward sexual minorities, queer migrants in Japan have to simultaneously navigate discrimination based on xenophobia. They are consequently subjected to a "double layer of discrimination": one is directed to their sexualities, and the other is boosted by their ethnicities or nationalities (Hibbins and Pease 2009). When Thuy (the aforesaid lesbian woman) first moved to a city in northern Japan for her undergraduate study, she disappointedly found out that very few students at her university were open about their sexual identities. The letdown was intensified when Thuy took part in a Pride parade in the city and saw several participants covering their faces with masks to avoid being identified. According to Thuy, many people whose faces were revealed were either foreigners or heterosexuals who wanted to show support. Such masking practices not only created a boundary between queers and non-queers, Japanese and non-Japanese, but also re-emphasized the homophobic and heterosexist barriers in Japanese society that Japanese people themselves have yet to overcome. Moreover, when Thuy tried using a dating app for lesbian women in Japan, she was made fully aware of her foreign status: "I was texting with this (Japanese) woman on the app, and of course, after a few sentences, she could tell that I am a *gaijin* (foreigner). She asked me where I am from. I texted back that I come from Vietnam, and she did not respond after that."

Comparable incidents were experienced by other participants on online dating platforms, where their sexual mobility (in term of sexual desirability and identity) is dictated by nationality, social class, and certain sets of capital. Even with participants who could communicate in Japanese fluently, their status as Vietnamese still hindered the facilitation of intimacies with Japanese locals. Nghi, a gay man in his early thirties, told me that although he had had countless sexual encounters while living in Japan for five years, he was not "the type that Japanese (gay men) like." The preferred "types" for many Japanese gay men, Nghi says, would be either Japanese nationals or white foreigners, whereas other Asians, especially Southeast Asians and South Asians, would be looked down on and considered as undesirable. Because of such racialized preferences in the Japanese queer dating scenes, foreign migrants have to develop suitable strategies to put their foreignness in a more favorable light. Most of the time, such strategies involve presenting themselves as possessing positive Western traits. For example, Nghi focused on showing his English skills on gay dating apps in Japan: "You have to steer the conversations toward English, since it means nothing to them (Japanese users) that you can use Japanese fluently. Although Japanese is very hard, they take it for granted that you should be able to speak Japanese. But if you can speak English, that is something superior." While English skill could be seen as an advantage, it is still important that migrants have to possess decent Japanese language skills in order to elevate their chances of finding sexual or intimate partners. Moreover, there are different queer dating apps catering to different user groups (Japanese, foreigners, tourists), and people choose the most suitable apps for their own needs, resources, and capabilities.

Immensely Oppressive? The (Sexual) Return of Queer Migrants to Vietnam

Migration is an intersecting site of dynamic considerations and negotiations. As this chapter shows, spatial mobilities are triggered not only by structural and sociocultural elements but also by countless facets in an individual's social life. Although emigration is dominant in migration literature, return migration patterns have started to attract scholarly attention. Similar to the determination to emigrate, the decision to return to the home country is characterized by tangling elements. Examining return migration patterns and experiences, therefore, widens the meanings of migration and mobility (Carling and Erdal 2014) and offers opportunities to critically reconsider common assumptions. For instance, while many non-heterosexual migrants are believed to migrate because of their sexualities, Hibbins (2005) observes that several heterosexual Chinese men wanted to go back home as their sexualities and masculinities were degraded after migrating to Australia. By contrast, Murray (2000) finds that some Martinican gays exchanged their sexual liberty in France for a non-racist and less stressful economic situation by returning home to Martinique, where most gays have to closet.

The decision to return and the post-migration experiences of queer Vietnamese migrants are shaped by a tangle of economic, familial, and sexual factors in both Vietnamese and Japanese contexts. In particular, as Vietnam has been turning into a promising business site for Japanese firms, job opportunities at home for high-skilled workers who possess sufficient linguistic skills and cultural competencies have increased, especially in manufacturing, retailing, and IT industries. Working for those companies and earning a Japanese salary while living in Vietnam is indeed attractive, considering the more affordable cost of living. At the same time, the stressful working environment in Japan also makes migrants consider going back. Many who have worked in Japan mentioned how they disliked Japanese corporate culture, where there was "no work-life balance, no emotion between people, and too much gossip."[5] Moreover, Japanese workplaces still remain ethnocentric, and offer limited career opportunities for foreign workers (Liu-Farrer and Shire 2020). Having worked for a Japanese technology firm for eight years, Tai saw no promotion chance for him because foreign workers were not trusted as much as Japanese in his company, "so I'd rather go back (to Vietnam)," he stated. Family-related concerns also motivate queer migrants to return. In the end, they still want to be closer to their families and to take care of their parents, which reflects a consistent traditional expectation for filial piety in contemporary Vietnam.

Sexuality, too, is a powerful driver facilitating return migration flows. The development of LGBTQ movements in Vietnam has fostered a more open public attitude toward sexual minorities. For participants who initially escaped Vietnam because of the oppressive environment for sexual minorities, such change was meaningful. Their idea of returning developed as a result of what they had experienced during home visit trips. Not only did they witness the changing public attitudes toward queerness but they also enjoyed more lively queer scenes and sexual experiences. Tai, the aforementioned translator in his late thirties, expressed that he felt more liberated when visiting Vietnam, which was in opposition to his limited sexual experiences in Japan: "I saw, wow, plenty of 'fish'[6] on the gay dating app when I opened it in Vietnam." He also thought that many potential dating or sexual partners were interested in him partly because he used to be abroad. The recent changes in how queerness and LGBTQ matters are perceived in Vietnam as well as the development of queer scenes in big cities therefore altered many participants' perceptions of a sexually oppressive Vietnamese society that they had had in the past.

Upon returning to Vietnam, many participants came out to their families and friends, took part in social activities for the LGBTQ community, cultivated intimate relationships, and expressed that they felt more at ease about their sexual identities and practices compared to when they were still in Japan. Some even said that it was easier to be queer in Vietnam than in Japan, as sexual minorities in Vietnam have been given a greater voice, and can express their own sexual orientations more freely. Being physically in Vietnam also means returned migrants do not have to negotiate the linguistic or cultural unfamiliarity, and therefore enjoy easier access to sexual opportunities. Phong, an IT engineer who spent seven years in Japan, shared that only by speaking in Vietnamese could he fully convey his affection to intimate partners. Furthermore, having dated several Japanese while living in Japan, Phong thought Japanese people were "too cold," and he consequently put "more trust in Vietnamese people" when it came to intimacy. When asked about whether he wanted to migrate again, Phong replied without reluctance: "To be honest, I did not go to Japan because of my sexuality. But now I have come back to Vietnam, it is my sexuality that keeps me here. I feel comfortable living in Vietnam, and I do not want to move away—at least not in the near future."

Moreover, overseas Vietnamese have a special status in Vietnam. In his works about money and marriageability, Thai (2014) describes how some low-income Vietnamese-American men, who were considered undesirable in the United States due to their racial and occupation status, were welcomed as good potential marriage partners in Vietnam. The shift in the way these men are seen is possible because the Vietnamese often perceive those living abroad as having greater financial power as a result of the economic gap between Vietnam and developed countries such as the US. Migrants, therefore, have access to symbolic, economic, and cultural capitals (Bourdieu 1986, 1989) that could easily be appreciated in a Vietnamese materialistic society. In addition, return migrants sometimes hold foreign education credentials and, together with their experiences of living abroad, project an image of modernized and competent individuals who possess foreign linguistic skills and cultural knowledge. Consequently, they usually have higher chances in earning better wages compared to the average Vietnamese salary upon return. Possessing these different capitals influences migrants' sexual expressions, desirabilities, and identities. The "major change" of Ben, a businessman in his mid-twenties, can clearly illustrate this point.

Ben only dated women before going to Japan and during the three years he lived in Tokyo. However, he started to date men, and just men, after returning to Vietnam. As we were chatting in a crowded Starbucks in the center of Ho Chi Minh City, Ben said that he had never thought of talking about his life as a gay man publicly. Indeed, his sexual practices and identity did not change until he returned, when a friend introduced him to a group of gay men in Ho Chi Minh City who also used to live in Japan. These people subsequently incorporated him into the city's queer scene, and since then, Ben has fully embraced the gay lifestyle. Ben relayed that the gay identity "had always been there," but he had not admitted it to avoid the childhood bullying of being an effeminate boy. When he returned to Vietnam and started to earn a good salary with his Japan-related job, he considered himself to be better off than other people in his social network. The economic superiority thus offered him upward social mobility upon his return, which has improved his self-esteem and social respectability. As a result, Ben now feels more comfortable expressing his true self.

Discussion: A Sexual Field Approach to Return Queer Migration

In order to make sense of how migrants' sexual desirabilities, identities, and practices are constructed in different stages of return migration, this chapter engages with the concept of "sexual field" (Green 2008, 2014, 2015). A sexual field "emerges when a subset of actors with potential romantic or sexual interests in one another congregate in physical or virtual space and orient themselves toward one another according to a logic of desirability imminent to their collective relations" (Green 2015: 27). The sexual field approach recognizes the power of field theory in explaining desire, desirability and sexual practices in contemporary sexual life. From the perspective of field theorists, a field is a relatively autonomous domain constructed with specific sets of rules by the participants, who struggle to claim recognition/rewards within it (Hilgers and Mangez 2015). Subsequently, within a sexual field, desire and desirability are products of ecological, social learning, and psychological processes that associate with the field itself. A key concept in the framework of sexual fields is "sexual capital," which refers to the ability to find intimate partners of one's choosing (Green 2014, 2015). As the sexual capital in a particular sexual field is the property of both field participants and the field itself, it could be seen as a fundamental factor that not only shapes but also allows individuals' positions in the field's structure of desire. Green's sexual field concept emerges from his studies of gay scenes in New York, and has been employed by scholars of queer and sexualities studies. This chapter engages with the concept by applying it to migration phenomena. Such an approach, I believe, allows a comprehensive understanding of migrants' negotiation of sexualities when they are positioned in different social contexts.

Despite the widely circulated images of an LGBT-friendly Japan, homophobic and heterosexist barriers still hinder sexual minorities in contemporary Japanese society from gaining full sexual expression and legal protections. Such barriers are even bigger for non-heterosexual migrants, who are confronted with racial and ethnic discrimination. The narratives of gay and lesbian Vietnamese returned migrants suggest that they are not favored in the Japanese queer sexual field. In other words, queer Vietnamese migrants do not possess a high position within a sexual field structured by a Japanese hierarchy of desirability. Within this hierarchy, Vietnamese nationals are not seen as the desirable "type," especially when compared with Japanese or white foreigners. In order to gain recognition in the field, queer Vietnamese migrants have to develop strategies that can help them win appreciation from other field participants, such as presenting the ability to communicate in English, cultivating Japanese language proficiency, or using suitable dating apps.

In contrast to their low position within the Japanese queer sexual fields, returned migrants occupy a relatively high position within contemporary Vietnamese queer sexual fields. This upward sexual mobility is a result of the process of capital conversion (Bourdieu 1986). In particular, upon their return from Japan, migrants are given higher social status thanks to the Vietnamese association of those who have lived abroad with greater economic resources, good education credentials, sophisticated mannerisms and modern worldviews. The financial and cultural capital they are thought to possess can be converted into symbolic capital, which in turn can then be converted into sexual capital, which allows these returned migrants to be considered as desirable within the structure of desire in Vietnamese queer sexual fields. While some might enjoy the changes in sexual experiences and desirability after coming back, a few participants concern about whether people in Vietnam approach them because of their sexual attractiveness or just because of their status as returned migrants.

From a mobility perspective, spatial mobility to and from Japan affects the social and sexual mobilities of queer Vietnamese migrants differently. Emigration from Vietnam to Japan might result in downward social mobility and sexual (im)mobility as migrants face discrimination based on not only their sexuality but also their ethnicity and nationality. On the other hand, returning from Japan to Vietnam offers queer migrants a chance to elevate their social and sexual statuses in the home society thanks to the conversion between different forms of capital. Consequently, in return migration, spatial mobility might lead to upward social and sexual mobility. This chapter's engagement with the sexual field concept from a migratory and mobility perspective therefore not only expands the meanings of migration and mobility but also sheds light on the systems of social meanings, institutions, and practices that shape queer migrants' experiences.

Conclusion

Transnational migration in the contemporary world is mainly a response to economic and/or demographic pushes and pulls, but it is also a process contingent on tangling factors. By exploring the return migration of queer Vietnamese from Japan, this chapter has shown that sexualities are influential in every phase of transnational relocation, and that their journeys diverge from the reductive assumption about the migration motivation as being committed to material betterment. The chapter, therefore, responds to the growing need to reflect on the tangled conundrums of mobilities and sexualities, and how these notions are conditioned by sociocultural structures and individuals' agencies (Howe, Zaraysky, and Lorentzen 2008; Groes and Fernandez 2018). It argues that the sexualities of queer migrants should be seen as susceptible to intersecting and tangled influences of diverse factors, ranging from an institutional level, such as employment and education markets, and dominant ideologies of gender and sexuality, to an individual level, such as sexual and gender identities, race and ethnicity, social class, and possessed capital.

In addition, the chapter's focus on returned queer migrants challenges the commonly assumed unidirectionality of cross-national queer migration, and provides more nuanced perspectives to the studies of sexualities in migration. The return migration of queer migrants who had initially wanted to "escape" from Vietnam but in the end found more sexual freedom in the home country subverts the designation of receiving and sending societies as respectively sexually liberal and sexually oppressive places. The chapter therefore puts into question whether Japan is truly liberal, and Vietnam immensely oppressive, for sexual minorities. It also suggests the necessity to understand queer migration as entailing tangled mobilities through the lenses of intersectionality, mobility, and transnationalism, because migrants negotiate their mobility trajectories in accordance with not only changing social contexts at both ends of the migration channel, but also the kinds of mobility available in different phases of their lives.

Acknowledgments

The Mercator Research Center Ruhr (MECUR) funded the research on which this chapter is based.

An Huy Tran is a PhD candidate at the Institute of East Asian Studies, University of Duisburg-Essen. His current research focuses on the interrelation of sexualities, masculinities, and transnational migration, but his broader research interests also include student mobilities, intermediaries/brokerage in the migration industry, and transnationalism.

NOTES

1. The term LGBTQ stands for the group of people who identify themselves as Lesbian, Gay, Bisexual, Transgendered and Queer.
2. By the end of 2019, the number of Vietnamese nationals residing in Japan was 411,968. The biggest foreign population in Japan was Chinese (813,675), followed by Korean (446,364) (Ministry of Justice 2020).
3. The Social Evil Campaign in the 1990s and early 2000s was considered to be an effort to reinforce a Vietnamese tradition and social morality by the Communist Party. This campaign focused on the curtailing of acts that are considered to cause social harms such as drug using, gambling, engaging in prostitution and homosexual sex, etc.
4. There have been quite a few television reality shows in Vietnam that featured participants who identified as members of the LGBTQ community, such as *Nguoi Ay La Ai* [Who Is That], The Voice Vietnam, and Vietnam Idol. These shows have all received positive feedback from audiences and possessed high viewing rates.
5. Extract from interview with Phong, a 29-year-old IT engineer in Hanoi, 17 September 2018.
6. The term "fish" could be used as a slang term in Vietnam for a possible intimate partner.

REFERENCES

Ahmad, Ali Nobil. 2009. "Bodies That (Don't) Matter: Desire, Eroticism and Melancholia in Pakistani Labor Migration." *Mobilities* 4(3): 309–27.

Baas, Michiel. 2018. "Queer Temporalities: The Past, Present and Future of 'Gay' Migrants from India in Singapore." *Current Sociology* 67(2): 206–24.

Basch, Linda G., Nina Glick Schiller, and Cristina Szanton Blanc. 1994. *Nations Unbound: Transnational Projects, Postcolonial Predicaments, and Deterritorialized Nation-States*. London: Routledge, Taylor & Francis Group (Gordon & Breach).

Baudinette, Thomas. 2016. "Ethnosexual Frontiers in Queer Tokyo: The Production of Racialized Desire in Japan." *Japan Forum* 28(4): 465–85.

Bourdieu, Pierre. 1986. "The Forms of Capital." In *Handbook of Theory and Research for the Sociology of Education*, ed. J. Richardson, 241–58. New York: Greenwood.

———. 1989. "Social Space and Symbolic Power." *Sociological Theory* 7(1): 14–25.

Cantú, Lionel. 2009. *The Sexuality of Migration: Border Crossings and Mexican Immigrant Men*, ed. Nancy A. Naples and Salvador Vidal-Ortiz. New York: New York University Press.

Carling, Jørgen, and Francis Collins. 2018. "Aspiration, Desire and Drivers of Migration." *Journal of Ethnic and Migration Studies* 44(6): 909–26.

Carling, Jørgen, and Marta B. Erdal. 2014. "Return Migration and Transnationalism: How Are the Two Connected?" *International Migration* 52(6): 2–12.

Carling, Jørgen, Marta B. Erdal, and Rojan Ezzati. 2014. "Beyond the Insider-Outsider Divide in Migration Research." *Migration Studies* 2(1): 36–54.

Carpenter, Laura M. 2015. "Studying Sexualities from a Life Course Perspective." In *Handbook of the Sociology of Sexualities*, ed. John DeLamater and Rebecca F. Plante, 65–92. Cham, Switzerland: Springer International Publishing.

Carrillo, Hector. 2004. "Sexual Migration, Cross-Cultural Sexual Encounters, and Sexual Health." *Sexuality Research & Social Policy* 1(3): 58–70.

———. 2017. *Pathways of Desire: The Sexual Migration of Mexican Gay Men*. Chicago: The University of Chicago Press.

Carrillo, Hector, and Jorge Fontdevila. 2014. "Border Crossings and Shifting Sexualities among Mexican Gay Immigrant Men: Beyond Monolithic Conceptions." *Sexualities* 17(8): 919–38.

Chiang, Howard, and Alvin K. Wong. 2017. "Asia is Burning: Queer Asia as Critique." *Culture, Theory and Critique* 58(2): 121–26.

Dasgupta, Romit. 2017. "Acting Straight? Non-heterosexual Salarymen Working with Heteronormativity in the Japanese Workplace." In *East Asian Men: Masculinity, Sexuality and Desire*, ed. Xiaodong Lin, Chris Haywood, and M. Mac an Ghaill, 31–50. London: Palgrave Macmillan.

Dhoest, Alexander, and Lukasz Szulc. 2016. "Navigating Online Selves: Social, Cultural, and Material Contexts of Social Media Use by Diasporic Gay Men." *Social Media + Society* 2(4): 1–10.

Favell, Adrian, and Ettore Recchi. 2011. "Social Mobility and Spatial Mobility." In *Sociology of the European Union*, ed. Adrian Favell and Virginie Guiraudon, 50–75. Basingstoke, UK: Palgrave Macmillan.

Goffman, Erving. 1956. *The Presentation of Self in Everyday Life*. Edinburgh: Social Sciences Research Centre, University of Edinburgh.

Gorman-Murray, Andrew. 2007. "Rethinking Queer Migration Through the Body." *Social & Cultural Geography* 8(1): 105–21.

———. 2009. "Intimate Mobilities: Emotional Embodiment and Queer Migration." *Social & Cultural Geography* 10(4): 441–60.

Green, Adam Isaiah. 2008. "The Social Organization of Desire: The Sexual Fields Approach." *Sociological Theory* 26(1): 25–50.

———. 2014. "Introduction: Toward a Sociology of Collective Sexual Life." In *Sexual Fields: Toward a Sociology of Collective Sexual Life*, ed. Adam Isaiah Green, 1–25. Chicago: University of Chicago Press.

———. 2015. "Sexual Fields." In *Handbook of the Sociology of Sexualities*, ed. John DeLamater and Rebecca F. Plante, 23–40. Cham, Switzerland: Springer International Publishing.

Groes, Christian, and Nadine T. Fernandez. 2018. "Intimate Mobilities and Mobile Intimacies." In *Intimate Mobilities: Sexual Economies, Marriage and Migration in a Disparate World*, ed. Christian Groes and Nadine T. Fernandez, 1–27. New York: Berghahn Books.

Han, Chong-suk. 2006. "Geisha of a Different Kind: Gay Asian Men and the Gendering of Sexual Identity." *Sexuality & Culture* 10(3): 3–28.

Hibbins, Raymond. 2005. "Migration and Gender Identity among Chinese Skilled Male Migrants to Australia." *Geoforum* 36(2): 167–80.

Hibbins, Raymond, and Bob Pease. 2009. "Men and Masculinities on the Move." In *Migrant Men Critical Studies of Masculinities and the Migration Experience*, ed. Mike Donaldson, Raymond Hibbins, Richard Howson and Bob Pease, 1–19. New York: Routledge.

Hilgers, Mathieu, and Éric Mangez, eds. 2015. *Bourdieu's Theory of Social Fields: Concepts and Applications*. New York: Routledge, Taylor & Francis Group.

Hirano, Kunisuke. 2014. "In Search of Dreams: Narratives of Japanese Gay Men on Migration to the United States." In *Queering Migrations Toward, From and Beyond Asia*, ed. Hugo C. Quero, Joseph N. Goh, and Michael S. Campos, 77–90. New York: Palgrave Macmillan.

Hoang, Lan Anh, and Brenda S. A. Yeoh. 2015. "'I'd Do It for Love or for Money': Vietnamese Women in Taiwan and the Social Construction of Female Migrant Sexuality." *Gender, Place & Culture* 22(5): 591–607.

Howe, Cymena, Susana Zaraysky, and Lois Lorentzen. 2008. "Transgender Sex Workers and Sexual Transmigration between Guadalajara and San Francisco." *Latin American Perspectives* 35(1): 31–50.

iSEE (Institute for Studies of Society, Economy and Environment) and AJC (Academy of Journalism and Communication). 2009. *Thong diep Truyen thong ve Dong Tinh Luyen Ai tren Bao in va Bao mang* [Media messages on homosexuality in print and online press]. Hanoi: World Publishing House.

Kawasaka, Kazuyoshi. 2018. "Contradictory Discourses on Sexual Normality and National Identity in Japanese Modernity." *Sexuality & Culture* 22(2): 593–613.

Kazawa, Takashi, and Kazuya Kawaguchi. 2003. "HIV Risks and the (Im)permeability of the Male Body: Representations and Realities of Gay Men in Japan." In *Men and Masculinities in Contemporary Japan: Dislocating the Salaryman Doxa*, ed. James E. Roberson and Nobue Suzuki, 188–97. London: Routledge.

Khuat, Thu Hong, Bach Duong Le, and Ngoc Huong Nguyen. 2010. *Easy to Joke About, but Hard to Talk About: Sexuality in Contemporary Vietnam*. Hanoi: World Publishing House.

Kong, Travis S. K. 2002. "The Seduction of the Golden Boy: The Body Politics of Hong Kong Gay Men." *Body & Society* 8(1): 29–48.

Levitt, Peggy, and B. Nadya Jaworsky. 2007. "Transnational Migration Studies: Past Developments and Future Trends." *Annual Review of Sociology* 33: 129–56.

Lewis, Nathaniel M. 2014. "Moving 'Out,' Moving On: Gay Men's Migrations Through the Life Course." *Annals of the Association of American Geographers* 104(2): 225–33.

Lewis, Rachel A., and Nancy A. Naples. 2014. "Introduction: Queer Migration, Asylum, and Displacement." *Sexualities* 17(8): 911–18.

Liu-Farrer, Gracia. 2010. "The Absent Spouses: Gender, Sex, Race and the Extramarital Sexuality among Chinese Migrants in Japan." *Sexualities* 13(1): 97–121.

———. 2020. *Immigrant Japan: Mobility and Belonging in an Ethno-nationalist Society*. Ithaca, NY: Cornell University Press.

Liu-Farrer, Gracia, and Karen Shire. 2020. "Who Are the Fittest? The Question of Skills in National Employment Systems in an Age of Global Labor Mobility." *Journal of Ethnic and Migration Studies* 47(10): 2305–22.

Liu-Farrer, Gracia, and An Huy Tran. 2019. "Bridging the Institutional Gap: International Education as a Migration Industry." *International Migration* 57(3): 235–49.

Luibhéid, Eithne. 2008. "Queer/Migration: An Unruly Body of Scholarship." *GLQ: A Journal of Lesbian and Gay Studies* 14(2–3): 169–90.

Lunsing, Wim. 2001. *Beyond Common Sense: Sexuality and Gender in Contemporary Japan*. London: Kegan Paul.

Mackintosh, Jonathan D. 2010. *Homosexuality and Manliness in Postwar Japan*. London: Routledge.

Mai, Nicola, and Russel King. 2009. "Love, Sexuality and Migration: Mapping the Issue(s)." *Mobilities* 4(3): 295–307.

Manalansan IV, Martin. 2006. "Queer Intersections: Sexuality and Gender in Migration Studies." *The International Migration Review* 40(1): 224–49.

McLelland, Mark J. 2000. *Male Homosexuality in Modern Japan: Cultural Myths and Social Realities*. Richmond: Curzon.

———. 2005. *Queer Japan from the Pacific War to the Internet Age*. Lanham, MD: Rowman & Littlefield.

McLelland, Mark J., and Romit Dasgupta, eds. 2005. *Genders, Transgenders and Sexualities in Japan*. London: Routledge.

McLelland, Mark J., Katsuhiko Suganuma, and James Welker, eds. 2007. *Queer Voices from Japan: First Person Narratives from Japan's Sexual Minorities*. Lanham, MD: Lexington Books.

Ministry of Justice. 2020. "Heisei Gannen Mae Genzai Ni Okeru Zairyuu Gaikokujin Kazu Ni Tsuite" [About the current number of residing foreigners at the beginning of Heisei era]. 27 March. Retrieved 26 April 2020 from http://www.moj.go.jp/nyuukokukanri/kouhou/nyuukokukanri04_00003.html.

Murray, David A. B. 2000. "Between a Rock and a Hard Place: The Power and Powerlessness of Transnational Narratives among Gay Martinican Men." *American Anthropologist* 102(2): 261–70.

Newton, Natalie. 2017. "Homosexuality and Transgenderism in Vietnam." In *Handbook of Sexuality Studies in East Asia*, ed. Mark J. McLelland and Vera Mackie, 255–67. London: Routledge.

Nguyen, Tan Hoang. 2014. *A View from the Bottom: Asian American Masculinity and Sexual Representation*. Durham, NC: Duke University Press.

Paquin, Jamie. 2014. "Should I Stay or Should I Go? Racial Sexual Preferences and Migration in Japan." In *Queering Migrations Toward, From and Beyond Asia*, ed. Hugo C. Quero, Joseph N. Goh, and Michael S. Campos, 21–40. New York: Palgrave Macmillan.

Plummer, Ken. 1995. *Telling Sexual Stories: Power, Change and Social Worlds*. New York: Routledge.

Quero, Hugo Córdova. 2014. "Made in Brazil? Sexuality, Intimacy, and Identity Formation among Japanese Brazilian Queer Immigrants in Japan." In *Queering Migrations Toward, From and Beyond Asia*, ed. Hugo C. Quero, Joseph N. Goh, and Michael S. Campos, 41–60. New York: Palgrave Macmillan.

Ryan, Louise. 2015. "'Inside' and 'Outside' of What or Where? Researching Migration through Multi-positionalities." *Forum Qualitative Sozialforschung / Forum: Qualitative Social Research* 16(2): Art. 17.

Sheller, Mimi, and John Urry. 2006. "The New Mobilities Paradigm." *Environment and Planning A: Economy and Space* 38(2): 207-26.

Suganuma, Katsuhiko. 2012. *Contact Moments: The Politics of Intercultural Desire in Japanese Male-Queer Cultures*. Hong Kong: Hong Kong University Press.

———. 2017. "Sexual Minority Studies in Japan." In *Handbook of Sexuality Studies in East Asia*, ed. Mark J. McLelland and Vera Mackie, 244-54. London: Routledge.

Thai, Hung Cam. 2014. *Insufficient Funds: The Culture of Money in Low-Wage Transnational Families*. Stanford, CA: Stanford University Press.

Vertovec, Steven. 2009. *Transnationalism*. London: Routledge.

Vu Thanh Long, Do Quynh Anh, and Chu Lan Anh. 2019. *Song Chung Cung Gioi: Tinh Yeu va Quan he Chung song cua Nguoi Dong tinh, Song tinh va Chuyen gioi o Viet Nam* [Living with gender: Love and co-habitat relationship of homosexuals, bisexuals and transgenders in Vietnam]. Hanoi: Institute for the Studies of Society, Economics and Environment (iSEE).

Wimark, Thomas. 2016. "Migration Motives of Gay Men in the New Acceptance Era: A Cohort Study from Malmö, Sweden." *Social & Cultural Geography* 17(5): 605-22.

CHAPTER
9

Social Mobility and Labor Migration under Recession
Exploring Generational Differences among Japanese Migrants in China

Kumiko Kawashima

Introduction

There is a bias toward the youth in the literature on labor migration experience in a post-economic crisis context. By positioning young adults as one of the hardest hit population groups, scholars have frequently examined the relationship between youth un(der)employment, motivations for migration, and future aspirations (Salamońska and Czeranowska 2019; Van Mol 2016). Studies on highly skilled youth in Southern Europe have found that increased motivations for emigration are not only associated with economic factors but also dissatisfaction with their quality of life under a recession, and poor future prospects (Bartolini, Gropas, and Triandafyllidou 2017; Domínguez-Mujica, Díaz-Hernández, and Parreño-Castellano 2016). Cross-national comparisons have revealed that patterns of the labor market incorporation and experiences of migration vary significantly, depending on the local context (Cairns 2017; Mendoza 2018). Notwithstanding their diverse findings, these studies share a broader and ongoing concern about the precarious youth (migrant) labor in times of uncertainty, and the widening wealth gap (Heggli, Haukanes, and Tjomsland 2013; McDowell, Batnitzky, and Dyer 2009).

Compared to the youth, the migration of the older generations is rarely studied through the lens of labor mobility, even though economic recessions equally affect their working lives. Following years of relative stability of Fordist employment, older generations of workers in many industrialized economies were hit with the Global Financial Crisis of 2008 and its aftermath in midlife. This has brought into sharp focus numerous disadvantages that older workers, as a marginalized group, face under an economic recession (Bank 2009; O'Loughlin, Humpel, and Kendig 2010; Solem 2012; Vickerstaff 2010). The extent to which they experience career interruptions, unemployment, and increased anxiety about their and their children's economic security and well-being in the future are dependent on their socioeconomic and institutional positions (Dingemans, Henkens, and Van Solinge 2016; McDaniel, Gazso, and Um 2013; Visser et al. 2016). While some scholars advocate for increased labor market participation by providing better training to older workers (Hancock 2006), others point out that reducing their access to employment or "productive work" to a question of skills and dispositions ignores the gendered and classed nature of cultural capital accumulation (Bowman et al. 2017; Loretto and Vickerstaff 2015). However, questions of older workers' employment under an economic crisis have rarely been researched explicitly in relation to labor migration.

In recent years, more scholars have highlighted the value of transnational perspectives for studies of aging (Horn and Sweppe 2015). Ciobanu and Hunter (2017) contemplate the potential mutual benefits between the "mobilities paradigm" in the social sciences and the study of older migrants. Commonly, studies divide geographically mobile older people into (former) migrant workers who have "aged in place" and non-labor migrants who move in old age for family or lifestyle reasons. For example, Warnes et al. (2004) separate older international migrants in Europe into European and non-European labor migrants, and family- or amenity-oriented retirement migrants. Benson (2011), Benson and O'Reilly (2009), and Oliver (2008) spotlight retirees as "lifestyle migrants" who move abroad in search of a better quality of life. Common concerns regarding "migrants who age in place" include their social and economic integration and well-being, including in retirement, and their care needs (Blakemore 1999; Steinbach 2018; Ramos and Martins 2020). For those who move in old age, their geographical mobility is frequently examined as part of transnational householding (Bolzman, Kaeser, and Christe 2017; Toyota 2006) or the outsourcing of aged care to institutions abroad where wages are cheaper (Horn, Schweppe, and Bender 2015; Schwiter, Brütsch, and Pratt 2020). Retirement and "amenity-seeking" migration have been debated as an opportunity to seek leisure, new lifestyles and identities, volunteer work, or affordable social care (Botterill 2017; Haas 2013; Thang, Sone, and Toyota 2012; Toyota and Xiang 2012). It is noteworthy that these approaches to studying older migrants collectively reflect and further promote a dominant conceptual divide between workers and non-workers (Huete, Mantecón, and Estévez 2013).

What remains under-researched is people who engage in labor migration in later life. In particular, the experiences of aging workers during trying economic times have not been adequately discussed in relation to labor migration. How does the experience of recession impact on the patterns of career trajectories and geographical mobility among different generations of migrants? How does their geographical mobility as transnational labor migrants intersect with their social mobility?

This chapter examines the experiences of both aging and younger skilled Japanese migrants in China to consider the impact of an economic downturn on the patterns of social and geographical mobility from a comparative perspective. Japan experienced a severe, large-scale market crash in the early 1990s when the asset bubble burst. Nearly three decades on, the national economy continues to stagnate, and it can be said that the "post"-crisis period is ongoing (Chiavacci and Hommerich 2017; Funabashi and Kushner 2015). In my study, the older migrant group came of age as the national economy surged, and were middle-aged when the recession hit, while the younger group completed their education and entered the labor market after the recession had begun. My findings show that the working conditions under a recession were a major factor that motivated both groups to initiate their migration, but the timing of the recession had a significant influence on each cohort's experience of the labor market, social mobility, and subsequently, labor migration. Viewing labor migration as part of a migrant's broader career trajectory helps elucidate the effect of a recession on geographical mobility and its entanglement with social mobility (see Fresnoza-Flot in this volume). A generational perspective is fruitful because it demonstrates that changing life course patterns are shaped historically and institutionally.

Methods and Data

This research is part of larger ethnographic studies that examined two groups of skilled Japanese migrants in the north-eastern Chinese city of Dalian. The findings discussed in this chapter are based on the fieldwork I conducted between 2012 and 2017. Semi-structured and unstructured interviews were carried out with thirty-nine younger migrants (sixteen females, twenty-three males) and twenty-two older migrants (all males). They all held renewable visas that allowed them to live and work in Dalian as skilled professionals. In 2012, just under 6,000 Japanese nationals were residing in Dalian as long-term residents (MOFA 2012). In 2015, there were 838 Japanese men in their sixties or over living in the city (MOFA 2016). There is no officially available figure for the kind of skilled migrants interviewed for this study. However, during interviews in 2012, Japanese consulate staff and labor recruiters estimated that up to a couple of thousand Japanese men and women in their twenties to forties belonged to this category, and that the gender ratio among this group was fairly equal. Therefore, my data on the younger migrant group is slightly skewed towards the males than the overall population. In contrast, older skilled Japanese migrants are extremely male-dominated, and therefore my data on this group is representative of the general population. As discussed in a later section, the male domination of this migration stems from the fact that lifelong career opportunities as skilled corporate workers have long been closed to most women in Japan, even after the Equal Employment Opportunity Law came into effect in 1986. The only older female corporate worker I met during my repeated visits to Dalian had initially arrived in the city as the spouse of a company transferee, and later studied Japanese language teaching before landing a trainer job for a locally based outsourcing firm. Her experience contrasts with the older migrants in my study, who all found a job in the city due to a lifetime of working in the same industry.

The younger migrants were aged between twenty-four and forty-four at the time of the interview, and the most common age on arrival was twenty-five. Apart from two single mothers with a young child, all were childless at the time. The median length of stay in the destination was four years, but ranged from two to nine years. Approximately two-thirds had a four-year university degree, slightly under a quarter had a vocational college certificate, and two had a master's degree. Both genders were well-represented among college and university graduates in my data. In the older group, the median age on arrival was sixty. The median period of residence was six years; it ranged from two to thirteen years, although the exact length was difficult to calculate because some of these migrants had taken frequent business trips to the destination city or been stationed there before they eventually migrated to it. Most men were married to a Japanese woman at the time of their arrival, but one was single and three were divorced. Except for one divorcee, all had grown-up children, whom they left behind in Japan together with their wife. Only one man migrated with his wife.

I conducted interviews in public places such as cafes and fast-food outlets, and sometimes at the interviewee's workplace or home. As part of participant observation, I visited research participants at both work and home, and joined them at eateries and parks during social outings. All interview excerpts have been translated from Japanese by the author, and the names attributed are pseudonyms.

Below, I will first explain both migrant groups' positions in the local labor market, and their roles in the Chinese city's economy. While both groups emigrated in order to access an employment opportunity rare in the home country, their differential roles in the workplace and occupational statuses stemmed from the patterns of social mobility distinctive to each generation.

Labor Migration to a Transnational Ethnic Niche

The Japanese migrants in this study had migrated to the Chinese city of Dalian as skilled workers. This section explains the importance of its trade relationship with Japan for its economic development, and the Japanese skilled migrants' place in the city's transnational economy.

My Japanese migrant interviewees were heavily concentrated in Dalian's key sectors: manufacturing and Information Technology. Dalian has been a key manufacturing base for China's economic development plan since the opening up of the national economy to foreign investment. The Dalian Development Area (DDA) was the first Economic and Technological Development Zone in the country, and it grew exponentially by attracting foreign capital, most notably from Japan (Seki 2000: 16–17). More recently, the city has become one of the twenty-one service outsourcing model cities in China, and the Dalian High-tech Industrial Zone (DHZ) has been celebrated as one of the most successful special economic zones focusing on service outsourcing (Zheng, Willcocks, and Yang 2010). Both zones represent numerous leading Japanese firms, which have significantly contributed to the host city's rapid growth as a regional economic hub. Knowledge and technology transfer from Japan has been instrumental in strengthening key industries such as digital outsourcing and electrical equipment and electronics manufacturing (Seki 2000: 49).

The Dalian-Japan trade ties in these and other key industries have created a demand for Japanese labor to facilitate and strengthen business relationships between the two countries. Chinese firms in Dalian hire Japanese migrants to accelerate knowledge transfer and develop domestic talent. These skilled migrants possess not only occupational expertise but also linguistic and embodied cultural knowledge; and as native-born workers, they are accustomed to the Japanese business conventions. Barring a few exceptions, both groups of migrants were monolingual and exclusively used the

Japanese language in the workplace. The Japanese ethnic niche in Dalian played a key role in regional economic development, and became embedded in global production chains.

While migration motivations are always complex, both groups stressed that their choice to migrate was a way of dealing with the stagnation or stalled upward mobility in the Japanese labor market under a prolonged recession. Following the economic crisis of the early 1990s, job security has weakened, precarious forms of employment have expanded, unemployment and suicide rates have increased, and rates of marriage and reproduction have declined (Allison 2012; Gordon 2015; Piotrowski, Kalleberg, and Rindfuss 2015). Jobs in an ethnic niche in Dalian, in comparison, provided a chance to create a favorable lifestyle with a better work-life balance without chronic overtime work or long commutes,[1] a higher salary level relative to the average local population, and the better living conditions this afforded them. Besides, the Japanese migrants enjoyed their status in China of being highly skilled foreign talent, as well as the excitement of being part of a burgeoning economy. These location-specific benefits were sufficient to offset the drawbacks, such as a substantially reduced salary compared to their previous job in Japan, and the provincial status of the host city. Unlike high-profile global cities such as London, New York, and Shanghai, where migrants become invested in their creative and entrepreneurial aspirations (Farrer 2020; Fujita 2009; Sooudi 2014), Dalian was virtually unknown among the young Japanese in my study, and the older migrants' wives and adult children frequently declared that the city lacked sufficient appeal to warrant a visit compared to other Chinese cities such as Shanghai and Beijing. My previous writing on the younger migrant group examined the intersection of economic, social, and cultural factors that motivated and shaped their migration experience in gendered ways (Kawashima 2018, 2020). By contrast, the remainder of this chapter will focus on the labor market issues in an economic downturn, with particular interest in a comparison between career trajectories of the older and younger migrant groups.

Despite both holding the role as a native-born Japanese expert in their respective workplaces, the two groups had a different occupational status. All the older migrants found work in their career fields as seasoned professionals, and the majority were formerly connected to large and reputable firms. For the local Chinese enterprises who hired them, their cultural and social capital help expand their business, develop the local workforce, and gain status and credentials in the eyes of their Japanese client firms. To compensate for the significantly lower salaries than they used to receive in Japan, the Chinese firms offered subsidized or free apartment accommodation, return flights to Japan at regular intervals, an interpreter, and even a chauffeur for those who worked at factories in isolated areas. Those aged over sixty were ineligible for the skill work visa. Usually, their employers arranged a Foreign Expert Certificate (a 'Z' visa) so that the aging workers could work, for example, as foreign technical experts in advisory roles at a local firm.

By comparison, the majority of the younger migrants worked in customer service roles, answering calls from Japanese users of digital or computer products such as virus software and industrial printers. While some were able to negotiate a better salary based on their prior industry experience in Japan, most were hired into entry-level positions, and became embedded in the lower echelons of the IT industry. Hence, the two groups of migrants in my study fulfilled distinctive roles in the global production chain, even as they all contributed to the development of the transnational economy between China and Japan, and the trade relationship between these two countries.

The difference between the two groups of migrants in terms of occupational types, remunerations, and positions in the workplace hierarchy stems from not only their age difference but also the different patterns of career trajectories that developed in the contrasting social, economic, and organizational contexts. The onset of the recession in the early 1990s hit the two groups at different points in their life course, and this had a lasting impact on their career development. In the next section, I will trace the older Japanese migrants' transitions from education to employment and subsequent career progression, to "retirement" in Japan.

Career Trajectories of Older Japanese Migrants between the 1960s and the 2010s

Education-Employment Transitions during the Economic Growth Era

The older migrants came of age when the Japanese national economy was growing rapidly. They completed formal education in the 1960s or 1970s, when manufacturing was thriving, labor supply was in shortage, and access to education was becoming more egalitarian (Brinton and Ikemura 2008). As stated earlier, the majority of these men completed a four-year university course, despite many coming from a modest family background. They overwhelmingly majored in technological fields such as electrical or mechanical engineering, and engineering management. The remaining commonly attended reputable industrial high schools at a time when the number of such schools and enrolled students was peaking (between 1965 and 1970), which served to meet the growing demand for labor in manufacturing and other key sectors (Sasaki 2000: 21–22). All the interviewees, including the high school leavers, made a smooth transition to full-time permanent employment, most commonly in positions related to producing goods such as computer hardware, home appliances, automobile parts, and mechanical equipment. The majority were hired by a large and reputable firm that was an ancillary company or a subsidiary in the conglomerate (*keiretsu*) system. Takafumi's reflection on his earlier years illustrates the positive impact of the expanding economy on career opportunities for male workers in the past. After graduating from university as an economics major, he joined a trading company in his native northern Japan and gained wide-ranging experience by being stationed at various affiliated companies. By his thirties, Takafumi was in charge of merchandising for home electronics and car accessory retailers, at a time when consumer spending had been soaring, and domestic manufacturing of consumer goods had taken over the imported goods (Gordon 2012). He commented: "It was a good time. Targets for sales and inventory turnovers were easy to meet, and I got a bonus every time I cleared a target, which was often."

The older migrants in my study were beneficiaries of the highly institutionalized, gendered, and rigidly age-based sequencing of career progression, which was the norm in this high-growth era (Kelly and White 2006; Brinton and Ikemura 2008; Gordon 2017). As young males, they followed the normative path to adulthood by becoming incorporated into the system of what is often referred to as Japanese-style management. Its key features include a seniority-based system of wages and promotions (*nenkō joretsu*) and long-term employment, or so-called lifetime employment (*shūshin koyō*). It echoes the American "baby boomer" generation's experience of Fordism in the postwar period, which is associated with job security, the gendered division of labor in the household, and increased welfare provision (McCormick 2007; Neilson and Rossiter 2005).[2] Men were routinely hired as permanent workers on the "management track" (*sōgōshoku*), which offered training, promotion, wages, and decision-making power that increased over time. The older men in my study certainly enjoyed these benefits. Teruyoshi completed a five-year industrial education at a prestigious national institute of technology and then found employment at a reputable machine tools manufacturer at the age of twenty, as did all his schoolfriends. He married when he was twenty-eight and had the first child at thirty, followed by two more children in the next few years. His promotion raised his salary and funded the purchase of a family home and the children's education.

Female workers in the same historical period were largely excluded from career advancement due to their routine assignment to the female-dominated general clerical track (*ippanshoku*). This track denied workers access to training and promotion, and therefore to pay increases and managerial positions. The two-track system has directly caused the gender pay gap in Japan (Zacharias-Walsh 2016). Thus, the relatively uniform manner in which male corporate workers in the postwar era met typical milestones of middle-class adulthood, including marriage, breadwinning, fathering children, and homeownership, was made possible at the expense of women's economic independence. The older migrants in my study benefited from the meteoric rise in the national economy led by manufacturing in the Golden Sixties and beyond. They enjoyed upward social mobility as part of the "new middle class" (Vogel 1963), when it was a real possibility for a larger segment of male-headed households than today, including those from working-class backgrounds (Gordon 2017; Kelly 1993).

Impacts of the Recession on the Experience of Retirement in Japan

The baby boomer and adjacent generations benefited from expanding career opportunities in these good economic times, and the normative gender roles supported their successes in the public domain of employment. However, the older migrants in this study left Japan, where it was difficult to continue working in their career field with the same level of remuneration and authority. Key structural factors are at play. First, firms in Japan routinely and systematically demote non-executive members in their mid-to-late-fifties by stripping them of their manager status and significantly reducing their salaries. This is called "retirement from a managerial post" (*yakushoku teinen*), and is designed to reduce labor costs in exchange for keeping permanent employees in the workforce until retirement. This practice became widespread as firms sought to manage the increased cost pressure due to the staged extension of the mandatory retirement age from fifty-five to sixty in the 1980s and 1990s (Oka and Kimura 2003: 602–3; Osako 1988). It is not uncommon for workers who have been "retired" from managerial posts to be given menial tasks outside the area of expertise, or else pressured to resign "voluntarily" (Berggren 1995: 65; Yamada and Higo 2011: 163). Second, the mandatory retirement age is very much the norm in Japan, and chances to extend one's career employment beyond this age with the same working conditions are hard to come by. In most cases, retirement-age workers are re-employed on a renewable contract or shifted to subsidiaries or client firms (Clarke et al. 2015; Yamada and Higo 2011).[3] Under these institutional measures, all but a select few spend the twilight of their careers in a reduced capacity and on a reduced salary. Osako (1988) aptly called this "downward mobility as a form of phased retirement in Japan."

In my data, Hidehiko was the only interviewee who could extend permanent full-time employment beyond the mandatory retirement age. For two years, he continued to work for his career employer, a large electronics manufacturer, as a trainer for junior staff, until he chose to work for a China-based company as a general manager of its Japan Business Department. For most other interviewed migrants, the institutional practice of enforced demotion curtailed their ability to end their lifelong employment on a high note. Kentaro was fifty-two years old when he was instructed to "retire" from his managerial post at the headquarters of a major electronics company, and to move to a smaller client firm as a rank-and-file software developer. In the new workplace, he felt marginalized as an outsider, and found the tasks unstimulating. He recalled this time as follows: "I wanted to stay where I was, but my manager was pushing for my resignation. I took the position and clung to it for eight years until I retired at sixty."

All the aging interviewees wished to continue working beyond the age of sixty. Approximately half took early retirement to seek a more rewarding work environment before they aged further. In these cases, an early retirement package was a bonus that softened the financial risk of jumping ship. Those without higher education credentials are more likely to face obstacles to desirable pathways to eventual retirement because they are underrepresented among higher-level managerial posts (Clarke et al. 2015). This tendency was also observed among the interviewed migrants. Shunsuke was already discontented that his job title "assistant manager" did not reflect his responsibility, and that he was barred from a higher status because he did not have a university degree. At fifty-five years old, he was transferred to a small affiliated company as its "president." There, he became answerable to his former subordinate at the headquarters, and his salary decreased to the level of a starting salary for a university graduate. Shunsuke found this humiliating: "No matter how skilled, those older than fifty-five are treated as a burden in Japan." Three months into this new role, he embarked on a job search in Asia and eventually found a factory manager job in Dalian, where an acquaintance was working. This example shows that, to the men who wished to continue working in old age, labor migration presented an alternative to an anticlimax to their lifelong career in Japan.

Transnational Mobility as Cultural and Social Capital in Globalizing Asia

What helped the aging men find professional employment in Dalian despite their stalled labor market mobility in Japan was their experience in working abroad and the transnational professional network they cultivated. By the time they were middle managers, all but one had a role that required working closely with firms abroad, taking long and frequent overseas business trips, or being transferred to subsidiaries in foreign cities. For example, Akihiko worked as a software developer, and his first employer, an ancillary company in a Japanese multinational conglomerate, collaborated with a computer research institute in Tianjin in the 1980s. Following this first overseas assignment, he regularly worked in Beijing and other major Chinese cities to collaborate with local IT engineers. These networks became integral to his decision to leave his first employer at the age of fifty-six and work for a small IT firm in Dalian, where his expertise was highly valued and he could have greater autonomy and control over the business.

Half of the older migrants had the experience of being stationed in Asia for multiple years. This was against the backdrop of the changing political economy in Asia. By the mid-1980s, Japan's national economy had become the second-largest in the world after the United States, and Japan-based business headquarters dispatched managers to oversee relocations of production sites to East and South East Asia. Those interviewees engaged in employer-initiated overseas transfers in order to set up and/or manage new factory operations to produce goods such as car parts, machine tools, and video cassette recorders. This experience of managing a foreign workforce turned out to be highly useful in their post-retirement work in Dalian. Their former colleagues, clients, and acquaintances were equally transnationally mobile, and circulated among Asian cities such as Shenzhen, Beijing, Penang, and Ho Chi Minh City. The Japanese IT sector had seen increased collaborations with overseas production sites due to globalization since the 1960s. Men such as Kentaro, Hiroki, and Hidehiko all recalled intensively studying English as young employees to read untranslated materials, attend overseas conferences, and collaborate with foreign engineers based in the United States.

As former full-time permanent members of corporations who had established a lifelong career in thriving occupational fields, the older migrants had two major advantages that the younger group did not. One was that they possessed skills and technical knowledge that would aid technology transfer from Japan to Chinese firms. The other was transnational professional ties that became an effective source of recruitment information. Such institutional forms of cultural capital and social capital (Bourdieu 1986) had been accumulated over the preceding decades, thanks to the men's status as core members of firms at a time when Japanese businesses were rapidly globalizing. The older migrants had long been part of the transnational Japanese business networks that later became an effective recruitment source. Over two-thirds of them found employment in Dalian because a former client or colleague had put them in contact with their new employer or had approached them with a job offer. Others registered with recruitment agencies and were quickly matched with jobs in China.

In summary, the older migrants in my study benefited from being the core workforce of corporate Japan during its economic ascension. It provided them with a stable income to support their family, skill training, assistance with gaining professional qualifications, and management experience. When they were posted in overseas locations, they gained knowledge of global production, international trade, and diverse business cultures. As permanent full-time employees at corporations, they monopolized the kind of opportunities and protections from which part-timers, contractors, and other precarious workers were excluded. By fully utilizing such cultural and social capital, they opened up a pathway to career employment abroad, not only to earn an income but also to enjoy the last years of working as valued professionals. Their transnational career trajectories differ significantly from those of younger Japanese migrants, shown in the next section, due to the timing of the economic downturn and the associated social and cultural changes in education and in labor market practices.

Career Trajectories of Younger Japanese Migrants

The younger group of migrants in my study all transitioned from education to employment between the mid-1990s and the early 2000s. They entered a dual labor market where the growing labor casualization produced a greater proportion of insecurely employed youth, and the lasting negative impacts of such marginalization on future career prospects intensified under the recession (Genda and Kurosawa 2001; Altonji, Kahn, and Speer 2016; Liu, Salvanes, and Sørensen 2016). This was a time when the large majority of high school graduates in Japan progressed to higher education (MEXT 2015). All but one of the younger migrants interviewed proceeded to tertiary education after high school. As in the majority of the general youth population in Japan, they tended to attend low- to mid-ranked private institutions, or to choose fields of study with high acceptance rates. A few others attended a vocational training school to learn skills such as bookkeeping, art, music, and languages, while a small minority dropped out of tertiary education. When these young people made their transition to the labor market, they found their tertiary education was insufficient for them to secure quality employment.

Two main factors contributed to their worsened employment situation, despite their tertiary education. One was labor casualization in the expanding service sector. In the context of growing global competition, outsourcing and other trends have hollowed out the manufacturing sector, significantly reducing secure manufacturing jobs within the country. By the 2000s, wholesale and retail sectors employed more people than all of the manufacturing combined (Gordon 2017: 20). Much of the demand for labor was for a heavily casualized workforce comprised of youth and women. Since the mid-1980s, the young casual labor force has more than doubled (MHLW 2013: 183–84), and encroached into the long-protected male workforce during the deepening recession in the 2000s (Statistics Bureau 2008). Among the younger interviewees, half had experienced casual or temporary work at least once before migrating to China. Every single one of those who had completed high school, vocational college, or a two-year university course had had a low-wage customer service occupation at one point in their career trajectories, such as retail assistant or fast-food restaurant manager. Even some four-year university graduates found themselves in such jobs. The migrants' education-to-employment transitions reflect the broader trend in Japan's post-crisis economy: mass tertiary education frequently produces labor for the low-wage service sector, and that labor casualization, which has long been the norm for women, has increasingly targeted young men during the recession (Brinton and Ikemura 2008).

The other contributing factor was the deterioration in working conditions, which reduced retention rates. The downsizing of the permanent workforce by neoliberal "reforms" has not only reduced job security and welfare privileges but also intensified mismatches between employers and employees (Genda, Kuroda, and Ohta 2015; Kambayashi and Kato 2017). The younger interviewees frequently complained about enforced overtime without pay, stress-related health problems, and putting the needs of the employer and clients above their own. While half of the younger interviewees successfully gained permanent employment as fresh graduates, they all left their first career job within three years. They are part of the 30 percent of all fresh university graduates in Japan who have done the same since 1995 (Nakajima 2015: 57; also see Ohta 2010: 520–24). This is despite the high cultural value attached to perseverance, commitment, and resolve (Matanle 2006: 248), and the resulting stigma attached to those who resign "prematurely." Concerned about the compromised prospects for future job applications, Yoshitaka mulled over for a year whether or not to leave his first career job in the agricultural machinery industry ("I knew I shouldn't quit"). As a graduate jobseeker, he hoped to find secure employment in an urban area. However, the competitive job market meant he had to settle with a medium enterprise in a rural area. Due to long working hours and an unglamorous working environment, his doubt about his future there grew, and he lasted a total of only two years before migrating to Dalian. Others like Masayuki struggled to find a position in his field of electrical engineering in Japan after resigning from his first job "too soon."

In the past, the Japanese-style management rewarded long-serving employees with stability, skill formation, subsidized housing costs, and other perks of "welfare corporatism" (Dore 1973). This significantly expanded the middle classes. As Gordon (2015: 95) concludes, "postwar Japan circa the

1960s through 1990s was far more egalitarian than it is today." Despite the diverse education-employment transition patterns, their migration in their twenties and thirties was a turning point in their life courses. They felt the need to disrupt the status quo (Kawashima 2018) because a sense of alienation, fatigue, boredom, and disengagement dominated their pre-migration work experience. The labor migration presented them with a novel chance to work for a large corporation without the need for foreign language skills or specific expertise, and to (re)launch a white-collar career (Kawashima 2020).

Unlike the older migrants interviewed, the younger group did not have prior experience of employment abroad or transnational connections. They usually found opportunities through job advertisements on digital media platforms or via a recruitment agent, and went through a formal application process. As an interview quote below reveals, the novel job opening in Dalian was an attractive alternative to staying in Japan: "I'd had enough of my previous job [as a recruitment agent] and wanted to try a new line of work. But at my age, there weren't a lot of choices. I was curious about working abroad, and thought this job offer [from Dalian] gave me the last chance to do that" (Akina, thirty years old at the time of departure).

Without exception, the young migrants explained that this was the only overseas position they could apply for without either foreign language proficiency or sought-after industry experience. Their prior exposure to foreign environments was largely limited to short-term tourism or higher education study, which one-third of all the migrants had experienced at private colleges in North America or universities in Asia, for between one month and four years. In the context of the commodification of international youth mobility, such as study abroad (Liu-Farrer 2011) and new forms of tourism (Beech 2018; Simpson 2005), the young Japanese primarily engaged with their overseas experience as consumers. By their own account, such experience was not considered relevant to their employment in China, and it did not add to their credentials.

Without Chinese language proficiency or technical qualifications, the migrants in my study tended to remain in the lower strata of the workplace hierarchy (Kawashima 2018). The precarity of labor produces continuous mobility, which together gives rise to future uncertainty (Standing 2011; Allison 2012; Anagnost, Arai, and Ren 2013). As years went by, it was not uncommon for the younger Japanese migrants to develop a strong sense of being cornered into a marginal space in their workplace, especially for those in their mid-thirties and older (Kawashima 2018). Such stalled career mobility experience prompted an interest in further geographical mobility, either through return migration to Japan or onward migration to a third location (ibid.).

Conclusion

In this chapter, I have discussed the contrasting experience of labor migration in the younger and older groups of Japanese skilled corporate workers in the city of Dalian in north-east China. The comparative approach connects the related but largely separate scholarly discussions about precarious youth labor, aging workers, and labor migration under a recession. On the one hand, the ongoing effects of a long-term recession erode the middle-class privileges and marginalize both the young and the aging in the Japanese labor markets. On the other hand, the onset of the economic downturn in the 1990s hit the two generations at different life course stages, and this has had a lasting impact on the patterns of social mobility. Geographical mobility across national borders offered both groups an alternative to a deflationary economy and neoliberal labor control in Japan. However, their contrasting career mobilities before arriving in their destination society are crucial in understanding their different economic and occupational positions there.

The older generation built lifelong careers after successfully transitioning from education to employment in a more egalitarian social environment. Being permanent full-time male workers, they embodied the ideal citizen model of the time. As core members of reputable corporations, they accumulated sufficient cultural, social, and economic capital to access an ethnic niche in the global economy as highly skilled professionals. Their internationally mobile careers gave them valued industrial and managerial expertise and transnational business contacts that proved highly beneficial, even after (early) retirement in Japan. Their earlier ascendance in the domestic labor market was underpinned by the gendered labor management system prevalent in the postwar economic boom. This functioned as their springboard for further transnational career advancement through skilled labor migration. As a result, the older men reported high levels of satisfaction about continuing work and experiencing a growing economy once again, albeit this time in China.

By contrast, the younger generation began their adulthood in an era of austerity, and their education-employment transitions reflected the broader precarization of youth labor in Japan and other post-Fordist economies. This group's upward social mobility in Japan was limited, which was a catalyst for their migration to Dalian. Without technical expertise or managerial experience, their principal value for Chinese employers was their native tongue and their ability to provide services for the Japanese market in culturally appropriate ways. The limitation of their marketable skills, however, constrained their upward career mobility in the destination society.

Even as the individualization of society is said to allow considerable variations in life course patterns (see Shanahan 2000), normative life course milestones are still strongly associated with biological age in Japan. As in the industrialized West, middle-class ideals in Japan have conceptualized a successful life trajectory in terms of the linear progression from completing education and becoming a full-time wage earner to leaving the natal family home, getting married, and becoming a parent (Arnett 2001; Rosenberger 2007). This "transition regime" (Walther 2006) problematizes "disrupted" social mobility, the avoidance of which heavily depends on securing an income from full-time permanent employment. This makes upward mobility in the (internal) labor market particularly important. My investigation of the two migrant groups' transnational career trajectories brought to the fore the tangled nature of geographical, life-course, and social mobilities.

One aspect that this study did not examine in depth was the influence of marital or civil status, nor the presence of children on career trajectories and migration decisions. Future research on the entanglement of labor and social class mobilities would benefit from the consideration of not only generational difference but also the gender and family dimensions of skilled migration.

Kumiko Kawashima is Associate Professor at the Department of Culture and Tourism Studies, Rikkyo University, Japan. Her research to date has focused on the everyday experiences of labor and consumption in postindustrial contexts, transnational migration, and global capitalism. Kumiko is the author of "Japanese Labour Migration to China and IT Service Outsourcing: The Case of Dalian," in *Destination China: Immigration to China in the Post-Reform Era* (edited by Angela Lehman and Pauline Leonard, 2019), among others. She also co-edited "Mobilities and Exceptional Spaces in Asia" in a special section of *Asian Anthropology* (with Brenda Yeoh, 2017).

NOTES

1. Those interviewed typically worked from 8 AM to 4 PM, which corresponds to 9 AM to 5 PM in Japan time. They reported that working overtime was relatively rare, and where it occurred, it was mostly among those in leadership positions.
2. Scholars have debated the extent to which these two are similar—see, for example, Kato and Steven 1993, and Naruse 1991; for a history of a related anthropological debate on the Japanese management, see Hamada 2007.

3. Approximately one-third of the older migrants interviewed had left their employment in Japan before the law reform in 2004 that required firms to continue employing workers until the age of sixty-five if they wished to stay (Taguchi 2016). Under this law, some employees can extend their retirement age and therefore continue to work under the same conditions, while others are re-employed as contract workers.

REFERENCES

Allison, Anne. 2012. "Ordinary Refugees: Social Precarity and Soul in 21st Century Japan." *Anthropological Quarterly* 85(2): 345-70.

Altonji, Joseph G., Lisa B. Kahn, and Jamin D. Speer. 2016. "Cashier or Consultant? Entry Labor Market Conditions, Field of Study, and Career Success." *Journal of Labor Economics* 34(S1): S361-401.

Anagnost, Ann, Andrea Arai, and Hai Ren. 2013. *Global Futures in East Asia: Youth, Nation, and the New Economy in Uncertain Times*. Stanford, CA: Stanford University Press.

Arnett, Jeffrey Jensen. 2001. "Conceptions of the Transition to Adulthood: Perspectives from Adolescence through Midlife." *Journal of Adult Development* 8(2): 133-43.

Bank, David. 2009. "Encore Careers and the Economic Crisis." *Generations* 33(3): 69-73.

Bartolini, Laura, Ruby Gropas, and Anna Triandafyllidou. 2017. "Drivers of Highly Skilled Mobility from Southern Europe: Escaping the Crisis and Emancipating Oneself." *Journal of Ethnic and Migration Studies* 43(4): 652-73.

Beech, Suzanne E. 2018. "Adapting to Change in the Higher Education System: International Student Mobility as a Migration Industry." *Journal of Ethnic and Migration Studies* 44(4): 610-25.

Benson, Michaela. 2011. *The British in Rural France*. Manchester, UK: Manchester University Press.

Benson, Michaela, and Karen O'Reilly. 2009. "Migration and the Search for a Better Way of Life: A Critical Exploration of Lifestyle Migration." *The Sociological Review* 57(4): 608-25.

Berggren, Christian. 1995. "Japan as Number Two: Competitive Problems and the Future of Alliance Capitalism after the Burst of the Bubble Boom." *Work Employment & Society* 9(1): 53-95.

Blakemore, Ken. 1999. "International Migration in Later Life: Social Care and Policy Implications." *Ageing and Society* 19(6): 761-74.

Bolzman, Claudio, Laure Kaeser, and Etienne Christe. 2017. "Transnational Mobilities as a Way of Life among Older Migrants from Southern Europe." *Population, Space and Place* 23(5): e2016.

Botterill, Kate. 2017. "Discordant Lifestyle Mobilities in East Asia: Privilege and Precarity of British Retirement in Thailand." *Population, Space and Place* 23(5): e2011.

Bourdieu, Pierre. 1986. "The Forms of Capital." In *Handbook of Theory and Research for the Sociology of Education*, ed. John G Richardson, 241-58. New York: Greenwood Press.

Bowman, Dina, Michael McGann, Helen Kimberley, and Simon Biggs. 2017. "'Rusty, Invisible and Threatening': Ageing, Capital and Employability." *Work, Employment and Society* 31(3): 465-82.

Brinton, Mary C., and Chiaki Ikemura. 2008. *Ushinawareta Ba o Sagashite: Rosuto Jenerēshon no Shakaigaku* [Lost in Transition: Youth, Work, and Instability in Postindustrial Japan]. Tokyo: NTT Shuppan.

Cairns, David. 2017. "Exploring Student Mobility and Graduate Migration: Undergraduate Mobility Propensities in Two Economic Crisis Contexts." *Social & Cultural Geography* 18(3): 336-53.

Chiavacci, David, and Carola Hommerich, eds. 2017. *Social Inequality in Post-Growth Japan: Transformation during Economic and Demographic Stagnation*. Abingdon, Oxon: Routledge.

Ciobanu, Ruxandra Oana, and Alistair Hunter. 2017. "Older Migrants and (Im)Mobilities of Ageing: An Introduction." *Population, Space and Place* 23(5): 1-10.

Clark, Robert L., Rikiya Matsukura, Naohiro Ogawa, and Satoshi Shimizutani. 2015. "Retirement Transitions in Japan." *Public Policy & Aging Report* 25(4): 129-31.

Dingemans, Ellen, Kène Henkens, and Hanna Van Solinge. 2016. "Access to Bridge Employment: Who Finds and Who Does Not Find Work after Retirement?" *Gerontologist* 56(4): 630-40.

Domínguez-Mujica, Josefina, Ramón Díaz-Hernández, and Juan Parreño-Castellano. 2016. "Migrating Abroad to Get Ahead: The Emigration of Young Spanish Adults during the Financial Crisis (2008-2013)." In *Global Change and Human Mobility*, ed. Josefina Domínguez-Mujica, 203-23. Singapore: Springer.

Dore, Ronald P. 1973. *British Factory – Japanese Factory: The Origins of National Diversity in Industrial Relations*. London: George Allen & Unwin.

Farrer, James. 2020. "From Cooks to Chefs: Skilled Migrants in a Globalising Culinary Field." *Journal of Ethnic and Migration Studies* 47(2): 1-17.

Fujita, Yuiko. 2009. *Cultural Migrants from Japan: Youth, Media, and Migration in New York and London*. Lanham, MD: Lexington Books.

Funabashi, Yoichi, and Barak Kushner, eds. 2015. *Examining Japan's Lost Decades*. London: Routledge.

Genda, Yuji, Sachiko Kuroda, and Souichi Ohta. 2015. "Does Downsizing Take a Toll on Retained Staff? An Analysis of Increased Working Hours in the Early 2000s in Japan." *Journal of the Japanese and International Economies* 36: 1-24.

Genda, Yuji, and Masako Kurosawa. 2001. "Transition from School to Work in Japan." *Journal of the Japanese and International Economies* 15(4): 465-88.

Gordon, Andrew. 2012. "Consumption, Consumerism, and Japanese Modernity." In *The Oxford Handbook of the History of Consumption*, ed. Frank Trentmann, 485-504. Oxford: Oxford University Press.

———. 2015. "Making Sense of the Lost Decades: Workplaces and Schools, Men and Women, Young and Old, Rich and Poor." In *Examining Japan's Lost Decades*, ed. Yoichi Funabashi and Barak Kushner, 77-100. London: Routledge.

———. 2017. "New and Enduring Dual Structures of Employment in Japan: The Rise of Non-Regular Labor, 1980s-2010s." *Social Science Japan Journal* 20(1): 9-36.

Haas, Heiko. 2013. "Volunteering in Retirement Migration: Meanings and Functions of Charitable Activities for Older British Residents in Spain." *Ageing and Society* 33(8): 1374–400.

Hamada, Tomoko. 2007. "The Anthropology of Japanese Corporate Management." In *A Companion to the Anthropology of Japan*, ed. Jennifer Robertson, 125–52. Maiden, MA: Blackmore Publishing Ltd.

Hancock, Linda B. T. 2006. "Mature Workers, Training and Using TLM Frameworks." *Australian Bulletin of Labour* 32(3): 257–79.

Heggli, Gry, Haldis Haukanes, and Marit Tjomsland. 2013. "Fearing the Future? Young People Envisioning their Working Lives in the Czech Republic, Norway and Tunisia." *Journal of Youth Studies* 16(7): 916–31.

Horn, Vincent, and Cornelia Schweppe. 2015. *Transnational Aging: Current Insights and Future Challenges*. New York: Routledge.

Horn, Vincent, Cornelia Schweppe, and Désirée Bender. 2015. "'Moving (for) Elder Care Abroad': The Fragile Promises of Old-Age Care Facilities for Elderly Germans in Thailand." In *Transnational Aging: Current Insights and Future Challenges*, ed. Vincent Horn and Cornelia Schweppe, 175–89. New York: Routledge.

Huete, Raquel, Alejandro Mantecón, and Jesús Estévez. 2013. "Challenges in Lifestyle Migration Research: Reflections and Findings about the Spanish Crisis." *Mobilities* 8(3): 331–48.

Kambayashi, Ryo, and Takao Kato. 2017. "Long-Term Employment and Job Security over the Past 25 Years: A Comparative Study of Japan and the United States." *ILR Review* 70(2): 359–94.

Kato, Tetsuro, and Rob Steven. 1993. *Is Japanese Management Post-Fordism? An International Debate*. Tokyo: Mado-Sha.

Kawashima, Kumiko. 2018. "Longer-Term Consequences of 'Youth' Migration: Japanese Temporary Migrants in China and the Life Course." *Journal of Intercultural Studies* 39(6): 658–72.

———. 2020. "Why Migrate to Earn Less? Changing Tertiary Education, Skilled Migration and Class Slippage in an Economic Downturn." *Journal of Ethnic and Migration Studies* 47(13): 3131–49. DOI:10.1080/1369183X.2020.1720629

Kelly, William W. 1993. "Finding a Place in Metropolitan Japan: Ideologies, Institutions, and Everyday Life." In *Postwar Japan as History*, ed. Andrew Gordon, 189–216. Berkeley: University of California Press.

Kelly, William W., and Merry I. White. 2006. "Students, Slackers, Singles, Seniors, and Strangers: Transforming a Family-Nation." In *Beyond Japan: The Dynamics of East Asian Regionalism*, ed. Peter J. Katzenstein and Takashi Shiraishi, 63–82. Ithaca, NY: Cornell University Press.

Liu, Kai, Kjell G. Salvanes, and Erik Ø. Sørensen. 2016. "Good Skills in Bad Times: Cyclical Skill Mismatch and the Long-Term Effects of Graduating in a Recession." *European Economic Review* 84: 3–17.

Liu-Farrer, Gracia. 2011. *Labor Migration from China to Japan: International Students, Transnational Migrants*. New York: Routledge.

Loretto, Wendy, and Sarah Vickerstaff. 2015. "Gender, Age and Flexible Working in Later Life." *Work, Employment and Society* 29(2): 233-49.
Matanle, Peter. 2006. "The Habit of a Lifetime? Japanese and British University Students' Attitudes to Permanent Employment." *Japan Forum* 18(2): 229-54.
McCormick, Kevin. 2007. "Sociologists and 'the Japanese Model': A Passing Enthusiasm?" *Work, Employment and Society* 21(4): 751-71.
McDaniel, Susan A., Amber Gazso, and Seonggee Um. 2013. "Generationing Relations in Challenging Times: Americans and Canadians in Mid-Life in the Great Recession." *Current Sociology* 61(3): 301-21.
McDowell, Linda, Adina Batnitzky, and Sarah Dyer. 2009. "Precarious Work and Economic Migration: Emerging Immigrant Divisions of Labour in Greater London's Service Sector." *International Journal of Urban and Regional Research* 33(1): 3-25.
Mendoza, Cristóbal. 2018. "Southern Europe Skilled Migration into Mexico: The Impact of the Economic Crisis." *Regional Studies* 54(4): 495-504.
MEXT (Ministry of Education, Culture, Sports, Science and Technology). 2015. "Heisei Nijūnananendo Gakkō Kihon Chōsa (Sokuhochi) No Kōhyō Ni Tsuite" [Discussion of the publication of initial findings from the 2015 school survey]. Retrieved 30 October 2020 from http://www.mext.go.jp/component/b_menu/houdou/__icsFiles/afieldfile/2015/12/25/1365647_01.pdf.
MOFA (Ministry of Foreign Affairs of Japan). 2012. "Annual Report of Statistics on Japanese Nationals Overseas." Retrieved 30 October 2020 from https://www.mofa.go.jp/mofaj/toko/page22_003338.html.
———. 2016. "Annual Report of Statistics on Japanese Nationals Overseas." Retrieved 30 October 2020 from https://www.mofa.go.jp/mofaj/toko/page22_003338.html.
MHLW (Ministry of Health, Labor and Welfare). 2013. "Heisei 25 Nenban Rōdō Keizai No Bunseki: Kōzō Henka No Naka Deno Koyō, Jinzai to Hatarakikata" [The 2013 White Paper on the labor economy: Employment, human resources and work amid structural changes]. Retrieved 30 October 2020 from https://www.mhlw.go.jp/wp/hakusyo/roudou/13/13-1.html.
Nakajima, Hiroshi. 2015. "Kyaria Kyōiku to Jyakunen Rishokuritsu: Tōkei Bunseki Kara No Ikkōsatsu" [Career education and the turnover rates among youth: A study based on a statistical analysis]. *Kansai Daigaku Kōtō Kyōiku Kenkyū* 6: 57-68.
Naruse, Tatsuo. 1991. "Taylorism and Fordism in Japan." *International Journal of Political Economy* 21(3): 32-48.
Neilson, Brett, and Ned Rossiter. 2005. "From Precarity to Precariousness and Back Again: Labour, Life and Unstable Networks." *Fiberculture* 5(022): 1-19.
Ohta, Sōichi. 2010. "Jyakunen Koyō Mondai to Sedai Kōka" [Youth employment issues and generational effects]. In *Rōdō Shijō to Shotoku Bunpai* [Labor markets and income distributions], ed. Yoshio Higuchi, and editorial supervision by the Economic and Social Research Institute Japan, 514-39. Tokyo: Keiōgijukudaigakushuppankai.
Oka, Masato, and Takeshi Kimura. 2003. "Managing an Ageing Labour Force: The Interplay between Public Policies and the Firm's Logic of Action — The Case of Japan." *The Geneva Papers on Risk and Insurance – Issues and Practice* 28(4): 596-611.

Oliver, Caroline. 2008. *Retirement Migration: Paradoxes of Ageing*. New York: Routledge.
O'Loughlin, Kate, Nancy Humpel, and Hal Kendig. 2010. "Impact of the Global Financial Crisis on Employed Australian Baby Boomers: A National Survey." *Australasian Journal on Ageing* 29(2): 88-91.
Osako, Masako M. 1988. "'Downward Mobility' as a Form of Phased Retirement in Japan." *Ageing International* 15(2): 19-22.
Piotrowski, Martin, Arne Kalleberg, and Ronald R. Rindfuss. 2015. "Contingent Work Rising: Implications for the Timing of Marriage in Japan." *Journal of Marriage and Family* 77(5): 1039-56.
Ramos, Anne Carolina, and Heidi Rodrigues Martins. 2020. "First-Generation Migrants Become Grandparents: How Migration Backgrounds Affect Intergenerational Relationships." *Global Networks* 20(2): 325-42.
Rosenberger, Nancy. 2007. "Rethinking Emerging Adulthood in Japan: Perspectives from Long-Term Single Women." *Child Development Perspectives* 1(2): 92-95.
Salamońska, Justyna, and Olga Czeranowska. 2019. "Janus-Faced Mobilities: Motivations for Migration among European Youth in Times of Crisis." *Journal of Youth Studies* 22(9): 1167-83.
Sasaki, Susumu. 2000. "Kōgyō Kōtōgakkō No Ryūsei to Suitai: 50 Nen No Kiseki o Kaerimiru" [The rise and decline of industrial high schools: Looking back on the 50-year trajectory]. *Sangyō Kyōikugaku Kenkyū* 30(2): 20-26.
Schwiter, Karin, Jill Brütsch, and Geraldine Pratt. 2020. "Sending Granny to Chiang Mai: Debating Global Outsourcing of Care for the Elderly." *Global Networks* 20(1): 106-25.
Seki, Mitsuhiro. 2000. *Nihon Kigyō/Chūgoku Shinshutsu No Shin Jidai* [Japanese corporations: The new era of entering the Chinese markets]. Tokyo: Shinhyoron Publishing Inc.
Shanahan, Michael J. 2000. "Pathways to Adulthood in Changing Societies: Variability and Mechanisms in Life Course Perspective." *Annual Review of Sociology* 26(1): 667-92.
Simpson, Kate. 2005. "Dropping Out or Signing Up? The Professionalisation of Youth Travel." *Antipode* 37(3): 447-69.
Solem, Per Erik. 2012. "Possible Effects of the Financial Crisis on Managers' Attitudes to Older Workers." *Nordic Journal of Working Life Studies* 2(3): 129-42.
Sooudi, Olga Kanzaki. 2014. *Japanese New York: Self-Reinvention and Migrant Artists on the World Stage*. Honolulu: University of Hawai'i Press.
Standing, Guy. 2011. *The Precariat: The Dangerous New Class*. London: Bloomsbury Academic.
Statistics Bureau. 2008. "Rōdōryoku Chōsa Nenpō Heisei 20 Nen (2008 Nen)" [Annual survey on Labor Force Survey 2008]. Statistics Bureau. Retrieved 30 October 2020 from http://www.stat.go.jp/data/roudou/report/index.html.
Steinbach, Anja. 2018. "Older Migrants in Germany." *Journal of Population Ageing* 11(3): 285-306.
Taguchi, Kazuo. 2016. "Kōreisha Koyō Shisaku no Tokuchō to Kadai: Keizoku Koyō Seido Dōnyū Kigyō Sansha no Jirei Kenkyū o Moto ni [Characteristics and problems

of employment policies for older workers: Lessons from a case study of three corporations that implemented a system of continuous employment]." *Nihon Rōdō Kenkyū Zasshi* 670: 90–100.
Thang, Leng Leng, Sachiko Sone, and Mika Toyota. 2012. "Freedom Found? The Later-Life Transnational Migration of Japanese Women to Western Australia and Thailand." *Asian and Pacific Migration Journal* 21(2): 239–62.
Toyota, Mika. 2006. "Ageing and Transnational Householding: Japanese Retirees in Southeast Asia." *International Development Planning Review* 28(4): 515–31.
Toyota, Mika, and Biao Xiang. 2012. "The Emerging Transnational 'Retirement Industry' in Southeast Asia." *International Journal of Sociology and Social Policy* 32(11/12): 708–19.
Van Mol, Christof. 2016. "Migration Aspirations of European Youth in Times of Crisis." *Journal of Youth Studies* 19(10): 1303–20.
Vickerstaff, Sarah. 2010. "Older Workers: The 'Unavoidable Obligation' of Extending Our Working Lives?" *Sociology Compass* 4(10): 869–79.
Visser, Mark, Maurice Gesthuizen, Gerbert Kraaykamp, and Maarten H. J. Wolbers. 2016. "Inequality among Older Workers in the Netherlands: A Life Course and Social Stratification Perspective on Early Retirement." *European Sociological Review* 32(3): 370–82.
Vogel, Ezra. 1963. *Japan's New Middle Class: The Salary Man and his Family in a Tokyo Suburb*. Berkeley: University of California Press.
Walther, Andreas. 2006. "Regimes of Youth Transitions: Choice, Flexibility and Security in Young People's Experiences across Different European Contexts." *Young* 14(2): 119–39.
Warnes, Anthony M., Klaus Friedrich, Leonie Kellaher, and Sandra Torres. 2004. "The Diversity and Welfare of Older Migrants in Europe." *Ageing and Society* 24(3): 307–26.
Yamada, Atsuhiro, and Masa Higo. 2011. "Institutional Barriers to Work beyond Retirement in an Aging Japan: Evidence from a Recent Employee Survey." *Contemporary Japan* 23(2): 157–86.
Zacharias-Walsh, Anne. 2016. *Our Unions, Our Lives: The Rise of Feminist Labor Unions in Japan*. Ithaca, NY: Cornell University Press.
Zheng, Yingqin, Leslie Willcocks, and Bo Yang. 2010. "China's Emerging Software Services Outsourcing Industry." In *China's Emerging Outsourcing Capabilities: The Services Challenge*, ed. Mary C. Lacity, Leslie P. Willcocks, and Yingqin Zheng, 17–36. Basingstoke: Palgrave Macmillan.

CHAPTER
10

Pursuing Respectability in Mobility
Marriage, Migration, and Divorce of Filipino Women in Belgium and the Netherlands

Asuncion Fresnoza-Flot

Introduction

In 2005, Caroline, a participant in a study I was conducting in Paris at that time, shared with me the story of Maria, a Filipino woman who had two children in France with an Algerian man. When the couple divorced, Maria's ex-husband obtained the custody of their children and decided to take them with him to Algeria. Caroline told me that she saw Maria crying, shouting, and running after the car of her ex-husband as he departed for Charles de Gaulle Airport with their children. Not being able to see her children again drove Maria "crazy," in the words of Caroline. In addition to the loss of her children, she lost her family home and suffered financially. Caroline expressed to me her pity for Maria, who had lost everything she had achieved, as well as her sanity.

Maria's case indicates how divorce can efface one's moral esteem. It engenders the sympathy of other Filipino migrants like Caroline, who view marriage and an intact family as sources of respectability—that is, the ideal Filipino womanhood satisfying the normative expectations for them in the

Philippines to marry, and build and maintain a family, as well as to fulfill their caregiving role to their natal families. How do Filipino women in the context of migration pursue respectability? What are the forces that influence them to do so?

To provide answers to these questions, I examine the experiences of Filipino migrant women; specifically, the way their pursuit of respectability results in different forms of mobility and immobility (spatial, social class, legal), and how these (im)mobilities trigger their quest for respectability during their marriage, divorce, and post-divorce lives. Through the lens of tangled mobility (see Introduction chapter to the present volume), I discuss (im)mobilities that these women simultaneously experience, and pay attention to the influence of gender norms in the Philippines on their lives overseas. Mobility is understood here as "change of condition" in terms of "movements, networks and motility" (Canzler, Kaufmann, and Kesselring 2008: 2). Among these three aspects, movements will be the focus of the present chapter. Specifically, I analyze transnational migration taking place in the Philippines and foreign countries, small-scale geographic motions that Filipino migrants are engaged in while in their receiving country (such as regular travel from home to workplace), these migrants' change of social class positions in professional terms, and the modification of their legal status linked to their migration.

For this chapter, I have drawn from the empirical data I gathered for a qualitative study of divorces involving Filipino migrant women in Belgium and the Netherlands (see Fresnoza-Flot 2018, 2019). I examine the data from thirty-four semi-structured interviews of Filipino women: fifteen in Belgium and nineteen in the Netherlands. I met these women through a snowballing approach in urban areas in both countries. Among these women, only three had been formerly married to Filipino men. Although the main focus here is women who had been in binational marriages, the case of these three women can also provide insights. The other thirty women were in "mixed couples" in which the partners have different nationalities and ethnicities. They had met their husbands through pen-pal correspondence, an intermediary, or the Internet. They were mostly university-educated, younger than their ex-partners, and in their forties at the time of my interviews. A majority had children, and three women had offspring from their previous non-marital unions in the Philippines. Except for two, all the informants acquired the nationality of their receiving country. Their marriages lasted about fifteen years on average. To protect their anonymity, I have replaced all their names with pseudonyms, and modified other identifiable characteristics, such as age, profession, and place of residence.

I chose to study the Filipino women in Belgium and the Netherlands because the migration flows of Filipinos in these two countries share many characteristics. First, both migration flows are composed mainly of women: 76 percent of 4,346 Filipinos in Belgium (Statbel 2019) and 78 percent of 14,546 Filipinos (first-generation with migration background) in the Netherlands (CBS 2019). These migration flows started after World War II. During the 1960s, Filipino nurses and midwives entered Belgium and the Netherlands as health workers in hospitals. During the 1970s and 1980s, many Filipino women arrived and concentrated in the service sector of the economy as domestic, entertainment, or sex workers. Second, although there have been Filipino men, especially seamen, who have married Belgian or Dutch women and stayed on in these two countries, the majority of the marriages took place between Filipino women and Belgian or Dutch men, and this pattern continues today. And third, the relatively long history of Filipino migration into Belgium and the Netherlands allows me to employ a longer temporal lens to study their tangled mobilities.

In the next sections, I delve into the literature of cross-border marriage and divorce to examine the mobilities and immobility entailed in the lives of mixed couples. After this literature review, I revisit the scholarly works on respectability in the context of migration to provide some insights on how migrants pursue it. The central part of the chapter presents the tangled mobilities that Filipino migrant women experience during their marriage and divorce, and thereafter. It also uncovers the way these women experience respectability during each phase of their lives.

Marriage, Breakup, and (Im)mobilities in the Context of Migration

Contrary to the strong scholarly interest in cross-border marriages, the divorce of mixed couples has only recently started to capture scientific interest. Marriage and divorce are intertwined institutions, which can cause individual mobilities as well as immobility spatially, socially, and economically.

Spatial mobility has been observed in many cases of binational marriages, as marriage often precedes or entails migration. Studies most often explain these marriages and migrations as part of a social class mobility project of migrant spouses from economically developing countries (see Palriwala and Uberoi 2008; Ricordeau 2012; Tosakul 2010). These migrants' marriages are therefore considered a form of hypergamy. However, this does not mean these individual migrants originate from a lower social class background than their spouses from developed countries. A few studies show the contrary: some migrant spouses from the so-called Global South had a university education and a middle-class family background in their own countries (see Constable 2005; Thai 2008). By marrying working-class men from the Global North, their binational marriage appears to engender downward social class mobility, and this situation can be dubbed as hypogamy—that is, marrying someone with a lower socioeconomic status than one's own (see Almanzar 2016). Moreover, many migrant spouses experience social class and spatial immobility after their relocation due to their economic and legal dependence on their citizen partners, notably during the beginning of their immigration (Strasser et al. 2009; Ishii 2016). Although their economic dependence on their citizen spouse does not make it easy for them to send financial support to their natal family back home, their legal status linked to their partner requires them to maintain their union and to be spatially immobile for a certain period of time to prove the veracity of their marriage to their receiving state. If their marriage breaks down before it reaches the required duration to be eligible for their receiving country's citizenship or permanent residency, they would be in a legally precarious situation and, in the worst case, could be deported.

The few works on the issue of marital breakdown demonstrate how migrant spouses and their partners are caught in the web of laws, institutions, and sociocultural norms in their cross-border social spaces. For example, Sportel (2013) demonstrates that transnational divorce among Dutch-Moroccan and Dutch-Egyptian couples not only concerns the partners but also involves institutions in their countries of origin. During the divorce process, mixed couples often interact with two legal systems (one in their country of origin and the other in their country of residence) and with intermediary structures such as embassies, public or private organizations, and associations (ibid.; see also Sportel 2016). These breakups can lead to lengthy legal battles over the custody of children, and can affect the financial situation, social networks, and psychological well-being of the individuals concerned (Kim 2010; Singh 2008; Singla 2015; Suzuki 2003). In this case, marital breakdown entails immobility in social class and spatial terms in many aspects of an ex-couple's lives. Despite the challenges of divorce, migrant partners in mixed couples find ways (for example, labor market engagement and re-coupling) to adjust to their situation.

Relationship breakups not only concern mixed couples, but also partners in "transnational families" (Bryceson and Vuorela 2002) in which the members are geographically separated from one another but keep a sense of unity across time and spaces. Unlike the dissolution of mixed couples, which remains understudied, marital breakups in ethnically homogeneous families are documented in many societies: first, in the context of "parental migration" involving mothers, fathers, or both (Frank and Wildsmith 2005; Pribilsky 2004); and second, in the case of diasporic migrant communities in which the members originate from one country (Mand 2005; Qureshi

2016). In this literature, we observe how divorce mostly leads to downward social class mobility for women, especially among those with children (for instance, see Mortelmans 2020).

The scholarly works cited above unveil that marriage and marital breakup entail various forms of mobilities (spatial, social, economic, and legal) and also immobility linked to the often-marginal economic and legal situation of the migrant partner in the couple. They also have a gendered dimension in which migrant spouses (mainly women) experience subordination and become "emerging minorities" due to the restrictive migration and citizenship policies of their receiving societies (Ishii 2016). I argue that to illuminate better the different forms of (im)mobility, and their tanglement during marriage, divorce, and post-divorce lives, one should not solely focus on marital breakup itself—the dominant scholarly approach so far—but rather locate it within the conjugal life course of the couple. This approach facilitates an understanding of the logics of marriage, migration, and breakup, as well as the dynamics of power relations in the couple prior to, during, and after its demise. It is in this vein that the present chapter scrutinizes the experiences of marriage and divorce of Filipino women in Belgium and the Netherlands as they pursue respectability.

Understanding Respectability in the Context of Migration

Many studies document how migrants aspire to respectability following the gender expectations in their country of origin. During the migration process, migrants try to achieve or maintain the ideal manhood or womanhood that their respective countries of origin uphold. In effect, migration itself is most often considered as a pathway toward the respected gender status they wish to acquire.

Respectability—the quality of being socially accepted—appears to depend on migrants' capacity to satisfy the gender norms and expectations in their countries of origin. In societies where men are expected to fulfill the breadwinning role in the family, it is often by migrating and working abroad that they accomplish such a role, thereby becoming in the process a "good" father, son, or brother (for example, see Pande 2017). For instance, Filipino and Ecuadorian migrant men successfully fulfill their father role through remittance sending and visits to home (McKay 2015; Pribilsky 2012). Migration also allows some men to increase the chance of finding a bride in their country of origin. Low-wage Vietnamese migrant men convert their low status "in their pursuit of marriage" in the United States of America to high status in Vietnam through "everyday drinking," "eating activities," and "simple gift-giving practices" (Thai 2005: 317).

This social class dimension of respectability can also be observed in the case of migrant women. For example, Malagasy women coupled with French men convert their "migrant social status and wages" in France "into the quasi-mystical force of someone who 'has the first word' in Madagascar" (Cole 2014: S93). Likewise, Thai women in relationships with Belgian men strive to satisfy their obligations and duties not only toward their nuclear family in Belgium but also toward their natal family in Thailand, which make them "good" wives and mothers as well as filial daughters (Fresnoza-Flot and Merla 2018). *Curtidoras* in Mozambique—"women who look for white men in downtown Maputo and engage in transactional sex with them, and sometimes marry and move with them to Europe" (Groes 2018: 123)—pursue a middle-class position in their country of origin or destination through intimate relations with white men. For these women, respectability comes with their access to money and possibilities to learn "good behaviour, charm, and stylish appearance" from their white partners (ibid.: 131).

The above studies indicate that gender role fulfillment and upward social class mobility are constitutive elements of respectability. These elements can also be found in the case of Filipino migrants, whose country of origin views Filipino women as the emblem of its national honor and reproducers of the nation. Many studies of Filipino women's migration reveal that they become "good" mothers and filial daughters through their transnational caregiving practices toward their nuclear and extended families, such as regular communication with them and the sending of financial support and gifts (e.g., Francisco-Menchavez 2018; Fresnoza-Flot 2009, 2017). The Philippine government also hails them and their Filipino male counterparts as "modern-day heroes" (*bagong bayani*) of the country because of their remittances boosting the local economy (Guevarra 2010). The respect gained from their entourage and the Philippine state symbolizes Filipino migrant women's upward social class mobility. This valorized social status only declines when they fail to fulfill their family obligations or other gendered expectations (Yea 2008). Considering all these elements of respectability in the context of the Philippine international migration, I examine in the following sections how Filipino migrant women in Belgium and the Netherlands gain, maintain, lose, or reacquire respectability in mobility.

Marriage and "Ideal" Filipino Womanhood: Understanding Spatial and Social Class Mobilities

Womanhood in the Philippines means satisfying certain social expectations, including that of building a family based on marriage, and at the "right" time (biologically speaking). Such expectations, together with the desire for improved social status, influenced each informant's decision to find a partner to construct their family unit, which subsequently led to their tangled (im)mobilities across national borders in spatial and social class terms.

Joan was born to a working-class family in the southern Philippines. Due to her academic excellence and her parents' support, she was able to obtain a bachelor's degree in engineering and passed the national licensure examination for engineers. She dedicated herself to working as an engineer for a local company, which allowed her to provide for the needs of her natal family. She was approaching thirty when one of her office co-workers put her in letter contact with a Dutchman. After a few months of correspondence, this man invited her in 1991 to live with him in the Netherlands to get to know each other. "Out of curiosity," Joan left her stable job as an engineer and moved to the Netherlands with a "fiancée" visa. However, this relationship did not work out, and she returned to the Philippines in 1993. Before her return, one of her Filipino friends introduced to her a potential Dutch partner, with whom she stayed in contact by mail. This man visited her in the Philippines in 1994 and asked her hand from her father: "My father was so eager that I get married. He said to him, 'no problem.'" It was her father who was encouraging her to get married "to have a child," particularly as she was almost thirty-two years old. Asked whether she had feelings for her soon-to-be husband at that time, Joan replied:

> Love was absent. My goal was to get married in order to have a child. My mother told me that romantic feelings could develop later. But I met someone (in the Philippines) with whom I fell in love, but he had a girlfriend at that time. So, I was crying and crying. So, which one will you choose, the one you love but is not there (available) or the one who loves you and is willing to get married with you?

Joan chose the latter option. In 1994, she got married and migrated to the Netherlands to start a family with her Dutch husband. Due to her low proficiency in Dutch and her husband's disapproval of her working, Joan decided not to engage in the labor market, and instead became a housewife. However, not being able to work frustrated her as she could not afford to support her natal family or acquire socially valued possessions back home.

Joan's experience demonstrates how the family pressure on her to get married due to her age and to have a child in wedlock influenced her decision to tie the knot with a man she was not in love with and to move with him to the Netherlands. Her previous live-in relationship with a Dutchman also decreased her attractiveness in the local marriage market as it practically announced that she was no longer a virgin or a sexually inexperienced woman. In the largely Catholic Philippine society, regardless of social class background, not only do single mothers encounter difficulty in finding a prospective "good" partner in the local marriage market (see Ricordeau 2012), but highly educated women and those over thirty years of age, like Joan, also confront the same challenge. This situation drives some of them to get married to non-Filipino men (Angeles and Sunanta 2007), who are, as Suzuki observes, "more lenient about their sexuality" and live "in a foreign place where the women could escape from the moral punishment against their suspected sexual deviancy" (Suzuki 2017: 131). Although binational marriage allowed Joan to attain an ideal Filipino womanhood (that is, becoming a wedded wife and mother), it impeded her professional career. For Filipino migrants with a working-class background like her, becoming a stay-at-home wife and mother without economic resources makes it difficult to move up the social class ladder in the Philippines. In this case, Joan's spatial movement, which ensued from her binational marriage, tangled with her social class immobility.

Unlike Joan who had a professional career before migration but stopped working after marriage, a few other informants, like Trina below, were engaged in the Dutch labor market either part-time or full-time following their marriage, which allowed them to slowly fulfill their dream of upward social class mobility in economic terms in the Philippines.

Trina came from a working-class family in a province adjacent to Manila. She did not finish her secondary education because of the economic difficulties experienced by her parents. Although not married, she became a mother at the ages of seventeen and then twenty. Her relationship with the father of her two children did not last long. To support her children's needs, she worked as a cashier in a supermarket while applying to migrate to another Asian country to work there. Her plan to go abroad did not materialize as she decided to pursue a new relationship with another Filipino man with whom she said she had fallen in love. During that time, a friend of her cousin introduced her to David, a Belgian man ten years older than her who was on vacation in the Philippines. David became interested in her and kept contact with her when he returned to Belgium. Once, David asked her if she would like to go to Belgium: "I replied, 'Yes, why not?' What I did not know was that when I said 'yes, why not?', he started processing (my travel) papers." David sent her plane tickets, and Trina had to decide "in the last minute" whether to go to Belgium or not. Her married Filipino boyfriend at that time persuaded her to leave the Philippines; he told her, "You don't [wouldn't] have [a] future with me. If you would like to go, just do it." Upon hearing this, Trina made up her mind to go to Belgium "for the future" of her children. When she arrived in Belgium, Trina worked part-time as a home cleaner, which allowed her to send remittances for her children back home, who were under the care of her mother and offered them a comfortable life.

Three informants, including Trina, had children outside of wedlock, which decreased their chances of good marriage prospects in the Philippines. Due to this situation and to their concern over the future of their children from previous relationships in the Philippines, they decided to migrate and marry non-Filipino men. Becoming a wife living in an economically developed country opened up possibilities for their offspring to migrate to that country, study there, and enjoy certain social rights. In this case, a mother's spatial mobility is tangled with not only their children's spatial mobility but also with these young people's social class mobility. This relational mobility echoes Ogaya's (2015) finding regarding the connection between motherhood and childhood in Filipino transnational families in Canada: the mobile motherhood of Filipino migrant women converges with their children's mobile childhood during family reunification.

The case of Trina above unveils how her migration and binational marriage facilitated her upward social class mobility in the Philippines. Unlike Joan, Trina was able to send financial support back home thanks to her paid employment, which provided a comfortable life to her children, thereby increasing her social status. Taking into account Trina's case and that of those who marry to become wives-mothers like Joan, there appear to be two faces of the "ideal" Filipino womanhood: wifehood and motherhood alongside upward social class mobility. The gender and family norms in the Philippines, where women are expected to fulfill reproductive and care roles in the family, fashion these faces and provide the framework through which to identify those that are worthy of social respect. In this case, pursuing respectability is tantamount to the quest for the "ideal" Filipino womanhood, and it is this quest that brings the Filipino women in the present study to Europe. During this process, their spatial movement tangled with their social class mobility and, in a few cases, also with their children's spatial and social mobilities.

Furthermore, other informants married non-Filipino men because they felt in love and/or aspired to attain a better socioeconomic situation by migrating. Suzuki (2017) qualifies the latter reason as a "postcolonial desire"—that is, a yearning to experience a "modern" lifestyle similar to that of people in the United States, the past colonial power in the Philippines. Hence, being a "good," "modern" woman in the Philippine context implies, on the one hand, that one becomes a wife and a mother and satisfies one's reproductive/care role in one's natal family, and on the other hand, that one attains the "postcolonial desire" of migration to an economically developed country like Belgium or the Netherlands. In the next section, I uncover how Filipino migrant women in my study attempted to conform to the "ideal" wife-mother figure during their conjugal lives, while experiencing in many cases tangled (im)mobilities.

Migration, (Im)mobilities, and Marital Breakdown

After they had moved to their husbands' countries, the women interviewed in the present study each experienced settlement differently in their new country: some became stay-at-home wives, like Joan, whereas others engaged in the labor market, like Trina. This situation evolved along with the life courses of the women interviewed—most notably when they became fluent in the language of their receiving country and when they gave birth. Nonetheless, regardless of whether they worked or not, many informants experienced an unequal gendered division of labor in the home, where they were mainly in charge of the reproductive work. This care obligation limited the informants' spatial movement, and made it difficult for them to enhance their natal families' economic situation back in the Philippines.

Aida had met Bernard (a Belgian man four years older than her) through exchanging correspondence, and they got married in the Philippines in 1992. She had a university degree in engineering and a stable job, whereas Bernard had only finished senior high school and was working as a farmer. After their marriage, Aida moved to Belgium and became unemployed. She decided to study and master French while looking for job possibilities. At home, she was in charge of domestic chores: cleaning the house, cooking, and washing clothes. Her husband was spending most of his time on the farm, and the main household task they did together was going to the supermarket to buy food. At that time, Aida's only spatial mobility was between her home and the supermarket. Not being able to continue her engineering profession in Belgium in the form of salaried employment, she looked for a job in the service sector, and applied for a driving license. She became a part-time office cleaner at a company situated in the next town from where she was residing, and she obtained her driving license. Her job neither changed her housewife role at home nor improved her social class status, but her driving license did improve her spatial mobility. When Aida became a mother, her family obligations suddenly increased, but she did not receive support from her husband:

> It was fine for me to [take] and pick up the kids (in school). I knew already how to drive; I did not have a problem with that. So, when Bernard arrived at home, he would eat; the kids were already there. I had already washed them. What was becoming the problem was that

after [some time], all [the responsibility] was falling on me because he was on the farm.

When Aida found out that her husband was cheating on her, she did not hesitate to separate from him and filed for divorce. She found a full-time office job and brought her children with her to a new home in Brussels to start afresh.

Aida's story shows that one form of mobility sometimes results in immobilities. Her migration from the Philippines to Belgium kept her in the beginning within the confines of home, and hampered her engagement in the labor market. These spatial and professional immobilities changed as she strived to master the language of the receiving society, looked for a job, and applied to get a driving license. Aida's spatial and professional mobilities contributed to her courage to end her marriage and pursue a life with her children as a single mother (at least for a short period, as she later re-partnered with a divorced Belgian man). Like Aida, many informants found themselves caught in spatial and professional immobilities during the early period of their immigration—one characterized by the unequal division of household chores.

Only a few informants started their immigration experience with both spatial and professional mobilities. For example, those Filipino care workers who migrated to these countries with a work contract as a nurse or au pair were able to improve the lives of their natal family in the Philippines via regular remittances. Then, before their work contract finished, they met and fell in love with a Belgian or a Dutchman, and decided to stay in their receiving country to form a family.

Another case is that of Helen, who became the principal family breadwinner. While working as an architect in the Philippines, she had met her Dutch husband via correspondence through one of her friends. After a few months of exchanges, the man went to see her in the Philippines and proposed marriage to her. In 1987, they got married there, and Helen migrated to the Netherlands in the same year. It was only after she had arrived in this country that she found out that her husband had in fact resigned from his job before going to the Philippines. As a result, they did not have enough money to rent an apartment for themselves. They lived for a while in the house of her husband's mother. In the meantime, Helen found an office-cleaning job to help with their financial difficulties. Helen got pregnant, but continued to work even after her child was born. Her husband worked sometimes, and they mostly relied on his unemployment benefits and her salary to sustain their needs. They later moved to an apartment, and Helen remained the breadwinner of the family. She described the division of labor at her home: "Mostly, I did the household chores," and from time to time her husband "did the shopping." She added that she also went shopping sometimes: "It was okay for me. I don't mind those [things]. I was just hoping that he had the motivation to look for a job. That's it, because mostly, I don't know if it was depression, he was always sleeping." One day, she discovered that her husband was cheating on her, which became the final push for their divorce. She moved out with her child to a new apartment and looked for a job that suited her university education. She found the job she was looking for—an architect in a private company—thanks to her Dutch proficiency. She eventually reached a high position in the company, which moved her up the social class ladder, not only in the Netherlands but also in the Philippines. On top of it, her new salary allowed her to visit the Philippines or other countries whenever she wished, unlike before when she was an office cleaner.

Helen's family trajectory is marked with tangled spatial mobility and professional immobility at the beginning, but later by both spatial and professional mobilities. Her experience, and that of Aida and other informants, shows that although marriage with non-Filipino men leads to spatial movement from a less developed country to a more developed one, it does not always result in financial betterment, either for them or for their natal families in the Philippines. More often, the Filipino women informants underwent either downward social class mobility or immobility coupled with limited spatial movements. In the latter case, stay-at-home informants felt stuck in their situation: they could not exercise their profession in their receiving country, and had no economic resources of their own. By fulfilling the vast bulk of reproductive work in their homes, they satisfy at least the "ideal" Filipino womanhood as "the light of home" (*ilaw ng tahanan*) and in charge of care work in the family. However, in many cases, the respectability gained from binational marriage and migration to Europe was challenging to maintain in the Philippines without economic resources in the receiving country to improve their natal family's socioeconomic situation. When they engaged in the labor market, the informants could keep their respectability by financially providing for their natal families' needs. Nonetheless, despite their paid employment, their care work at home remained the same, and they still strived to fulfill them both. Hochschild (1989) describes this situation as "double shifts" in which women perform productive (first shift) and reproductive labor (second shift). Among the informants, only a few declared to be on an equal footing with their husbands in terms of division of labor, and only one confided that it was her husband who was doing more household tasks than her, saying that "he's much better" at it than her.

The pursuit of respectability can also be observed when informants decided to end their marital union after discovering that their husband had transgressed certain moral expectations. In the section that follows, I unveil the tangled (im)mobilities that the informants underwent after divorce, and the way they regained or maintained respectability.

Divorce and Its Underlying (Im)Mobilities

Most of the informants were the ones who decided to put an end to their conjugal lives. This gendered aspect of marital dissolution echoes previous studies' observation that it is the women who predominantly decide and initiate divorce among heterosexual couples (e.g., Boylan 2007; Kalmijn and Poortman 2006). Such gender gap highlights women's agency to introduce a radical change in their family life trajectories. This change took place after several years of trying to keep their relationships afloat—behavior shaped by the Catholicism-influenced ideology in the informants' natal country, which values the marital bond and family unity.

Anticipated disapproval from natal family members drives some informants to conceal their plan of divorce, and only to contact them after their marriage has been dissolved—proof that the dominant family ideology in the Philippines can cross national borders. As Joan, the mother of two introduced before, relayed, "My family knew (about my situation); then my father advised me: 'Don't divorce', but I said that I didn't like this situation."

A few informants who had retained an idealistic image of the family aligned with the ideology in the Philippines expressed their sadness and regret about what had transpired in their marriage, whereas others shared how they and their entourage viewed divorce.

> I never expected that I would end up in this situation when I arrived here (Belgium). I told myself, "If I only knew, I would not have come here." (Rosa, mother of one)
>
> They (natal family members) could not accept (my divorce), but it was really done. I even heard my brother saying (angrily) like, "If I were your husband and you leave me, you'll see (what I will do)!" It was fine; my (Dutch) husband and I were already divorced (at that time). I was only waiting for the (social) housing (I had applied for). My family could not imagine it. They could not accept it. (Lila, mother of two)
>
> My former classmates in high school (in the Philippines) ... When we had a reunion, it was like, hello, difficult (to say). I did not really tell (about my divorce) to other classmates because their mentality was different. They would not understand, or they had a different (life) framework. (Rita, mother of one)

Divorce affected many informants' respectability in the eyes of their kin and friends in the Philippines, and this was especially the case when the cause of the divorce could be traced back to the women's behavior. For instance, one informant confided that she fell in love with another man and that her mother could not accept her divorce with her husband because of this. Losing respectability due to divorce appears also linked to the fact that many informants struggled economically after their marital breakdown. Only seven informants with children aged eighteen years and below received monthly child financial support from their former husbands (see Fresnoza-Flot 2021). The rest of the informants underwent abrupt downward social class mobility immediately after conjugal separation. This situation was aggravated when, as in many cases, the informants moved out of the family home and needed to find a new place to live with their children. Women who were not earning an income at the time of separation encountered difficulties: some sought refuge in a friend's home, while others obtained assistance from their friendship networks, government agencies, or associations to get an affordable apartment or social housing. For example, Helen borrowed money from her employer to be able to rent an apartment for her and her child as well as to take care of her divorce process. She asked her employer to deduct the money she borrowed from her monthly salary.

The informants' spatial mobility within their respective receiving countries increased after a marital breakdown. This increase can be attributed to two often overlapping factors: first, shared child custody with the ex-husband, and second, engagement in the labor market. In the first situation, depending on the arrangement with their ex-husbands, fourteen informants regularly brought their children to their ex-husband's place or picked them up after from there. In the second case, many informants entered the labor market after divorce, and for this, they needed to take their car or public transportation to go to their workplace. Despite their employment, most informants could no longer afford to regularly take their children to visit their natal families in the Philippines, as their husbands were usually the ones who took care of the round-trip plane tickets for the whole family. Hence, it is evident that the informants' increased spatial mobility within the borders of their receiving country existed simultaneously with the decrease in their transnational mobility.

As downward social class mobility tangled with their spatial mobility at the local level and with transnational immobility, legal immobility emerged following an informant's divorce. This form of immobility arises when a law or policy of a state impedes the change of one particular legal status to another, which subsequently triggers constraints in the lives of individuals concerned. The Family Code of the Philippines for non-Muslim Filipinos is an interesting example to evoke here. Compared to their non-migrant husbands, all the informants but one (a Muslim Filipino woman) were subjected to this law, particularly those who still possessed Filipino nationality and/or maintained active social ties with the Philippines. This represents another gendered aspect of these women's marital breakups. When a divorce is not registered in the country where the marriage was solemnized, it may lead to challenges in the post-divorce lives of the former partners. Many informants in my study ended up after divorce having two different legal identities—that is, "divorced (or, in one case, widowed) 'here' but married or single 'there'" (Fresnoza-Flot 2019: 526). These dual legal identities complicated the lives of a few of the women interviewed who intended to acquire properties in the Philippines or to regain their family name when they were single. The Family Code of the Philippines requires that a migrant with Filipino nationality needs to obtain a divorce in his/her country of residence, which must be initiated by his/her foreign partner (see Article 26 of the Family Code). If the migrant concerned is no longer a Filipino citizen, (s)he can directly file the divorce by him/herself and then seek the judicial recognition of this overseas divorce from the Philippine court. Not doing so means that if they remarry abroad, their former husbands can file bigamy against them in the Philippine court.

Moreover, legal immobility appears in the life of a few informants when family law intersects with religion, so remarrying may be difficult for Filipino migrants, notably the ones who were formerly married to a Filipino man. For instance, Darla and her Filipino partner got married religiously in the Philippines in 1991 and migrated to the Netherlands afterwards. They acquired Dutch nationality in 1996 and 1997, respectively. Due to the emotional gap between them, they divorced in 2011. Darla stayed in the Netherlands with her child, whereas her ex-husband renounced his Dutch nationality and decided to reside in the Philippines permanently. A few years later, via a social networking site, Darla met Roman, a former school classmate in the Philippines who was informally separated from his wife. They started a long-distance relationship and planned to get married. The problem was that they were still considered married to their respective former spouses in the eyes of the Philippine law as well as of the Catholic Church, and therefore could not get married there, neither in a civil nor a religious way.

As many Filipinos like Darla and her former husband get married through a religious ceremony, which is legally recognized in the Philippines, nullifying, voiding, or dissolving their marriage in a civil way does not allow them to remarry in a church. Those who decide to keep their marriage due to the costly and lengthy procedure to terminate it usually opt for an informal live-in arrangement with a new partner. This strategy allows these migrants to counter the legal immobility that the Philippine family law produces. The post-divorce lives of women like Darla show, on the one hand, the tangled mobilities and immobilities they are experiencing, and on the other hand, how the institution of marriage and the procedures of divorce are interlinked, like two sides of one coin (Fresnoza-Flot 2019).

Conclusion and Discussion

This chapter has investigated the pursuit of respectability by Filipino migrant women in Belgium and the Netherlands, resulting in and from tangled (im) mobilities they incurred during their family trajectory. Such a pursuit stems from their desire to achieve or the pressure to conform to an "ideal" Filipino womanhood that the gendered and family norms of their country of origin dynamically shape.

The normative expectations for them to marry, build a family, and give birth to children push them to enter a legal union. Among my informants, except for care workers or tourists who migrated to their receiving country before getting married, many women interviewed migrated after their marriage, especially after marrying foreign spouses. Although marriage allowed them to be "good" Filipino women, it also brought them frustrations for various reasons, including professional immobility. The religious ideology that values the marital bond and family unity in the Philippines often prevents them from introducing immediate changes in their conjugal lives, notably regarding whether or not to break their marital vows. My interview data reveal how important maintaining a united family is to Filipino migrant women. Whereas marriage is both a resource and an effective way to attain "ideal" Filipino womanhood, divorce is an avenue for emancipation from an unhappy marriage—but at the same time, it indicates a failure to meet the "ideal" Filipino family in the Philippine context. When their marriages ended in divorce, the women interviewed turned to the labor market, thereby showing their flexibility and readiness for mobility, as well as their intention to regain respectability. The way they live with and confront their situation indicates their agency to move forward and give meaning to their lives.

It is not only the gender and family norms in their country of origin but also the legal norms in terms of marriage and conjugal separation that shaped the lives of the Filipino women interviewed. The Philippine family law requiring them to apply for judicial recognition of their divorce in the Philippines produces dual legal identities, which creates legal immobility when Filipino migrants intend to remarry in their country of origin where they remain "married," or in a religious wedding that should be preceded by a civil wedding in their receiving country. Legal immobility does not stop Filipino migrant informants from pursuing their projects, notably in maintaining or reinforcing their respectability.

The case of these migrants underlines the forms of mobility and immobility that can become tangled during their family and migration trajectories, as well as the different modes of entanglement. First, spatial mobility becomes associated with social class mobility in the Philippines, notably when the informants marry non-Filipinos who are citizens of an economically more developed country, and when they migrate to this country. Second, spatial mobility can nonetheless lead to downward social class mobility when some informants become stay-at-home wives/mothers and cannot realize their caregiving roles toward their natal families back in the Philippines. This combination usually takes place when migration to a new country prevents individuals from practicing their profession or being engaged in the labor market. Third, spatial immobility and downward social class mobility occur during the married lives of many informants, when they become confined within the four walls of their home, are not engaged in the labor market, and have no driving license. Fourth, spatial mobility, downward social class mobility, and legal immobility coexisted at one point following divorce. All these crisscrossing (im)mobilities imply that individuals can simultaneously experience two or more forms of (im)mobility during their life course in the context of migration. Aside from social and legal norms, life course events such as marriage, migration, the arrival of children, and divorce exert influence on this process. Comparing tangled (im)mobilities in the context of migration with those in non-migration settings can yield additional insights on how (im)mobilities are produced and reproduced in various social situations, as well as how gender and power are incorporated during the process.

Acknowledgments

The Radboud Excellence Initiative fellowship (2016–17) of the Radboud University Nijmegen in the Netherlands supported the present study. The success of this research would not have been possible without the intellectual guidance of Betty de Hart and the trust of all the study informants. Previous versions of this chapter were presented at the conferences "Gender in the Philippines: Challenges within the domestic sphere and beyond" (21 November 2017) and "Intimacy, Sexuality and Family in the Process of Migration: European/Asian experiences compared" (18 December 2018) at the Université libre de Bruxelles.

Asuncion Fresnoza-Flot is a tenured Associate Researcher of the Belgian National Fund for Scientific Research (F.R.S.-FNRS) and a Senior Lecturer (*maîtresse de conference*) at the Laboratory of Anthropology of Contemporary Worlds (LAMC) at the Université libre de Bruxelles (ULB) in Belgium. Her recent works include the co-edited volumes *Mobile Childhoods in Filipino Transnational Families: Migrant Children with Similar Roots in Different Routes* (with Itaru Nagasaka, 2015) and *International Marriages and Marital Citizenship: Southeast Asian Women on the Move* (with Gwenola Ricordeau, 2017). Her other publications deal with transnational family dynamics, conjugal mixedness, and intergenerational transmission, as well as marriage and divorce involving Filipino and Thai migrants in selected European countries. Her ongoing research focuses on the contextual mobility of Belgian-Asian couples within their cross-border social spaces.

REFERENCES

Almanzar, Josephine Marie. 2016. "Hypogamy." In *Encyclopedia of Family Studies* (vol. II), ed. Constance L. Shehan and Melanie Duncan, 1087–89. West Sussex: John Wiley & Sons, Inc.

Angeles, Leonora, and Sirijit Sunanta. 2007. "Exotic Love at Your Fingertips: Intermarriage Websites, Gendered Representation, and the Transnational Migration of Filipino and Thai Women." *Kasarinlan: Philippine Journal of Third World Studies* 22(1): 3–31.

Boylan, Kristina A. 2007. "Revolutionary and Not-so-Revolutionary Negotiations in Catholic Annulment, Bigamy, and Divorce Trials: The Archdiocese of Mexico, 1929–40." In *Faith and Impiety in Revolutionary Mexico*, ed. Matthew Butler, 167–83. New York: Palgrave Macmillan.

Bryceson, Deborah, and Ulla Vuorela. 2002. *The Transnational Family: New European Frontiers and Global Networks*. Oxford: Berg.

Canzler, Weert, Vincent Kaufmann, and Sven Kesselring. 2008. *Tracing Mobilities: Towards a Cosmopolitan Perspective*. Farnham: Ashgate.

CBS (Centraal Bureau voor de Statistiek). 2019. "Population; Sex, Age, Migration Background and Generation, 1 January." Retrieved 10 July 2020 from https://opendata.cbs.nl/statline/#/CBS/en/dataset/37325eng/table?ts=1594917093288.

Cole, Jennifer. 2014. "Producing Value among Malagasy Marriage Migrants in France." *Current Anthropology* 55(9): 85–94.

Constable, Nicole, ed. 2005. *Cross-Border Marriages: Gender and Mobility in Transnational Asia*. Philadelphia: University of Pennsylvania Press.

Francisco-Menchavez, Valerie. 2018. *The Labor of Care: Filipina Migrants and Transnational Families in the Digital Age*. Urbana: University of Illinois Press.

Frank, Reanne, and Elizabeth Wildsmith. 2005. "The Grass Widows of Mexico: Migration and Union Dissolution in a Binational Context." *Social Forces* 83(3): 919–47.

Fresnoza-Flot, Asuncion. 2009. "Migration Status and Transnational Mothering: The Case of Filipino Migrants in France." *Global Networks* 9(2): 252–70.
———. 2017. "Gender- and Social Class-based Transnationalism of Migrant Filipinas in Binational Unions." *Journal of Ethnic and Migration Studies* 43(6): 885–901.
———. 2018. "Social Citizenship and Divorce: Filipino Migrant Women (Un)claiming Social Rights in the Netherlands and in Belgium." *Nijmegen Migration Law Working Papers*, series no. 2018/01. Nijmegen, The Netherlands: Radboud University Nijmegen.
———. 2019. "Interacting Legal Norms and Cross-Border Divorce: Stories of Filipino Migrant Women in the Netherlands." *Migration Letters* 16(4): 521–29.
———. 2021. "The Best Interests of the Child in 'Mixed' Couples' Divorce in Belgium and the Netherlands: Filipino Mothers' Socio-Legal Encounters about their Children." *Oñati Socio-Legal Series* 11(4): 990–1011.
Fresnoza-Flot, Asuncion, and Laura Merla. 2018. "Global Householding in Mixed Families: The Case of Thai Migrant Women in Belgium." In *Making Multicultural Families in Europe: Gender and Generational Relations in Transnational and Inter-Ethnic Families*, ed. Isabella Crespi, Stefania Giada Meda, and Laura Merla, 25–37. New York: Palgrave Macmillan.
Groes, Christian. 2018. "Mobility through the Sexual Economy Exchanging Sexual Capital for Respectability in Mozambican Women's Marriage Migration to Europe." In *Intimate Mobilities: Sexual Economies, Marriage and Migration in a Disparate World*, ed. Christian Groes and Nadine T. Fernandez, 122–42. New York: Berghahn Books.
Guevarra, Anna Romina. 2010. *Marketing Dreams, Manufacturing Heroes: The Transnational Labor Brokering of Filipino Workers*. New Brunswick, NJ: Rutgers University Press.
Hochschild, Arlie. 1989. *The Second Shift: Working Parents and the Revolution at Home*. New York: Viking.
Ishii, Sari K., ed. 2016. *Marriage Migration in Asia: Emerging Minorities at the Frontiers of Nation-States*. Singapore and Kyoto: NUS Press and Kyoto University Press.
Kalmijn, Matthijs, and Anne-Rigt Poortman. 2006. "His or Her Divorce? The Gendered Nature of Divorce and its Determinants." *European Sociological Review* 22(2): 201–14.
Kim, Doo-Sub. 2010. "The Rise of Cross-Border Marriage and Divorce in Contemporary Korea." In *Asian Cross-Border Marriage Migration: Demographic Patterns and Social Issues*, ed. Wen-Shan Yang and Melody Chia-Wen Lu, 127–53. Amsterdam: Amsterdam University Press.
Mand, Kanwal. 2005. "Marriage and Migration through the Life Course Experiences of Widowhood, Separation and Divorce amongst Transnational Sikh Women." *Indian Journal of Gender Studies* 12(2–3): 407–25.
McKay, Steven. 2015. "'So They Remember Me When I'm Gone': Remittances, Fatherhood and Gender Relations of Filipino Migrant Men." In *Transnational Labour Migration, Remittances and the Changing Family in Asia*, ed. Lahn Ann Hoang and Brenda S. A. Yeoh, 111–35. New York: Palgrave Macmillan.
Mortelmans, Dimitri. 2020. "Economic Consequences of Divorce: A Review." In *Parental Life Courses after Separation and Divorce in Europe*, ed. Michaela Kreyenfeld and Heike Trappe, 23–41. Cham, Switzerland: Springer.

Official Gazette. 1987. "The Family Code of the Philippines." Government of the Philippines. Manila: Presidential Management Staff. Retrieved 19 July 2020 from https://www.officialgazette.gov.ph/1987/07/06/executive-order-no-209-s-1987/.

Ogaya, Chiho. 2015. "When Mobile Motherhoods and Mobile Childhoods Converge: The Case of Filipino Youth and their Transmigrant Mothers in Toronto, Canada." In *Mobile Childhoods in Filipino Transnational Families: Migrant Children with Similar Roots in Different Routes*, ed. Itaru Nagasaka and Asuncion Fresnoza-Flot, 205–21. Basingstoke and New York: Palgrave Macmillan.

Palriwala, Rajni, and Patricia Uberoi, eds. 2008. *Marriage, Migration and Gender* (vol. 5). Los Angeles: Sage.

Pande, Amrita. 2017. "Mobile Masculinities: Migrant Bangladeshi Men in South Africa." *Gender & Society* 31(3): 383–406.

Pribilsky, Jason. 2004. "'Aprendemos a Convivir': Conjugal Relations, Co-Parenting, and Family Life among Ecuadorian Transnational Migrants in New York City and the Ecuadorian Andes." *Global Networks* 4(3): 313–34.

———. 2012. "Consumption Dilemmas: Tracking Masculinity, Money and Transnational Fatherhood between the Ecuadorian Andes and New York City." *Journal of Ethnic and Migration Studies* 38(2): 323–43.

Qureshi, Kaveri. 2016. *Marital Breakdown among British Asians: Conjugality, Legal Pluralism and New Kinship*. Basingstoke: Palgrave Macmillan.

Ricordeau, Gwénola. 2012. "Devenir une First World Woman: Stratégies Migratoires et Migrations par le Marriage" [Becoming a First World Woman: Migratory strategies and migrations by marriage]. *SociologieS*. Retrieved 20 August 2019 from http://sociologies.revues.org/3908.

Singh, Kirti. 2008. "Child Custody Cases in the Context of International Migration." In *Marriage, Migration and Gender* (vol. 5), ed. Rajni Palriwala and Patricia Uberoi, 326–47. Los Angeles: Sage.

Singla, Rashmi. 2015. *Intermarriage and Mixed Parenting, Promoting Mental Health and Wellbeing: Crossover Love*. Basingstoke: Palgrave Macmillan.

Sportel, Iris. 2013. "'Because it's an Islamic Marriage': Conditions Upon Marriage and After Divorce in Transnational Dutch-Moroccan and Dutch-Egyptian Marriages." *Oñati Socio-Legal Series* 3: 1091–110.

———. 2016. *Divorce in Transnational Families: Marriage, Migration and Family Law*. Basingstoke: Palgrave Macmillan.

Statbel (Office Belge de Statistique). 2019. "Population par Commune Selon la Nationalité et le Sexe depuis 1992" [Population by municipality based on nationality and sex since 1992]. Retrieved 20 November 2019 from https://statbel.fgov.be/sites/default/files/files/documents/bevolking/5.1%20Structuur%20van%20de%20bevolking/popstranger-1992-fr.xlsx.

Strasser, Elisabeth, Albert Kraler, Saskia Bonjour, and Veronika Bilger. 2009. "Doing Family." *The History of the Family* 14(2): 165–76.

Suzuki, Nobue. 2003. "Transgressing 'Victims': Reading Narratives of 'Filipina Brides' in Japan." *Critical Asian Studies* 35(3): 399–420.

———. 2017. "Postcolonial Desires, Partial Citizenship, and Transnational 'Un-Mothers': Contexts and Lives of Filipina Marriage Migrants in Japan." In *International Marriages and Marital Citizenship: Southeast Asian Women on the Move*, ed. Asuncion Fresnoza-Flot and Gwénola Ricordeau, 121–39. New York: Palgrave Macmillan.

Thai, Hung Cam. 2005. "Globalization as a Gender Strategy: Respectability, Masculinity, and Convertibility across the Vietnamese Diaspora." In *Critical Globalization Studies*, ed. Richard P. Appelbaum and William I. Robinson, 313–23. London: Routledge.

———. 2008. *For Better or for Worse: Vietnamese International Marriages in the New Global Economy*. New Brunswick, NJ: Rutgers University Press.

Tosakul, Ratana. 2010. "Cross-Border Marriages: Experiences of Village Women from Northeastern Thailand with Western Men." In *Asian Cross-Border Marriage Migration: Demographic Patterns and Social Issues*, ed. Wen-Shan Yang and Melody Chia-Wen Lu, 179–99. Amsterdam: Amsterdam University Press.

Yea, Sallie. 2008. "Married to the Military: Filipinas Negotiating Transnational Families." *International Migration* 46(4): 111–44.

CONCLUSION

Empirical Insights, Policy Implications, and COVID-19 Influences

Gracia Liu-Farrer and Asuncion Fresnoza-Flot

This volume showcases the effectiveness of an ethnographic approach in capturing the tangled nature of mobilities in diverse contexts. In this concluding chapter, we highlight the insights from the case studies in our volume to outline some future research directions on tangled mobilities. We also discuss the policy implications of the volume's empirical insights. Although our case studies were conducted before the global outbreak of COVID-19 (Coronavirus disease discovered in 2019), we offer some reflections on the impact of this pandemic on tangled mobilities.

Empirical Insights from Asian Migratory Movements

Mobility as an Emotional Journey

The international workshop that eventually set off the process of putting together the present edited volume was entitled "Intimacy, sexuality and family in the process of migration: European/Asian experiences compared." In organizing this event in 2018, and embarking afterwards on the publication of our volume, we understand that intimate relationships, both their presence and absence, have potent emotional consequences that drive people's mobility decisions.

The chapters in this volume collectively demonstrate that the emotions of intimate partners and family members are entangled, exercising influences on one another's migration decisions. Emotions, developed through the practical experiences in the mobility process and physical environments of the places, can also be a powerful driving force for migration or settlement decisions. Highly educated migrants' mobility decisions often boil down to the choice of places (Liu-Farrer, this volume). The uneven mobilities cause migrants to have different emotional responses toward the places they move to; however, negative emotions about that place or, in particular, their life in that place, compel individuals to move despite instrumental rationality. In the case of mixed marriages and transnational families, the exchanges of money, objects, information or services from the kin construct the affective circuits (Cole and Groes 2016) across borders, perpetuating mobilities by sustaining material and emotional bonds. The Japanese-Filipino adult children returning to Japan feel obligated to repay the emotional debts of their kin caregivers in the Philippines (Celero, this volume). A son of a Japanese mother and a Pakistani father who grew up in Karachi forsook his education opportunity to study in the UK and enrolled into a Japanese university instead to allow his mother and sister to move back to Japan. He did so partly because he felt indebted to his mother, who had raised him alone in his father's natal home in Pakistan, and because of his sympathy toward his mother's and sister's suffering in a social environment where women's freedom is severely restricted (Kudo, this volume).

It is evident that emotions are simultaneously the causes and consequences of mobilities. Emotions reveal affects—that is, the "intensity" and "duration" (Massumi 1995) of the impact of im/mobilities on the lives of migrants and/or their family members. The emotional and affective aspects of tangled mobilities appear therefore indispensable in the study of transnational migration. To easily grasp them, emotions/affects-focused data gathering and analytical methodologies should be encouraged and further developed alongside an ethnographic approach and thematic analysis, as the contributors in this volume have adopted.

Uneven Mobilities in Multiple Social Fields

Our volume unveils that mobilities in all their forms (spatial, legal, social, economic, educational, intimate, and sexual) are uneven across multiple social fields, as all have different directions, degrees and speeds. These uneven mobilities go beyond a dichotomy of movement and stasis.

Migration policies can explain uneven mobilities and their tanglement. Some individuals have the facility to move from one country to another due to their (former) legal unions with citizens inside their destination country (Celero, Fresnoza-Flot, Kudo, and Seiger, this volume) and/or due to their socioeconomic resources and cultural capital (Farrer, Kawashima, Liu-Farrer, and Tran, this volume). Others rely on their socioeconomic resources and social networks to make the transnational movement of their material possessions possible (Marilla, this volume).

Uneven mobilities can also be interpreted as resulting from the incompatible logics for (upward) social class mobility in distinct fields, as well as the values and significance of the various forms of "capital" (Bourdieu 1997) present in these fields. While such unevenness exists for all people, regardless of their migratory status, international migration intensifies and even distorts it. International migrants, by crossing national borders, also traverse sociocultural borders. They find themselves differently positioned in each context (Kawashima, this volume), and confronted with unfamiliar sets of logic for social class mobility. Consequently, in the migratory trajectory, migrants often experience trade-offs between mobilities.

This trade-off is manifested in Japanese senior salarymen's migration into a northeastern Chinese city where their previous professional experience of Japanese corporations allows them to recuperate the social status that they had been deprived of in their natal country, but at the same time depresses their economic earnings (Kawashima, this volume). Similarly, the middle-class Filipino women's desire for respectability—a form of social status in the Philippines—motivates them to become marriage migrants in Europe, only to then experience occupational downward mobility and be stuck on the lower rungs of the social ladder—and even have spatial immobility—in the destination countries (Fresnoza-Flot, this volume). Trade-offs also take place between economic gain, social recognition, and sexual opportunity (Farrer and Tran, this volume). In such instances, not only do countries have their distinct social and sexual fields, and migrants occupy different positions in these fields, but also countries undergo the complex evolution of their multiple fields and thereby the valuation of various forms of capital. We witness this process in the case of Japanese-Pakistani couples: the migrant men gain legal status and economic independence, which often means that their Japanese spouses experience decreased power in the family (Kudo, this volume). This takes place alongside these women's devalued cultural capital and downward social class mobility.

Hence, uneven mobilities not only occur in multiple fields but also in different social spheres, notably within the realm of the family. They have gender dimensions that need to be unpacked in the future studies of tangled mobilities as part of the engendering of transnational migration scholarship (see Pessar and Mahler 2003).

Temporality of Tangled Mobilities

Resonating with migration studies' increasing attention to the impact of life stages on migratory trajectories and outcomes, several studies in this volume show that different forms of mobilities have varied significance at each stage of one's life course, and that distinct priorities motivate migration or settlement accordingly.

While children of Filipino-Japanese couples migrate to the Philippines as receivers of care, they migrate back to Japan when they reach adulthood to be the caregivers for the extended families in the Philippines (Celero, this volume). While education, career, and economic gain might drive people to seek opportunities overseas while younger, sexual desire and a longing for marriage and family make them either return to their home country or drive them to search for a new place (Liu-Farrer and Tran, this volume). Similarly, unmarried middle-class Filipino women moved downward in terms of occupational or class hierarchy to marry men of lower socioeconomic standing in Belgium or the Netherlands to fulfill their religion-inflected normative gender expectations in their natal country. When their marriage ended in divorce, they pursued social class and spatial mobilities in the destination countries in order to regain respectability (Fresnoza-Flot, this volume).

Moreover, the migration project continues over generations, as revealed in several chapters in this volume. The legal and institutional constraints that have produced irregular migrants among the mothers continue to perpetuate the precarious migratory circumstances for the children (Madhavi, this volume). The shifting power positions in the marriage and the cultural negotiations taking place in Japanese-Pakistani households sometimes drive the children to continue the transnational mobility, either to conform to the cultural expectation of the father or to rescue the mother out of a powerless social position (Kudo, this volume). The Japanese-Filipino families also see the intergenerational continuity of the migration project: while the mother may have first migrated to Japan as an entertainer, and given birth to children fathered by a Japanese man, the children can later use the newly revised nationality law to claim citizenship and residency in Japan, thereby allowing the mother to re-enter Japan as a labor migrant (Seiger, this volume). Finally, the mobility of objects, both spatially and temporally, serves the purpose of enforcing the cultural identity and individual biography of the migrants themselves, as well as intergenerationally (Marilla, this volume).

In brief, the entanglement of individual trajectories across generations seems to characterize mobilities. This temporal dimension should be further examined to uncover at what point of an individual's life course two or more forms of mobility bifurcate, conflate, and tangle, as well as how these processes take place and shape family dynamics in a migration setting.

Policy Implications: Rethinking Suspension and Compartmentalization

The current migration policies, especially those in Asian countries, are driven primarily by the concerns about labor and marriage market demands. Migrants are primarily considered as either productive workers (with skills of varying desirability in different sectors of the economy) or reproductive laborers (with character traits suitable for marriage partners). These migration policies essentially demand the potential migrants to enter a state of "suspension" upon immigration—a condition in which migrants pause their routines and detach themselves from other human concerns and social attachments to focus on accomplishing a particular goal, be it economic accumulation, career building, or home making (Xiang 2021). In our volume, we witness how migration policies affect migrants' lives in the destination country, and make their residence contingent upon their employment or marital situation.

The policy that demands or imposes "suspension" is obviously unaware of the actual process of migration and the affective consequences of tangled mobilities. The empirical studies in this volume emphatically argue that migrants have complex desires and aspirations (for example, see Kawashima, Farrer, and Tran, this volume), and they are embedded in transnational households, kinship networks, and social relations. Migrants are not individual actors free of social contexts, and therefore it is impossible to "suspend" their complex needs and wants to extract their economic labor for long, or even at all. In particular, several chapters in this volume point out the centrality of sexual intimacy in a migrant's mobility decision, and how migrants might change their migratory trajectories to seek assurance of their sexual desirability or in pursuit of romantic relationships (Farrer and Tran, this volume). This reality has not been factored into government policymaking. Consequently, states are confronted with unexpected outcomes of their migration policies: either the inability to attract and retain workers that they desire, or the long-term stay of workers—in many cases without legal residency and in precarity (Mahdavi, this volume)—that they originally hoped to only use and dispose of, or even those that they try to get rid of.

Some labor migration policies make family reunification impossible, and force migrants to leave when they lose their employment. However, some migrants stay, look for other jobs, and sometimes start a new (single-parent or not) family in the receiving country (Mahdavi, this volume).

The increasingly diverse patterns of cross-border migration also challenge social institutions, notably marriage and divorce. In spite or because of their (former) mixed marriages, Filipino and Japanese women were able to migrate, create a family, and/or engage in productive labor (Celero, Kudo, and Seiger, this volume). The dissolution of a marriage might mean that the migrant spouse is not able to continue to stay, specifically if the years of marriage do not reach the receiving state's required duration for the migrant to apply for citizenship acquisition of their new country. It could also mean failing to obtain the custody of their children, losing their home, and having an unstable financial condition, any of which would put the woman in an economically challenging situation (Fresnoza-Flot, this volume).

In addition, our volume highlights the entanglement of mobilities among family members across generations, as well as the involvement of different actors interested in moving people across borders, which make policy attempts to restrict, select, or compartmentalize migration myopic, if not outright impractical. Families in economically developing countries often see emigration as an effective means to gain social mobility in economic terms, and so are willing to strategize around migration policies to achieve spatial mobility. In addition, a range of intermediary actors, such as labor recruiters, migration agencies, and non-profit organizations (NPOs), enter the migration industry to facilitate cross-border human mobilities. The Filipino-Japanese children's journey demonstrates this phenomenon: a revised nationality law has allowed diverse actors with different objectives and interests to participate in the migratory process of these children, who are seeking their Japanese fathers and Filipino mothers as guardians but aiming to engage in the labor market (see Seiger and Celero, this volume).

Migrants and material objects are tangled too, as state policies affect their spatial mobility. The emotional impact on migrants of separation of these two entities suggests that the spatial mobility of objects is equally important as that of human beings (Marilla, this volume). Hence, states should go beyond their anthropocentric policies on transnational mobility by becoming considerate of the impact of their policies on other non-human entities and the environment in which spatial im/mobility takes place.

Hence, our volume yet again highlights the importance of dialogues between policymakers and researchers. Bridging the gap between state migration policies and the reality of migrants' lives—in other words, between law in books and law in action—is an urgent necessity, particularly at the present time of a global COVID-19 pandemic.

Tangled Mobilities in the COVID-19 Pandemic

Since the first quarter of 2020, nation-states worldwide have implemented restrictive controls of their national borders to prevent the propagation of COVID-19 infections within their respective territories. These restrictions have slowed human geographical movements, with about "two million fewer international migrants" (IOM 2021: 1). This situation suggests that the pandemic and the border controls it triggered may have also affected different social spheres, other forms of mobility, and the entanglement of stasis with mobility.

Several studies have shown an important increase of gender inequality during lockdown periods in many countries, with women receiving the strongest blow in terms of reduced labor market participation and heightened reproductive role at home (see, for example, Inno, Rotundi, and Piccialli 2020; Landivar et al. 2020). In the context of migration, migrant women who are breadwinners to their stay-behind families and who work as carers for the elderly in their receiving countries chose to keep their employment, despite being locked up in their client's home, performing "heavy tasks without any external support … no time off, permanent availability, isolation, no social contact" and "no access to basic services" (Giordano 2021: 146). Other migrant workers lost employment, returned to their countries of origin, or remained in their receiving countries without a possibility to go back home (Suhardiman et al. 2021). These situations affect migrants' capacity to financially support their stay-behind families. The COVID-19 pandemic has reinforced "regimes of immobility" (Glick Schiller and Salazar 2013) everywhere, amplifying consequently not only socioeconomic difficulties among migrants but also family precariousness, characterized by an inability to fulfill the (re)productive role from afar. Hence, the private and public spheres, as well as the productive and reproductive realms, appear more tangled than ever during the global pandemic. How do migrants and their family members undergo this entanglement? As many of them become immobile in spatial and social class terms, how do they experience stasis or suspension? To what extent does this stasis modify or invigorate their emotional attachment to specific places and social spaces?

Pandemic-related border controls also affect other forms of mobility. On the one hand, they disentangle linked mobilities: for example, legal and economic mobilities incurred through migration pre-pandemic do not anymore facilitate other spatial movements or intimate mobility. As states increasingly emphasize borders at regional, national, and city levels, they make these borders intricately entangled with one another, rendering spatial mobility more challenging for individuals and families. On the other hand, states' restrictions on the spatial movements of people intensify two specific mobility forms: virtual and material. As geographical mobility became almost impossible during lockdowns, individuals and families relied heavily on digital technologies to maintain contacts and support one another. Virtual mobility became a norm for migrant workers, as did material mobility—that is, the flows of material objects across borders. Many of these objects perhaps served as "proxy" (Baldassar 2008) to migrants whose physical absence from home became more uncertain than before the pandemic. The breadth of virtual and material mobilities in which migrants started to engage at the advent of the pandemic suggests that they are not individual footloose people but rather are connected to different networks and institutional contexts. This embeddedness of migrants in networks and contexts needs to be examined, most notably the question of how it complicates or facilitates their lives in times of global crisis.

Finally, the abrupt interruption to the global movements of people in the early 2020s due to the pandemic and the consequent border controls highlights the inseparability of mobility and stasis. It is stasis that makes mobility stand out, be socially valued, and be longed for. In other words, it is through stasis that one understands the importance of mobility, and vice versa. In the present times, the salience of stasis necessitates scholarly investigations to find out if stasis, like mobility, presents several forms, and if so, how they are related to those of mobility.

Gracia Liu-Farrer is Professor of Sociology at the Graduate School of Asia-Pacific Studies, and Director of the Institute of Asian Migrations, Waseda University, Japan. Her research examines immigrants' economic, social, and political practices in Japan, and the spatial and social mobility of students and professional migrants in Asia and Europe. She is the co-editor of the *Routledge Handbook of Asian Migration* (with Brenda Yeoh, 2018), and the author of *Labour Migration from China to Japan: International Students, Transnational Migrants* (Routledge, 2011) and *Immigrant Japan: Mobility and Belonging in an Ethno-nationalist Society* (Cornell University Press, 2020). Her ORCID is: 0000-0003-3241-8703.

Asuncion Fresnoza-Flot is a tenured Associate Researcher of the Belgian National Fund for Scientific Research (F.R.S.-FNRS) and a Senior Lecturer (*maîtresse de conference*) at the Laboratory of Anthropology of Contemporary Worlds (LAMC) at the Université libre de Bruxelles (ULB) in Belgium.

Her recent works include the co-edited volumes *Mobile Childhoods in Filipino Transnational Families: Migrant Children with Similar Roots in Different Routes* (with Itaru Nagasaka, 2015) and *International Marriages and Marital Citizenship: Southeast Asian Women on the Move* (with Gwenola Ricordeau, 2017). Her other publications deal with transnational family dynamics, conjugal mixedness, and intergenerational transmission, as well as marriage and divorce involving Filipino and Thai migrants in selected European countries. Her ongoing research focuses on the contextual mobility of Belgian-Asian couples within their cross-border social spaces.

REFERENCES

Baldassar, Loretta. 2008. "Missing Kin and Longing to be Together: Emotions and the Construction of Copresence in Transnational Relationships." *Journal of Intercultural Studies* 29: 247–66.

Bourdieu, Pierre. 1997. "The Forms of Capital." In *Education: Culture, Economy, Society*, ed. Albert Henry Halsey, Hugh Lauder, Phillip Brown, and Amy Stuart Wells, 46–58. New York: Oxford University Press.

Cole, Jennifer, and Christian Groes, eds. 2016. *Affective Circuits: African Migrations to Europe and the Pursuit of Social Regeneration*. Chicago: University of Chicago Press.

Giordano, Chiara. 2021. "Freedom or Money? The Dilemma of Migrant Live-in Elderly Carers in Times of COVID-19." *Gender, Work & Organization* 28: 137–50.

Glick Schiller, Nina, and Noel B. Salazar. 2013 "Regimes of Mobility across the Globe." *Journal of Ethnic and Migration Studies* 39(2): 183–200.

Inno, Laura, Alessandra Rotundi, and Arianna Piccialli. 2020. "COVID-19 Lockdown Effects on Gender Inequality." *Nature Astronomy* 4(12): 1114.

International Organization for Migration (IOM). 2021. "Updates to International Migration Data Reflect COVID-19 Impacts." *COVID-19 Analytical Snapshot* 64: 1–2. https://www.iom.int/sites/g/files/tmzbdl486/files/documents/covid-19_analytical_snapshot_64_international_migrants.pdf.

Landivar, Liana Christin, Leah Ruppanner, William J. Scarborough, and Caitlyn Collins. 2020. "Early Signs Indicate that COVID-19 is Exacerbating Gender Inequality in the Labor Force." *Socius* 6: 1–3.

Massumi, Brian. 1995. "The Autonomy of Affect." *Cultural Critique* (3): 83–109.

Pessar, Patricia R., and Sarah J. Mahler. 2003. "Transnational Migration: Bringing Gender In." *International Migration Review* 37(3): 812–46.

Suhardiman, Diana, Jonathan Rigg, Marcel Bandur, Melissa Marschke, Michelle Ann Miller, Noudsavanh Pheuangsavanh, Mayvong Sayatham, and David Taylor. 2021. "On the Coattails of Globalization: Migration, Migrants and COVID-19 in Asia." *Journal of Ethnic and Migration Studies* 47(1): 88–109.

Xiang, B. 2021. "Suspension: Seeking Agency for Change in the Hypermobile World." *Pacific Affairs* 94(2): 233–50.

Index

affective circuits: across borders, 141–46; creating complex social web, 150; definition of, 135; in intimacy, 135

affects: affective drive in, 114–17; definition of, 5, 118; as entangled, 149; migration, personhood and, 7–9; mobilities, places and, 128–29; physical, social, institutional environment and, 126–28; place and, 122–28, 249; structuring relations in, 123–26

agency: of art, 71; of objects, 71–74, 84. *See also* sexual agency; situated agency

altar, 82–83, 87n7

Andrikopoulos, Apostolos, 135

Appadurai, Arjun, 71

Asian migration, 2; colonization and, 9–10; emotional dimension of, 8–9; empirical insights from, 248–52; existential, 8; feminization of, 6–7; marriage migration in, 8–9; mediated and tangled mobilities in, 9–10; mobility, personhood, and affects in, 7–9; mobility as emotional journey in, 248–49; mobility research on, 6–11; tangled mobility lens on, 11, 19; tangled social spheres, mobilities, and stasis in, 11–17; temporality of tangled mobilities for, 251–52; uneven mobilities in multiple social fields for, 249–51

aspirations, 115, 122; entangled affects and, 149; triggering transnationally split families, 143

Baldassar, Loretta, 116
Barber, Tamsin, 76
better lives: overseas employment in, 97; sacrifice for, 93, 95–96, 108
Bloch, Maurice, 73
Boccagni, Paolo, 73, 84
Bourdieu, Pierre, 27, 43n2, 72
breadwinning: by Filipino migrant women, 237–38; by Japanese-Filipino children, 170–72, 175; *utang na loob* through, 170–72
Brickell, Katherine, 76
brokerage, 12; female workers exploited in, 99–100, 110n10; for Filipino migrant "entertainers," 108; of Filipino migrant women, 92, 95, 98

capital conversion: in queer migration, 198; sexual agency, shifting entanglements and, 38–40; as sexual agency, 31; in sexual field, 31. *See also* sexual capital
care trajectories, 142
care work, 110n6; Filipino migrant women in, 92, 237; labor recruitment for, 100; primary carers in, 12
Catholicism, 101–2, 234, 239
Celero, Jocelyn O.: on entwined mobility and stasis, 16–17; on interweaving

Celero, Jocelyn O. (*cont.*)
  social spheres, 13; profile of, 176; research methods of, 163–64
Center for Japanese-Filipino Families (CJFF), 159
childhoods: migrant motherhoods and, 93–95; migration and (im)mobility shaping, 94. *See also* "good childhoods"; Japanese-Filipino children; migrant children
China: *fuerdai* in, 17, 39; marriage expectations in, 33; patriarchy in, 39–40; transnational sexual field in, 32–35. *See also* Dalian; Shanghai
China Inc. (Fishman), 35
Ciobanu, Ruxandra Oana, 206
circuits of intimacy and care, 161, 173, 176
citizenship: human trafficking and, 52; migrants lacking, 48–51; renouncing of, 136, 152n2; in UAE and Kuwait, 57–58
CJFF. *See* Center for Japanese-Filipino Families
Cole, Jennifer, 135
Collet, Beate, 70
colonization, 9–10
conjugal mixedness, 69–70. *See also* mixed couples
Conradson, David, 115
Constable, Nicole, 41, 134
contemporary Japan. *See* Japan
Contractual Sterilization Laws in Other Gulf Cooperation Council Countries, 59
contradictory class mobility, 169, 175
COVID-19 pandemic, 19, 248; gender inequality in, 254; tangled mobilities in, 254–55

Dalian: favorable lifestyle in, 210, 220n1; Japan trade with, 209; key sectors in, 209; transnational ethnic niche in, 209–11; transnational mobility as cultural and social capital in, 214–16. *See also* China
Dalian Development Area (DDA), 209
Dalian High-tech Industrial Zone (DHZ), 209
Darwin, Charles, 3–4
DDA. *See* Dalian Development Area
Department of Labor and Employment (DOLE), 57, 65n3
DHZ. *See* Dalian High-tech Industrial Zone
Ding, Yu, 40
Dirty Linen (Kaufmann), 72–73
discrimination: cycles in, 54; in Germany, 128; in Japan, 139–40; in Japanese-Pakistani marriages, 139–40; queer migration avoiding, 184; of sexuality and ethnicity, 193
divorce: in Japan, 144, 148, 153n14; for mixed couples, 230; (im)mobilities underlying, 239–42; in Philippines, 239–40; polygamy and, 147–48, 153n15; respectability affected by, 240; spatial mobility increased after, 240; women initiating, 239. *See also* marriage
DOLE. *See* Department of Labor and Employment
domestic object, 86n3
domestic workers: as illegal, 54; *kefala* on, 56; legal protection lacking for, 56; pregnancy of, 58; in UAE, 55–56; women as, 12, 48–50, 55
Dubai: abortion illegal in, 58; gender inequality in, 55; human trafficking in, 60–61; sexual field in, 123; UAE, Kuwait, irregular migration and, 55–58
Duyvendak, Jan Willem, 135

educational mobility, 146–47
emotion: definition of, 5, 118, 123; materiality entangled with, 135; migration as journey of, 248–49;

in migration decisions, 118–21; negative, 15, 114, 129; positive, 15, 119–20, 122; as tangled, 121–22, 249. See also affects
emotional dimension, 8–9
emotional distress, 107–8
emotional labor, 104, 106–7, 110n9
Equal Employment Opportunity Law, 208
erotic capital. See sexual capital
erotic habitus. See sexual habitus
ethic of reciprocity, 162, 166
Ethiopia, 60
ethnography: of home objects, 70–71, 84; interviews in, 70

family, 12; asymmetrical power in, 135; in Japan, 98–100, 160; migration of, 92–93; in Philippines, 159; power dynamics shaping trajectories of, 144–46; reconfigurations of, 98–100. See also Japanese-Filipino families; Japanese-Pakistani families; transnationally split family
Family Code of the Philippines, 240–41
Farmer, Paul, 54
Farrer, James: on entwined mobility and stasis, 17; fieldwork by, 32; profile of, 42–43; on tanglement of mobility forms, 14
Fernandez, Nadine T., 3, 185–86
Fielding, Tony, 172
Filipino migrant women, 55; as breadwinners, 237–38; brokerage of, 12, 92, 95, 98–100, 108, 110n10; in care work, 92, 237; Catholicism influencing, 101–2, 234, 239; divorce and underlying (im)mobilities for, 239–42; employment for, 97; on "good motherhood," 93–94, 101–4; legal mobility decreasing for, 240–41, 243; limited social mobility of, 97; marriage and "ideal" womanhood for, 232–36, 242; migration, (im)mobilities, and marital breakdown for, 236–39, 243; migration flows of, 228–29; postcolonial desire of, 235; profiles of, 228; reasons for returning to Japan by, 96–98, 110n5; reconfigurations of family life for, 98–100; respectability of, 227–28, 232, 238–39, 242, 250; sacrifice by, 101–2, 107; as single mothers, 95, 109n2; spatial mobility increasing for, 240; spatial mobility lacking for, 236–37, 243; as talents, 98, 110n8; tangled mobilities of, 251; tangled spatial mobility of, 107–9
Fishman, Ted, 35
Fligstein, Neil, 38, 43n2
Fordism, 212, 220n2
Francisco-Menchavez, Valerie, 106–7
Fresnoza-Flot, Asuncion, 19–20, 85; on entwined mobility and stasis, 16; methods of, 228–29; *Mobile Childhoods in Filipino Transnational Families* by, 94; profile of, 244, 255–56
fuerdai, 17, 39

Garcés-Mascareñas, Blanca, 52
GCC. See Gulf Cooperation Council
Gell, Alfred, 71, 78
gender: Asian migration feminization in, 6–7; in house and home, 75–76; in Islam, 143, 148–49; in migration, 51; patriarchy in, 39–40, 145; respectability, migration and, 231–32; roles in, 75–76, 82, 93; in sexual mobility, 35–38. See also women
gender inequality: COVID-19 increasing, 254; in Dubai, 55; in Japan, 140; in transnational families, 147
Germany: built environment and sociocultural milieu in, 127; fieldwork in, 117; migrant intimate relations in, 123–24; positive

Germany *(cont.)*
    emotions in, 119–20, 122; racial discrimination in, 128
Giddens, Anthony, 80
Goffman, Erving, 191
gong ganh, 191
"good childhoods," 93, 96. *See also* childhoods
"good motherhood," 93–94; concerns over, 101–4; ideals of, 102
Gordon, Andrew, 217–18
Gorman-Murray, Andrew, 184
Green, Adam Isaiah, 197
Groes, Christian, 3, 135, 185–86
Gulf Cooperation Council (GCC), 50, 59

hadith, 141, 153n12
happiness studies, 115–16
Hernes, Tor, 4
Hibbins, Raymond, 194
highly educated migrants: emotions in migration decisions for, 118–21; intimate relationships for, 121–22, 129; motivations for, 113–14; place and affects for, 122–28, 249
highly skilled migrants: affects, physical, social, institutional environment and, 126–28; intimate relations for, 123–24, 129; motivations for, 117; social relations for, 124–26. *See also* Japanese migrants
Ho, Petula Sik Ying, 40
Hochschild, Arlie, 238
home, 86n3; altars in, 82–83, 87n7; definition of, 69, 73; ethnography of objects in, 70–71; gender in, 75–76; homing in, 73, 84; *vs.* house, 72, 86n2; making of, 84; materiality of, 71–74, 84; objects' mobility within, 79–80; as private space, 77–79
Horton, Sarah, 93–94, 106
house, 72, 86n2
human trafficking: citizenship and, 52; Ethiopia against, 60; law and lived experience in, 58–64; moral panic about, 51–52, 60, 64, 65n1; regulation of, 60; sex work after, 60–61
Hunter, Alistair, 206
Hurdley, Rachel, 72, 78
hypogamy, 230

immigration controls, 57–58
immigration policy: illegality produced by, 52–53; in Japan, 98, 175; suspension and compartmentalization in, 252–54
im/mobilities, 16; in childhoods, 94; in divorce, 239–42; intimate, 164–67, 175; legal and social, 167–72; marriage, breakup, migration and, 229–31; migration, marital breakdown and, 236–39, 243; of objects, 77, 84. *See also* mobility
Inglis, David, 72
Ingold, Tim, 4–5, 81
intergenerational intimacies, 157, 162, 175–76
intergenerational reciprocity, 158, 161–62
International Migrant Population in Kuwait and the UAE, (2019), 55
International Organization for Migration (IOM), 159
InterNations, 125
interpretive communities, 83
intimacy: affective circuits in, 135; centrality of, 121–22; intimate relationships, 123–24, 129; in mobility, 3; sexual, 26–27, 43n1
intimate laborers: *kefala* on, 55–56; women as, 54
intimate mobilities, 3; definition of, 27, 158, 185–86; in irregular migration, 64, 65n4
IOM. *See* International Organization for Migration
irregular migration: Contractual

Sterilization Laws in, 59; Countries to Host Country—Female Migrant Stock in, 56; cycles of, 64-65; in Dubai, UAE, and Kuwait, 55-58; as intergenerational, 51-54; International Migrant Population in, 55; intimate mobilities in, 64, 65n4; law and lived experience in, 58-64; legally produced illegality in, 48-51; research on, 54. See also migration

Islam: education in, 143, 153n13; gender norms in, 143, 148-49; hadith in, 141, 153n12; in Japan, 140-41; Japanese wives converting to, 140-41, 153n11; marriage requirements in, 140; "true Islam," 141

Japan: built environment and sociocultural milieu in, 126-27; corporate culture in, 195; Dalian trade ties with, 209; divorce in, 144, 148, 153n14; economic growth era of, 211-13, 215; Equal Employment Opportunity Law in, 208; as "escape" destination, 190-92; existential mobility in, 8; family in, 98-100, 160; fathers in, 165; fieldwork in, 117; foreign workers in, 139, 195; "gay boom" in, 187-88; gender inequality in, 140; homophobic and heterosexist barriers in, 193, 197; homosexuality history in, 186-87; immigration and residency policies in, 98, 175; international marriages in, 137, 152n4, 152n9; Japanese-style management in, 212, 217-18, 220n2; labor migration in, 92, 97-98; on LGBTQ issues, 182, 187, 200n1; middle class ideals in, 220; Muslims in, 140-41; Nationality Law in, 152n2, 167, 176n1; negative emotion-driven migration in, 120-21; nightclubs in, 110n8; 1.5-generation migrants in, 91-92; as oppressive, 194-97; positive emotions in, 122; queerness in, 186-89, 192-94; racial discrimination in, 139-40; racialized sexual preferences in, 193-94; reasons for returning to, 96-98, 110n5; recession in, 207, 210-11, 213-14; reconfigurations of family life in, 98-100; retirement in, 213-14, 221n3; sexual field in, 197-98; spousal visa in, 140, 152nn6-7; two-track system in, 212-13; unskilled labor in, 138, 152n5; Vietnamese migrants in, 188, 200n2; youth career trajectories in, 216-18

Japanese-Filipino children: breadwinning by, 170-72, 175; care and reciprocity among, 161-62; on coming to terms with moving, 104-7; definition of, 159; education delayed for, 171-72; emotional distress of, 107-8; emotional labor of, 104, 106-7, 110n9; ethic of reciprocity of, 162; with extended kin, 166-67, 169, 173-74; in family migration, 92; hardships for, 93; ideational shifts in, 174, 177n3; legal mobility of, 167-68, 176n2; as lonely, 98-99; mothers of, 98; as 1.5-generation migrants, 91-92; reconfigurations of family life for, 98-100; sacrifice by, 105-6; situated agency of, 161-62, 176; spatial mobility of, 107-9; in transnational families, 157-58; *utang na loob* by, 166, 169, 173. See also childhoods; Philippines

Japanese-Filipino families, 13; blue-collar workers in, 170; circuits of intimacy and care in, 161, 173, 176; fathering deficit in, 165, 173;

Japanese-Filipino families (*cont.*)
intergenerational intimacies in, 157, 162, 175–76; legal status of, 159, 175; mobile motherhood in, 160; multiple im/mobilities, legal and social im/mobilities in, 167–72; multiple im/mobilities, spatial mobility of extended kin, spatial and intimate im/mobilities in, 164–67, 175; profile of, 163–64; remarriage in, 168–69; single mothers in, 161; tangled mobilities of, 251; as transnational families, 159–61, 175–76; transnational family relations of, 164–72

Japanese migrants: methods and data on, 207–9; status differences in, 210–11; in transnational ethnic niche, 209–11

Japanese migrants, older: advantages for, 215; career trajectories of, 211–16; education-employment transitions for, 211–13, 219; female, 212–13; in labor migration, 206–7, 250; recession impacting retirement for, 213–14; transnational mobility as cultural and social capital for, 214–16; in two-track system, 212–13; upward social mobility of, 213

Japanese migrants, younger: career trajectories of, 216–18; experience and expertise lacking for, 218–19; labor casualization impacting, 216–17; roles for, 211; in tertiary education, 216; work condition deterioration impacting, 217

Japanese-Pakistani families, 134, 249; affective circuits of, 150; children's journeys in, 148–49, 151; divorce and polygamy in, 147–48, 153n15; educational mobility of, 146–47; entangled affects and multifaceted aspirations in, 149; gender norms in, 144–45; moral force in, 150; mothering techniques in, 145–46; Pakistani citizenship renounced in, 136, 152n2; patriarchal bargaining in, 145; personhood transforming in, 150–51; power dynamics shaping trajectories of, 144–46; tangled mobilities of, 251; transactions across borders by, 135, 152n1; as transnationally split family, 142–44

Japanese-Pakistani marriages, 250; affective circuits across borders for, 141–46; barriers to, 138–39; care trajectories in, 142; Islam conversion in, 140–41, 153n11; law, economy, religion and, 137–41; motives for, 138; racial discrimination in, 139–40; reciprocal visa exemption increasing, 137–38; spousal visa in, 140, 152nn6–7; transnational entrepreneurs in, 141–42. *See also* marriage

Japanese-style management, 212, 217–18, 220n2

Japan-Philippine Economic Partnership Agreement (JPEPA), 110n6

kafeel, 56–57
Kaufmann, Jean-Claude, 72–73
Kawashima, Kumiko: on interweaving social spheres, 13; methods and data of, 207–9; profile of, 220; on tanglement of mobility forms, 14
kefala, 12; abolishment of, 56; definition of, 54; on domestic workers, 56; on intimate laborers, 55–56; reformation of, 56–57
Kelly, Philip, 97
King, Victor T., 76
kin-objects, 83
Kudo, Masako: on interweaving social spheres, 13; profile of, 151; on research methodology and

participants, 136–37; on tanglement of mobility forms, 15
Kuwait, 12; adoption in, 62; citizenship in, 57–58; Contractual Sterilization Laws in, 59; Countries to Host Country–Female Migrant Stock on, 56; DOLE against, 57; immigration controls in, 57–58; International Migrant Population in, 55; migrant children in, 61–63; research in, 54; UAE, Dubai, irregular migration and, 55–58; women migrants in, 49–50, 55–56

labor migration: in Japan, 92, 97–98; older generations in, 206–7, 219, 250; to transnational ethnic niche, 209–11; youth bias in, 205–6. *See also* Dalian; Japanese migrants, older; Japanese migrants, younger
Latham, Alan, 115
legal mobility: definition of, 158; for Filipino migrant women, 240–41, 243; of Japanese-Filipino children, 167–68, 176n2; social mobility and, 167–72
LGBTQ: definition of, 200n1; Japan on, 182, 187, 200n1; in Vietnam, 188–89, 195, 200n6, 200nn3–4. *See also* queer migrants; queer migration
life-history interview, 189
Liu-Farrer, Gracia, 20, 145; data, methods, and labeling by, 117–18; on entwined mobility and stasis, 16; profile of, 129, 255; on tanglement of mobility forms, 15
longitudinal research, 134, 136

Madison, Greg, 8
Mahdavi, Pardis: fieldwork by, 51–52, 54; on interweaving social spheres, 12; profile of, 65
Marilla, Angelie: on entwined mobility and stasis, 17; fieldwork by, 70–71, 87n8; profile of, 86; on tanglement of mobility forms, 15
marriage: in China, 33; "ideal" womanhood and, 232–36, 242; in Islam, 140; in Japan, 137, 152n4, 152n9; migration, breakup, (im)mobilities and, 229–31; migration, (im)mobility, and breakdown of, 236–39, 243; polygamy and, 147–48, 153n15; religious, 241; remarriage, 168–69; spatial and social class mobilities in, 232–36. *See also* divorce; Japanese-Pakistani marriages; mixed couples
marriage migration, 8–9, 152n8; motives in, 26; scholarly works on, 134–35
materiality: emotions entangled with, 134; of home, 71–74, 84; reflecting social meanings, 72
McAdam, Doug, 38, 43n2
migrant children, 51–52; coming to terms with moving, 104–7; in Japanese-Pakistani families, 148–49, 151; in Kuwait, 61–63. *See also* childhoods
migrant motherhoods: childhoods and, 93–95; gift-giving in, 94; as remote, 95, 110n3
migrants: aging in place by, 206; COVID-19 impacting, 254–55; as illegal, 52–53; lacking citizenship, 48–51; law and lived experience of, 58–64; as older, 206; outpass for, 61; policing and disciplining of, 57; sexual intimacy for, 26–27, 43n1; as single status, 53–54; suspension for, 252. *See also* migrant children
Migrants' Rights, 56–57, 65n2
migration: affective drive for, 115–17; affects, mobilities and places for, 128–29; amenity-seeking in, 206–7; categories of, 53; decision making in, 114; as emotional journey, 248–49; as gendered, 51, 64–65; happiness and, 115–16; identity

migration (cont.)
disruption in, 127; marriage, breakup, (im)mobilities and, 229-31; migration infrastructure, 9; (im)mobilities, marital breakdown and, 236-39, 243; mobility turn in, 185; motherhood and childhood in, 93-95; motivation of, 113, 115; negative and positive emotions in decision for, 118-21; personhood, affects and, 7-9; place and affects in, 122-28; postcolonial desire in, 235; respectability within, 231-32; sexualities in, 184-86; sexual mobility as framework for study of, 28-31; trade-offs in, 250; uneven mobility in, 250. *See also* irregular migration

migration policy. *See* immigration policy

Miller, Daniel, 72

mixed couples, 69; agency of objects and materiality of home for, 71-74; divorce process for, 230; ethnography of home objects for, 70-71; marriage, breakup, (im)mobilities, migration and, 229-31; meanings and material-social relations of, 82-84; migration, (im)mobilities, and marital breakdown for, 236-39, 243; mobility of home objects for, 77-79; objects crossing borders for, 74-77; objects for, 73-74; objects' mobility within home of, 79-80; objects' ongoingness and decay for, 80-82; in restaurants, 77; spatial mobility of, 229-30; spatial mobility of objects for, 74-80. *See also* conjugal mixedness; marriage

Mobile Childhoods in Filipino Transnational Families (Nagasaka & Fresnoza-Flot), 94

mobile motherhood, 160

mobility: affect, places and, 128-29; as assemblage, 19; definition of, 158, 228; educational, 146-47; as existential, 8; of home objects in public spaces, 77-79; intimacy in, 3; of material objects, 15; in multiple social fields, 249-51; "new mobilities paradigm" on, 3, 206; of objects, 15, 71, 73; of objects within home, 79-80; regimes of, 77, 94, 109n1, 254; relational aspects of, 18; sexualities in, 185-86; stasis inseparable from, 255; trade-offs in, 250; trajectory in, 118-19; virtual, 255. *See also* im/mobilities; spatial mobility; tangled mobility

mobility lattice, 31

mobility research: of Asian migration, 6-11; mediated and tangled mobilities in, 9-10; migration, personhood, and affects in, 7-9; tangled mobility lens in, 11, 19

Murray, David A. B., 194

Nagasaka, Itaru, 94

Nationality Law, 152n2, 167, 176n1

Newell, Sasha, 83

nikah nama, 140

Nohl, Arnd-Michael, 128

Nowok, Beata, 116

objects, 86n3; agency of, 71-74, 84; binaries of, 75; biography of, 81; crossing borders, 74-77; domestic, 86n3; ethnography of, 70-71, 84; im/mobilities of, 77, 84; kin-objects, 83; meanings and material-social relations of, 82-84; as mediants, 71; for mixed couples, 73-74; mobility of, 15, 71, 73; mobility within home of, 79-80; ongoingness and decay of, 80-82, 85; as personal, 80; from private spaces to (semi-)public spaces, 77-79; spatial mobility of, 74-80, 253

OFWs. *See* overseas Filipina workers
Ogaya, Chiho, 110n10
1.5 generation migrants , 91–92
Ong, Aihwa, 145
The Origin of Species (Darwin), 3–4
outpass, 61
overseas Filipina workers (OFWs), 57, 101–2

parda, 143, 145
Parreñas, Rhacel Salazar, 93
passport consciousness, 98
patriarchal bargaining, 145
personhood: definition of, 5; migration, affects and, 7–9; transformation of, 148–49, 150–51
Philippines, 2; brokers from, 92, 95, 99–100, 108, 110n10; Catholic influence in, 101–2, 234, 239; divorce in, 239–40; DOLE in, 57, 65n3; Embassy of, 49–50; Family Code of the Philippines in, 240–41; family relationships in, 159; "good motherhood" in, 93; labor export from, 97–98; marriage and "ideal" womanhood in, 232–36; OFWs from, 57, 101–2; 1.5-generation migrants from, 91–92; reason for returning to Japan from, 96–98, 110n5; religious marriages in, 241; stay-behind children in, 164–67, 176. *See also* Filipino migrant women; Japanese-Filipino children; Japanese-Filipino families
place: affect, mobilities and, 128–29; affects, physical, social, institutional environment and, 126–28; affects and, 122–28, 249; aging in, 206; attachment to, 116–17; built environment in, 126–27; definition of, 5, 122–23; intimate relations and, 123–24, 129; sexual field and, 123; social landscape in, 127–28; social relations and, 124–26; on structuring relations, 123–26
place-belongingness, 116
politics of mobility, 253–54
postcolonial desire, 235

queer migrants, 15; Japan as "escape" for, 190–92; motivations for, 184–85, 199; negotiating queer sexualities in Japan by, 192–94; profiles of, 189; return to Vietnam by, 194–97; reverse migration of, 183–84, 199; sexual capital of, 198; sexual field of, 197–98; sexuality and, 184–86; sexual mobility of, 193–94. *See also* LGBTQ; Vietnamese migrants
queer migration, 15; capital conversion in, 198; definition of, 184; discrimination and, 184; isolation or social exclusion in, 192–93; sexual field of, 197–98; sexualities in, 184–86; studies lacking on, 183, 186; tangled mobilities in, 199; as transnational, 186. *See also* LGBTQ; Vietnamese migrants

racial hierarchy, 10
racial preference, 14–15, 30
relations: intimate, 123–24, 129; social, 124–26; structuring of, 123–26
relativizing, 158, 166
respectability: definition of, 231; divorce affecting, 240; for Filipino migrant women, 227–28, 232, 238–39, 242, 250; within migration, 231–32; social class dimension of, 231–32
return migration, 116; economic factors in, 194–95; queer migrants in, 183–84, 194–97, 199; reasons for, 96–98, 110n5; sexual field approach to, 197–98; sexuality factors in, 195–96; tangled elements in, 194–95; in transnational migration, 198–99; upward mobility in, 196–97

Sabban, Rima, 55
sacrifice: for "better life," 93, 95–96, 108; by Filipino migrant women, 101–2, 107; by Japanese-Filipino children, 105–6
sari-sari store, 96, 110n4
Seiger, Fiona-Katharina: fieldwork by, 95–96; on interweaving social spheres, 12–13; profile of, 109
self-making, 18, 148–49, 151
sexual agency: capital conversions as, 31; shifting entanglements and capital conversions in, 38–40. *See also* agency
sexual capital, 10, 27; conversion of, 31, 40; definition of, 29, 197; of queer migrants, 198; Whiteness as, 36. *See also* capital conversion
sexual field: boundaries in, 30; capital conversion in, 31; in China, 32–35; definition of, 27, 43n2, 184, 197; in Dubai, 123; existential considerations in, 38, 43n2; as framework for study, 28–29, 43n4; in Japan, 197–98; patriarchy in, 39; place and, 123; premodern, 29; of queer migrants, 197–98; sexual mobility and, 26–28; in Shanghai, 32–35, 123; stratification in, 29–30; urban, 41. *See also* transnational sexual fields
sexual habitus, 27, 30–31
sexual hierarchy: economics influencing, 38; in Japan, 197–98; racial preference in, 14–15, 30; in Shanghai, 35, 37
sexual migrants, 26
sexual migration, 26–27; definition of, 184; queer migrants in, 184–86
sexual mobility: definition of, 14, 26–27; entangled mobilities and, 41–42; as framework for studying migration, 28–31; gendered experiences of, 35–38; immobility in, 17; marginalization in, 41–42; sexual fields and, 26–28; sexual hierarchy in, 14–15, 30; sexual intimacy in, 26–27, 43n1; sex work in, 28
sex work: criminalization of, 40; human trafficking leading to, 60–61; in sexual mobility, 28; women migrants in, 48–49
Shanghai: gendered experiences of sexual mobility in, 35–38; local sexual field in, 35, 123; nightclubs in, 36, 38–39; power migrants in, 34; sexual hierarchies in, 35, 37; transnational sexual field in, 32–35; upward sexual mobility in, 35–37; Western male expatriates in, 34. *See also* China
situated agency, 161–62, 176
Social Evil Campaign, 188, 200n3
social mobility: as contradictory, 175; definition of, 158; interweaving spheres in, 12–13, 18; of Japanese migrants, older, 213; legal mobility and, 167–72; as limited, 97; marriage and "ideal" Filipino womanhood in, 232–36
social relationship, 124; affects, physical, institutional environment and, 126–28; learning skills for, 126; social organizations for, 125
spaces: as private and (semi-)public, 77–79; sexual, 29; workspace, 78–79
spatial mobility: COVID-19 impacting, 254–55; definition of, 6; after divorce, 240; increasing of, 240; lacking, 236–37, 243; marriage and "ideal" Filipino womanhood in, 232–36; in mixed couples, 229–30; of objects, 74–80, 253; of objects within home, 79–80; reproductive work limiting, 236; as strategy for upward class mobility, 7–8; tangled, 107–9; in transnational families, 164–67, 175. *See also* mobility
Sportel, Iris, 230

stasis: entwined mobility and, 16–17; mobility inseparable from, 255; tangled social spheres, mobilities and, 11–17
stateless. *See* citizenship
structural violence, 54
sukli, 107
Suzuki, Nobue, 235

Takahata, Sachi, 172
Takaya, Sachi, 170, 172
tangled mobility, 2; in COVID-19 pandemic, 254–55; of Filipino migrant women, 251; forms of, 13–16, 27; of Japanese-Filipino families, 251; of Japanese-Pakistani families, 251; as lens, 11, 19; mediated and, 9–10; in queer migration, 199; sexual mobility and, 41–42; social spheres, mobility forms, and stasis in, 11; stasis and entwined mobility in, 16–17; temporality of, 251–52; in transnational migration, 3–6. *See also* mobility
A Theory of Fields (Fligstein & McAdam), 38, 43n2
Thiếu nữ bên hoa huệ, 77–78
Thổ Công, 82
Thomson, Alistair, 116
Thrift, Nigel, 5
Tô Ngọc Vân, 77–78
Top Five Sending Countries to Host Country—Female Migrant Stock, (2019), 56
Tran, An Huy: on entwined mobility and stasis, 17; methodological approach by, 189–90; profile of, 199; on tanglement of mobility forms, 14–15
transnational division of labor, 161
transnational families: care and reciprocity among children in, 161–62; children in, 157; divorce and polygamy in, 147–48, 153n15; educational mobility in, 146–47; evolving trajectories of, 146–48; gender inequality in, 147; immobilities of children, spatial mobility of kin, spatial and intimate im/mobilities of parents in, 164–67, 175; im/mobilities of Japanese-Filipinos, legal and social im/mobilities of Filipino parents in Japan in, 167–72; intergenerational affinities in, 173; Japanese-Filipino children in, 157–58; Japanese-Filipino families as, 159–61, 175–76; making of, 135–36; relationship breakups impacting, 230–31; relations in, 164–72; spatial mobility in, 164–67, 175
transnationally split family: economic implications for, 143; emergence of, 142–44; Islamic education in, 143, 153n13; patriarchal bargaining in, 145. *See also* family
transnational migration, 1–2; children in, 94; immobility in, 16; intersectionality in, 5; return migration in, 198–99; sexualities in, 185; tangled mobility in, 3–6
transnational sexual fields: boundaries in, 30; capital conversion in, 31; in China, 32–35; gendered experiences of sexual mobility in, 35–38; heterosexual, 32; patriarchy in, 39; sexual agency, capital conversion and, 38–40; in Shanghai, 32–35; socialization in, 30–31; urban dating culture in, 32. *See also* sexual field

United Arab Emirates (UAE), 12; citizenship in, 57–58; Contractual Sterilization Laws in, 59; Countries to Host Country—Female Migrants on, 56; domestic workers in, 55–56; Dubai, Kuwait and, 55–58; immigration controls in, 57–58;

United Arab Emeriates (UAE) (*cont.*)
International Migrant Population in, 55; *kefala* reformed in, 56–57; Kuwait, Dubai, irregular migration and, 55–58; 1980 UAE labor law in, 56; on pregnancy, 58; research in, 54; women migrants in, 55–56; women sex workers in, 48–49

United States (US): Fordism in, 212, 220n2; urban dating culture in, 32

utang na loob: breadwinning reinforcing, 170–72; definition of, 13, 107; in intergenerational relations, 162, 174; Japanese-Filipino children developing, 166, 169, 173

Việt Kiều, 76, 86n4

Vietnam: homophobic views in, 191; homosexuality as social evil in, 188, 200n3; LGBTQ movement in, 188–89, 195, 200n6, 200nn3–4; overseas Vietnamese in, 196; queer sexualities in, 186–89; Social Evil Campaign in, 188, 200n3

Vietnamese Law of Marriage and Family, 188

Vietnamese migrants: gender roles in, 75–76; home altars of, 82–83, 87n7; as homophobic, 192–93; in Japan, 188, 200n2; Japan as "escape" destination for, 190–92; as queer, 182–83; restaurants of, 77, 86n5; return migration by, 189, 194–97; sexual capital of, 198; sexual field of, 197–98; as *Việt Kiều*, 76, 86n4; in Vietnam, 196. *See also* queer migrants

Walsh, Katie, 126
Warnier, Jean-Pierre, 79
Whiteness, 36
Wilder, William D., 76
women: abuse of, 49–50, 60; children of, 51–52; Contractual Sterilization Laws on, 59; Countries to Host Country–Female Migrants on, 56; COVID-19 impacting, 254; cycles of irregularity for, 64–65; divorce initiated by, 239; as domestic workers, 12, 48–50, 55; downward sexual mobility of, 37; in Dubai, UAE, and Kuwait, 55–58; gender roles for, 75–76, 82; intergenerational irregular migration of, 51–54; International Migrant Population on, 55; as intimate laborers, 54; in Islam, 140–41, 153n11; in Kuwait, 49–50, 55–56; law and lived experience of, 58–64; "leftover women," 39; legally produced illegality for, 48–51; as migrants, 51; mothers of, 43n5; patriarchy against, 39–40; performing "double shifts," 238; pregnancy of, 58; sexual agency for, 39–40; in sex work, 48–49; as stateless and immobile, 48–51; upward sexual mobility of, 36; in urban US dating culture, 32. *See also* Filipino migrant women; gender

Yaoi, 191

www.ingramcontent.com/pod-product-compliance
Lightning Source LLC
Chambersburg PA
CBHW051532020426
42333CB00016B/1887